TECHNICAL READOUT:™

3 ▸ 0 ▸ 8 ▸ 5

TABLE OF CONTENTS

CREDITS

Writing

Joel Bancroft-Connors
Herb A. Beas II
Randall Bills
Roland Boshnack
Craig Erne
Johannes Heidler
Ken' Horner
David McCulloch
Luke Robertson
Ben H. Rome
Jason Schmetzer
Paul Sjardjin
Joel Steverson
Geoff Swift
Chris Wheeler

Additional Writing

Brent Evans

Additional Unit Designs

Johannes Heidler
Daniel Isberner
Chris Marti

Product Development

Joel Bancroft-Connors

Production Editing

Jason Schmetzer
Diane Piron-Gelman

BattleTech Line Developer

Herb A. Beas II

Production Staff

Art Direction

Brent Evans

Cover Art

Doug Chaffee

Cover Design

Ray Arrastia

Layout

Ray Arrastia

Illustrations

Doug Chaffee
Brent Evans
Joel Hardwick
Stephen Huda
Alex Iglesias
Chris Lewis
Justin Nelson
Eric Ou
Matt Plog
Chad Segesketter
Stanley VonMedvey
David White

Maps

Øystein Tvedten

Evolved Faction Logos Design

Jason Vargas

BattleTech Logo Design

Shane Hartley
Matt Heerdt
Steve Walker

Proofers and Core Fact Checkers

Roland "ColBosch" Boshnack, Joshua "NCKestrel" Franklin, William "Mad Capellan" Gauthier, Keith "Xotl" Hann, Johannes "jymset" Heidler, Daniel "DarkISI" Isberner, Chris "Alexander Knight" Marti, Mike Miller, Luke "Jellico" Robertson, Chris "Chunga" Smith, Øystein Tvedten, Chris Wheeler, Patrick Wynne.

Additional Fact Checkers and Playtesters

Paul Bowman, Duane "Boilerman" Bywaters, Rich Cencarik, Blake "Topgun505" Cetnar, Tami Elder, John "Worktroll" Haward, Jan-Hendrik "isatlas" Kalusche and the OPFOR Kiel playtesting group, Darrell "FlailingDeath" Myers, Craig "TrboTurtle" Reed, Andreas "Gaiiten" Rudolph, Christopher K. Searls, Jeff Skidmore, Mark Yingling.

Special Thanks

To Herb and Randall, for showing me a truly incredible amount of trust. I never truly realized how "big" a TRO is to the universe and they trusted me to bring it to life. Thank you.

To the Master Unit List Team, Roland, Josh, William, Keith, Jo, Dan, Chris "Alexander Knight", Luke, Chris "Chinless" and of course Pat the indomitable Roosterboy. This TRO would truly not have been possible without their incredible work and research. From finding just the right name for a new Plasma Rifle, to practically hand building every unit to double check it, they did it all and were ready to do it all over again. Thank you, guys.

To Joel Steverson and the rest of the Aerospace Cabal, Mike "Cray", Chris "Goose", Luke "Jellico", Térence "Weirdo", and Jason "GiovanniBlasini", without whose efforts we would not have had the rules that would allow us to bring Land-Air BattleMechs back.

Formatting is one of the hidden nightmares of any BT book and TROs doubly so. Chris Wheeler and Mike Miller literally wrote the book on TRO formatting and reviewed every single TRO entry.

Most fans know him as Kit or Ken', but to me he's "Yes I can". Thank you, Ken', for being there ready to pick up anything that needed doing.

I can't in good conscience close this thanks without an extreme bow to Pat Wynne, AKA "Roosterboy". One of the quiet ones, there isn't a product that publishes that Pat's not been indispensable on. Having him working with the MUL and looking over my virtual shoulder was a boon I can't describe.

And finally, to all of you whose entries inspired the Old is the New New section, be you Catalyst Demo Team, Fact Checker or BattleCorps subscriber, your entries made this section possible.

Brent Evans would like to thank Stephen Huda for bringing his LAM sketches to life.

Ray Arrastia would like to thank his wife Ibis, Herb Beas, Jose Piniella, Ben H. Rome, Jason Schmetzer, and *all* the guys at CamoSpecs.com for their moral support when work on this project seemed bleak.

Dedication

To my incredible wife, Jesai, thank you for being you. Without you, I would not be half the man I am today. You give me focus, belief and love. You are the world.

Corrected Second Printing.

Published by Catalyst Game Labs, an imprint of InMediaRes Productions, LLC
PMB 202 • 303 91st Ave NE • G701 • Lake Stevens, WA 98258

FIND US ONLINE:

Precentor_martial@classicbattletech.com
    (e-mail address for any Classic BattleTech questions)
http://www.classicbattletech.com
    (official Classic BattleTech web pages)
http://www.CatalystGameLabs.com
    (Catalyst web pages)
http://www.battlecorps.com/catalog
    (online ordering)

INCOMING MESSAGE

SEND

SAVE

CANCEL

DELETE

With every ending, one almost always finds a new beginning. So it was with the ending of what history would come to know as the Jihad. The year 3085 marks an ending and a beginning for humankind. While Terra was liberated in 3078, it has taken the last seven years for the Inner Sphere to return to some semblance of normalcy. For the Republic of the Sphere, the signing of the Tikonov Treaty represented the final pieces of our new nation. 3085 also marks two years since the formal creation of The Republic Armed Forces. Formed not only from Devlin Stone's personal warriors, but also including warriors from all over the Inner Sphere and beyond, the RAF finds more in common with the old Star League than with any of her modern counterparts.

3075 was a watershed year, the year the Inner Sphere began to strike back against the madness of the Word. Devlin Stone's coalition grew from a loose handful of the like-minded, to a Sphere-wide alliance capable of mounting a concentrated offensive against the "Master" and his cybernetic monsters. Supported by nearly every major nation and many of the most famous mercenary units of history, Stone tightened the noose on Blakist-held Terra and, in August of 3078, the second liberation of Terra began. Hauntingly similar to Kerensky's long-ago liberation of humanity's birthworld, the five-month battle saw the fall of major Word opposition, but not without a crippling cost in men and materiel felt by every nation involved.

There, however, Kerensky's liberation and Stone's diverge. Whereas Kerensky's victory signaled the beginning of the end, the start of three hundred years of world-destroying Succession Wars, Stone's victory heralded the beginning of a new era. His formation of the Republic of the Sphere has signaled a new age of peace and prosperity, an age when war is not the first and only solution. The elite Knights of The Republic and the larger Republic Armed Forces are not an army of conquest, but of protection and stability.

The last ten years have seen more than the fall of the Word and the rise of The Republic. They have seen an explosion of innovation forged by the fires of war and destruction. From cutting-edge designs like the RAF Winston Combat Vehicle, to necessity-bred upgrades like aquatic armor conversions, to the new BattleMech "Phoenixization" that swept through front-line units of every nation in the final drive to Terra, the last decade has seen greater advances in military technology than were achieved in an entire century of the Star League.

While by no means comprehensive, this tactical briefing document summarizes the major innovations and equipment changes for The Republic Armed Forces and those of the major Houses and powers that surround us. The current Archon of the Lyran state may have made famous the phrase "information is ammunition," but that does not make it any less valid. The Republic is built on the best of all nations, and we shall use all the "ammunition" we have available to us.

—General Albrecht Hoft
RAF Department of Military Intelligence
1 December 3085

INTRODUCTION

GAME NOTES

Technical Readout: 3085 covers the widest breadth of units and equipment of any previously published Technical Readout. As such, to understand how these various units plug into the core *BattleTech* rulebooks, it's useful to cover how the various rulebooks interact.

Standard Rules

The *Total Warfare* (*TW*) and *TechManual* (*TM*) rulebooks present the core game and construction rules for *BattleTech* (*BT*), otherwise referred to as the standard rules.

Advanced Rules

Beyond the standard rules, a legion of advanced rules exists, allowing players to expand their games in any direction they desire. In an effort to bring these rules to players in the most logical form possible, the advanced rules are contained in three "staging" core rulebooks, each one staging up and building off of the previous rules set.

Tactical Operations: *Tactical Operations* (*TO*) is the first in the "staging" Advanced Rulebooks. Its focus is during game play, and applies directly to a game as it unfolds on a world in the *BattleTech* universe.

Strategic Operations: *Strategic Operations* (*SO*) is the second "staging" Advanced Rulebook. It stages a player up to the next logical area of play, focusing on "in a solar system" and multi-game play.

Interstellar Operations: *Interstellar Operations* (*IO*) is the third and final "staging" Advanced Rulebook. Players are staged up to the final level of play, where they can assume the roles of a House Lord or Clan Khan and dominate the galaxy.

How To Use This Technical Readout

Complete rules for using 'Mechs, vehicles, infantry, battle armor, fighters, and DropShips in *BattleTech* game play can be found in *Total Warfare*, while the rules for their construction can be found in *TechManual*; some of the equipment found on some units is detailed in *Tactical Operations*. The rules for using JumpShips and WarShips, as well as their construction rules, can be found in *Strategic Operations*.

The following three definitions are used to clarify the various types of equipment that appear in *Technical Readout: 3085* and are presented in the Standard and Advanced Rulebooks.

- **Standard:** Any equipment mass produced "in universe"; can be used with *Total Warfare* rules alone.
- **Advanced:** Any equipment mass produced "in universe"; must have *Tactical Operations* and/or *Strategic Operations*, in addition to *Total Warfare*, to use.
- **Experimental Rules:** Any equipment not mass produced "in universe" because it is prohibitively expensive, extraordinarily sophisticated, exceedingly difficult to maintain or simply deemed too unreliable or restrictive for widespread deployment; must have *Tactical Operations* and/or *Strategic Operations*, in addition to *Total Warfare*, to use.

Land-Air BattleMech Quick-Start Rules are found in *Record Sheets: 3085*; the complete rules are found in *Interstellar Operations*.

All Battle Values listed in this book for unit types appearing in *Total Warfare* were generated using the Battle Value system as it appears in *TechManual*; if it mounts Advanced equipment, Battle Values were generated using the addendum rules from *Tactical Operations*. Battle Values for those units appearing in *Strategic Operations* were generated using the addendum rules found in that rulebook.

INCOMING MESSAGE

SEND

SAVE

CANCEL

DELETE

THE CUTTING EDGE

The years between 3060 and 3070 saw an explosion of technological advancements on a scale not seen since the height of the Star League. Where the decade of the Clans saw the Inner Sphere in a desperate race to counter the Clans' technological edge, the subsequent ten years saw new technologies emerge that would rival anything previously created. Yet for all these advancements, much of that technology was relegated to proving grounds or limited production runs. Even weapons we now take for granted, like the heavy PPC, were slow to make their way to the field despite their reliability and obvious tactical value.

It would take a war that nearly ended modern civilization to move these technologies from the proving grounds to the battlefield. The decade-long Jihad saw not only an immense proliferation of technologies, but also gave them much-needed "real world" tests. Technologies that might have taken decades to make their way into popular use under more peaceful conditions became household names overnight. The liberation of Terra would not slow down this new fire of development. Projects begun in the heat of the war, as well as those designed as a result of the war's lessons, would continue for several years. Only with the Military Materiel Redemption Program did we finally see a slowdown in innovation here in The Republic. Similar slowdowns in new designs have begun with all the other major governments as rebuilding and peace-focused technologies move to the forefront of all our priorities.

Ranging from battle armor suits to massive assault DropShips, the military hardware introduced in the past decade has pushed the limits of technology into new territory. We must now wait and see if that new territory is indeed the realm of peace envisioned by Exarch Stone. If not, these machines will be among the first to see a new era of warfare.

—General Albrecht Hoft
RAF Department of Military Intelligence
1 December 3085

THE INNER SPHERE

The first years of the Jihad saw the Great Houses scrambling to shore up their shattered infrastructures and put into the field whatever they could cobble together, re-purpose, rig up or pull from mothballs. Many innovations and new military designs appeared, but often they began with the resurrection of a previously shelved design or the modification of a well-known platform, as was the case with the *Patriot* and the *Mongoose II*, respectively. During this time, a large number of conventional vehicles and battle armor were also becoming available, the first signs of the shift from the BattleMech as undisputed ruler of the battlefield.

As the tide of the Jihad turned, the nations of the Inner Sphere gained ground in their dogged efforts to rebuild. The last three years of the drive toward Terra saw the debut of an unprecedented number of new designs, a pace that is only now slackening as Exarch Stone continues to push the Inner Sphere toward greater demilitarization. At the same time, the Word of Blake, with its access to Terra's industrial might and the rebuilt factories on dozens of Protectorate worlds, fielded a startling amount of new technology during its final days. While many of these Blakist weapons of war have been virtually eradicated, others live on in one form or another. More than one of the RAF's key combat vehicles owes its origins to the Word. While the Blakists' quest for interstellar dominion marked them as the most dangerous of religious zealots, the quality of their military designs cannot be ignored.

We have the dubious honor of thanking the Word of Blake for the current renaissance in military hardware. Their technological innovations, coupled with an intelligence service that stole seemingly every single military advance made elsewhere during the past twenty years, gave them an unprecedented technological edge. Only when the Coalition joined forces were we able to match the diversity of technology the Word could field. With Terra liberated, those technological secrets have fallen to The Republic and, to a great extent, to the rest of the Inner Sphere. Where ten years ago it would have been unheard of for a stealth armored vehicle to be produced anywhere except the Capellan Confederation, they are now being made in the factories of at least three other nations. Rotary autocannons in the Free Worlds and heavy Gauss rifles on Combine tanks are two other examples of the ever-widening diffusion of new technology.

With all sides in the Jihad innovating at a frenetic pace and technology spreading across borders, it is not surprising that the military designs of the past decade are some of the most advanced since the fall of the Star League.

—General Albrecht Hoft
RAF Department of Military Intelligence
1 December 3085

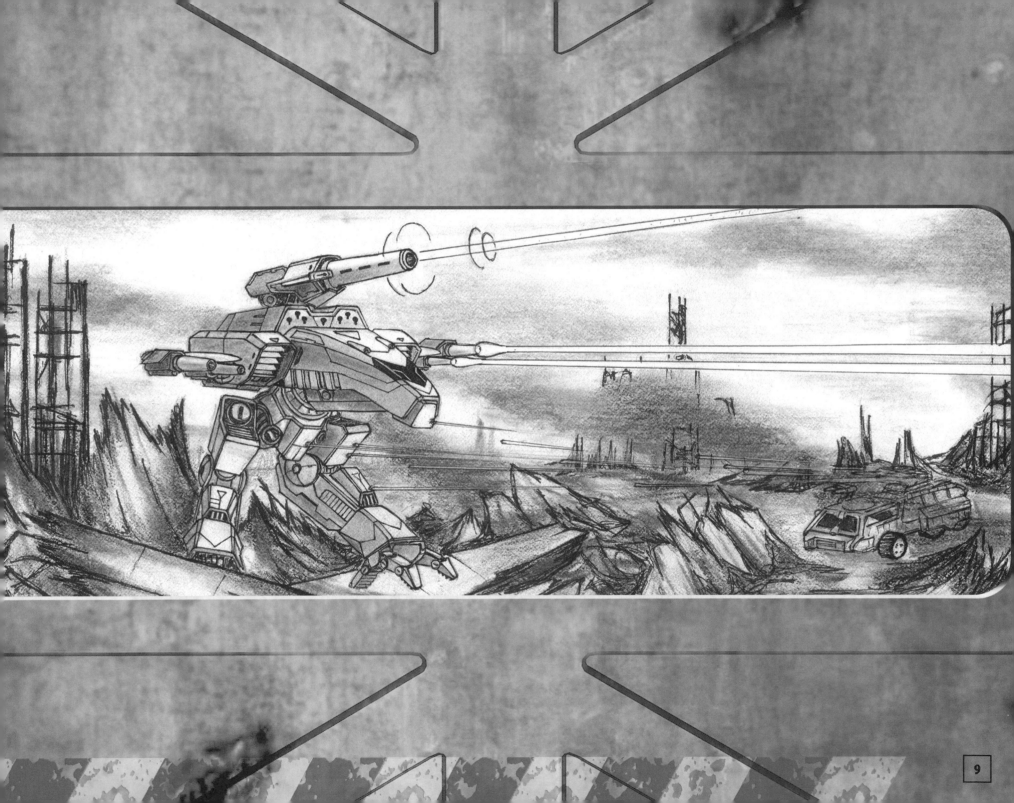

ANGERONA SCOUT SUIT

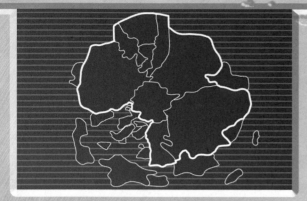

As a scouting unit the Purifier's greatest asset is also its greatest weakness. For the Purifier to be most effective, it has to stand perfectly still, thus limiting its ability as a mobile scout unit. At the other end of the spectrum, the Draconis Combine puts their faith in the Kage battle armor for its recon squads. The flaw in this plan, however, is that the Kage must use its jump jets to move quickly about the battlefield, and no matter how stealthy the armor it carried, jumping from point to point will alert even the greenest troops to your presence. Based on lessons learned from the Coalition campaign, the new Republic Armed Forces needed an infantry scout that was mobile and stealthy when doing so. StarCorps, still enjoying popular success with their first entry into the battle armor market, the Kopis, was invited to expand their small Terran facility and create just such a unit.

Borrowing concepts from the Capellans' Trinity battle armor, the Angerona mounts no jump jets but has instead been designed to travel over thirty kilometer per hour on the ground. The lack of jump jets was a purposeful decision, despite the loss of tactical mobility, as they are counter to the suit's core misson: to move overland and operate with maximum stealth in open or city terrain. Likewise, the Angerona's design team steered away from mimetic armor. While the technology is now well-understood, and Purifier suits make up a good portion

of the RAF's battle armor forces, the armor's inability to mask a moving unit kept it from being used optimally. Instead the Angerona combines improved stealth armor with a full camouflage system that allows the suit to be nearly invisible to most sensors. Despite being rated as a medium-class suit, the Angerona's overall armor protection is more in keeping with its primary mission as a battlefield scout.

A light recoilless rifle provides the suit's primary offensive armament. Comparable to the Magshot in damage, the loss of range was a necessary trade off on a suit already at risk of having no room left for the operator. Backup firepower is provided by an AP weapons mount affixed under the left arm to provide anti-infantry or mission specific weapons. Basic manipulators allow the Angerona to ride BattleMechs and vehicles. However, for added stability, the weapon casing wraps around the right hand manipulator. This requires the rifle to be un-limbered if the Angerona is to best ride on the exterior of another unit.

Recently, a pure recon suit has begun field testing. This recon version drops the rifle for an improved sensor package and replaces the manipulators with armored gloves that allow for carrying standard infantry weapons and special mission equipment.

Though only in production for the last two years, the Angerona has still managed to become a well-known and popular suit. Even before full production the Angerona made a name for itself with the Eighth Hastati Sentinels. On Shipka, heavily armed militants, believed to be Capellan-backed, were threatening to destabilize the planet's Foxborough continent. Not wishing to put Shipka's Republic militia, who were still largely ex-Capellan citizens, to the test, the Eighth Hastati was sent in to deal with the threat. Two squads of Hastati battle armor, one a Purifier squad and the other Angerona suits undergoing field trials, were doing recon of a small town believed to be hiding a large concentration of militants.

Penetrating the perimeter, the Hastati troopers discovered the rogue militants and were preparing to withdraw when the Purifier suits were wiped out in a rapid fusillade from two squads of Ying Long battle armor. Watching their brothers gunned down, the Angerona squad quickly retook the initiative and began carefully stalking the Capellan mimetic suits. Able to move nearly undetected, the Angeronas used their stealthy mobility and patience to wait for the Capellan-made suits to move and thereby reveal themselves. After an hour-long game of cat and mouse, only three of the Ying Longs managed to flee the city.

Deployment remains limited to active line units, primarily the Hastati Sentinels, Stone's Lament and Liberators. The Quartermaster's office has begun accepting requisitions from other units, but there is no specific time table for these requests to be filled.

ANGERONA SCOUT SUIT

Type: Angerona
Manufacturer: StarCorps Industries
    Primary Factory: Terra

Tech Base: Inner Sphere
Chassis Type: Humanoid
Weight Class: Medium
Maximum Weight: 1000 kg
Battle Value:
    46 (Standard)
    33 (Recon)
Swarm/Leg Attack/Mechanized/AP: Yes/Yes/Yes/Yes*
Notes: *Recon variant may not make Anti-'Mech attacks or use Mechanized deployment.

Equipment		Slots	Mass
Chassis:			175 kg
Motive System:			
Ground MP:	3		80 kg
Jump MP:	0		0 kg
Manipulators (Standard):			
Left Arm:	Basic Manipulator		0 kg
Right Arm:	Basic Manipulator		0 kg
Manipulators (Recon):			
Left Arm:	Armored Glove		0 kg
Right Arm:	Armored Glove		0 kg
Armor:	Improved Stealth	5	360 kg
Armor Value: 6 + 1 (Trooper)			

Weapons and Equipment	Location	Slots (Capacity)	Tonnage
Standard			
Light Recoilless Rifle (20)	RA	2	175 kg
Anti-Personnel Weapon Mount	LA	1	5 kg
Camo System	Body	2	200 kg
Recon			
Light Machine Gun (50)	LA	1	75 kg
Improved Sensors	Body	1	65 kg
Remote Sensor Dispenser	Body	1	40 kg
Camo System	Body	2	200 kg

S.HUDA 2010

KOPIS ASSAULT BATTLE ARMOR

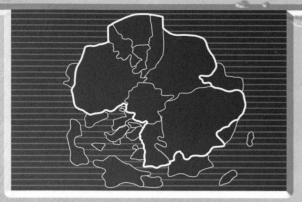

When Etna Foundries' Longinus factory on Oriente was sabotaged by suspected Blakist operatives, Thomas Halas became keenly aware of the need for alternate production facilities. Halas approached StarCorps to provide the manufacturing base. Their Emris IV facility had been producing industrial exoskeletons for some time, with the Gorilla exoskeleton having a near universal acceptance. StarCorps was more than willing to produce a battle armor suit. Previous attempts to move into this market had been stymied by the Free Worlds government and likely Blakist influence to maintain control of the League's battle armor designs. Securing manufacturing facilities was only the first hurdle. Powered exoskeletons were one thing; to produce a high-end assault suit required a level of technical expertise StarCorps had yet to acquire.

StarCorps solved this problem by reaching out to Duchess Alys Rousset-Marik. In exchange for access to production units, Rousset-Marik agreed to help acquire that technical know-how that StarCorps needed. Using her extensive resistance network Rousset-Marik was able to contact a leading scientist from Irian BattleMechs. Having escaped the Blakist-controlled Irian but still on the run, Dr. Hyram Sundahar was more than happy to accept employment with StarCorps, and quickly headed up their battle armor research. With Blakist technical documents, also obtained by Rousset-Marik's resistance, Sundahar quickly had a prototype assault suit ready for field trials.

Based on an assault suit that Irian had been developing,

the Kopis stresses firepower over all else. Lightly armored compared to other assault suits, it still possesses protection equal to the standard Clan Elemental. This tradeoff of protection and ground speed allows the Kopis to devote than half its mass to offensive equipment. Twin heavy battle claws enable it to rip through nearly any armor as well as buildings and other obstacles. In its favored urban environment, this means it can move nearly anywhere it needs to in order to carry out its primary mission.

Moving away from the trend in missile-heavy assault suits, Kopis designers were prepared to trade single-salvo firepower for longer battlefield endurance. What they settled on gave both raw firepower and the ability to fire at targets of opportunity without fear of squandering a handful of missile reloads. Two modified Martell medium lasers form the Kopis' primary firepower. These two over-the-shoulder lasers give the Kopis the ability to take down ninety percent of other Inner Sphere battlesuits in a single attack and a full squad is a deadly threat to any light BattleMech. Two arm-mounted anti-personnel weapon mounts complete the Kopis' offensive capabilities.

Released just days before the final assault on Terra the only Kopis variant saw limited use before the Liberation of Terra. The anti-personnel variant was built to deal with the fanatical Word infantry expected to defend Terra's urban centers. It replaces the twin medium lasers with a pulse laser and a flamer.

The first suits were fielded in late 3077. Assigned to the Twelfth Atrean Dragoons, under direct command of Alys Rousset-Marik, the suits were there when Alys liberated Outreach. In a series of brief pitched battles, Wannamaker's Widowmakers were devastated by the Dragoons and other units of the Free Worlds Group I. The Kopis suits saw their first combat here when a mixed company of Widowmakers attempted to break out of Rousset-Marik's encirclement. Two squads of the suits were dispatched by VTOL ahead of the retreating mercenaries. The Kopis suits used their heavy battle claws to quickly drag debris into the roadways and then laid an ambush against the retreating company. When the Widowmakers slowed to navigate the debris field,

sixteen lasers lanced out to cripple or destroy the leading and trailing elements of the retreating mercenaries. When Coalition forces arrived two minutes later, the eight Kopis suits had destroyed eighty percent of the Widowmaker company for the loss of only three of their suits.

The Kopis was present at the Liberation of Terra in significant numbers and has since become the backbone of Marik and Oriente battle armor units. Using the highly capable suit as a bargaining chip, Oriente is selling Kopis suits to The Republic in exchange for access to Achileus and Phalanx suits from the factories now in Republic space. It is believed the pairing of Kopis suits with Federated Suns Grenadiers will make for a highly effective urban defense squad and plans are underway to deploy two to three squads of these mixed battle armor teams to each planetary militia in The Republic.

KOPIS ASSAULT BATTLE ARMOR

Type: Kopis
Manufacturer: StarCorps Industries
    Primary Factory: Emris IV

Tech Base: Inner Sphere
Chassis Type: Humanoid
Weight Class: Assault
Maximum Weight: 2000 kg
Battle Value:
    78 (Standard)
    57 (Anti-Infantry)
Swarm/Leg Attack/Mechanized/AP: No/No/ No/ Yes
Notes: None

Equipment		Slots	Mass
Chassis:			550 kg
Motive System:			
Ground MP:	1		0 kg
Jump MP:	0		0 kg
Manipulators:			
Left Arm:	Heavy Battle Claw		20 kg
Right Arm:	Heavy Battle Claw		20 kg
Armor:	Advanced	5	400 kg
Armor Value: 10 + 1 (Trooper)			

Weapons and Equipment	Location	Slots (Capacity)	Mass
Standard			
Anti-Personnel Weapon Mount	RA	1	5 kg
Anti-Personnel Weapon Mount	LA	1	5 kg
2 Medium Lasers (30 x2)	Body	6	1,000 kg
Anti-Infantry			
Anti-Personnel Weapon Mount	RA	1	5 kg
Anti-Personnel Weapon Mount	LA	1	5 kg
Medium Pulse Laser (24)	Body	3	805 kg
Flamer (30)	Body	1	160 kg

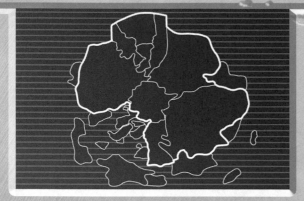

Mass: 20 tons
Movement Type: Hover
Power Plant: Nissan 195 Extralight Fusion
Cruising Speed: 151 kph
Flank Speed: 226 kph
Armor: StarSlab/2
Armament:
    1 Bright-Bloom ER Medium Laser
    2 Magna 200P Small Pulse Lasers
Manufacturer: Valiant Systems
    Primary Factory: Johnsondale, Achernar
Communications System: QuasComm 5.3
Targeting and Tracking System: TacTOM IV

Overview

The civil war that engulfed the Federated Commonwealth led to many hardships and problems, and those that affected war machines were given top priority. No longer able to procure the cheap and effective Savannah Master, Valiant Systems was tasked by the AFFS with replicating the design in conjunction with the Department of the Quartermaster. The relatively simple design of the Savannah Master made the task seem easy and not many resources were devoted to it. However, the Quartermaster kept expanding the scope of the project until it no longer resembled the Savannah. First, more armor was added. Then a more advanced laser were used,

and finally anti-infantry weaponry. By the time it was ready to prototype the war was over and the supply lines reestablished, so the entire design was shelved.

With the destruction inflicted by the Jihad, Valiant once again looked to supply the AFFS with weaponry they were lacking. With the plans already in place and development costs already sunk, they quickly moved forward and in 3084 released the Fox Armored Car. Initial reception was positive, especially from our own RAF procurement office. The RAF Quartermaster subsidized Valiant's partial reconstruction of the destroyed Achernar BattleMech factory on Achernar in order to produce the Fox. Only Valiant's marketing staff had difficulty with the task of bringing the Fox to production; they had to work overtime to convey the fact that the Fox was actually a hovercraft and not a wheeled vehicle, despite the name insisted upon by the RAF Quartermaster.

Capabilities

In the end the Fox does what it aimed to do—for a price. The extralight engine gives it more speed than the Savannah Master, while the extended-range medium laser gives it more reach. Over five tons of armor will allow it to weather some heavy blows, though the fragility of the hovercraft design will likely leave it immobile before it is completely destroyed. A pair of small pulse lasers offer a short-ranged sting as well as powerful anti-infantry weaponry without dependence on ammunition. The energy-based weapons load combined with a fusion engine allows the design to be very independent.

The Fox is more effective as a threat than in actual ability. The medium laser is a concern to many combat units, but with the speed of the Fox it can suppress a large portion of the battlefield. A good commander should be able to use the Fox to slow down the enemy and force them to adopt more conservative tactics. The Fox likely won't be used primarily in an infantry-hunting role, as competent infantry forces will avoid placing themselves in a position where the Fox will thrive, but as a reaction force the Fox can be very effective.

Deployment

Armor units attached to the Davion Guards were the first to receive the Fox Armored Car, followed by the Crucis Lancers. Due to a logistical error, six were assigned to the defunct Third Crucis Lancers and were lost in the AFFS inventory system for months. When this error was finally rectified the Foxes in question were donated to the Interstellar Red Cross for use as armed ambulances. So far, forty percent of Foxes have gone to the RAF and the rest to Federated forces.

Variants

There are two factory variants of the Fox. The simplest variant replaces one of the pulse lasers with a flamer, giving it added utility and more powerful, if less accurate, anti-personnel firepower. The second variant attempts to upgrade the mediocre firepower against hard targets. The two pulse lasers are replaced by a single variable-speed pulse laser. The additional range compensates for the loss of hitting power. The use of machine guns rather than the more complex pulse lasers has been brought up but not yet gone past the discussion phase.

FOX ARMORED CAR

Type: **Fox**
Technology Base: Inner Sphere
Movement Type: Hover
Tonnage: 20
Battle Value: 549

Equipment		Mass
Internal Structure:		2
Engine:	195	6
Type:	XL Fusion	
Cruising MP:	14	
Flank MP:	21	
Heat Sinks:	10	0
Control Equipment:		1
Lift Equipment:		2

Equipment		Mass
Power Amplifier:		0
Turret:		.5
Armor Factor:	88	5.5

	Armor Value
Front	27
R/L Side	17/17
Rear	12
Turret	15

Weapons and Ammo	Location	Tonnage
ER Medium Laser	Turret	1
2 Small Pulse Lasers	Turret	2

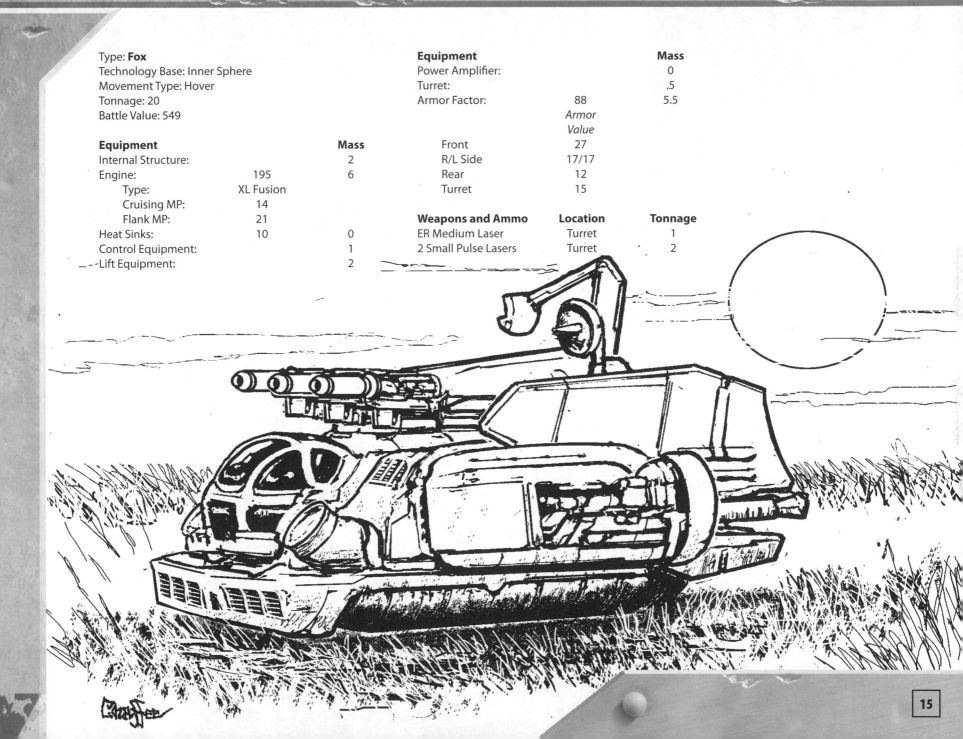

15

PANDION COMBAT WIGE

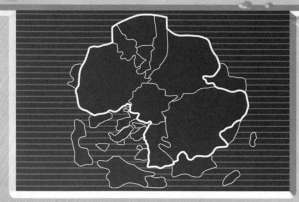

Mass: 20 tons
Movement Type: WiGE
Power Plant: GM 120 XL Fusion
Cruising Speed: 108 kph
Flank Speed: 162 kph
Armor: StarSlab/4 Ferro-Fibrous
Armament:
    2 Bright Bloom Extended Range Medium Lasers
    1 Hovertec Streak SRM 4
Manufacturer: General Motors
    Primary Factory: Kathil, Salem, New Valencia
Communications System: Garret Supremesound
Targeting and Tracking System: Trackmaster VIII
    with Beagle Active Probe

Overview

General Motors suffered considerable losses during the Jihad. Countless plants were damaged or destroyed, with BattleMech production most affected. While working to rebuild their factories, GM turned to high-volume sales in order to keep business going. The best performing sales came from combat vehicles, both proven designs like the Challenger MBT and new models like the Pandion. Simple construction techniques allow GM to churn out WiGEs the way smaller companies deliver RetroTech units. Conservative estimates suggest that GM is capable of producing three Pandions for every Challenger MBT.

The design was prototyped at the Salem plant, entering trials in 3076 with full production following in early 3078. While the WiGE is a newer platform for GM, the underlying technology is proven, reliable and easy to produce. The New Valencia plant went live in 3080, followed by the newly repaired Kathil line in 3083.

In 3084, the Pandion infantry variant competed against the Giggins APC for an RAF APC contract. The Pandion outperformed the Giggins in virtually every trial, but ultimately the Giggins was chosen. According to the official RAF explanation, the Giggins' armament is better suited to dealing with conventional infantry. This has created a rift between GM and the RAF, as GM contends a backroom arrangement with Hohiro Kurita led to the Giggins' selection. GM retaliated against the Giggins, calling it a "dragon-built death-trap" through the voices of several retired mercenaries, but analysts predict this effort will be short-lived, as GM can ill afford a lengthy negative media campaign.

Capabilities

Marketing material describes the Pandion as cross between a Badger transport and a Beagle hovercraft. A GM 120 extralight engine powers a brace of turret-mounted Diverse Optics extended-range lasers and gives the Pandion a maximum speed of 162 kph. A trustworthy Hovertec Streak rack backs up the lasers and a GM Trackmaster ties all three together for precise allocation of firepower.

The Trackmaster VIII is a significant upgrade over the older Trackmaster VII, which had serious problems tracking airborne and ground-based targets simultaneously. An exploitable glitch in the VII that failed to execute the firing routine under certain circumstances has been patched in the VIII, though some crews remain skeptical. Another new feature of the VIII is the inclusion of a Beagle hardware and software suite that can accurately detect hidden, camouflaged and shut-down units. Given the expense of the targeting and tracking system, it's curious that GM chose the Garret Supremesound suite. Though perfectly serviceable, it's an older model and lacks some modern amenities.

Four tons of ferro-fibrous armor are arranged so that the Pandion can withstand a PPC strike on any armor facing without a breach. The WiGE is intended for scouting and skirmishing, making this configuration more than adequate.

Deployment

The Pandion has been deployed to numerous Federated Suns units including the Avalon Hussars, Davion Guards and Crucis Lancers. Aside from the failed bid for the RAF contract, the WiGE has not been offered outside the Suns.

Variants

GM manufactures two additional variants of the Pandion. Both feature significant subterfuge in their construction. Specifically, they sport cosmetic features that make them visually indistinguishable from the standard model. The infantry variant removes the Streak launcher and ammunition and installs an infantry transport bay capable of carrying a squad of battle armor soldiers. The prototype featured four individual compartments arranged port and starboard on the ventral hull, but this configuration was scrapped as it failed to adequately accommodate conventional infantry and visibly differed from the standard model. Instead, a rear-mounted door was installed. Containing no exterior handles, the door is remotely operated by the vehicle commander. The small size makes egress difficult for bulky battlesuits. Of particular concern for infantry, ingress is just as cumbersome. Though the missile launcher is removed in this configuration, the turret size is unaltered, and dummy missile tubes adorn the turret face between the laser ports.

The C³ variant strips out both ER medium lasers. A TAG designator is installed in place of the starboard laser, with a C³ slave computer and fake barrel filling the space vacated by the port laser. The design is indistinguishable from the standard model and infantry variant.

PANDION COMBAT WIGE

Type: Pandion
Technology Base: Inner Sphere
Movement Type: WiGE
Tonnage: 20
Battle Value: 658

Weapons and Ammo	Location	Tonnage
2 ER Medium Lasers	Turret	2
Streak SRM 4	Turret	3
Ammo (Streak) 25	Body	1
Beagle Active Probe	Body	1.5

Equipment		Mass
Internal Structure:		2
Engine:	120	3
Type:	XL Fusion	
Cruising MP:	10	
Flanking MP:	15	
Heat Sinks:	10	0
Control Equipment:		1
Lift Equipment:		2
Power Amplifier:		0
Turret:		.5
Armor Factor (Ferro):	71	4

	Armor Value
Front	20
R/L Side	13/13
Rear	13
Turret	12

S.HUDA 2010

YASHA VTOL

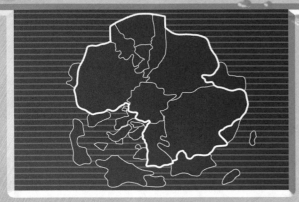

Mass: 30 tons
Movement Type: VTOL
Power Plant: Indy 70 Extralight
Cruising Speed: 76 kph
Flank Speed: 119 kph
Armor New Samarkand Royal Ferro-Fibrous with CASE
Armament:
    1 Lord's Light 3 Heavy Particle Beam Weapon
    1 Series 14NC-B Light Machine Gun
Manufacturer: Wakazashi Enterprises
    Primary Factory: Dover
Communications System: Sony MSF-23 with C^3
Targeting and Tracking System: Radcom T11

Overview

Like many things war-oriented in the Draconis Combine, the Yasha started off in the hands of Luthien Armor Works. In the mid-3060s, the company tried to develop an Omni VTOL, but were unable to achieve that goal. After the chaos that engulfed LAW, aerospace manufacturer Wakazashi Enterprises bought the rights to this VTOL for a minimal sum. Wakazashi likewise failed to produce a successful Omni platform, but its engineers realized that the Yasha was a stable platform that could be used for multiple factory variants. Rather than write off the entire project, the company told its designers to go forward with three versions that could fill various roles. To reflect the framework's multi-role flexibility, the marketing department named it after a class of nature spirits from Buddhist and Hindu mythology.

Capabilities

Though slow when compared to most VTOLs and many WiGE, the Yasha is swift enough to stay away from most enemy fire and still line up a decent shot. Its strategic speed is even faster, enabling it to ignore ground terrain and cover a larger area. In addition to the axiom that VTOLs use speed for armor, Wakazashi has done a good job protecting the Yasha in case that primary protection fails. Three and a half tons of heavy ferro-fibrous armor protects it better than four tons of standard armor would. Should its ammunition be detonated, the crew and vehicle can still be salvaged thanks to CASE protecting the ammunition bays (depending, of course, on how high they were flying).

The main feature of the Yasha is its weaponry. A heavy particle cannon mounted in the nose gives it plenty of penetration power with no need to worry about ammunition. The cannon's range allows the VTOL to avoid close-range enemy fire, but its C^3 slave module gives it high accuracy at longer distances. A light machine gun was added as a back-up weapon and to provide anti-infantry capability. Some eyebrows were raised when Wakazashi purchased the Yasha's machine gun system from Clan Nova Cat manufacturers, but it has since been proved to be a downgraded version in line with Inner Sphere models. Designers wanted to use another energy weapon, but the heat load on the Yasha was already using up almost 20 percent of its mass.

Deployment

With the state of the Combine economy, purchasing VTOLs, no matter how good, was not a high priority. Collecting taxes was, and so Wakazashi received approval to sell the Yasha not only to all Inner Sphere powers, but to some Clans as well. Given the design's connection to the Nova Cats, it is expected that the Cats will be heavy buyers of the Yasha.

Variants

While plans exist for several variants, only two are currently being manufactured. The first is an interdictor platform, outfitted with large amounts of electronic warfare hardware. An active probe enhances detection, while the ECM can disrupt enemy systems or defend against enemy ECM disruption of friendly networks. A pair of seven-tube multi-missile launchers with three tons of ammunition provides considerable flexibility and decent firepower. An Artemis IV targeting system increases precision, and this variant retains the hefty armor of the PPC Yasha.

The third version is being marketed as the Spectre, and it lives up to that name. While most warriors are lukewarm about the light Gauss rifle, all are wary of the range it possesses. The addition of stealth armor and the light Gauss allows this variant to become a deadly battlefield sniper while remaining almost untouchable. A targeting computer was added to increase accuracy. The stealth armor does not provide nearly as much protection as the thick heavy ferro-fibrous armor of the standard Yasha, but this version properly used should never be in a position to take nearly as many hits as the other variants.

YASHA VTOL

Type: **Yasha**
Technology Base: Inner Sphere
Movement Type: VTOL
Tonnage: 30
Battle Value: 799

Equipment		Mass
Internal Structure:		3
Engine:	70 XL	1.5
Type:	VTOL	
Cruising MP:	7	
Flanking MP:	11	
Heat Sinks:	15	5
Control Equipment:		1.5
Lift Equipment:		3

Equipment		Mass
Armor Factor (Heavy Ferro):	69	3.5
	Armor	
	Value	
Front	21	
R/L Side	18/18	
Rear	10	
Rotor	2	

Weapons and Ammo	Location	Tonnage
Heavy PPC	Front	10
C³ Slave	Body	1
Light Machine Gun	Front	.5
Ammo (Light MG) 100	Body	.5
CASE	Body	.5

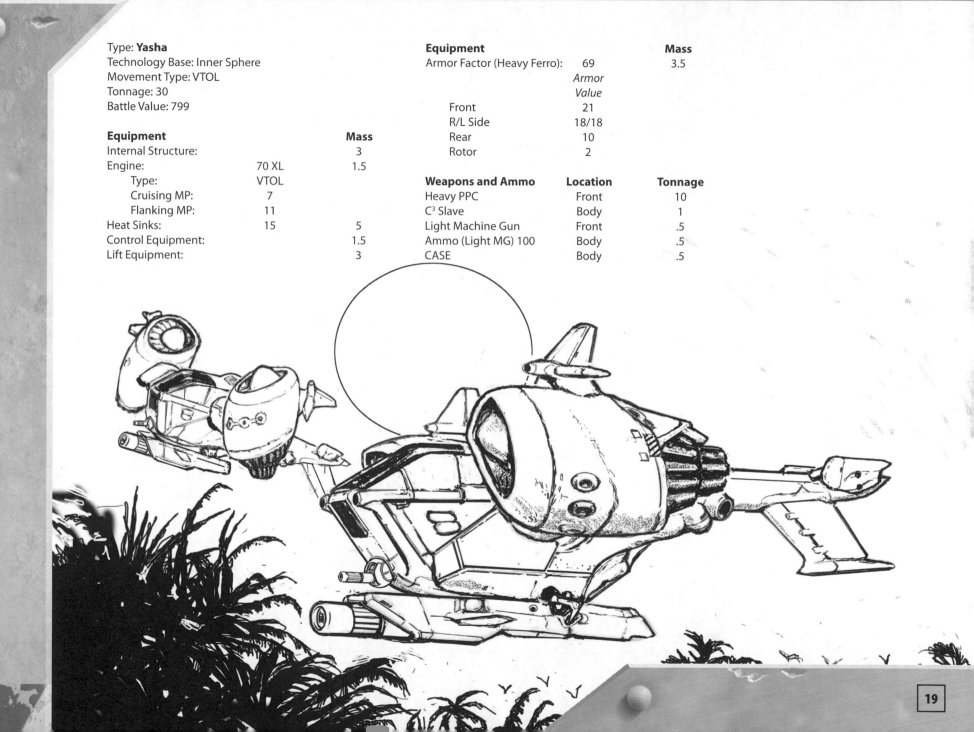

TUFANA HOVERCRAFT

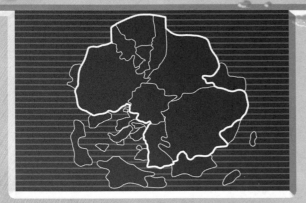

Mass: 35 tons
Movement Type: Hover
Power Plant: Pitban 210 XL Fusion
Cruising Speed: 119 kph
Flank Speed: 184 kph
Armor: Valiant Chainmail Ferro-Fibrous
Armament:
    1 Doombud Multi-Missile Launcher 7
    1 Octagon Missile-Magnet Narc Beacon
Manufacturer: Ronin Incorporated
    Primary Factory: Wallis
Communications System: Garrett T21-C
Targeting and Tracking System: Wasat Watchdog W105
    with A-Trac

Overview

With a large amount of missile firing units, the Regulans wanted a way to improve their efficiency. From that idea, the Tufana was born: a hovercraft that would focus on making its teammates better. This interesting unit is not without its challenges. The screening of crews for the Tufana is more thorough than most, as the Regulan armed forces do not want personnel too eager to attempt to take down the enemy by themselves, but rather to play a role as part of a larger team.

Capabilities

Named after the Hindi word for storm, the Tufana is based around speed. Designers used an extralight engine to greatly increase the craft's speed while allowing for a specific weapons load. Capable of speeds over 180 kilometers an hour, the Tufana can outpace almost any battlefield unit short of airborne units, including some VTOLs. Though speed is the Tufana's primary advantage, Ronin Incorporated also thought to provide some armor protection. Four and a half tons of ferro-fibrous armor can deflect a lucky Gauss round in most locations.

The Tufana uses two pieces of equipment to accomplish its goal: a dozen-shot Narc launcher and target acquisition gear. The crew must carefully husband their shots, making sure each one counts and choosing their targets wisely as the Tufana's comrades will follow their lead. In fact, the Tufana may be the only unit that sees the target, with the rest of the formation able to fire indirectly from behind cover. TAG allows the Tufana to spot for artillery and semi-guided LRMs.

Unfortunately, the effectiveness of the Tufana's equipment can make it a bigger target than the massive war machines firing the missiles and artillery it is guiding. To defend itself, designers equipped it with a multi-missile launcher capable of firing seven missiles in a salvo. It also carries three tons of ammunition, a costly but useful expense. In addition to having many of the options common to most units carrying MMLs, the Tufana may have both Narc and semi-guided missiles on board. A crew caught away from the rest of its unit may use the Narc to mark an enemy it encounters and retreat behind cover to shell indirectly, homing in on the beacon.

Deployment

The first Tufanas were sent to Regulan units, particularly those engaging in border skirmishes. The hovertank worked well with the *Patriot*, targeting for the 'Mech's Arrow IV rounds. Presently, all Regulan Hussar units as well as most other Regulan units are believed to have Tufanas in their order of battle. Ronin has now opened up sales to most of the former Free Worlds League as well as the Capellan Confederation and Magistracy of Canopus. Canopian forces have started pairing up their new Tufanas with their massive heavy LRM and heavy MML carriers.

Fighting with the Regulan Principality, the Tufana made an impression. A lance of three Tufanas and an LRM Harasser were headed to join a larger unit when they came across four Oriente scout 'Mechs. The Tufanas kept making passes to distract the 'Mechs while the Harasser hid and rained missiles down on them. A *Phoenix Hawk* made a lucky shot with a pulse laser that blew out the air skirt on one of the Tufanas, but the tank got its revenge as two salvos of SRMs crippled the *Hawk*. One *Hermes II* managed to retreat while the Regulan forces held the area long enough to recover the downed hovercraft.

Variants

Ronin has also had requests for a variant with the improved Narc system. To free up more tonnage and keep the same ammo load, the multi-missile system had to be removed. Rather than replacing it with an anemic three-tube launcher, Ronin took advantage of the Tufana's fusion engine and used energy weapons. Two medium pulse lasers are located in the turret, perfect for high-speed passes. An extended-range small laser mounted in front of the cockpit rounds out the weapons load. This model has seen higher sales to the Capellan Confederation than to any other customer.

TUFANA HOVERCRAFT

Type: **Tufana**
Technology Base: Inner Sphere
Movement Type: Hover
Tonnage: 35
Battle Value: 583

Equipment		Mass
Internal Structure:		3.5
Engine:	210	7
Type:	XL Fusion	
Cruising MP:	11	
Flanking MP:	17	
Heat Sinks:	10	0
Control Equipment:		2
Lift Equipment:		3.5
Power Amplifier:		0
Turret:		1
Armor Factor (Ferro):	80	4.5

	Armor Value
Front	25
R/L Side	15/15
Rear	10
Turret	15

Weapons and Ammo	Location	Tonnage
MML 7	Turret	4.5
Ammo (MML) 51/42	Body	3
Narc Missile Beacon	Turret	3
Ammo (Narc) 12	Body	2
TAG	Turret	1

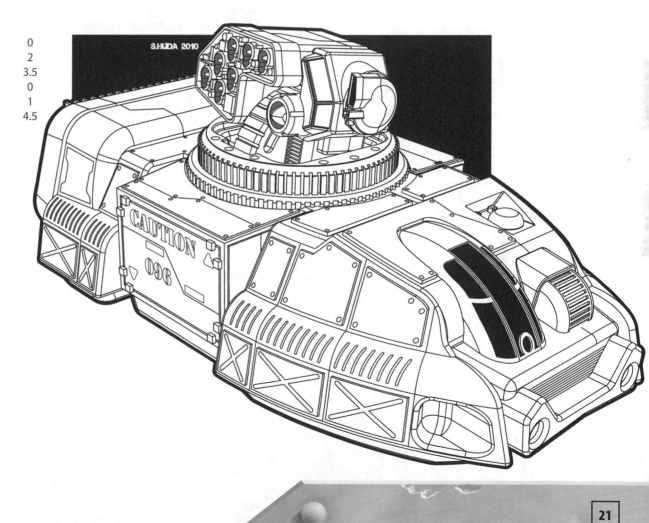

S.HUDA 2010

CAUTION

096

GIGGINS APC

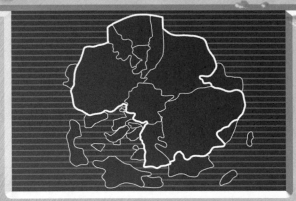

Mass: 40 tons
Movement Type: Wheeled
Power Plant: DAV 220 Fusion
Cruising Speed: 64 kph
Flank Speed: 97 kph
Armor: StarSlab/7 Heavy Ferro-Fibrous
Armament:
    2 SuperFire Minigun Heavy Machine Guns
Manufacturer: Duncan Enterprises
    Primary Factory: Moore
Communications System: Exeter LongScan with ECM
Targeting and Tracking System: Standard SmarTrack

Overview

The rise of battle armor in modern combat has changed the face of conflict and appears unlikely to disappear in the foreseeable future. This has resulted in the need for a whole line of support for battle armor, from trained technicians to transport. As the Republic of the Sphere planned for the future of its armed forces, the need for battle armor transport was recognized. Duncan Enterprises of Moore was chosen, a planet gifted to The Republic from the Coordinator of the Combine, his only request that the dead soldiers of the DCMS be remembered for their sacrifice. This new armored personnel carrier was named after *Sho-sa* Charles Giggins, killed in the infamous Day of Fire. While reception of the APC has been good, the use of the name has disturbed the Giggins family, with two of his children, John and Kelly, praising the honorific while their sisters, Jill and Sabrina, have filed suit to claim royalties. It may take a few years for Charles Giggins' legacy to be completely decided.

Capabilities

The first thing a perceptive observer will notice about the Giggins is the unique armor placement. Typically the armor on the front of an armored vehicle is much heavier than the rear, with the sides and turret being somewhere in the middle. While this is true on the Giggins, the differences are much smaller. This is in part due to its mission profile. With battle armor being relatively slow for the most part on the battle field, the Giggins needs to be able to endure shots as it approaches the battle and then even more from all sides as it moves into the middle of the conflict to unload its troops.

Speed is another necessity and with a top speed of over ninety kilometers per hour, the Giggins succeeds there. To accomplish this goal a pricey fusion engine was used but designers declined to drive the price higher with a light or extralight model. With an eight-ton infantry bay the Giggins can deliver two squads of battle armor into battle. A squad of mechanized infantry or even a pair of platoons of foot infantry can be carried instead, with room left over for extra supplies.

To protect its charges the Giggins is equipped with a pair of heavy machine guns. While not significant against armored targets, these two weapons will create a hundred-meter-bubble that enemy infantry will avoid at all costs. Despite their limited range the guns can destroy a whole platoon caught in the open. Even more useful is an ECM suite that disrupts enemy electronics. Some critics worry that 'Mech-centric commanders may sacrifice a Giggins and its troops to disrupt enemy C^3 systems, but given the integrated tactics the RAF favors these fears seem overblown.

Deployment

The first Giggins was presented as a gift to the DCMS in memory of Charles Giggins. It is currently being used by the Coordinator as his armored conveyance when reviewing military units. After it is retired from this role it will be sent to the DCMS museum on Luthien. The remainder of the production run has been deployed to RAF forces with battle armor on the Confederation and former League borders. In the future, all units should receive the Giggins as the standard battle armor transport vehicle.

Variants

The fire support version is usually issued one for every three standard APCs. Removing half of the infantry compartment and the ECM system, the heavy machine guns are replaced by dual extended-range medium lasers. Accompanying them is a five-tube multi-missile launcher, allowing close-range fire or long-range coverage. With two tons of ammunition, it can be equipped for any mission. An expected close-range confrontation may call for regular SRMs and infernos or fragmentation rounds, while between cities standard LRMs and Thunder munitions might be used. This version can be used to transport smaller numbers of infantry and actively support them.

GIGGINS APC

Type: **Giggins**
Technology Base: Inner Sphere
Movement Type: Wheeled
Tonnage: 40
Battle Value: 476

Equipment		Mass
Internal Structure:		4
Engine:	220	15
Type:	Fusion	
Cruising MP:	6	
Flank MP:	9	
Heat Sinks:	10	0
Control Equipment:		2
Lift Equipment:		0
Power Amplifier:		0
Turret:		.5

Equipment		Mass
Armor Factor (Heavy Ferro):	128	6.5
	Armor Value	
Front	28	
R/L Side	25/25	
Rear	25	
Turret	25	

Weapons and Ammo	Location	Tonnage
2 Heavy Machine Guns	Turret	2
Ammo (Heavy MG) 50	Body	.5
Guardian ECM Suite	Body	1.5
Infantry Transport Bay	Body	8

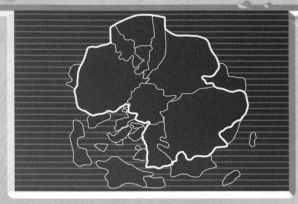

Mass: 45 tons
Movement Type: Wheeled
Power Plant: GM 295 Fusion
Cruising Speed: 76 kph
Flanking Speed: 119 kph
Armor: Leopard II Heavy Ferro-Fibrous
Armament:
    2 Tronel XII Medium Pulse Lasers
    2 Zippo Conventional Flamers
    2 GM Light Machine Guns
Manufacturer: Brigadier Corporation
    Primary Factory: Oliver
Communications System: Exeter LongScan
Targeting and Tracking System: Standard TargetTrack

Overview

As the modern RAF's predecessors finished conquering the Blakist Protectorate, the greater urban density of the Core systems compared to the rest of the Inner Sphere became a critical factor in outfitting the RAF. To assist with this added challenge of defending Republic worlds, Devlin Stone called for a new urban armor vehicle to be produced at the recently captured Brigadier Corporation factory on Oliver. Designers went with a more efficient wheeled design over treads, since the Demon would be primarily an urban vehicle. This brought dissent from some armor commanders. CEO Joseph Zimmal finally settled the argument by offering to show all the allied armor officers recordings from the trials.

The recordings won over the design's opponents, as the prototypes met all the claims Brigadier had made. The trials showed the Demon to be a successful fighter against infantry and smaller armored enemies. The company was able to quickly get the Demon out to the troops as they started to hit heavily urbanized worlds.

The original Demon was an ancient design, first introduced in 2716 for use with the Star League Defense Force. The name was chosen again in an effort to instill its crew with a sense of history and esprit de corps.

Capabilities

When the shooting starts, the Demon needs to be under cover. Designed for urban warfare, it excels at tight-quarters combat, but its weapons have little reach—less than a fifth of a kilometer of effective range. Dual turret-mounted medium pulse lasers give it accurate close-range fire. For anti-infantry work, a pair of light machine guns supplements the lasers and can threaten infantry formations at ranges too far for most to return fire. Two conventional flamers round out the weapons array. They can devastate infantry at close range, inhibit enemy 'Mech performance and even start fires if needed. A ton of flamer fuel is plenty for a single engagement. However, in a longer campaign numerous refills will be needed.

The Demon's most important asset is speed. Powered by a fusion engine to avoid the tonnage of heat sinks, the Demon is faster than many medium-weight tanks, for a significant price. With a safe speed of over 70 kph, the driver can accelerate to up to 118 kph in emergencies. Many of the Demon's non-hovertank contemporaries cannot exceed 90 kph with the throttle wide open. Opponents must choose between being outmaneuvered by the Demon or risking a collision by moving at flanking speed.

In case it is outflanked or mistakenly drives close to a Zhukov, the Demon mounts three tons of heavy ferro-fibrous armor. This is enough to survive a chance encounter with heavier enemies, but not enough for sustained combat. The armor plating is bulky, but the engineers designed the tank so it would still be easy to maintain. While this design makes life easier on technicians, crews complain that it makes some of their systems more vulnerable to incoming fire that might bypass the thick armor. Brigadier officials say this has never occurred in all the trials and tests they have performed.

Deployment

The Demon was first issued to armor forces as they needed replacements. As time goes on, it will be concentrated in units that specialize in urban or other close-quarters combat. The tank's excellent performance has encouraged The Republic to purchase all the Demons that Brigadier has so far manufactured. With the advent of peace, the Demon has been dispersed mostly to militia units and the few prototypical urban specialists. In fact, it's as common to find a Demon loaded with coolant or fire-fighting foam as incendiary fuel.

Variants

As our militia role has expanded, the RAF wished to extend the reach of the Demon. Not wanting to use less accurate missiles in a unit that often serves in populated areas and does not have enough of payload for most large ballistic weapons. Brigadier therefore turned to old-style rifled cannons. Less efficient against military-grade armor, the cannon still makes an effective deterrent for a militia vehicle. In addition to removing all the standard weapons for a medium rifle and two tons of ammunition, this variant adds another half ton of armor.

DEMON MEDIUM TANK

Type: **Demon**
Technology Base: Inner Sphere
Movement Type: Wheeled
Tonnage: 45
Battle Value: 454

Equipment		Mass
Internal Structure:		4.5
Engine:	295	27
Type:	Fusion	
Cruising MP:	7	
Flanking MP:	11	
Heat Sinks:	10	0
Control Equipment:		2.5
Lift Equipment:		0
Power Amplifier:		0
Turret:		.5
Armor Factor (Heavy Ferro):	59	3
	Armor Value	
Front	18	
R/L Side	12/12	
Rear	7	
Turret	10	

Weapons and Ammo	Location	Tonnage
2 Medium Pulse Lasers	Turret	4
2 Vehicular Flamers	Front	1
Ammo (Flamer) 20	Body	1
2 Light Machine Guns	Front	1
Ammo (Light MG) 100	Body	.5

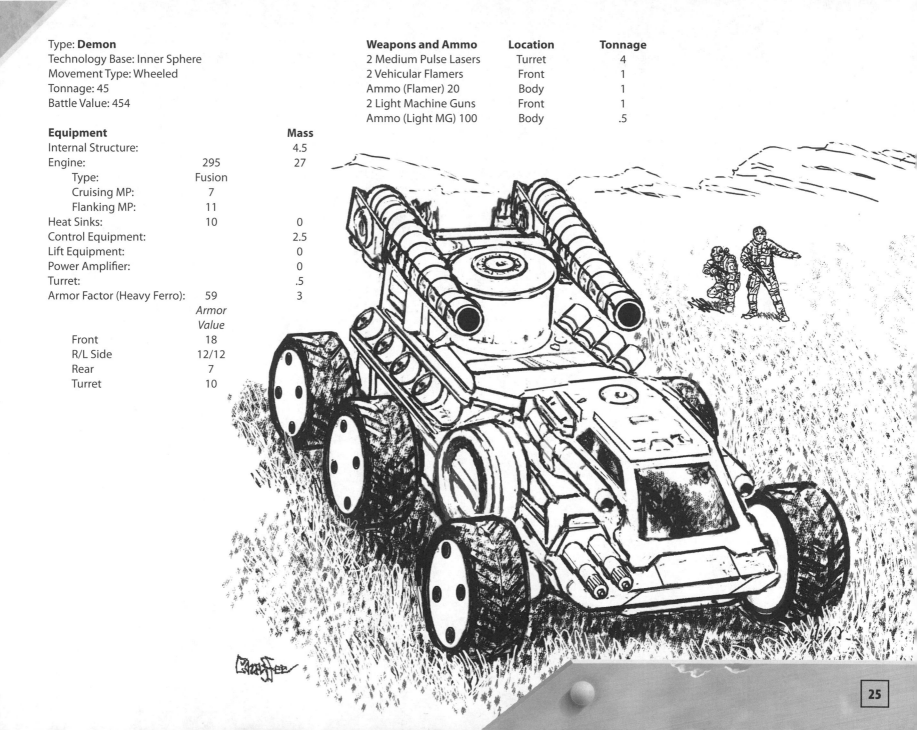

25

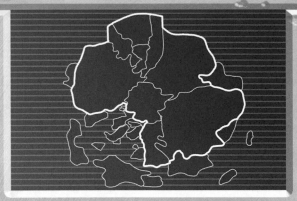

Mass: 45 tons
Movement Type: Wheeled
Power Plant: GM 250 Fusion
Cruising Speed: 64 kph
Flank Speed: 97 kph
Armor: Valiant Buckler
Armament:
    4 Johnston Miniguns
    4 Johnston Light Miniguns
    2 Johnston SlavTrack Arrays
    2 Exostar ER Small Lasers
Manufacturer: Valiant Systems
    Primary Factory: Johnsondale
Communications System: Wunderland XXI-3 series
Targeting and Tracking System: Salamander Systems
    CommPhase Unit

Overview

Unlike the Fox Armored Car, Valiant Systems' final design for the Ranger VV1 was exactly what the original design specifications called for. Heavier and more costly than its Striker predecessor and with an effective combat range of less than 120 meters, the Ranger is a vehicle that exactly fits the niche it was built for and, as a result, has seen limited success in the market. And like the Fox, naming confusions have also affected market sales.

Capabilities

The Ranger came together relatively quickly. Using the Striker chassis as a starting point, the third axle allowed it to handle the additional weight of the Ranger. Weighing nearly twice the Striker's engine, the Shipil 250 is capable of propelling the Ranger up to ninety-seven kilometers per hour. This allows the Ranger to easily keep up with its Striker lancemates and quickly navigate urban environments. Ten tons of standard armor provide thirty percent more protection to the Ranger—a welcome boon when crews realize just how close they need to get to the enemy to hit them.

The primary armament is built around two linked machine gun arrays. Mixing light and standard machine guns allows light engagement out to 120 meters, while giving considerable firepower at point blank ranges. The arrays allow the machine guns to link fire, making them a valid weapon against conventional and battle armored infantry alike. Taking advantage of the fusion engine, two extended-range small lasers were added to the front of the hull.

Deployment

First available in late 3076, the Ranger's relative low cost made it an attractive purchase by Coalition forces. The Ranger was quickly pushed into gaps in orders of battle with a focus on reinforcing Coalition infantry and battle armor forces. Unfortunately, the limited range of its weaponry was quickly recognized and the majority of Rangers that survived their first combat missions were pulled out of the line to be used only in urban combat.

Within the narrow environment of a city, the Ranger performed surprisingly well. Its mobility and thick armor allowed it to survive encounters with Word of Blake tanks such as the Trajan. The massed machine gun batteries proved highly effective against battle armor in the tight urban environment. In the AFFS nearly all Rangers were transferred from armor regiments to infantry regiments where they were grouped with APCs and their heavy infantry.

During the intense fighting at the Achernar BattleMech factory on Achernar, two ComStar Rangers were instrumental in taking down a lance of Protectorate *Locust*s. The Rangers encountered the lance and lured them back into a deadly crossfire from their Morningstar Command Tank lancemates and the two squads of Grenadier battle armor. When a Level I of Achileuses attempted to overpower one of the Morningstars, the Rangers made quick work of the Word suits with a point-blank fusillade of machine gun fire.

Post-Jihad sales of the Ranger have remained low but steady. The limited versatility of the design keeps orders low, but the low cost to purchase and maintain a Ranger still makes them attractive. Mercenaries and corporations have shown a higher interest than most House armies, although The Republic continues to purchase a steady number for deployment to planetary militias for urban defense.

Variants

Answering calls for better range, Valiant released an update to the Ranger. The VV2 removed the machine guns for eight Magshot Gauss rifles. This nearly tripled the effective range of the IFV's main guns at the cost of volume of fire. The tradeoff has so far garnered positive reviews. Able to better deal with battle armor, the VV2 is often paired with two or three VV1s in urban defense lances.

With the machine gun arrays requiring a high level of maintenance, a common field variant removes these and upgrades the four Johnson light machine guns to standard miniguns. The more expensive ER lasers are replaced with four standard small lasers. As a field modification it is still designated VV1.

Recently Valiant has been experimenting with installing a second turret ring for the lasers. Only available as a modification of the VV2, the laser turret is lightly armored compared to the rest of the chassis, even after upgrading the VV2's armor to ferro-fibrous. The expense and increased maintenance of the second turret has limited this model's popularity.

Type: **Ranger**
Technology Base: Inner Sphere
Movement Type: Wheeled
Tonnage: 45
Battle Value: 664

Equipment		Mass
Internal Structure:		4.5
Engine:	250	19
Type:	Fusion	
Cruising MP:	6	
Flank MP:	9	
Heat Sinks:	10	0
Control Equipment:		2.5
Lift Equipment:		0
Power Amplifier:		0
Turret:		.5
Armor Factor:	160	10

	Armor Value
Front	36
R/L Side	32/32
Rear	28
Turret	32

Weapons and Ammo	Location	Tonnage
4 Light Machine Guns	Turret	2
Ammo (Light MG) 300	Body	1.5
Light Machine Gun Array	Turret	.5
4 Machine Guns	Turret	2
Ammo (MG) 200	Body	1
Machine Gun Array	Turret	.5
2 ER Small Lasers	Front	1

MAXIM MK II TRANSPORT

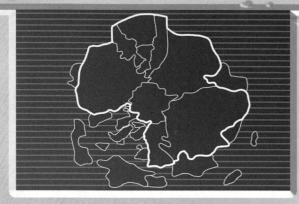

Mass: 50 tons
Movement Type: Hover
Power Plant: PowerTech 165 Highlift Fusion
Cruising Speed: 86 kph
Flank Speed: 129 kph
Armor: ArcShield Heavy Ferro-Fibrous with CASE
Armament:
    2 Helga Series Three-Tube Multi-Missile Launchers
Manufacturer: Cyclops Industries, Inc.,
    Scarborough Manufacturers
    Primary Factory: Skye (Cyclops), Al Na'ir (Scarborough)
Communications System: Cyclops Surelink
Targeting and Tracking System: Scarborough Tracky 3

Overview

When Devlin Stone's "Anyone Can Be a Hero" recruiting campaign created the need for an RAF heavy infantry carrier, both Cyclops Industries and Scarborough Manufacturers bid the Maxim Heavy Hover Transport—a favorite of conventional infantry forces since the days of the first Star League. Praised for its spacious and comfortable transport bay, powerful support weaponry, flexible deployment options, and multiple variants, the Maxim was everything the average soldier could want. The RAF selected the Maxim, but neither Scarborough nor Cyclops could deliver. Scarborough—owing to damage suffered during the Jihad—could not meet production requirements, and although Cyclops escaped the 3075 orbital bombardment of Skye with minor damage they weren't licensed to produce the Maxim.

Hoping to salvage the contract, Scarborough approached Cyclops and proposed a joint venture to develop the Maxim Mk II. Heated debates ensued over the appropriate battlefield role for the Mk II. Amidst a flurry of media coverage, Cyclops's executive VP of development, Shiloh Connolly, resigned, stating the final specifications "…ignored the Maxim's lengthy and successful history of combat support roles and created a tank designed to lose a fist fight." Scarborough's rebuttal argued that the lack of weaponry would keep the Mk II out of combat and prolong the service life of the vehicle. The RAF sided with Scarborough, and the Maxim Mk II was born.

Capabilities

The Mk II's spacious infantry compartment is designed for battle armor soldiers. Adjustable handholds and equipment hooks line the walls while storage bins offer space for ammunition, power packs, support weapons, and other combat essentials. Each multifunction, fold-down station has configurable restraints for both biped and quad suits and a quick release system for egress. These stations can also accommodate various types of conventional infantry, giving the Mk II considerable flexibility as a multi-role transport.

RAF standard procedure is to transport a full platoon of battle armor. Additional configurations include two motorized infantry platoons, four platoons of jump infantry, or five platoons of conventional foot soldiers. Multi-role loadouts usually include two squads of battle armor and two platoons of jump or foot infantry, or one platoon of motorized infantry.

Armed with a pair of MML 3s, the Mk II can engage targets effectively at any range and two tons of ammo ensure combat endurance. Critics observe this is equivalent to the firepower of a foot LRM infantry platoon, making the Mk II one of the few heavy infantry transports outgunned by its compliment of soldiers. Five and a half tons of heavy ferro-fibrous armor provide above-average protection for an infantry transport, and the installation of CASE protects crew and passengers in the event its ammo bin is breached. With a top speed of only 129 kph, the Mk II is average for its weight class. Commanders are advised to avoid light hunter-killer units at all costs.

Deployment

The entire first production run of Mk IIs went to the regiments of the Hastati Sentinels. Subsequent runs have been equally divided between the Sentinels, Triarii Protectors and Principes Guards and are ninety percent standard Mk IIs. Beginning in 3088 the RAF will deploy Mk IIs to prefecture militias. The Mk II Infantry Support variant—produced exclusively on Skye since '84—is exported to the Lyran Commonwealth where it's assigned to the Bolan and Donegal provinces, although rumors suggest that the Mk II will soon see service in Coventry and other parts of the Commonwealth.

Variants

Only one variant of the Mk II has been produced. Cyclops officially calls it the Infantry Support variant though it's known colloquially in the Lyran Commonwealth as the Shiloh. Cargo capacity is sacrificed by half and the turret is enlarged to accommodate two light PPCs and a pair of machine guns, the former providing adequate firepower to screen the advance of deployed soldiers and the latter to discourage close assault by conventional infantry.

Type: **Maxim**
Technology Base: Inner Sphere
Movement Type: Hover
Tonnage: 50
Battle Value: 476

Equipment		Mass
Internal Structure:		5
Engine:	165	10
Type:	Fusion	
Cruising MP:	8	
Flank MP:	12	
Heat Sinks:	10	0
Control Equipment:		2.5
Lift Equipment:		5
Power Amplifier:		0

Equipment		Mass
Turret:		.5
Armor Factor (Heavy Ferro):	109	5.5
	Armor Value	
Front	30	
R/L Side	20/20	
Rear	19	
Turret	20	

Weapons and Ammo	Location	Tonnage
2 MML 3	Turret	3
Ammo (MML) 80/66	Body	2
CASE	Body	.5
Infantry Transport Bay	Body	16

REGULATOR II HOVER TANK

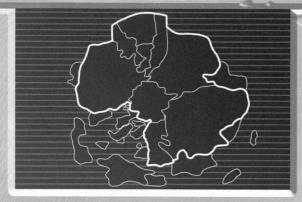

Mass: 50 tons
Movement Type: Hover
Power Plant: GM 265 XL Fusion
Cruising Speed: 108 kph
Flank Speed: 162 kph
Armor: Hellespont Heavy Ferro-Fibrous
Armament:
    1 M-7 Gauss Rifle (Republic)
    1 Inokuma Gauss Rifle (Capellan)
Manufacturer: Aldis Industries
    Primary Factory: Terra (RotS), Betelgeuse (CC)
Communications System: Olmstead 37
Targeting and Tracking System: Virtutrak S1

Overview

The Word of Blake rarely respected intellectual property rights, patents and corporate courtesy. Like robber barons of ancient Terra, they cultivated the art of "I see, I like, I take." Such was the case when the Word provided the Terra-based Aldis Industries with full schematics, including factory retooling guidelines, for the Regulator Hovertank. Not content merely to copy the flagship Capellan hovertank, the Word directed Aldis to improve the design. Unconstrained by resource limitations and with access to anything Terra could produce, Aldis rose to the challenge, introducing the Regulator II on Christmas Day 3076.

Capabilities

Leveraging the Regulator's already-heavy chassis, Aldis increased the Regulator II's mass to fifty tons. Aldis then identified key weaknesses of the Regulator and worked to address these. The first task was to improve its armor protection with eight and a half tons of heavy ferro-fibrous armor, which provides the Regulator II with 150% greater protection. To free tonnage for the additional armor, Aldis upgraded the fusion engine to an extralight model, increasing it to a 265-rated in the process. The additional power allows the Regulator II to achieve speeds up to 162 kph.

In field tests against standard Regulators the Regulator II was able to consistently outperform the older model, using the added maneuverability to flank its slower brethren. Able to easily withstand return fire, the Regulator II easily won over ninety-five percent of its field trials.

Deployment

The Regulator II quickly became a staple of the Blakist Protectorate Militia. Coalition forces came to expect these heavily armored Regulators and devised elaborate traps to deal with them. One preferred tactic used by the Federated Suns offensive was to use Grenadier battlesuits as mobile land mines. Placed strategically by VTOL, the Grenadiers would lie in wait and fire on the Regulator IIs as they raced in to strike the main formations.

While many were destroyed in combat, the Regulator II became a very popular salvage item among Coalition forces. This was not to last though. In an effort to smooth over the tensions between the burgeoning Republic and the Capellan Confederation, David Lear brokered an agreement with the Confederation: in exchange for dropping any legal or corporate retaliation against Aldis and The Republic, Lear provided the Confederation with full schematics for the Regulator II. The deal also required The Republic to purchase all surviving Regulator IIs from Coalition allies and resell half of those to the Confederation. While requiring extensive negotiations and no small amount of arm twisting—the Federated Suns was particularly loathe to surrender their Regulator IIs—the final deal is credited with paving the way for the Treaty of Tikonov.

Regulator IIs can be found in all three RAF brigades, with the Principes Guard having the highest percentage. While too expensive for planetary militias, Aldis is manufacturing the original Regulator for deployment to planetary defense units. In the Capellan Confederation, McCarron's Armored Cavalry and the regiments of the Confederation Reserve Cavalry have seen the largest shipments of Regulator IIs.

Variants

The Republic and Confederation have gone in divergent directions with their respective follow-on Regulator II models. The Republic's updated model moves from sniper to close-in fighter, relying on speed and heavy armor to protect it. The RAF's new Regulator uses a rotary autocannon married to a Federated Suns-licensed targeting computer. A Guardian ECM suite is also installed, enabling it to upset communications networks as it gets in close to pummel targets with the RAC. Eschewing their earlier use of rotary autocannons in field refits as counter to Xin Sheng, the Strategios instructed Aldis to instead develop an improved sniper platform. Replacing the Inokuma Gauss rifle with a lighter model based on the Marik light Gauss gives the Capellan model the ability to strike from outside almost any other weapon's range. Wrapping the vehicle in stealth armor makes the Regulator Stealth an extremely difficult target to hit. While unwilling to use the Davion-invented rotary autocannon in a production unit, Aldis-Betelgeuse and the Strategios had no compunction about using a reverse-engineered targeting computer to increase the accuracy of their updated Regulator.

REGULATOR II HOVER TANK

Type: Regulator II
Technology Base: Inner Sphere
Movement Type: Hover
Tonnage: 50
Battle Value: 1,426

Equipment		Mass
Internal Structure:		5
Engine:	265	10.5
Type:	XL Fusion	
Cruising MP:	10	
Flank MP:	15	
Heat Sinks:	10	0
Control Equipment:		2.5
Lift Equipment:		5
Power Amplifier:		0

Equipment		Mass
Turret:		1.5
Armor Factor (Heavy Ferro):	168	8.5
	Armor Value	
Front	38	
R/L Side	33/33	
Rear	30	
Turret	34	

Weapons and Ammo	Location	Tonnage
Gauss Rifle	Turret	15
Ammo (Gauss) 16	Body	2

PADILLA TUBE ARTILLERY TANK

Mass: 55 tons
Movement Type: Wheeled
Power Plant: Leenex 145 Light Fusion
Cruising Speed: 32 kph
Flank Speed: 54 kph
Armor: StarSlab/3
Armament:
    1 Sniper Artillery Piece
    2 Magna 200P Small Pulse Lasers
    2 Delta Dart Long Range Missile 5-Racks
Manufacturer: Aldis Industries
    Primary Factory: Terra
Communications System: COMSET 9c
Targeting and Tracking System: Aldis TTS 7

Overview

As the Jihad started to turn against the Word of Blake, Precentor Martial Cameron St. Jamais put several plans in motion preparing for the eventuality of Coalition forces reaching Terra. One such plan was the commissioning of a new tube version of the Padilla artillery vehicle. Designed under the watchful guidance of senior engineer James Richard, the Padilla entered service too late to significantly affect the outcome of the Jihad.

Richard succeeded in producing the vehicle as quickly as possible through masterful leveraging of existing resources. With St. Jamais' approval, he based the new Padilla on the chassis of the Thor artillery vehicle then in production by Aldis Industries, instead of the heavier tracked chassis of the original Padilla. This saved valuable months of development time and significantly reduced R&D costs. Once St. Jamais approved the new variant, Richard ordered most Thor chassis production diverted to Padilla construction. Aldis then installed the smaller Leenex light fusion engine, weaponry and StarSlab armor. The resulting vehicle was in production less than six months after being commissioned and on the battlefield shortly after.

The Blakists deployed the Padilla alongside the Thor and their rare heavy Padillas in mixed-artillery Level IIs. The combination gave Blakist commanders highly configurable support options. All three vehicles being somewhat fragile, an additional Level II was usually assigned to support the artillery units.

Capabilities

The tube-equipped Padilla is built around the second most powerful tube-based fire support weapon common in the Inner Sphere. A turret-mounted Sniper artillery piece consumes nearly one-third of the vehicle's mass. The Sniper has an effective range of just over nine klicks—roughly double that of the Arrow IV system mounted by the Padilla's "big brother" of SLDF fame. With only twenty rounds available for the Sniper, artillery crews must be judicious with their fire.

For defense weaponry, the Padilla mounts a pair of Delta Dart missile launchers that do little more than provide harassing fire to opposing forces. Close support is covered by matched Magna 200P pulse lasers. An effective anti-infantry weapon, the Magna has a solid service history and is popular among most crews.

The Leenex light fusion engine is an underpowered model and the Padilla suffers for the lack. Where the Thor and heavy Padilla are both capable of speeding along at nearly ninety kph, the Padilla's top end is a slugging fifty-four kph.

With seven and a half tons of StarSlab/3 armor, the Padilla has reasonable armor protection for a fire support vehicle, but lacks the ability to weather significant attacks. High-speed skirmishers such as the Pegasus hover tank and *Wight* 'Mech pose the biggest threat, as they can easily evade support units to strike at the Padillas.

Deployment

Appearing in the eventide of the Jihad, the Padilla never saw significant deployment within the Blakist Protectorate. The tank featured prominently in the failed defense of Terra and a significant number were captured by Stone's Coalition. Following the cessation of hostilities, they were deployed with Stone's Lament. Production resumed in late 3082 after the Aldis factory was repaired. New Padillas are currently shipping to the Triarii Protectors, Hastati Sentinels and Principes Guards. Aldis also offers the design to all non-Clan factions in the Inner Sphere.

Variants

The Long Tom Cannon (LTC) variant replaces the Sniper artillery piece with a Long Tom. The change results in a thirty-three percent increase in damage, but at a significant cost in range, as the Long Tom's effective range is shorter than that of conventional LRMs. This variant removes one of the LRM 5 racks and a ton of LRM ammo and replaces them with two additional tons of Long Tom ammo and a Guardian ECM suite. Lightly armored for a vehicle expecting direct combat, the LTC variant is often accompanied by a sizeable escort force or used as close-in protection for its Sniper-equipped brethren.

[Editor's note: Image pictured here is that of a Thumper and MML equipped model. - AH]

PADILLA TUBE ARTILLERY TANK

Type: **Padilla**
Technology Base: Inner Sphere (Advanced)
Movement Type: Wheeled
Tonnage: 55
Battle Value: 592

Weapons and Ammo	Location	Tonnage
Sniper Artillery Piece	Turret	20
Ammo (Sniper) 20	Body	2
2 Small Pulse Lasers	Turret	2
2 LRM 5	Turret	4
Ammo (LRM) 48	Body	2

Equipment		Mass
Internal Structure:		· 5.5
Engine:	145	6
Type:	Light Fusion	
Cruising MP:	3	
Flank MP:	5	
Heat Sinks:	10	0
Control Equipment:		3
Lift Equipment:		0
Power Amplifier:		0
Turret:		3
Armor Factor:	120	7.5
	Armor Value	
Front	28	
R/L Side	25/25	
Rear	20	
Turret	22	

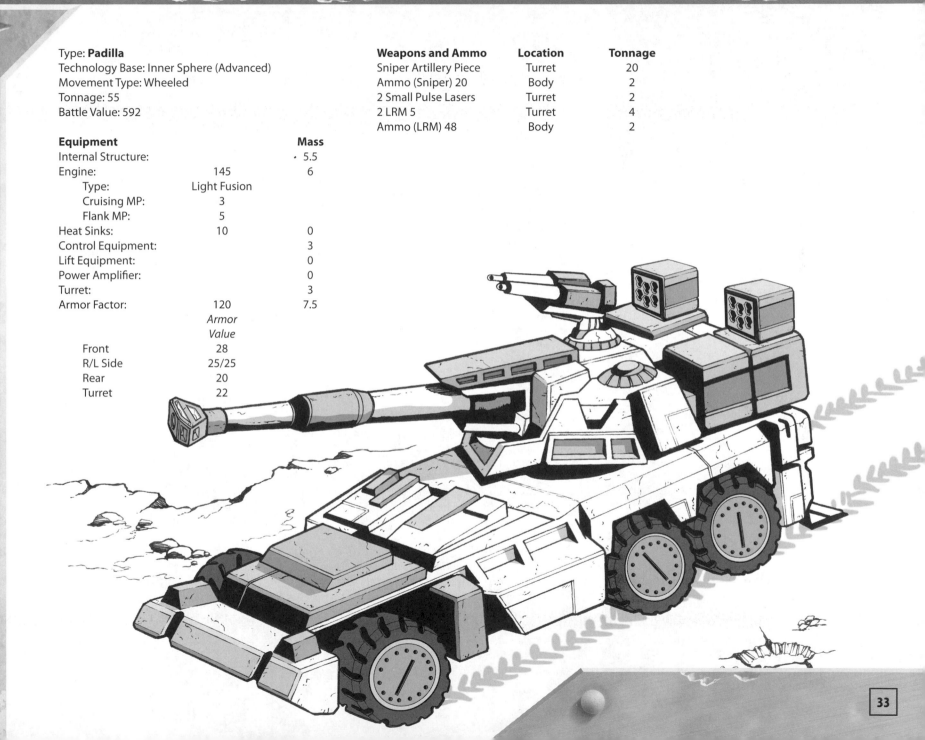

BOLLA STEALTH TANK

Mass: 60 tons
Movement Type: Wheeled
Power Plant: VOX 280 XL Fusion
Cruising Speed: 54 kph
Flank Speed: 86 kph
Armor: Krupp Stealth
Armament:
   1 Voelkers Machine Gun
   19.5 tons of pod space (maximum of 15 tons in turret)
Manufacturer: Maxwell-Pulaski Motors
   Primary Factory: Terra
Communications System: GPT Multi-Track Enhanced
   with Guardian ECM and C³
Targeting and Tracking System: Baltex K590

Overview

The Bolla was originally designed by the Word of Blake as a stealth tank tasked with infiltration and the insertion of a battle armor Level I behind enemy lines. The Coalition's discovery of the research facility where the Bolla was designed allowed for greater understanding of the underlying specifications than could be gleaned from attempts to reverse-engineer captured examples. At Stone's urging the original design was modified to correspond with the RAF organizational scheme and manufactured at a concealed facility on Terra in 3084 to supply our special forces units.

Capabilities

The first change in the redesigned Bolla was to make the unit more serviceable for the RAF. Since the Blakists used a base of six for their forces, the battle armor bay was sized

for a Level I squad of six battle armor troopers. The RAF's standard squad size of four meant that space was wasted, so the chassis was modified to reduce the bay. The C³i system was replaced with a standard C³ slave, although the stealth armor was retained. Also kept was the machine gun, though its ammunition load was halved, and the ECM required for the stealth armor. These reductions in fixed equipment give the new Bolla an additional four tons of pod space.

The primary configuration of the Bolla adds a second machine gun to bolster anti-infantry capability, while the turret carries a rotary AC/5 and two multi-missile 3 racks. This configuration also mounts a TAG system to allow the crew to guide artillery fire.

The A configuration is clearly designed around a long-range engagement philosophy. The turret mounts a light Gauss rifle and anti-missile system. A targeting computer enhances the accuracy of the light Gauss rifle, making the A an exceptional sniper. Like the primary configuration, the A also mounts a TAG system.

The Bolla B seeks to be a jack of all trades. Adding a C³-master computer allows the B to serve as a command unit for an entire lance of C³-slaved units, while its fixed C³ slave allows it to connect to another C³ master as part of a full C³ company. The B can serve as a close-in or long-range bombardier with paired turret-mounted MML 7s. A trio of Magshot Gauss rifles completes its armament, providing pinpoint accuracy at moderate range.

The Bolla C is a well-rounded configuration. A light autocannon paired with precision autocannon ammunition provides some long-range capability with moderate hitting power. A pair of Streak SRM 6 racks keeps enemies honest at short range, while a second machine gun dissuades enemy infantry from getting too close. The C also mounts a TAG system.

Deployment

The original configurations of the Bolla constructed by the Blakists can be found in the forces of those who fought against and salvaged them. Besides the number captured by our own RAF, the Lyran Commonwealth, Federated Suns, Draconis Combine and the former Free Worlds states are all known to have a small handful of Bollas. Though the RAF has the most, the new configurations have been kept secret and are deployed only among special forces units.

Variants

The Blakists constructed the Bolla in four commonly-encountered configurations. The primary (Invictus) was the most frequently seen, while the A (Dominus), B (Infernus), and C (Comminus) were also reported a number of times. Those original Bolla tanks all have a larger infantry bay and a fixed C³i system.

Type: **Bolla**
Technology Base: Inner Sphere (Experimental)
Movement Type: Wheeled
Tonnage: 60
Battle Value: 1,243

Equipment		Mass
Internal Structure:		6
Engine:	280	12
Type:	XL Fusion	
Cruising MP:	5	
Flank MP:	8	
Heat Sinks:	10	0
Control Equipment:		3
Lift Equipment:		0
Power Amplifier:		0
Turret:		1.5
Armor Factor (Stealth):	168	10.5

	Armor Value
Front	34
R/L Side	32/32
Rear	30
Turret	40

Fixed Equipment	Location	Tonnage
Machine Gun	Front	.5
Ammo (MG) 100	Body	.5
Guardian ECM Suite	Body	1.5
C³ Slave	Body	1
Infantry Transport Bay	Body	4

Weapons and Ammo Location Tonnage

Primary Configuration

Rotary AC/5	Turret	10
Ammo (RAC) 60	Body	3
2 MML 3	Turret	3
Ammo (MML) 40/33	Body	2
TAG	Turret	1
Machine Gun	Front	.5

Alternate Configuration A

Light Gauss Rifle	Turret	12
Ammo (Light Gauss) 32	Body	2
Anti-Missile System	Turret	.5
Ammo (AMS) 12	Body	1
TAG	Turret	1
Targeting Computer	Body	3
Battle Value: 1,059		

Alternate Configuration B

2 MML 7	Turret	9
Ammo (MML) 51/42	Body	3
3 Magshot Gauss Rifles	Turret	1.5
Ammo (Magshot) 50	Body	1
C³ Master Computer	Body	5
Battle Value: 961		

Weapons and Ammo Location Tonnage

Alternate Configuration C

2 Streak SRM 6	Turret	9
Ammo (Streak) 30	Body	2
Light AC/5	Turret	5
Ammo (Light AC) 40	Body	2
TAG	Turret	1
Machine Gun	Front	.5
Battle Value: 1,068		

PO II HEAVY TANK

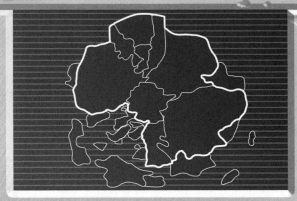

Mass: 60 tons
Movement Type: Tracked
Power Plant: Pitban 240 XL Fusion
Cruising Speed: 43 kph
Flanking Speed: 64 kph
Armor: Starshield V
Armament:
    1 Ceres Huang Di Ultra AC/20 Autocannon
    2 SperryBrowning Machine Guns
    2 LongFire V LRM 5
    2 Hovertec Streak SRM 2 Racks
Manufacturer: Ceres Metals Industries
    Primary Factory: Menke, St. Ives
Communications System: CeresCom Model 37-P
Targeting and Tracking System: Ceres/Maladev 3

Overview

St. Ives suffered grievous damage at the hands of the Word of Blake, with millions of Capellan civilians lost trying to keep the Blakists from the Commonality capital world. The St. Ives-based Ceres Metals facilities were heavily damaged during the fighting, with the turret assembly line completely annihilated. While suitable tooling systems were fabricated to replace the lost equipment, Capellan engineers took the opportunity to redesign the Po, and the re-designated Po II has been in standard production on St. Ives since 3077.

Capabilities

The original Po was designed as a cheap, readily available fighting vehicle to replenish the Confederation's depleted ranks after the Fourth Succession War, and the upgrades applied to it in the late 3060s did little except improve the basic weaponry. Strategios purchasers were loath to accept the loss in production (and attendant sales income) necessary to retool a line for more drastic redevelopment, but the destruction of the lines on St. Ives allowed them the necessary design time.

The core of the tank's new strength is the Pitban 240 extralight engine, which frees up enough mass to completely upgrade the old Po's weaponry. The Po II currently in production mounts a devastating class-twenty Ultra autocannon built from stolen Imperator Automatic Weaponry schematics. Two SperryBrowning machine guns provide an anti-infantry deterrent, and two five-tube long-range missile batteries provide distance strike capability. Two twin-rack Streak short-range missile launchers support the autocannon at close range.

All this weaponry is mounted in the turret, which drastically reduced design time. The interior work necessary to install the extralight engine necessitated some cosmetic changes, but the turret offers a massively different profile than the original Po. Where Maladev's Po was a simple machine with a simple task, the Po II is a successful all-aspect fighting vehicle.

Deployment

The first Po IIs off the line were placed immediately with the St. Ives Lancers, but several companies' worth were also spread across the Confederation for evaluation. Those facing The Republic in the old Tikonov worlds have caused significant disruption to Republic forces—units used to facing platoons of old Pos are surprised by the near-quadrupled firepower of the Po II. A Principes company was caught in an ambush recently, with a platoon of Capellan Po IIs on a ridge above them. Working in concert with Fa Shih battlesuit infantry, the Po IIs used their LRMs to lay a series of staggered minefields. Eight of the Principes' vehicles were disabled by mines before the Pos rolled close enough to aim their autocannons. The survivors surrendered.

Variants

One variant of the Po II has been observed in testing on Menke, leading our analysts to speculate that Ceres Metals may be considering switching all of their Po production facilities over to the Po II configuration. The tank on Menke was similar in all respects to the stock Po II, except that the Ultra autocannon was replaced by a Luxor Mobile Battery Arrow IV missile artillery system. The tank's body has been significantly altered to accept the missile reload bundles, but in observed test firings it was nearly flawless.

PO II HEAVY TANK

Type: Po II
Technology Base: Inner Sphere
Movement Type: Tracked
Tonnage: 60 tons
Battle Value: 1,181

Equipment		Mass
Internal Structure:		6
Engine:	240	9
Type:	XL Fusion	
Cruising MP:	4	
Flanking MP:	6	
Heat Sinks:	10	0
Control Equipment:		3
Lift Equipment:		0
Power Amplifier:		0
Turret:		2.5
Armor Factor:	176	11
	Armor	
	Value	
Front	40	
R/L Side	32/32	
Rear	30	
Turret	42	

Weapons and Ammo	Location	Tonnage
Ultra AC/20	Turret	15
Ammo (Ultra) 15	Body	3
2 Machine Guns	Turret	1
Ammo (MG) 100	Body	.5
2 LRM 5	Turret	4
Ammo (LRM) 24	Body	1
2 Streak SRM 2	Turret	3
Ammo (Streak) 50	Body	1

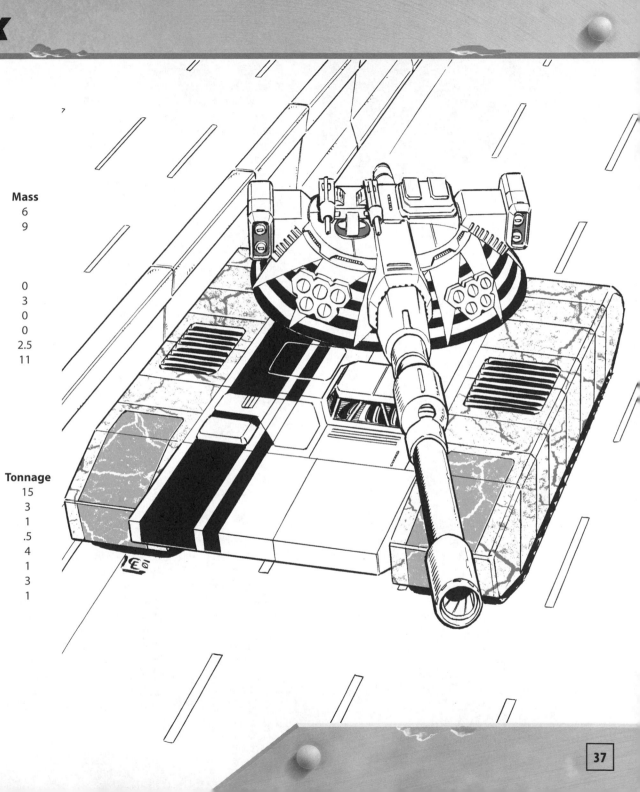

KINNOL MBT

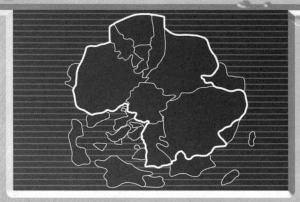

Mass: 70 tons
Movement Type: Tracked
Power Plant: GM 350 Extralight Fusion
Cruising Speed: 54 kph
Flank Speed: 86 kph
Armor: StarSlab/1 Ferro-Fibrous with CASE
Armament:
    1 Mydron Exel LB 10-X Autocannon
    2 Doombud MML 5s
    1 Diverse Optics Extended Range Medium Laser
Manufacturer: Aldis Industries
    Primary Factory: Terra
Communications System: Basix 220
Targeting and Tracking System: Scope 2000

Overview

A new nation needs an army. The Republic of the Sphere had some forces to work with, but nothing standard. With the focus of the new RAF on armor it was identified that a dedicated main battle tank such as the Patton or Schiltron was needed. The re-opened facility at Aldis offered to provide several design overviews and allow the RAF to choose between them. The Kinnol, named after the SLDF General of the Armies for the first half of the twenty-seventh century, was chosen. Aldis' designers had the luxury of not having to rush the next tank to production and had extensive field tests. Field trials were secretly conducted in covert anti-piracy missions to Astrokaszy and Tortuga before the Kinnol was accepted for full production in 3083.

Capabilities

The heart of the Kinnol is the powerful GM extralight engine. The 350-rated engine allows the Kinnol to achieve speeds of over eighty kph and mount a respectable array of weapons and armor. While an expensive outlay of resources, the RAF believes in smaller, high-tech armed forces. Protecting this investment is twelve tons of high-grade StarSlab/1 ferro-fibrous armor. Should the armor fail, the crew is protected from ammunition explosions by CASE. Given the relative frequency of ammunition explosions on the battlefield, being able to save a good crew will go a long way to improving the RAF's armor units. Between the speed and the armor, the Kinnol should be able to bring its firepower to bear.

The heart of the tank's firepower is the Mydron Exel autocannon. It has decent range and packs a good punch, able to destroy some smaller vehicles in a single shot. Mounted on the turret, it can fire at any target within range the tank's crew can see. Paired with the cannon is an extended-range medium laser, complementing the Mydron's power. However the weapons that give the Kinnol the most flexibility are the dual five-tube multi-missile launchers. With three tons of ammunition, the tank can load up to three different types of munitions. For general duty, two tons of LRMs and one of SRMs are often used. But if paired with a unit that has a TAG system, semi-guided LRMs might be used instead. In a close-quarters engagement, the LRMs might be swapped out for more SRMs or Inferno SRMs.

Deployment

The Kinnol has been sent to most of the militias in The Republic. They are usually assigned to the best crews, as the Kinnol's mobility and firepower mean it will likely see more combat than most vehicles. Subsidized sales to mercenary units working for The Republic have proven an enticing tool to keep them contracted. It is also available on the open market, as the RAF currently doesn't have the budget or the need for all of Aldis' output. The Kinnol can be found in most Inner Sphere armies, though often as a supplemental unit rather than the backbone of the force. Some have even been sold to the Capellan Confederation, though animosity between governments often causes long delays in getting contracts approved by both sides.

While not a publicly revealed mission, during the field trials on Astrokaszy a lance of Kinnols demolished a mixed company of pirates in the Periphery. The pirates weren't expecting the tanks to have such speed and allowed the Kinnols to flank them, crippling the pirates' heavier tanks with missile and autocannon fire. As their 'Mechs pulled back to regroup, the Kinnols followed them. Without the heavy guns of their armored units the 'Mechs were soon crushed. One Kinnol was immobilized in the fighting and had to be destroyed before the covert unit returned home with plenty of data to analyze.

Variants

While Aldis hasn't started manufacturing any variants at this time, they have been looking into alternatives to expand the usefulness of the Kinnol. The version that seems most likely to make it to market replaces the auto-cannon with a standard PPC and downgrades the laser to a standard version. Three machine guns would be added to improve the Kinnol's anti-personnel capabilities while a C[3] slave system would allow integration with C[3] networks for increased accuracy.

KINNOL MBT

Type: **Kinnol**
Technology Base: Inner Sphere
Movement Type: Tracked
Tonnage: 70
Battle Value: 1,226

Equipment		Mass
Internal Structure:		7
Engine:	350	22.5
Type:	XL Fusion	
Cruising MP:	5	
Flank MP:	8	
Heat Sinks:	10	0
Control Equipment:		3.5
Lift Equipment:		0
Power Amplifier:		0
Turret:		1.5
Armor Factor (Ferro):	215	12

	Armor Value
Front	65
R/L Side	40/40
Rear	30
Turret	40

Weapons and Ammo	Location	Tonnage
LB 10-X AC	Turret	11
Ammo (LB-X) 20	Body	2
ER Medium Laser	Turret	1
2 MML 5	Front	6
Ammo (MML) 48/20	Body	3
CASE	Body	.5

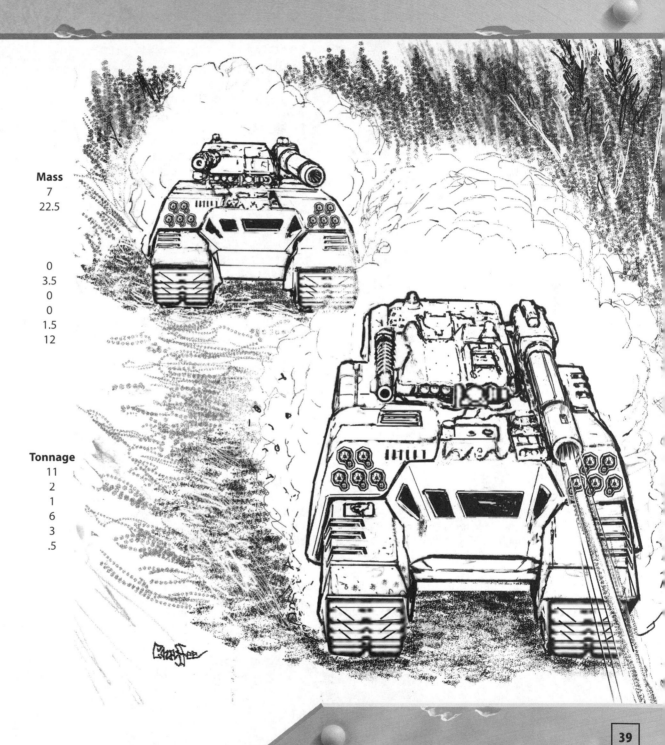

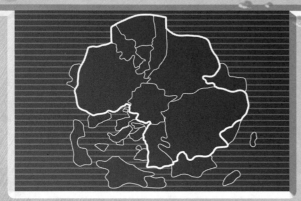

Mass: 70 tons
Movement Type: Tracked
Power Plant: Pitban Light 210 Fusion
Cruising Speed: 32 kph
Maximum Speed: 54 kph
Armor: AmberStar Weave Heavy Ferro with CASE
Armament:
    2 Donal Technologies Light PPC
    2 Holly LRM 15
    1 Holly Streak SRM 6
    1 Buzzsaw Anti-Missile System
Manufacturer: Pandora 'Mech Works
    Primary Factory: Terra
Communications System: COMTEC 400E
Targeting and Tracking System: GroundTracker EE-4

Overview

The Winston Combat Vehicle began life as the Stone main battle tank. As a one-hit wonder company producing the Puma assault tank, Pandora 'Mech Works was desperate to expand their product lines. Though an acclaimed tank, the Puma is still very much identified with the Word of Blake, and post-Jihad sales have been dismal. Facing possible bankruptcy or government-ordered closure, Pandora needed to come up with something to save the company. The result was the Stone MBT, a multi-role combat tank. It was more affordable, better armored and comparably armed to the heavier Puma, and possessed none of the Word of Blake baggage. When Pandora presented the Stone in field trials earlier this year, it was well received by RAF procurement; when Exarch Stone learned of the name, however, he ordered the design rejected because he did not want any military machine named after him. Fortunately for Pandora, former Commanding General and now Paladin Steiner-Davion, has been overseeing military procurement at the request of current RAF commander Belle Lee. He was impressed with the tank and, after consulting with Pandora's board, the Winston Combat Vehicle entered field trials in November 3085.

Capabilities

Named for the famous soldier/statesman Winston Churchill, the name is still clearly a nod to Exarch Stone. A seventy-ton tracked chassis places the Winston in the middle range for a traditional main battle tank, but the Pitban light fusion engine frees up tonnage to allow it to compete with tanks ten and fifteen tons heavier. Fourteen and a half tons of heavy ferro-fibrous armor makes the Winston one of the best-armored tanks ever produced. A vehicular CASE system further protects the tank and extends its lifespan in the event its ammunition stores are hit. A fore-mounted Buzzsaw anti-missile system rounds out the Winston's impressive defensive abilities.

Some have questioned whether the Winston's weapons systems are sufficient for a main battle tank. The two light PPCs only provide half the penetration power of a standard PPC and at first appear light for the tank's mass, even backed by the targeting computer as they are. Designers intentionally went with the two lighter weapons in an effort to create redundancy. The widely spaced Holly long-range missile racks likewise serve as their own backup, and even with half its turret weapons disabled, the Winston remains an effective battle tank. Finally, a Holly Streak launcher is mounted on the front deck, giving the Winston an added short-range bite.

Deployment

The Office of Procurement has yet to announce publicly if they will issue purchase requests for the Winston. After its highly successful field trials, however, the RAF is expected to issue a full purchase order as part of the procurement budget for the second half of 3086.

After the Winston's above-average performance in all standard qualification trials, Paladin General Steiner-Davion asked to see how it would do against BattleMechs of similar firepower. A *Phoenix Hawk* PXH-6D and *Dervish* DV-8D were sent into an urban test range to test the mettle of the two Winston prototypes. The BattleMechs easily outmaneuvered the tanks, and early on scored several telling blows. Then the tanks parked side by side, facing opposite directions, in a broad thoroughfare. The *Dervish* attempted to pepper them at range, but their AMS and heavy armor allowed them to absorb the fire while sending back nearly double the 'Mech's return fire. The *Phoenix Hawk* attempted to close, nullifying the advantage of the tanks' LRMs—but at point-blank range, the Streak SRMs and MML launchers of the LAC variant added a devastating level of firepower that dropped the *Phoenix Hawk* before it could retreat.

Immediate rollout of the Winston to all three front-line combat brigades is expected, and the Winston is reportedly under consideration to become the standard MBT of planetary militia heavy armor companies.

Variants

In an effort to make their design more appealing, Pandora quickly rolled out a second prototype with an alternate weapons load. Both the original and LAC prototypes took part in the November 3085 field trials. The dual light PPCs are traded for shorter-ranged light autocannons, which make up for in accuracy what they lose in range when loaded with precision ammunition. Long-range missile firepower is cut in half by the use of dual seven-tube multi-missile launchers, but this loss is made up for in the increased damage offered by the missile volley at shorter ranges. The LAC variant is specifically designed to defend key intersections in urban combat.

Type: Winston
Technology Base: Inner Sphere
Movement Type: Tracked
Tonnage: 70
Battle Value: 1,551

Equipment		Mass
Internal Structure:		7
Engine:	210	10.5
Type:	Light Fusion	
Cruising MP:	3	
Flank MP:	5	
Heat Sinks:	10	0
Control Equipment:		3.5
Lift Equipment:		0
Power Amplifier:		0
Turret:		2
Armor Factor (Heavy Ferro):	285	14.5

	Armor Value
Front	65
R/L Side	58/58
Rear	50
Turret	54

Weapons and Ammo	Location	Tonnage
2 Light PPCs	Turret	6
2 LRM 15	Turret	14
Ammo (LRM) 24	Body	3
Streak SRM 6	Front	4.5
Ammo (Streak) 15	Body	1
Anti-Missile System	Front	.5
Ammo (AMS) 12	Body	1
Targeting Computer	Body	2
CASE	Body	.5

MOLTKE MBT

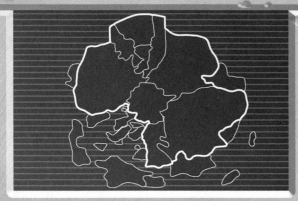

Mass: 75 tons
Movement Type: Tracked
Power Plant: Vlar 300 XL Fusion
Cruising Speed: 43 kph
Flanking Speed: 64 kph
Armor: StarSlab/7 Heavy Ferro-Fibrous
Armament:
2 Kali Yama Weapons Industries LB 10-X ACs
1 FlameTech Inferno Plasma Rifle
Manufacturer: Brooks Incorporated
Primary Factory: Andurien
Communications System: Maxell 650
Targeting and Tracking System: Maxell TA 85 with TAG

Overview

Desperate to supplement Andurien's meager forces with long-ranged support, Brooks revised the ancient Augustus tank to create the Moltke. The design more than did its job, though the Jihad took a further toll on Andurien forces. Rather than risk relying on foreign imports to replace losses, the Anduriens looked to internal sources. While the two existing Moltke versions were shown to be effective, they focused on ranged support. The M2 could unleash a short-range barrage, but versatility was its strength. Brooks offered to reconfigure its base design to provide a version better suited to getting deep into the heat of battle. The new tank would provide considerable savings in design and maintenance.

Capabilities

Possessing the same engine, chassis and armor as its cousins, the M3 is tough and quick, just like the other models. It can keep up with opponents like a Rommel or a Po, and mounts the firepower of a Von Luckner or a Demolisher. Brooks kept the Y-shaped turret inherited from the Augustus and mounted three powerful weapons in it. A pair of versatile heavy autocannons gave it hitting power along with the option of increased accuracy and better damage spread with cluster munitions. Backing up the dual cannons is a newly designed plasma rifle devastating to vehicles, infantry and 'Mechs alike. As a side effect, this weapon raises the heat levels of 'Mechs, an asset in clashes with Capellan units that have stealth armor.

As a final addition to the M3, Brooks' designers added a TAG system to spot for artillery and make units equipped with semi-guided LRMs, like the M2, more effective. With five tons of ammunition, the Moltke can last most engagements without its ammo bins running empty. Often the hardest decision is what ratio of cluster and slug ammunition to load for the autocannons.

The biggest vulnerability for the M3, and all the Moltkes, is a lack of anti-infantry weapons. While the plasma rifle can ravage an infantry unit, it is an expensive way to fight infantry. However, the M3 remains an improvement over other versions of the Moltke in this regard.

Deployment

The first Moltkes were sold to Andurien militia forces, especially those working heavily with 'Mech units. After approval from the Duchy, Moltkes were also sold to the Abbey District, the Mosiro Archipelago and the Regulan Free States. After the cessation of Jihad fighting, sales were opened up to the Principality of Regulus and the Duchy of Oriente, though primarily of the M1 and M2 versions. Other parties have shown interest in the Moltke, but the Duchy has not authorized sales outside of former League worlds that are not hostile to it.

Variants

The original Moltke carries dual light Gauss rifles in the turret, accompanied by a Sunbeam extended-range laser. The M2 version replaces the dual rifles with four seven-tube multi-missile launchers, while the laser gives way to a snub-nose PPC. A fifth missile launcher is mounted on the front of the tank, which required some rework of the base chassis, one reason that Brooks designers have been reluctant to mount other weapons outside the turret.

Notable Crews

Triple Zero One: The first Moltke produced, serial number 0001, has an extended battle history along with its crew, Sergeant Lipscolm and Corporals Petty, Chu, Running Elk and Chavez. As part of the Shiro III militia, they were one of the few Andurien units to engage Blakist forces in the Jihad. Shattered remnants of a few fleeing Blakist forces landed on Shiro III in late 3080. Hiding on a hillside, this Moltke crew managed to cripple three Blakist armor units before pulling back out of their range. They then fought the remainder of the Blakist Level II to a standstill, leaving only two Blakist tanks to retreat with other surviving crews.

MOLTKE MBT

Type: **Moltke**
Technology Base: Inner Sphere
Movement Type: Tracked
Tonnage: 75
Battle Value: 1,438

Equipment		Mass
Internal Structure:		7.5
Engine:	300	14.5
Type:	XL Fusion	
Cruising MP:	4	
Flanking MP:	6	
Heat Sinks:	10	0
Control Equipment:		4
Lift Equipment:		0
Power Amplifier:		0
Turret:		3
Armor Factor (Heavy Ferro):	238	12
	Armor Value	
Front	62	
R/L Side	47/47	
Rear	32	
Turret	50	

Weapons and Ammo	Location	Tonnage
2 LB 10-X AC	Turret	22
Ammo (LB-X) 30	Body	3
Plasma Rifle	Turret	6
Ammo (Plasma) 20	Body	2
TAG	Turret	1

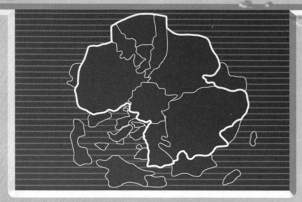

Mass: 80 tons
Movement Type: WiGE
Power Plant: Hermes 260 XL Fusion
Cruising Speed: 54 kph
Flanking Speed: 86 kph
Armor: Johnston Duraweave 8000 Ferro-Fibrous
Armament:
    1 Defiance Hammerfist Heavy Gauss Rifle
    2 Devastator Selectable 7 Tube
    2 BlazeFire Longshot Extended Range Medium Lasers
Manufacturer: Nashan Diversified, WC Site 4
    Primary Factory: Furillo (LC), Arc-Royal (CWiE)
Communications System: Nashan Optichat
Targeting and Tracking System: T-800 Series 5

Overview

The Taurian nuclear bombardment of New Syrtis in October of 3076 nearly finished Johnston Industries. Unlike their contemporaries who saw production facilities razed during the attack, Johnston found their factory complex contaminated by fallout. By January of 3077 their insurance company was insolvent, and clean-up costs had more than doubled initial estimates. Watching their reserves dwindle faster than the Blake Protectorate, Johnston turned to joint ventures. From 3077 to 3080, they approached more than a dozen manufacturers in the Lyran Commonwealth, Federated Suns and the increasingly unstable Free Worlds League.

Nashan Diversified met with Johnston executives in early 3078. It seemed a good match, as Nashan had been looking to expand in the combat vehicle market, but six months of difficult negotiations followed. Johnston wanted an assault-class tank to compete against StarCorp's Manteuffel, but Nashan was developing a fifty-ton WiGE counterpart to the Maxim transport, and despite their vast holdings, didn't have the facilities to produce Johnston's vehicle.

The project was all but dead until Johnston suggested using Nashan's WiGE as alternative chassis. In the ensuing talks, Nashan agreed to increase mass by thirty tons, remove the turret and upgrade the weaponry. In exchange for these concessions, Nashan obtained exclusive rights to the vehicle for ten years. The original WiGE died with only one chassis partially completed, and the Fensalir development began. The first prototype was delivered in 3083 and full production started in 3084.

The Fensalir is the first Johnston joint-venture project to come to market, though several others are in field trials or late development stages as of this briefing. This vehicle is a new type of gamble for Lyran industrial giant Nashan, but one that so far looks promising.

Capabilities

At eighty tons, the Fensalir is the heaviest combat WiGE currently in production. Nashan assembles the craft on Furillo using more than fifty percent imported materials. A Hermes XL 260 engine is sourced from Kallon Industries on Asuncion. Two BlazeFire Longshot lasers and eleven and a half tons of Duraweave armor are brought in from Johnston's reclaimed facilities on New Syrtis, and a Defiance Hammerfist gives the Fensalir its offensive punch. Rumor has it that Nashan executives are unhappy with this weapon choice, but found it cheaper to purchase and ship the weapon from Defiance Industries on Hesperus II than to import the Johnston-made Poland Main Model C Gauss rifle.

Only the targeting and tracking systems, communications system, chassis and Devastator MML launchers are produced on Furillo. A four-ton infantry transport bay remains as a leftover from Nashan's original WiGE project. The compartment is utilitarian with quick-stow seating, five-point restraints and little else. Nashan delivers the Fensalir with the compartment pre-configured for battle armor, but sells a conventional infantry reconfiguration kit as an option.

Deployment

The Fensalir started shipping to Lyran units in Bolan and Donegal provinces last year. Republic Intelligence expects this year's production runs will go to units in the Melissia Theater and Coventry province.

The CWiE variant appears with the Kell Hounds and CWiE Galaxies in the Arc-Royal Theater.

Variants

Detailed analysis recently revealed that the new Clan Wolf in Exile WiGE—previously designated A88—is actually a Fensalir variant. Republic operatives have been unable to determine if the Wolves purchased the design from Nashan, or otherwise acquired the technology. Long-range reconnaissance scans suggest the CWiE Fensalir uses Inner Sphere technology for its chassis, engine and armor, but mounts Clan weaponry. It appears to be equipped with a HAG 30 in place of the Hammerfist. ATM 9 racks replace the MML 7s, and the BlazeFire Longshots are upgraded to Clan models. Transport capacity is also increased to carry a Point of battle armor infantry.

Additionally, Nashan produces an infantry transport variant of the Fensalir based on their original fifty-ton WiGE concept. It drops the MMLs and expands the infantry bay to carry a full platoon of battle armor. CASE and an additional half-ton of armor provide added protection. Finally, three machine guns cover the front and sides of the vehicle.

FENSALIR COMBAT WIGE

Type: **Fensalir**
Technology Base: Inner Sphere
Movement Type: WiGE
Tonnage: 80
Battle Value: 1,654

Equipment		Mass
Internal Structure: 8		
Engine:	260	10.5
Type:	XL Fusion	
Cruising MP:	5	
Flanking MP:	8	
Heat Sinks:	10	0
Control Equipment:		4
Lift Equipment:		8
Power Amplifier:		0

Equipment		Mass
Turret:		0
Armor Factor (Heavy Ferro):	228	11.5
	Armor	
	Value	
Front	60	
R/L Side	60/60	
Rear	48	

Weapons and Ammo	Location	Tonnage
Heavy Gauss Rifle	Front	18
Ammo (Heavy Gauss) 12	Body	3
2 MML 7	Front	9
Ammo (MML) 34/28	Body	2
2 ER Medium Lasers	Front	2
Infantry Transport Bay	Body	4

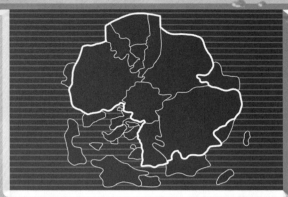

Mass: 85 tons
Movement Type: Tracked
Power Plant: GoreTex 255 Fusion
Cruising Speed: 32 kph
Flank Speed: 54 kph
Armor: ArchShield Maxi II
Armament:
    2 Holly MML 7
    1 SarLon MiniCannon Light Autocannon/5
    1 Kreiger ER Medium Laser
    4 MainFire Light Minigun Machine Guns
    2 SureFire 444 Anti-Missile Systems
Manufacturer: Aldis Industries
    Primary Factory: Terra
Communications System: Olmstead 3000
    with Guardian ECM and C^3 Slave
Targeting and Tracking System: Omicron X

Overview

The first encounter with a Palmoni AIFV provided an unpleasant surprise to the Coalition forces fighting on Wasat. With the outward appearance of a heavy combat tank, Duchess Rousset-Marik's forces were unprepared for the assault infantry that poured from the Palmoni's bay. Crippling fire from SRM-loaded MMLs, combined with the infantry attacks, wiped out nearly a company of the Home Guard in barely two minutes time.

Aldis Industries has a reputation for reliable and deadly, if unimaginative, designs, including the Behemoth Assault Tank, the Demolisher, and various weapons carriers. As all of these Aldis vehicles are reliable and venerable designs, with the only modern design to their name being the Zhukov and that through the Capellan branch of Aldis, there was some surprise that Aldis was the force behind the Palmoni. Most likely Aldis produced the Palmoni to specific requirements from the Word's own military designers and they were extremely eager to redesign it to Republic specifications. Renamed after a Roman Emperor/General, the Trajan has become a key vehicle in RAF battle armor units.

Capabilities

As with most multi-role vehicles, the Trajan does not excel at any one task. The Trajan's standard fusion engine grants a flank speed of just over fifty kilometers per hour. The low speed limits its ability to rapidly deploy its onboard infantry, up to two squads of battle armor or several platoons of conventional infantry. In RAF units this weakness is offset by assigning assault armor to support the Trajan.

The weapons systems of the Trajan are equally diverse, or confused. The twin Holly MML 7 launchers provide long-range firepower, but when compared to lighter dedicated missile units, like a thirty-five ton Striker, they come up wanting. This is mitigated somewhat at short range, where the MMLs, combined with the turreted extended-range medium laser and light autocannon—often loaded with precision ammunition—offer a healthy punch. In close the tank shifts roles to anti-infantry, with light machine guns ringing the chassis.

While the Trajan's weapons call for closing with its opponents, its thirteen-and-a-half tons of armor are deemed insufficient for a prolonged slugging match. This forces a Trajan crew to rely on cover and its own carried battle armor to keep it safe, limiting its usefulness in combat. The C^3 system mitigates this to some extent, allowing it to share targeting data with fellow company members. The Republic standard model's ECM grants it additional protection over the original Word Protectorate model.

What the Trajan does do effectively is provide a rounded multi-role vehicle in an easily built chassis with a relatively low cost.

Deployment

Heavily produced for Protectorate Militias, the Trajan was found on nearly every planet liberated by the Coalition in late 3077 and 3078. Their perceived limited usefulness made them relatively unwanted salvage by the Houses, leaving the Protectorate Trajans in the hands of the planetary militias set up in the wake of liberation. With the rebranding given by The Republic, the new battle armor command tracks quickly became key units in the RAF.

New Trajans are being used as the backbone of RAF battle armor transport units. One Trajan, two Giggins and a Maxim II can carry a complete battle armor company and provide the firepower to support them.

Variants

Intended to carry conventional infantry, the original Word of Blake Palmoni also had an eight-ton infantry bay. Typically used to carry a motorized platoon, it could carry foot infantry in a pinch. The Word's standard version used an Improved C^3 in the place of The Republic C^3 Slave and ECM suite. Few, if any, of the original Word models remain, with most salvaged models being field-refitted to RAF standard. Unchanged from the original Word second-line variant, the ICE-powered Trajan sacrifices firepower for cost savings. The multi-missile systems are dropped in favor of a Holly LRM 10 and a Streak SRM 6. The ICE version also gives up the medium laser and one of its SureFire Anti-Missile systems.

TRAJAN ASSAULT INFANTRY FIGHTING VEHICLE

Type: **Trajan**
Technology Base: Inner Sphere
Movement Type: Tracked
Tonnage: 85
Battle Value: 1,182

Equipment		**Mass**
Internal Structure:		8.5
Engine:	255	19.5
Type:	Fusion	
Cruising MP:	3	
Flank MP:	5	
Heat Sinks:	10	0
Control Equipment:		4.5
Turret:		1.5
Armor Factor:	216	13.5
	Armor Value	
Front	52	
R/L Side	44/44	
Rear	36	
Turret	40	

Weapons and Ammo	**Location**	**Tonnage**
2 MML 7	Turret	9
Ammo (MML) 68/56	Body	4
Light AC/5	Turret	5
Ammo (Light AC) 40	Body	2
ER Medium Laser	Turret	1
Light Machine Gun	Front	.5
Light Machine Gun	Right	.5
Light Machine Gun	Left	.5
Light Machine Gun	Rear	.5
Ammo (Light MG) 200	Body	1
2 Anti-Missile System	Front	1
Ammo (AMS) 24	Front	2
C^3 Slave	Body	1
Guardian ECM	Body	1.5
Infantry Transport Bay	Body	8

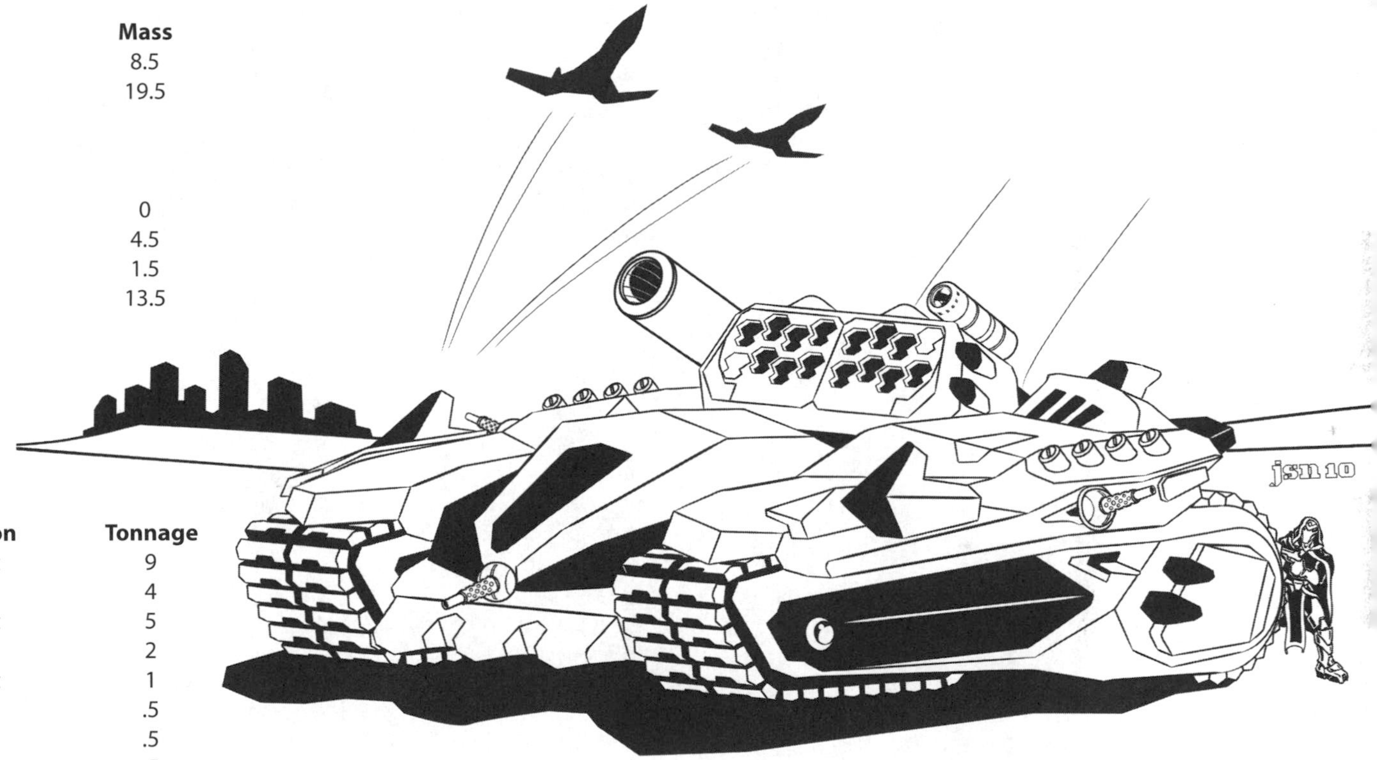

Mass: 95 tons
Movement Type: Tracked
Power Plant: DAV 190 Fusion
Cruising Speed: 21 kph
Flanking Speed: 32 kph
Armor: ArcShield Maxi IV
Armament:
  4 FarFire LRM 15 Launchers
  2 FarFire MML 9 Racks
  1 BlazeFire Longshot Extended-Range Medium Laser
Manufacturer: Joint Equipment Systems
  Primary Factory: Panpour
Communications System: Communicator
  with Guardian ECM and C³ Slave
Targeting and Tracking System: FireScan
  with IndirecTrack

Overview

The conquest of Alshain and the loss of their main production facility, combined with the loss of contracts for the upgraded SRM/LRM carriers in the mid-3050s, nearly killed Joint Equipment Systems. With debts spiraling, things looked bleak until an unlikely savior appeared in the form of Clan Ghost Bear.

In 3063, the Bears' merchant caste received permission from the Clan Council to approach JES and invite the company back to Alshain, to help bridge the gaps between the people of Rasalhague and the Clan. In exchange for the resources to refurbish and upgrade part of JES' large facilities, the Bears would exact hefty export

fees and JES would be restricted to exporting Inner Sphere-quality technology.

The Tyr infantry support tank was JES' "comeback vehicle" for the Clan market and provided a trickle of capital to keep their creditors at bay. With the onset of the Jihad, this trickle soon became a flood. Desperate for increased production, the Bears reduced the export tariffs and stepped up the facility's expansion and refurbishment. JES also upgraded their Panpour facilities to produce the radical but under-whelming tactical missile carrier in 3074.

With the completion of the new facilities in late 3074, and a near tripling of profits by 3076, JES was able to fully expand the Panpour facilities. Debuting in 3079, the strategic missile carrier represents a return to the market in which JES made their name—tracked missile carriers.

Capabilities

The JES II strategic missile carrier is built around four front-mounted FarFire LRM 15 launchers, matching the payload of the older carriers the company used to produce. A pair of side-mounted FarFire MML 9 racks expands the JES II's flexibility by providing additional long-range barrages and then switching to close-in support should the enemy get too near. A front-mounted BlazeFire Longshot ER medium laser rounds out the weaponry, and acts as a backup should ammo run low or as a deterrent to enemy infantry.

A cavernous eleven-ton LRM ammo bay provides almost four minutes of continuous fire, while a smaller four-ton bay supplies the MMLs—often split fifty-fifty between LRMs and SRMs. The multitude of alternate ammunition loads available on the current market vastly increases the JES II's usefulness, enabling commanders to outfit the unit to match specific requirements or conditions of battle. Ten and a half tons of ArcShield Maxi IV armor provides the JES II with ample protection—a good thing, considering its meager 32 kph maximum speed—and a Guardian ECM suite provides defensive countermeasures against enemy electronics.

The JES II works best from prepared positions with cover, either launching its LRMs indirectly at the enemy or utilizing its C³ system to use direct targeting data from a more agile skirmisher unit.

Deployment

Initial production runs were split between Clan Ghost Bear's Dominion and the Federated Suns, with later runs opened up to the Inner Sphere as a whole. The Suns has used the carriers to help implement its new defensive doctrine, while the Dominion's carriers have gone to shore up KungsArmé units that were damaged in the recent troubles.

Republic units have also picked up a number of production runs of the JES II, which provide the backbone of many militia units. Attempts are underway to persuade JES to build a factory in The Republic.

Variants

Only one variant currently exists. The Dominion units replace the C³ slave with another ton of LRM ammunition.

Given the simplicity of the design, Joint Equipment Systems is rumored to be looking into a number of variants. Likely options include alterations to the missile launchers or electronics systems to better suit individual customers' requirements, though a cheaper ICE-powered version may be possible.

While not a variant of the JES II, the expansion of the Cartago engine production facility has given JES a chance to finally rectify the primary flaw of the tactical missile carrier: its speed. Utilizing a 165-rated fusion engine, the JES I can now achieve a maximum speed of 129 kph. Even though this increases the cost of the vehicle by nearly 60 percent, the upgraded version has seen a dramatic upturn in sales and has become a welcome support unit to JES II platoons.

JES II STRATEGIC MISSILE CARRIER

Type: **JES II**
Technology Base: Inner Sphere
Movement Type: Tracked
Tonnage: 95
Battle Value: 1,349

Equipment		Mass
Internal Structure:		9.5
Engine:	190	11.5
Type:	Fusion	
Cruising MP:	2	
Flanking MP:	3	
Heat Sinks:	10	0
Control Equipment:		5
Lift Equipment:		0
Power Amplifier:		0
Turret:		0
Armor Factor:	168	10.5
	Armor Value	
Front	64	
R/L Side	35/35	
Rear	34	

Weapons and Ammo	Location	Tonnage
ER Medium Laser	Front	1
4 LRM 15	Front	28
Ammo (LRM) 88	Body	11
MML 9	Right	6
MML 9	Left	6
Ammo (MML) 52/44	Body	4
C³ Slave	Body	1
Guardian ECM Suite	Body	1.5

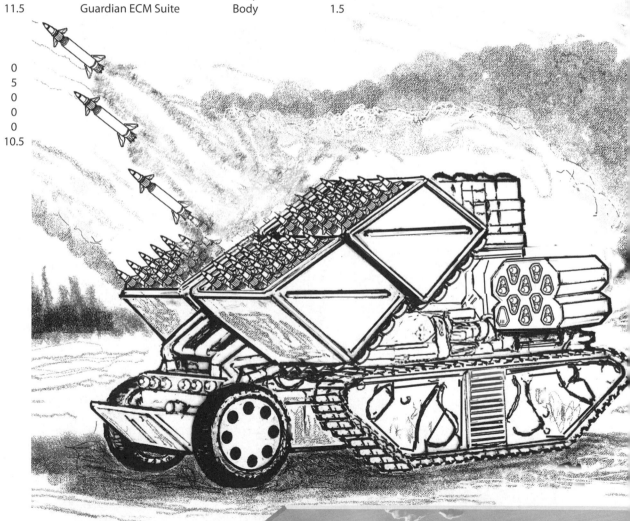

GÜRTELTIER MBT

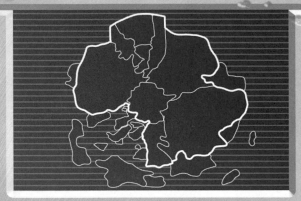

Mass: 100 tons
Movement Type: Tracked
Power Plant: Vlar 300 XL Fusion
Cruising Speed: 32 kph
Flank Speed: 54 kph
Armor: StarSlab/4 Heavy Ferro-Fibrous with CASE
Armament:
    1 Defiance 1001 Extended Range PPC
    1 Poland Main Model A Gauss Cannon
    1 TharHes Multi-Missile 7 Launcher
    3 Coventry Light Autoguns
Manufacturer: Defiance Industries
    Primary Factory: Hesperus II
Communications System: TharHes Muse 54-58K with
    Guardian ECM and C³ Slave
Targeting and Tracking System: TharHes Mars8.2
    with Targeting Computer

Overview

The Lyran armed forces have access to the multi-functional Rommel and Patton tanks as well as a great many specialist designs, but lacked a good multi-role tank to fill a similar role to the Rommel and Patton in the assault weight class. As the damaged facilities on Hesperus were rebuilt, a new line was constructed to manufacture a tank to fill this role. The Quartermaster's department studied recent tank battles, especially those involving the *EisenJäger* on Tharkad. The department then submitted a list of criteria to the design team, requiring thick armor and long-range weapons to keep the tank relevant if disabled. A weapon was needed to disable enemy armor units and exploit damage against BattleMechs. Finally, the department wanted a sophisticated electronic system for targeting and electronic warfare. The LAAF was pleased with the design submitted and named the heavily armored tank after the Terran armadillo, known for its thick protective shell.

Capabilities

The Gürteltier delivers on all counts and then some. Almost a fifth of the design's tonnage was allocated to armor, and designers used heavy ferro-fibrous armor to make it even tougher. CASE protects the crew and much of the more expensive parts of the tank from ammunition explosions. Finally, a trio of machine guns protects much of the tank from infantry attacks. To provide a long-distance one-two punch, an extended-range particle cannon is mated with a Gauss rifle in the turret, allowing the Gürteltier to engage targets at nearly three-quarters of a kilometer. Supplementing that is a seven-tube multi-missile system, allowing accompanying long-range fire as well as a close-range punch. With three tons of ammo for both ammo-based weapons, the tank has endurance as well as options. It typically carries one ton of long-range missiles and one ton of short-range missiles, with the third ton allocated depending on the mission. Mine-laying missiles can slow down or channel the enemy while on the defensive, or infernos can wreak havoc on enemy armor and infantry.

The Gürteltier has an ECM system capable of protecting it from enemy electronics or of disrupting enemy ECM. This capability grows even more powerful when the tank is part of a C³ network, thanks to the slave module built into the massive electronics suite. The last part of the electronics suite is an enhanced targeting computer, allowing the two devastating weapons in the turret to hit with improved precision. The entire package is a deadly war machine that has pleased the Lyran command and troops.

Deployment

The Gürteltier has been assigned to armor regiments in the front-line LCAF, most heavily among Royal and Lyran Guards units. It has yet to make an appearance in militia units, and the expense and maintenance will likely keep it out of their hands for some time. The tank is also sold to the Federated Suns and Republic of the Sphere, where it coordinates well with their C³ networks. The Gürteltier has seen limited action, mostly against pirates. However, a conflict on Surcin showed Clan Wolf forces that the Gürteltier is an enemy to be reckoned with. A Star of Wolf 'Mechs encountered a lance of Gürteltiers, and after the initial salvos destroyed a *Linebacker* and disabled a Gürteltier, the remaining Wolves closed on the damaged tank. Using their C³ systems, the Lyrans took down two more 'Mechs in the half minute that their enemy spent pouring fire into the immobile Gürteltier. The remainder of the Clan forces retreated and the Gürteltier was eventually repaired.

Variants

To coordinate with the standard Gürteltier, a C³ master version is also being manufactured. To make room to upgrade the C³ system, the Gauss rifle has been replaced with a Class-10 LB-X autocannon. With a lighter ballistic weapon, engineers were able to use a lighter turret and targeting computer. This allowed for an upgrade of the missile launcher with an Artemis IV system and the addition of a forward-firing machine gun.

GÜRTELTIER MBT

Type: **Gürteltier**
Technology Base: Inner Sphere
Movement Type: Tracked
Tonnage: 100
Battle Value: 2,125

Equipment		Mass
Internal Structure:		10
Engine:	300	14.5
Type:	XL Fusion	
Cruising MP:	3	
Flanking MP:	5	
Heat Sinks:	15	5
Control Equipment:		5
Turret:		3
Armor Factor (Heavy Ferro):	376	19

	Armor Value
Front	109
R/L Side	75/75
Rear	50
Turret	67

Weapons and Ammo	Location	Tonnage
ER PPC	Turret	7
Gauss Rifle	Turret	15
Ammo (Gauss) 24	Body	3
MML 7	Turret	4.5
Ammo (MML) 51/42	Body	3
Machine Gun	Right	.5
Machine Gun	Left	.5
Machine Gun	Rear	.5
Ammo (MG) 100	Body	.5
Guardian ECM Suite	Body	1.5
C³ Slave	Body	1
Targeting Computer	Body	6
CASE	Body	.5

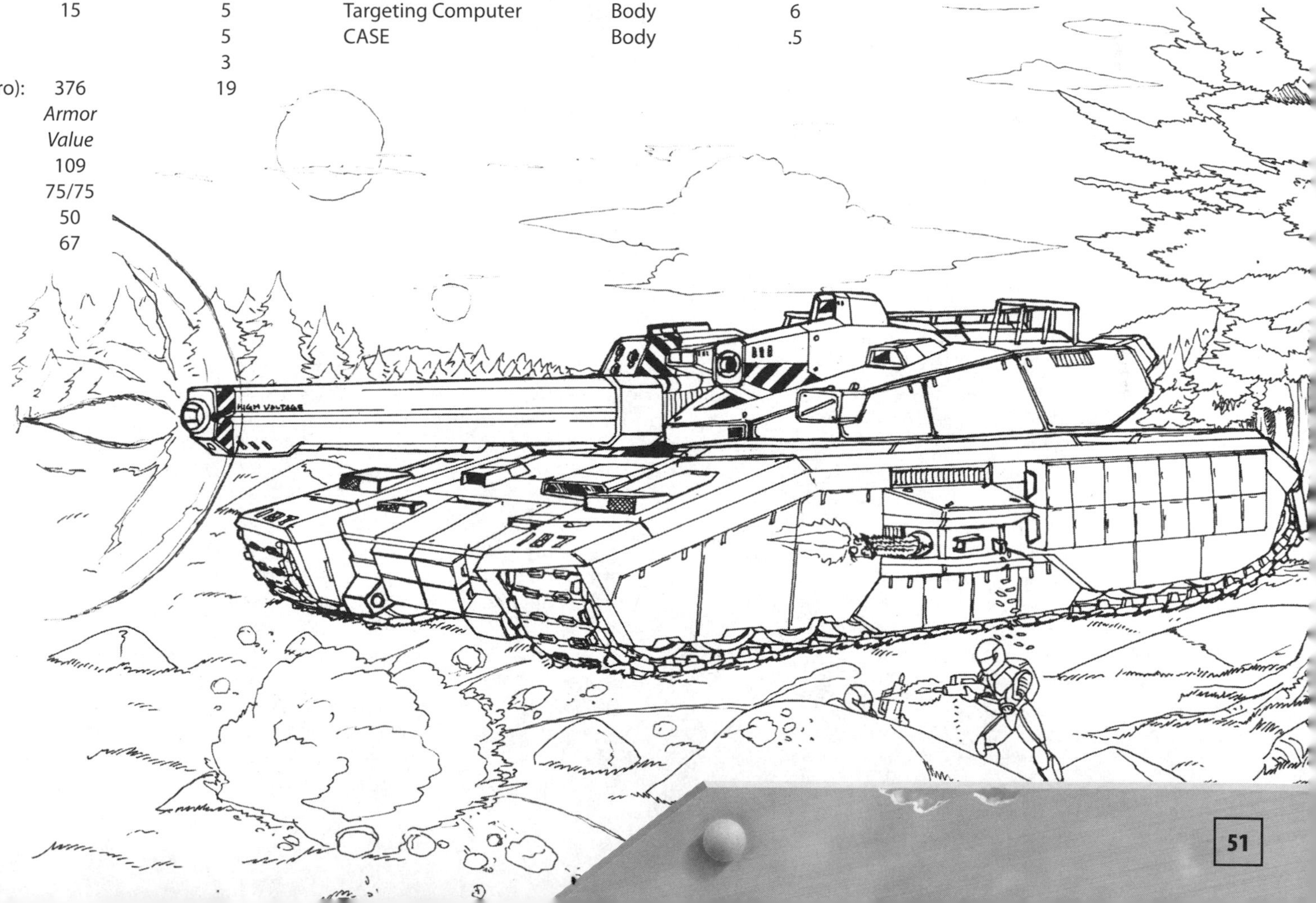

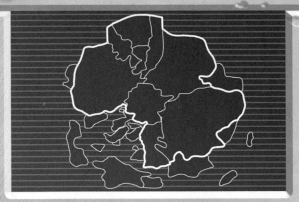

During Operation BULLDOG, foreign forces enjoyed full salvage rights on any planet liberated. Yet this salvage was often sorely disappointing, which generated a legend of hive-like DropShips landing and spewing forth insect swarms that picked clean nearby Smoke Jaguar depots. At first, these stories were dismissed as as the ravings of battle-weary 'Mech jocks, until a holopic taken by a Royal Guards recon camera on Avon surfaced in 3059. The picture showed an insectoid VTOL picking up a Mars assault tank and lifting it toward a nearby hovering airship. Despite the apparent Kurita markings on the units, the holopic merely fed stories throughout the 3060s and 3070s that ranged from the fantastic to the ridiculous.

Only in preparations for the Terran campaign was House Kurita's well-kept secret revealed. The aptly named Tonbo (Dragonfly) Superheavy Transport is a large support VTOL designed to conduct salvage in contested areas and combat transport in flanking assaults. Weighing in at 56 tons, the Tonbo uses four lift hoists to carry external loads of more than 100 tons. In addition to this heavy lift capacity, the Tonbo sports a full communications suite that serves as a command and control relay. Furthermore, a company of infantry can be carried in an internal bay, allowing for easy deployment of combat engineers or armored troops to support assaults or guarantee defense against headhunters when the Tonbo is grounded.

Wakazashi Enterprises developed the Tonbo based on DCMS specifications that called for a unit capable of recovering Clan salvage in any terrain. Operation BULLDOG was its field trial, deployed in company-sized formations by specially modified Rose DropShips. The existence of the Tonbo was kept secret, allowing the Combine to retain more than its fair share of salvage during BULLDOG. In the decades since, Tonbo-Roses have been attached to major Kurita units during bigger operations.

The mission briefings conducted before Stone's invasion of Terra changed this exclusive service. *Tai-sa* Albert Benton said his forces had Tonbo support that was not needed for the Athens campaign, and offered to divert his Roses to Geneva in support of General Redburn. After a quick demonstration of the Tonbo's capabilities, the offer was gladly accepted.

The Tonbo quickly proved invaluable to the Coalition troops making their way across southern Germany and Austria toward Bratislava. The Alps represented a potential fortress for Blakist forces, just to the south of the route Redburn's task force had to travel, and the danger of flank attacks was extremely high. Attacking the Alps directly would have been suicide; the mountain range's natural defenses were too strong, and passes had either been destroyed or booby-trapped. Redburn's task force sent out an armada of VTOLs: Tonbos and their escorts. Skirting the mountains, the VTOL fleet circumvented mountain passes and dropped Coalition elements right on top of Blakist supply depots. As huge aerospace fighter battles raged across Europe, tying up both sides, the close support by combat VTOLs was sufficient to protect the Tonbos' precious cargo.

The Coalition passed through Germany and Austria, while the task force cut straight into Austria and secured the Alps. After neutralizing Innsbruck as rallying point for the Blakists, the ground forces let the VTOL flotilla leave to meet up with the other Coalition forces once Graz was also secured. At that point, the Tonbos received a final task: to join the Liberators and Fox's Teeth as they chased Blakist survivors eastward. Both parties sidestepped Vienna as a battleground, but a city fight became inevitable as the chase continued toward Bratislava. The remaining Tonbos quickly loaded up 'Mechs and flew them over Carpathian outliers to attack Bratislava from the north. The relatively nimble craft managed to drop their loads right into the streets just as the surprised Blakists entered the city from the west. While the damage to urban areas was huge, this tactic allowed the Coalition to navigate the city on equal footing rather than having to enter a defended area, preventing further carnage among General Redburn's forces.

For the rest of the campaign, the Tonbos served in logistical roles, transporting munitions and salvage. The Terran campaign left Lord Kurita little choice but to allow Wakazashi to start selling the VTOL on the open market. The Tonbo's utility had proved equal to its previous mystique; refusal to sell it could have turned into a public-relations disaster for the Combine. By making it available to other buyers, the Tonbo has instead become a best-selling unit for Wakazashi Enterprises.

Type: Tonbo
Chassis Type: VTOL (Large)
Mass: 56 tons
Battle Value: 189
Equipment Rating: E/X-X-D/D

Equipment			Mass
Chassis/Controls:			14.5
Engine/Trans:	Fusion		7
Cruise MP:	6		
Flank MP:	9		
Heat Sinks:	0		0
Fuel:			0
Armor Factor (BAR 7):	60		2.5
	Internal Structure	Armor Value	
Front	6	18	
R/L Side	6	15/15	
Rear	6	10	
Rotor	6	2	

Weapons and Ammo	Location	Mass
4 Lift Hoists	Body	12
Searchlight	Front	.5
Searchlight	Rear	.5
Communications Equipment	Body	7

Crew: 12 (2 officers, 10 enlisted/non-rated)
Cargo
   Infantry Transport Bay (12 tons) 1 Door (rear)

Notes: Total carrying capacity of Lift Hoists (at 4/6) = 112 tons.

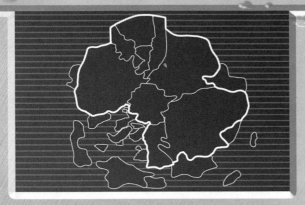

For every active combat vehicle in the Inner Sphere there are myriad vehicles supporting them. These, too, are adapted to the ever-changing demands of war. Two ubiquitous support units in particular saw (re-)introduction in the past decade

Acme Widget's J-27 has been the much-maligned "gold" standard of ammunition transport vehicles since the early days of the Star League. Its spread was assured by impossibly-low licensing fees that made illegal reverse-engineering look expensive. Thus, all larger military manufacturers have been producing the J-27 in huge numbers to counter the equally huge attrition rate of this fragile unit.

One of these producers is Ceres Metals. Though glad to have such a bestseller on its books, the company was not satisfied with the quality of the vehicle: despite Ceres Metals often advocating quantity over quality, the J-27's death-trap status was an entirely different PR problem. In response the company developed the J-37, supplementing their J-27 production starting in the late 28th Century.

The ordnance transport was quintupled in size and mounted armor that, while of lower quality than that found on a combat vehicle, nevertheless represented a huge increase compared to the older J-27. The biggest improvement was the large internal cargo hold that was capable of housing more cargo than the J-27 without relying on a fragile, exposed trailer system. A commercial fusion engine, not a rare commodity during the days of the Star League, allowed the new J-37 to stay logistically independent. A small laser as sole weapon traded the ability of infantry suppression for questionable firepower.

In marketing the J-37, Ceres stressed that life was cheap and machines were expensive—and so were munitions. While at first a huge success, the J-37 faced quick near-extinction as the Succession Wars and the Confederation's poor economy forced Ceres to revert back to the J-27. Single units did survive the ages, but it was not until the mid-3070s that the catastrophic loss of life of the Jihad had thoroughly changed old doctrines. Now, even support crews are seen as valuable members of a military. Production of the J-37 was restarted in 3076 in heavily modified form with an upgraded frame, an ER laser and combat-grade armor. The new J-37 has been achieving record sales, at first in the Confederation and, as of 3081, on the open Inner Sphere market.

Though most vehicles are conceived due to technological changes, some are constructed because of corporate dealings. In the latter half of the 3060s, Blue Bull, Inc. blatantly copied the JI-50 "Jifty" with its own "Nifty" Recovery Vehicle. Initially Johnston Industries attempted to stop its competitor via legal action, but quickly realized its superior R&D department could develop an improved design for military use with which to tie customers more closely to their company.

Following the simple dual paradigm of bigger and better, the new JI-100 would be a vehicle that resembled the JI-50 only in mission profile. The JI-100 utilizes a heavy, tracked tank chassis rather than the civilian truck-like chassis of the JI-50. This makes for a sturdier cross-country vehicle. Detractors immediately spotted that the armor, while of higher quality, is actually thinner than on its progenitor. Johnston Industries claims the JI-100 should never come close to an active battlefield, and its sturdy chassis merely guarantees longevity in hazardous salvage operations.

Military salvage sorties are where the JI-100 excels. It masses ten tons more than the previous Jifty and adds another lift hoist. These three impressive arms are found at the front of the JI-100, where they allow for immediate access to salvage as it is approached. This is quite contrary to the dual smaller arms attached to the back of the JI-50 Jifty's loading platform. The JI-100 is indeed an ideal recovery unit, with a combined cargo capacity that dwarfs that of other heavy BattleMech recovery vehicles.

The JI-100 was introduced in the first quarter of 3074 to great media fanfare and the response was enthusiastic. Military commands have mostly upgraded from the JI-50 to the JI-100. The years since then have proven Johnston Industries' plan to be successful: the JI-100 left no room on AFFS support rosters for the "fake" Nifty.

Type: **J-37**
Chassis Type: Wheeled (Medium)
Mass: 50 tons
Battle Value: 351
Equipment Rating: E/X-X-D/E

Equipment		Mass
Chassis/Controls:		14.5
Engine/Trans:	Fusion	8.5
Cruise MP:	5	
Flank MP:	8	
Heat Sinks:	2	2
Fuel:		0
Turret:		.5
Armor Factor (BAR 10):	98	5.5
	Armor Value	
Front	25	
R/L Side	25/25	
Rear	11	
Turret	12	

Weapons and Ammo	Location	Tonnage
ER Small Laser	Turret	.5
Advanced Fire Control	Body	.5

Crew: 3 (2 enlisted/non-rated, 1 gunner)
Cargo
   17 tons standard   1 Door (rear)
   Infantry Transport Bay (1 ton) 2 Doors (1 each side)

Notes: Features Armored and Off-Road Chassis and Controls Modifications

Type: **JI-100**
Technology Base: Inner Sphere
Movement Type: Tracked
Tonnage: 70
Battle Value: 210

Equipment		Mass
Internal Structure:		7
Engine:	Fusion	13.5
Cruising MP:	3	
Flank MP:	5	
Heat Sinks:	10	0
Control Equipment:		3.5
Lift Equipment:		0
Power Amplifier:		0
Turret:		0
Armor Factor:	40	2.5

	Armor Value
Front	10
R/L Side	10/10
Rear	10

Weapons and Ammo	Location	Tonnage
2 Machine Guns	Front	1
Ammo (MG) 100	Body	.5
3 Lift Hoists	Front	9
Cargo	Body	33

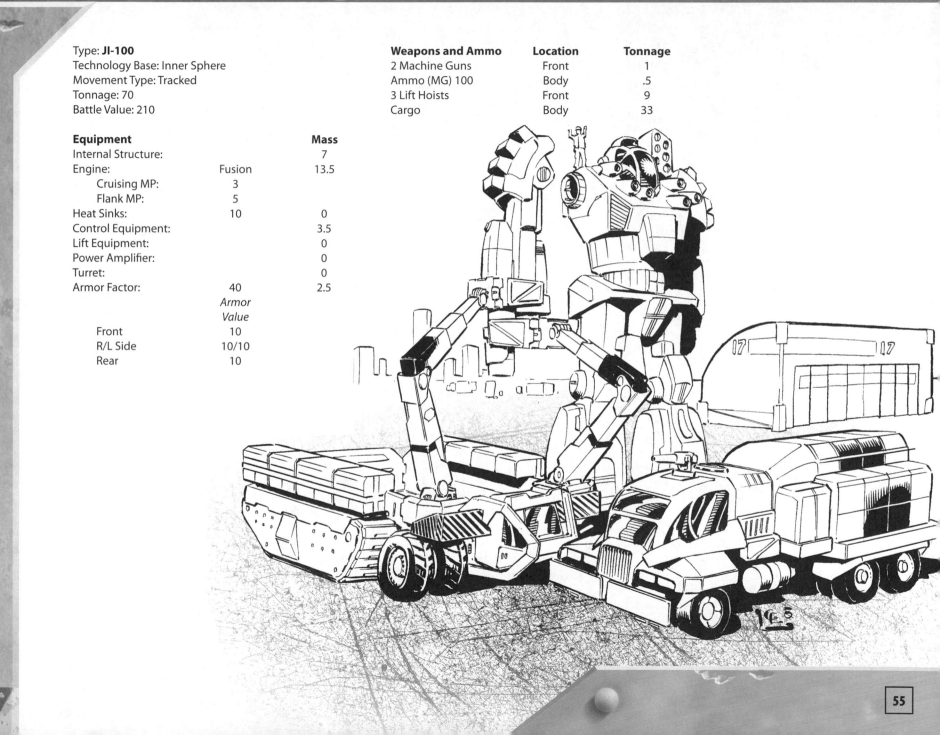

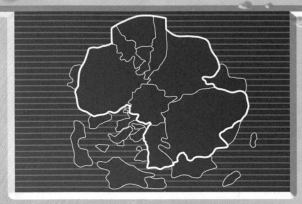

"Big guns and even bigger vehicles." When it comes to equipping its armed forces, the Lyrans have never been accused of being thrifty. With a bias to the largest, the best, and the most expensive equipment they can field, the Lyran armed forces also have one of the largest logistical trains in modern warfare. Constantly struggling to get the right 'Mech, tank, gun, or bullet to the right place, the LCAF Quartermaster Corps has become very adept at using every tool available to it. Over the centuries this has led to the Lyran military being one of the largest users of fixed wing support aircraft.

Long-time producers of support aircraft, Lockheed/CBM of Gibbs have more than once filled this need, with their KC-9 "King Karnov" being a mainstay of logistic units across Lyran space ever since it debuted in 3001. Over the years, the Lyran high command has made many requests for modifications to the KC series, with its large interior cargo bay being modified as a gunship, bomber, mobile command post, MASH and more. Each of these designs, however, required extensive after-market work or retooling of the manufacturing lines to create these often-limited production runs. Seeking to reduce their factory retooling costs and to streamline the number of manufacturing lines needed, Lockheed/CBM conceived the Zugvogel.

The Zugvogel solves these construction issues through the modularization of Omni construction. With more than seventy tons of pod space the Zug can be modified to fit nearly any mission role an army can come up with. Using an Edasich commercial-grade fusion engine, the KC-O-01 is twenty-five percent faster than its KC progenitor, carries twice the tonnage of military-grade armor and comes standard with advanced fire control and CASE reinforcement for any ammunition carried.

Five factory-produced Omni kits are available from Lockheed/CBM, with the most common configuration having the aircraft equipped as a heavily-armed transport. Two LRM 15 launchers backed by twin class-2 light autocannons make up the primary armament, with a medium pulse laser filling out the forward arc. To reduce the threat from light aerospace fighters a rear-mounted light Gauss rifle provides a nasty surprise for "tailgaters" at any range. Twenty-three tons of cargo is carried internally, more than enough to support the company of infantry and all its gear. The A configuration is a veritable technology warehouse that serves as an aerial command post with enough communications equipment, sensors and command and control equipment to lead an entire planetary campaign without ever touching the surface of the world. The B and C configurations are classic support designs; the B a mobile hospital with ten operating theatres and the C a self-transportable repair platform with two mobile field bases. Finally, the D variant is an aerial gunship designed to protect its fellow Zugvogels with twin Gauss rifles and a heavy PPC. The D configuration possesses enough firepower to threaten even the heaviest aerospace fighters.

Still going through final quartermaster trials, the Zugvogel is already earning praise from several circles. The Third Skye CMR, a paratrooper-trained combat unit, has been eagerly putting the Zugvogel through its paces as part of a series of ongoing RAF-LCAF war games. Using the mobile command post to avoid disruption of their command and control and relying on the primary configuration to move paratrooper squads quickly, the Third has been able to surprise its opposition several times. They have succeeded even so far as to force an entire combined arms battalion to surrender without firing a shot, thanks to a combination of aerial fire support and hit and run infantry tactics. The Lyran Quartermaster Corps is expected to requisition at least two hundred Zugvogels over the next five years and several other nations, including The Republic, have made inquires about possible purchases once field trials are complete.

Type: Zugvogel
Chassis Type: Fixed Wing (Large)
Mass: 200 tons
Equipment Rating: E/X-X-F/E
Battle Value: 1,159

Equipment		Mass
Chassis/Controls:		57.5
Engine/Trans:	Fusion	45
Cruise MP:	4	
Flank MP:	6	
Structural Integrity:	4	
Heat Sinks:	0	0
Fuel:	369	8.5
Armor Factor (BAR 10):	204	11.5
	Armor Value	
Front	51	
Wings	51/51	
Rear	51	

Weapons and Ammo	Location	Tonnage
Advanced Fire Control	Body	5.5

Base Crew: 3 (3 enlisted/non-rated)
Cargo
–	1 Door (rear)

Notes: Features Armored, Omni (71.5 tons, 24 slots), STOL Chassis and Control Modification, CASE (.5 tons), may carry up to 55 tons of weaponry.

Weapons and Ammo	Location	Tonnage
Primary Configuration [Combat Transport]		
2 LRM 15	Front	14
Ammo (LRM) 40	Body	5
Medium Pulse Laser	Front	2
4 Heat Sinks	Body	4
2 Light AC/2	Front	8
Ammo (Light AC) 90	Body	2
Light Gauss Rifle	Rear	12
Ammo (Light Gauss) 16	Body	1

Crew: 22 (4 officers, 3 enlisted/non-rated, 15 gunners)
Cargo
23.5 tons standard	1 Door (rear)

Weapons and Ammo	Location	Tonnage
Configuration A [High-Altitude, Long-range HQ] – Advanced		
Command Console	Body	3
Hi-Res Imager	Front	2.5
Hi-Res Imager	Left	2.5
Hi-Res Imager	Right	2.5
Hi-Res Imager	Rear	2.5
Hyperspectral Imager	Front	7.5
Infrared Imager	Front	5
Look-Down Radar	Front	5
C^3 Computer	Body	5
2 LB 2-X	Rear	12
Ammo (LB-X) 135	Body	3
Communications Equipment	Body	10
Medium VSP Laser	Front	4
7 Heat Sinks	Body	7

Crew: 23 (4 officers, 13 enlisted/non-rated, 6 gunners)
Cargo

None	1 Door (rear)	

Battle Value: 645

Weapons and Ammo	Location	Tonnage
Configuration B [M.A.S.H. Support Unit]		
MASH (10 theaters)	Body	12.5
4 Paramedic Equipment	Body	1
Field Kitchen	Body	3
Searchlight	Left	.5
Searchlight	Right	.5

Crew: 68 (12 officers, 56 enlisted/non-rated)
Cargo

Light Vehicle Bay 50 tons)	1 Door (rear)	
4 tons infantry		

Battle Value: 518

Weapons and Ammo	Location	Tonnage
Configuration C [Mobile Repair Base] – Advanced		
2 Mobile Field Bases	Body	40
Lift Hoist	Body	3
Searchlight	Rear	.5

Crew: 16 (3 officers, 13 enlisted/non-rated)
Cargo

20 tons standard	1 Door (rear)	
12 tons infantry		

Battle Value: 518

Weapons and Ammo	Location	Tonnage
Configuration D [Attack Craft] "Raubvogel"		
2 Gauss Rifles	Front	30
Ammo (Gauss) 56	Body	7
Heavy PPC	Front	10
15 Heat Sinks	Body	15
Ultra AC/2	Rear	7
Ammo (Ultra) 90	Body	2
Rocket Launcher 10	Front	.5

Crew: 28 (5 officers, 3 enlisted/non-rated, 20 gunners)
Cargo

None	1 Door (rear)	

Battle Value: 1,444

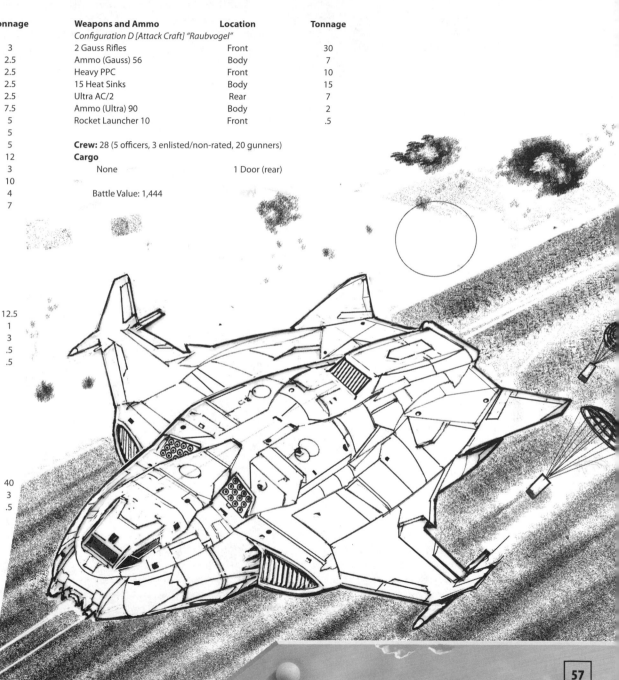

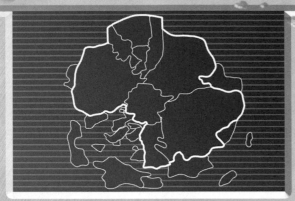

Mass: 25 tons
Chassis: Majesty MLIX Endo Steel
Power Plant: Magna 250 XL
Cruising Speed: 108 kph, 118 kph with TSM
Maximum Speed: 162 kph, 183 kph with TSM
Jump Jets: None
Jump Capacity: None
Armor: Hellespont Light Stealth
Armament:
   1 Ceres Arms Thrasher Snub-Nose PPC
Manufacturer: Majesty Metals and Manufacturing,
   Hellespont 'Mech Works
   Primary Factory: Canopus IV (MMM),
      Sian (Hellespont)
Communications System: Majesty COMSET
   with Guardian ECM
Targeting and Tracking System: Majesty 032-199

Overview

Hard proof of the Ebon Magistrate—an ultra-elite covert operations branch of the Magistracy Intelligence Ministry—first surfaced shortly before the Jihad. In the years since the downfall of the Blake Protectorate, the group remains shrouded in mystery but the existence of a namesake 'Mech appearing in the MAF and CCAF beginning in 3081 have been confirmed.

When or how the Magistracy developed the MEB-9 Ebony is as much an enigma as the Ebon Magistrate itself. Given that Canopus IV was occupied by Blakist forces until late 3075, and considering the significant damage

suffered during the occupation, it seems unlikely that Majesty Metals constructed a new manufacturing line and repaired damage to their existing facilities all in six short years—even with significant assistance from their Confederation partners.

Analysts' speculations vary widely. The most popular explanation posits that MMM has a hidden facility somewhere on Canopus IV, while the farthest-fetched analysis suggests the Blakists were building a new factory prior to being driven out. Another observation notes the use of Capellan stealth armor on a Magistracy design, suggesting that primary construction may be taking place in the Confederation with final assembly of the MEB-9 occurring somewhere on Canopus IV. Further investigation is needed.

On the Capellan front, Republic Intelligence has had little difficulty pinpointing construction of all three Ebony variants on Capella. Deployment information, however, has been significantly more elusive. The Ebony is notably rare in most Warrior Houses. Given the tension between The Republic and Confederation, it is noteworthy that the 'Mech has not been spotted along the borders of Prefectures V and VI. This lends credence to theories the Confederation is marshalling forces in preparation for military action to reclaim worlds lost to the Blakists. [The recent signing of the Tikonov Treaty rules out military action, but the stockpiling analysis may be accurate. –AH]

Capabilities

A huge Magna 250 extralight engine rockets the Ebony to a cruising speed of 108 kph, which only a handful of 'Mechs can match. When running hot enough to activate its triple-strength myomer the Ebony can reach sustained speeds of over 180 kph. A single Ceres Arms Snub-Nose PPC gives the Ebony highly accurate firepower to a range of 270 meters and a maximum standard engagement range of 450 meters. Ten double-strength freezers provide enough cooling power to balance the stealth armor, SN-PPC, and triple-strength myomer. Five tons of armor protect the Ebony with almost the best possible protection for its weight. Finally, the 'Mech's Guardian ECM system is capable of disrupting C^3 and other hostile electronics in an area just over 100,000 square meters.

Deployment

In the Magistracy, the MEB-9 is currently deployed in the Magistracy Royal Guard, Chasseurs á Cheval, and Canopian Fusiliers. Details of its deployment within the Capellan Confederation have been harder to ascertain. All Ebony variants spotted in the Confederation have been with the Prefectorate Guard and Second St. Ives Lancers. The Second McCarron's Armored Cavalry features the MEB-9 and MEB-10 in many recon lances. Among the Warrior Houses, the only confirmed deployment is of the MEB-11 with the still-rebuilding House Imarra, though it's believed the Ebony is shipping to all three of the other surviving Houses.

Variants

The MEB-10 features an ER large laser in place of the snub-nose PPC. The left arm receives a Capellan-styled sword, and an additional half ton of armor improves the already excellent protection. These improvements are fitted by exchanging the standard cockpit for a small model. While MechWarriors like the pairing of a physical attack weapon and TSM, the more challenging heat curve and cramped conditions have made the design somewhat unpopular.

Even less popular, and only found in the Capellan Confederation, the ammo-dependent MEB-11 exchanges the snub-nose PPC for a plasma rifle and a ton of ammo. Installing a small cockpit creates the necessary space to house the plasma rifle ammo, but the lack of secondary weaponry is the most common concern cited by MechWarriors assigned to this variant.

Type: **Ebony**
Technology Base: Inner Sphere
Tonnage: 25
Battle Value: 1,012

Equipment		Mass
Internal Structure:	Endo Steel	1.5
Engine:	250 XL	6.5
Walking MP:	10 (11)	
Running MP:	15 (17)	
Jumping MP:	0	
Heat Sinks:	10 [20]	0
Gyro (XL):		1.5
Cockpit:		3
Armor Factor (Stealth):	80	5

	Internal Structure	Armor Value
Head	3	7
Center Torso	8	12
Center Torso (rear)		3
R/L Torso	6	10
R/L Torso (rear)		2
R/L Arm	4	8
R/L Leg	6	9

Weapons and Ammo	Location	Critical	Tonnage
Snub-Nose PPC	RA	2	6
Guardian ECM Suite	LT	2	1.5
Triple-Strength Myomer	RT/LT	3/3	0

MLR-B2 MJOLNIR

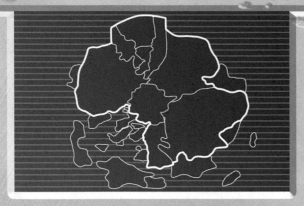

Mass: 25 tons
Chassis: Arc-Royal AR-7m
Power Plant: GM 150
Cruising Speed: 64 kph
Maximum Speed: 97 kph
Jump Jets: Luxor 2/Q
 Jump Capacity: 180 meters
Armor: Paulina Ferro-Fibrous
Armament:
 1 RAMTech 1500Z ER Medium Laser
 1 Diverse Optics Extended Range Small Laser
Manufacturer: Arc-Royal MechWorks
 Primary Factory: Arc-Royal
Communications System: O/P COM-22/H47
Targeting and Tracking System: Digital Scanlok 347

Overview

The wholesale destruction of the Word of Blake's Jihad devastated BattleMech production capabilities in every nation and territory including the Lyran Commonwealth (having reverted from the Alliance last year). The proud home of such BattleMech production juggernauts as Defiance Industries and Coventry Metal Works, the Lyran Commonwealth lost most of its industrial base in the effort to liberate its worlds from Blakist forces. Rebuilding the host of facilities that made the Lyrans an economic powerhouse has been one of the primary goals of Lyran reconstruction efforts.

While the Jihad cost dearly in terms of production capacity, it proved to be a boon in technical advancement, as several new and exciting BattleMech technologies emerged out of necessity. As the painful process of reconstruction took root, hard decisions had to be made about what units would be produced.

Fortunately for both Defiance Industries and Arc-Royal MechWorks, the facilities on Arc-Royal were still intact enough to restart production within a relatively short timeframe. Bitter arguments ensued over the best use of the repaired factories. Many argued that the LAAF should be rebuilt first and foremost while others felt an export product would generate revenues desperately needed to continue rebuilding the Lyran industrial base. An uneasy compromise determined that a portion of the facilities would be dedicated to rebuilding the BattleMech forces of the LAAF. At the same time a new light BattleMech design would be pushed into production for both internal use and external export. That new design would become the *Mjolnir*.

Capabilities

The chief concerns of the *Mjolnir*'s design team were available components and simplicity of construction. From that perspective they looked at some of the Lyran Alliance's historical successes, including the *Wolfhound* and *Commando* designs. Utilizing design elements of both as well as acquiring a list of components in ready supply helped the *Mjolnir* take shape quickly.

By far the simplest weapon at any BattleMech's disposal is the ability to cause damage from brute physical force. The *Hatchetman*'s inclusion of a built-in close combat weapon had made the tactic even more popular in recent decades. Close combat weapons became a staple of many designs during the 3050s and 3060s. The *Mjolnir*, it was decided, would feature this cheap yet effective weapon as its focal point. The 'Mech was built to marry triple-strength myomer with the particularly brutal mace, fashioned to look like the Norse thunder god's hammer. Despite its small size, this would allow the *Mjolnir* to deliver a potentially lethal blow to even the largest BattleMech opponents.

Speed and armor would be needed to get the mace to its targets. Worried about the fragility of extralight fusion engines, the designers chose to utilize the *Commando*'s reliable GM 150 power plant. They also installed ferro-fibrous armor that would allow maximum protection for less weight.

What little space remained was dedicated to energy weapons. Production of RAMTech extended-range medium lasers had recently resumed and Defiance Industries had enough Diverse Optics extended-range small lasers to keep the production lines moving. Not only would the laser weapons give the *Mjolnir* a semblance of ranged combat abilities, it would also keep the 'Mech independent of resupply constraints.

Deployment

Initial production of the *Mjolnir* went chiefly to Lyran Guards and Lyran Regulars regiments to help replace extensive combat losses. The fledgling Republic of the Sphere also requested a number of *Mjolnir*s in accordance with agreements made during the Coalition effort to free Terra from the Word of Blake. These *Mjolnir*s were assigned to Stone's Liberators and the Principes Guards.

Since the design was not considered vital to national defense, subsequent production runs of the *Mjolnir* were sold to the Federated Suns and the general mercenary market.

Variants

The Lyran Commonwealth utilizes an experimental version of the *Mjolnir*, the MLR-BX. This variant sheds the energy weapons and employs an extralight engine and extralight gyro in order to free up weight. This space is filled by a pair of short-range missile launchers intended to exploit holes in enemy armor created by the 'Mech's mace attacks.

Type: **Mjolnir**
Technology Base: Inner Sphere (Advanced)
Tonnage: 25
Battle Value: 655

Equipment		Mass
Internal Structure:		2.5
Engine:	150	5.5
Walking MP:	6 (7)	
Running MP:	9 (11)	
Jumping MP:	6	
Heat Sinks:	10	0
Gyro:		2
Cockpit:		3
Armor Factor (Ferro):	80	4.5

	Internal Structure	Armor Value
Head	3	8
Center Torso	8	11
Center Torso (rear)		3
R/L Torso	6	10
R/L Torso (rear)		2
R/L Arm	4	7
R/L Leg	6	10

Weapons and Ammo	Location	Critical	Tonnage
ER Small Laser	RA	1	.5
ER Medium Laser	CT	1	1
Mace	LA	3	3
Triple-Strength Myomer	RA/LA	3/3	0
Jump Jet	RL	1	.5
Jump Jets	RT	2	1
Jump Jets	LT	2	1
Jump Jet	LL	1	.5

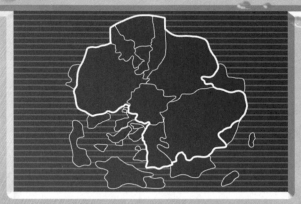

Mass: 30 tons
Chassis: Chariot Type I-B
Power Plant: Pitban 300 XL
Cruising Speed: 108 kph
Maximum Speed: 162 kph
Jump Jets: None
    Jump Capacity: None
Armor: Krupp 200 Ferro-Fibrous
Armament:
    1 Holly SRM 6
    2 Diverse Optics Extended Range Medium Lasers
    1 Diverse Optics Extended Range Small Laser
Manufacturer: Diplan MechYards, Krupp Armament Works
    Primary Factory: Aix-la-Chapelle (Diplan),
        Terra (Krupp)
Communications System: Corean Transband-J12
Targeting and Tracking System: Cat's Eye 5
    with Forward 1 BAP

Overview

The genesis of the *Nyx* was the Word of Blake. The project had reached the field testing stage when Quentin was liberated by Coalition forces. Buried in the detritus of the fighting was a full set of technical documentation for the *Nyx* as well as a mostly-functional prototype, which were spirited to Aix-la-Chapelle and given to Diplan 'Mechyards with the *Kanrei*'s instructions to make it work. Unfortunately for the Combine, many of the key components for the *Nyx* were highly specialized and only available from factories on Terra.

After Terra's liberation, production of the *Nyx* was much more feasible. Instead of relying on whatever substitute components they could scrounge, the DCMS approached The Republic. With Diplan 'Mechyards having the knowledge and Krupp Armament Works on Terra the components, the DCMS and the Republic of the Sphere agreed to make production of the *Nyx* a joint effort.

Capabilities

The *Nyx* was less a revolutionary design than an amalgamation of successful parts assembled into an impressive whole. With the marked increase of stealth technologies and the ever-increasing speed of light BattleMech units, the existing arsenal of reconnaissance-devoted BattleMechs had begun to fall short of battle-field necessities. The Word of Blake set out to make a fast, capable recon 'Mech with the ability to engage in combat if necessary.

Cognizant of the age-old battlefield maxim that speed is life, the Word of Blake engineers started with speed as the primary focus. The heart of the *Nyx* is a 300 XL fusion engine, which had to be specially redesigned to fit into the small chassis. The powerful nine and a half-ton engine gives the *Nyx* raw speed in excess of 160 kilometers per hour. That speed, coupled with the Beagle Active Probe, makes the *Nyx* an incredibly capable scout or pursuit 'Mech. It also gives the *Nyx* a natural ability to detect, and escape, ambush situations.

In order to further increase the speed of the *Nyx* every possible weight-saving measure was enacted. The frame was constructed of endo steel components to provide a lightweight internal structure. The armor, while a necessity, was comprised of lighter ferro-fibrous panels. Despite being lightweight, the Krupp 200 ferro-fibrous armor provides a surprisingly effective amount of protection.

The *Nyx* mounts an effective, if unimaginative, arsenal. A pair of Diverse Optics extended range medium lasers provide the primary firepower, while a Diverse Optics extended-range small laser is included as a defensive weapon. Finally, a tried-and-true Holly Short-Range Missile 6 launcher gives the 'Mech the ability to deliver a finishing punch. Given such a plethora of mission capabilities, it is easy to see why the liberators of Quentin went ahead with plans to push the design into production.

Deployment

Since full production of the *Nyx* was delayed until the liberation of Terra the design was late to deploy in significant numbers. Within the Draconis Combine it has been placed in the Sword of Light regiments where it has received enthusiastic reviews. The Republic of the Sphere has issued its supply of *Nyx* 'Mechs to its own forces and in small numbers to all of the members of the Coalition that helped liberate Terra, which was received with less than stellar enthusiasm from the Draconis Combine.

Variants

Design notes for a radical variant of the *Nyx*, the NX-90, were discovered by Combine engineers as more of the Independence Weaponry facilities were successfully repaired and rebuilt. The NX-90 strips the active probe and lasers from the 'Mech in order to mount a pair of BattleMech lances in the arms. The apparent vision of this variant was to use the *Nyx*'s speed to deliver armor piercing charge-style attacks. The DCMS is also fielding a C^3 variant that drops the SRM to a four-rack and places a C^3 slave under the launcher.

Type: **Nyx**
Technology Base: Inner Sphere
Tonnage: 30
Battle Value: 924

Equipment			Mass
Internal Structure:	Endo Steel		1.5
Engine:	300 XL		9.5
Walking MP:	10		
Running MP:	15		
Jumping MP:	0		
Heat Sinks:	10 [20]		0
Gyro:			3
Cockpit:			3
Armor Factor (Ferro):	89		5

	Internal Structure	Armor Value
Head	3	9
Center Torso	10	15
Center Torso (rear)		5
R/L Torso	7	10
R/L Torso (rear)		2
R/L Arm	5	8
R/L Leg	7	10

Weapons and Ammo	Location	Critical	Tonnage
ER Medium Laser	RA	1	1
Beagle Active Probe	RT	2	1.5
Ammo (SRM) 15	RT	1	1
SRM 6	CT	2	3
ER Small Laser	LT	1	.5
ER Medium Laser	LA	1	1

SDR-8R SPIDER

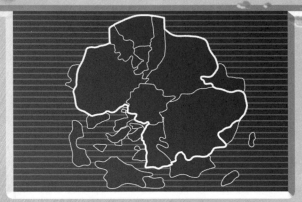

Mass: 30 tons
Chassis: Crucis-II Delux Endo Steel
Power Plant: GM 210 Light
Cruising Speed: 75 kph
Maximum Speed: 118 kph
Jump Jets: Pitban LFT-20X
    Jump Capacity: 300 meters
Armor: Durallex Light
Armament:
    2 Diverse Optics Extended Range Medium Lasers
Manufacturer: Krupp Armament Works
    Primary Factory: Terra (Budapest)
Communications System: O/P 500A
Targeting and Tracking System: O/P TA1240

Overview

In taking steps to plug what he considered to be a dangerous gap in the Knights of the Sphere's order of battle, which was predominantly filled with battlefield salvage, Commanding General Victor Steiner-Davion issued a call for a Republic-manufactured fast recon BattleMech. Commissioned originally for service with the First Star League's Special Operations units over four centuries before, the *Spider* was identified by Krupp Armament Works as a viable design that was well suited to The Republic's needs. More importantly, it was also a design that the company could still manufacture at its heavily-damaged Budapest plant using components readily available on Terra.

While the design borrows heavily from the antiquated SDR-5V model, the new SDR-8R *Spider* is based on a prototype field refit used by Stone's forces in the Liberation of Terra. Krupp purchased the prototype after the war and reverse-engineered the design's experimental technology into the production SDR-8R.

Capabilities

Speed and maneuverability have always been the *Spider's* strength. Although this new incarnation of the design sacrifices something in the way of top speed, the use of improved jump jets has increased the distance the SDR-8R can cover in a single jump by twenty-five percent. The initial prototype used a highly experimental partial wing system that, while highly effective, proved unworkable for mass production. The wing structure was retained for the added stability it provided in extended jumps. The new jump jets generate a lot of heat but double efficiency heat sinks ensure that the 'Mech can maintain a withering rate of fire from its twin Diverse Optics lasers. This energy-based weaponry and effective heat management system means the *Spider's* endurance is limited only by the physical limits of the MechWarrior in the cockpit.

Equally important to MechWarriors piloting this new *Spider* is the welcome news that the redesign of the BattleMech included the installation of an emergency ejection system. Long considered to be the only true flaw in an otherwise excellent design, this improvement has ensured that the *Spider* is getting positive reviews from the Knights who have piloted the BattleMech.

Deployment

The introduction of the new *Spider* has been bedeviled by a series of delays. In mid-3084 Krupp filed a lawsuit against The Republic over damages their Budapest plant suffered during the final battles to liberate Terra from the Word of Blake. Demanding reparations for the property damage and maintaining that their profits have been significantly reduced, Krupp took not only The Republic itself but also several prominent individuals (including Devlin Stone and Victor Steiner-Davion) to court. In the months that followed relations between the arms manufacturer and The Republic deteriorated steadily. Delivery of the first production run was tardy and the new BattleMechs have been coming at a painfully slow rate. Those 'Mechs that have been received to date are being deployed in Prefectures V and VI, the site of ongoing tensions with the Capellan Confederation. The need for reliable intelligence has seen the *Spider* being worked hard.

Nimakachi has continued to experiment with its own upgraded *Spiders* at their Lapida II production plant just across the frontier in the Draconis Combine. Some component shortages have impacted their production levels and output has so far been little better than that of troubled Krupp Armament Works. The bulk of Nimakachi's production has gone to the Sword of Light. Several Combine-built *Spiders* have also been sighted with Clan Ghost Bear's second-line Clusters as well as with the Rasalhague KungsArmé. This has led to speculation that the DCMS is trading some of its home-built equipment for spares to keep its precious Clantech equipment operational.

Variants

The Draconis Combine's Nimakachi Fusion Products Limited's upgraded SDR-8K *Spider* lacks the advanced jump jet technology of The Republic's version but it has a faster ground speed, nearly 130 kph. Employing a compact gyro and Pitban 240 XL fusion engine, armor protection has also been increased with four tons of New Samarkand ferro-fibrous armor. The weight savings from these changes allowed Nimakachi to replace the medium lasers with a single torso-mounted snub-nosed PPC augmented with a PPC capacitor.

Still produced in very limited numbers, the SDR-8X uses an Inner Sphere modified partial wing with standard jump jets and mounts nearly double the armor of the 8R. The wing weighs a ton more than the Clan version of the partial wing and has additional structural supports in the torso.

Seeing use in the final days of Operation SCOUR, a field refit of the SDR-7K replaced one of the lasers for an Angel ECM suite.

SDR-8R SPIDER

Type: **Spider**
Technology Base: Inner Sphere
Tonnage: 30
Battle Value: 694

Equipment			Mass
Internal Structure:	Endo-Steel		1.5
Engine:	210 Light		7
Walking MP:	7		
Running MP:	11		
Jumping MP:	10		
Heat Sinks:	10 [20]		0
Gyro:			3
Cockpit:			3
Armor Factor:	56		3.5

	Internal Structure	Armor Value
Head	3	8
Center Torso	10	8
Center Torso (rear)		2
R/L Torso	7	6
R/L Torso (rear)		2
R/L Arm	5	5
R/L Leg	7	6

Weapons and Ammo	Location	Critical	Tonnage
2 ER Medium Lasers	CT	2	2
Improved Jump Jets	RT	10	5
Improved Jump Jets	LT	10	5

PNT-13K PANTHER

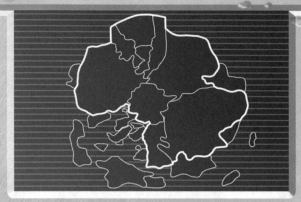

Mass: 35 tons
Chassis: Alshain 56A-Carrier
Power Plant: Omni 175 XL
Cruising Speed: 54 kph
Maximum Speed: 86 kph
Jump Jets: Lexington Heavy Lifters Improved Jump Jets
    Jump Capacity: 240 meters
Armor: Maximillian 42
Armament:
    1 Tiegart Incinerator Plasma Rifle
    1 Telos-4 Short-Range Missile Delivery System
Manufacturer: Wakizashi Enterprises
    Primary Factory: New Samarkand
Communications System: Sipher CommCon SCU-4
Targeting and Tracking System: Cat's Eyes 5

Overview

The *Panther* with the greatest jump capacity for the chassis was pioneered before the start of the Jihad but not put into production until after the Blakists' war against civilization began. Holding true to its original design concept, the PNT-13K *Panther* serves as a fire-support 'Mech for recon units. While the PNT-16K came off the New Samarkand assembly lines first, the -13K was conceived earlier, thus its lower numerical designation. Production of the -13K was stalled due to problems with reliability of its unproven jump jets. Once these issues were resolved, in part after examining Blakist PNT-14S *Panthers* salvaged on Dieron, the -13K was officially commissioned.

Capabilities

Unlike recent variants of the *Panther*, the PNT-13K uses a standard internal structure, freeing up the space needed for the extralight engine required to attain the speed called for by DCMS procurers. The -13K also uses a recently developed extralight gyroscope, reducing its weight by half. The bulkier gyroscope required moving the SRM 4 from its traditional center torso location to the left torso. The -13K's double-strength heat sinks ensure cool running even while firing its full complement of weapons. Two heat sinks are mounted directly on the plasma rifle in the right arm, enabling continuous firing in combat which pleased the MechWarriors who fought the Jihadists.

The -13K's 175 XL engine powers it to a respectable eighty-six kph, though this is still slow for a light 'Mech. The -13K makes up for its ground speed by mounting improved jump jets able to double the jumping capability of older *Panthers*. While the Blakists were successful in debuting their -14S variant on Dieron before the -13K completed development, the -13K has both greater ground speed and a longer jump.

The -13K's armament changed its role during the Jihad. Dispensing with the traditional PPC-type weapon for its right arm, it mounts a modern plasma rifle. The plasma rifle was an excellent weapon to pit against the snub-nose PPC carried by the Blakists' -14S, not only because of the plasma rifle's constant damage over range but also because it compounds its damage by superheating its targets. This benefit was quite effective when the -13K's MechWarriors loaded their SRM with Inferno missiles. The excess heat delivered by these weapons was often successful in overheating enemies to the point of shutdown, making it a worthy risk to carry the volatile Infernos.

Deployment

Given its recent vintage the -13K has only been seen in combat with Sword of Light and Genyosha regiments, with none reported among the rest of the DCMS. It has been reported that the Ghost Bear Dominion salvaged some -13Ks which were repaired and put into service. The -10K2 and -12K2 have been replacing the -10K at a high rate as the older *Panthers* are refitted after combat damage.

Variants

Other variants of the *Panther* have recently appeared. Due to the privations and extraordinary losses of the Jihad, these are generally upgrades of older variants. To put as many 'Mechs back in the field as possible the upgrades were kept simple. The two primary variants which premiered during the Jihad changed little from their standard configurations. One is the PNT-10K2, an upgrade of the PNT-10K, which had a significant presence in the Combine's light 'Mech ranks. The -10K2 upgrades the -10K's heat sinks to double-strength freezers, reducing the total to twelve which greatly aids cooling of the ER PPC and allows for the installation of a second missile rack. Dropping the Artemis IV system and its expensive ammo requirements, two standard SRM 4 racks were installed in the center torso, an intelligent use of the stockpiles of old PNT-9R parts.

The PNT-12K2 is actually a variant of the PNT-10K2 not the -12K, replacing the -10K2's SRM racks with a single MRM 10 rack, using the same CASE-protected left torso space for ammo. The PNT-12K2 was seen in units which either lacked spare SRM racks or which had excess MRM racks to give their *Panthers*.

Notable MechWarriors

***Chu-i* Deborah McEnglevan:** This young officer's first combat action was with the Eighth Dieron Regulars' assault on Fortress Dieron in November 3077. She was part of the stalwart defense against the Blakist counterattack after the Regulars breached the walls. She feared never being able to sit the command couch again after being blasted from her *Crusader*'s cockpit. Having recently learned to walk again, she was awarded a billet in the Second Genyosha. Though her PNT-13K packs much less firepower than her prior 'Mech, she is pleased to serve the Dragon once more.

PNT-13K PANTHER

Type: **Panther**
Technology Base: Inner Sphere
Tonnage: 35
Battle Value: 996

Equipment		Mass
Internal Structure:		3.5
Engine:	175 XL	3.5
Walking MP:	5	
Running MP:	8	
Jumping MP:	8	
Heat Sinks:	10 [20]	0
Gyro (XL):		1
Cockpit:		3
Armor Factor:	96	6

	Internal Structure	Armor Value
Head	3	9
Center Torso	11	11
Center Torso (rear)		4
R/L Torso	8	10
R/L Torso (rear)		3
R/L Arm	6	10
R/L Leg	8	13

Weapons and Ammo	Location	Critical	Tonnage
Plasma Rifle	RA	2	6
Ammo (Plasma) 10	RT	1	1
SRM 4	LT	1	2
Ammo (SRM) 25	LT	1	1
Improved Jump Jet	RL	2	1
Improved Jump Jets	RT	6	3
Improved Jump Jets	LT	6	3
Improved Jump Jet	LL	2	1

WLF-5 WOLFHOUND

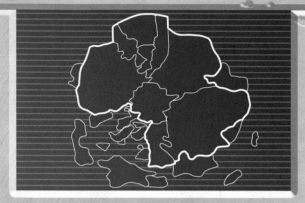

Mass: 35 tons
Chassis: Arc-Royal KH/3b Lite
Power Plant: GM 245 XL
Cruising Speed: 75 kph
Maximum Speed: 118 kph, 151 kph with MASC
Jump Jets: None
    Jump Capacity: None
Armor: Durallex Medium
Armament:
    1 Hound's-tooth Snub-Nose PPC
    2 Defiance 1002 Light PPCs
Manufacturer: Arc-Royal MechWorks
    Primary Factory: Arc-Royal
Communications System: O/P COM-22/H47
Targeting and Tracking System: Digital Scanlok 347

Overview

The *Wolfhound* has long-served as a fast scout 'Mech with a secondary goal of defending recon units from scout hunters like the *Panther*. The original WLF-1 *Wolfhound* was a pioneering effort to develop a new BattleMech following the technological stagnation of the Succession Wars. The *Wolfhound* has evolved from the initial WLF-1, which used only the technology which had survived the Succession Wars, to more recent variants which have increasingly incorporated recovered or newly-developed technology. The WLF-5 continues this evolution, using a new engine and primary weapon while relying on battle-tested components for its other systems.

The WLF-5 replaces the armament of the WLF-2 with an array of PPCs. As with all other production *Wolfhounds*, this 'Mech is an all-energy weapon combat machine, freeing it from supply lines. While the TharHes plant may construct this unit in the future, damage sustained in the Jihad has so far prevented this. The WLF-4W is still being built on Arc-Royal alongside the WLF-5, with both variants being observed in greater numbers as the factory has increased production to fill depleted ranks.

Capabilities

Replacing the large laser or ER PPC of prior variants, the WLF-5 uses a newly-developed snub-nose PPC in the right arm. This provides extreme accuracy compared to other types of PPC, though its decreasing destructive potential with distance remains a shortcoming. The medium lasers which once adorned the torso have been replaced by a pair of light PPCs. While they are just as powerful as the lasers, the increased range of these secondary weapons allows the WLF-5 to pepper enemies with fire while closing to optimum range for the snub-nose PPC. The freedom from supply lines allows the *Wolfhound* to remain in the field uninterrupted and perform the same mission it has excelled at for decades: scouting or supporting recon units.

Throughout the past six decades the *Wolfhound* has repeatedly matched up well against the Draconis Combine's slower *Panther*. When Arc-Royal engineers learned of the faster PNT-13K and its increased jump capacity, they were motivated to design a new, faster *Wolfhound*. The powerful GM 245 XL engine propels the WLF-5 along at nearly 120 kph. Given the likelihood of engaging Clan opponents, the Arc-Royal designers installed a MASC system to compensate for the enemy's greater speed. The circuitry gives the WLF-5 bursts greater than 150 kph, allowing it to pace and engage speedy Clan BattleMechs. Few 'Mechs can outrun the WLF-5 or its weapons.

Like its predecessors, the WLF-5 possesses the full-head ejection system first used on the *Hatchetman*. This system has proven invaluable in saving MechWarriors' lives. The armor and environmental sealing of the head, when battle damage has not compromised them, allows the MechWarrior to weather the combat still raging outside the decapitated head until friendly forces can arrive.

Deployment

The WLF-5 debuted with the Kell Hounds in 3079 and has since seen increased deployment among their allies and other mercenary units, including some as far away as the Federated Suns. The RAF has received several as a gift from the Arc-Royal government. The equally-new WLF-3M has only been seen in units of the former Free Worlds League along the Lyran border. Given that it is a field refit we don't expect to see greater distribution.

Variants

A field refit of the WLF-3S *Wolfhound*, the WLF-3M has been seen in small numbers in the former Free Worlds League. This variant sacrifices the energy weapons of other *Wolfhounds* for a single light Gauss Rifle mounted in the arm. Its one ton of ammo ensures it cannot spend a great deal of time in the field before retiring for reloads. To accommodate the heavy weapon, all the lasers and the ER PPC have been removed, along with two double heat sinks and one half-ton of armor. It does, however, extend its effective combat range compared to other *Wolfhounds*, enabling it to avoid close combat while scouting.

Notable MechWarriors

Agent John "Applecart" Randolph: This former SAFE agent, now in the service of Alys Rousset-Marik, distinguished himself as an advance scout. After planetary insertion, rather than scout the enemy from the cockpit of his WLF-3M, "The Lone Wolfhound," Randolph conceals and shuts down his *Wolfhound* and proceeds on foot to reconnoiter the area. He got his nickname after reportedly ascertaining the disposition of Blakist forces on Atreus in December 3078 by striking up a conversation with the proprietor of a small fruit stand. Randolph returned with the intelligence and a sack of apples.

Type: **Wolfhound**
Technology Base: Inner Sphere
Tonnage: 35
Battle Value: 1,290

Equipment		Mass
Internal Structure:	Endo Steel	2
Engine:	245 XL	6
Walking MP:	7	
Running MP:	11 (14)	
Jumping MP:	0	
Heat Sinks:	10 [20]	0
Gyro:		3
Cockpit:		3
Armor Factor:	112	7

	Internal Structure	Armor Value
Head	3	9
Center Torso	11	15
Center Torso (rear)		6
R/L Torso	8	10
R/L Torso (rear)		5
R/L Arm	6	11
R/L Leg	8	15

Weapons and Ammo	Location	Critical	Tonnage
Snub-Nose PPC	RA	2	6
Light PPC	RT	2	3
MASC	CT	2	2
Light PPC	LT	2	3

Note: If playing under Advanced Rules, treat head as having a Full-Head Ejection System.

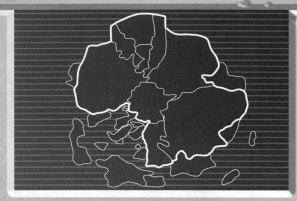

Mass: 40 tons
Chassis: Void Integrated MK II
Power Plant: VOX 280 XL
Cruising Speed: 75 kph
Maximum Speed: 118 kph, 151 kph with MASC
Jump Jets: None
   Jump Capacity: None
Armor: Void Integrated Light Ferro-Fibrous
Armament:
   2 Streak SRM 6s
   2 ER Medium Lasers
Manufacturer: CLASSIFIED
   Primary Factory: CLASSIFIED
Communications System: Black Box Com 7
   with Guardian ECM
Targeting and Tracking System: Night Fire 7

Overview

Along with the Bolla Stealth Tank, our forces were able to secure the design specifications and technical data for the *Raptor II*. While the Blakists destroyed the *Raptor II's* factory during the invasion of Terra, they failed to destroy the R&D laboratory where the specifications were first recorded. Using the Blakists' specs and salvaged *Raptor II*s, construction was initiated using modified specs at a classified R&D facility. This activity has been kept secret from the rest of the Inner Sphere. The *Raptor II*s emerging from the assembly line have been assigned to the most elite of our special forces. The RPT-3X serves the same mission as that of the Blakists' *Raptor*: infiltration by stealth.

Capabilities

Using the Blakists' innovative void-signature system, a merger of mimetic armor and original Star League null-signature system, the *Raptor II's* void-signature system enables it to evade not just electronic targeting systems but also the eyes of those who would do it harm. While fanciful tales have long been told to frighten children of ghost 'Mechs and invisible enemies, the *Raptor II* makes the tales reality. Devlin Stone was only too aware of the game-changing nature of such a cloaking system, taking all risks to ensure that his forces obtained all salvaged *Raptor II*s. He did not want to risk the technology falling into the hands of other nations whose scientists have demonstrated past expertise at reverse-engineering.

While the RPT-3X penetrates rear areas using its unmatched stealth, its already impressive speed is enhanced with a MASC system. The MASC is not necessary during infiltration operations, but should the *Raptor II* be required to flee, there are few enemy units able to mount an effective pursuit.

A pair of Streak SRM 6 racks provide the RPT-3X with accurate and efficient firepower for those operations when surveillance is not the only assigned task. More than one facility was targeted by Blakist *Raptor II*s during the Jihad, with great destruction resulting from the surprise nature of the attacks. Similar success is being enjoyed by RAF special forces seeking to deny insurgency and excessive military buildup amongst The Republic's neighbors. Two extended range medium lasers complete the armament of the RPT-3X.

The -3X uses the same armor as the Blakists' -2X, a light ferro-fibrous armor specially molded to the sensor-deflecting shapes necessary for the void-signature system's optimum functioning. The incorporation of mimetic characteristics slows the production of this armor, which has similarly delayed the manufacturing of new *Raptor II*s.

An interesting decision was made during the redesign period. The RPT-2X utilized CASE to protect its ammunition bays and ensure survival of the MechWarrior in the event of a catastrophic ammo explosion. However, the RPT-3X was to be assigned to covert reconnaissance and search-and-destroy missions, for which no accountability to The Republic could be tolerated. CASE contradicts this philosophy. The pilots who perform these missions enter with no identification or markings, accepting death as a consequence of failure. Should they come under significant enemy fire, they are expected to escape or die; capture must never occur. Thus, CASE was removed from the RPT-3X specifications. Similarly, the *Raptor II's* cramped cockpit was constructed with no ejection system, further reducing the chances of the pilot's capture by enemy forces. As a note to all RAF officers, should an intact *Raptor II* ever be found in the field, all efforts should be made to destroy it before it can fall into any other hands.

Deployment

Along with the -3X and -5X, all captured or salvaged RPT-2Xs and RPT-2X1s have been assigned exclusively to our covert units. No known *Raptor II*s are in the hands of any other nation.

Variants

In addition to the redesigned RPT-3X, RAF technical staff developed the RPT-5X for use in covert search and destroy missions. The -5X drops the MASC system, swaps the SRM racks for an MML 5, and upgrades the right arm laser to an extended range large laser. A 150-meter jumping range gives the -5X maneuverability in terrain where the -3X's MASC system might not enable suitably fast withdrawal. One heat sink is also removed to accommodate the weight of the large laser.

The Blakists mounted other experimental technology besides the stealth system on their *Raptor II*s. These include a 'Mech Taser and a pair of variable speed pulse lasers on the RPT-2X, and a Bloodhound probe on the RPT-2X1.

[Editor's Note: The unit pictured here is the RPT-5X variant. - AH]

Type: **Raptor II**
Technology Base: Inner Sphere (Experimental)
Tonnage: 40
Battle Value: 1,423

Equipment		Mass
Internal Structure:	Endo Steel	2
Engine:	280 XL	8
Walking MP:	7	
Running MP:	11 (14)	
Jumping MP:	0	
Heat Sinks:	11 [22]	1
Gyro:		3
Cockpit (Small):		2
Armor Factor (Light Ferro):	127	7.5

	Internal Structure	Armor Value
Head	3	9
Center Torso	12	20
Center Torso (rear)		4
R/L Torso	10	16
R/L Torso (rear)		4
R/L Arm	6	12
R/L Leg	10	15

Weapons and Ammo	Location	Critical	Tonnage
ER Medium Laser	RA	1	1
Streak SRM 6	RT	2	4.5
Streak SRM 6	LT	2	4.5
Ammo (Streak) 30	LT	2	2
ER Medium Laser	LA	1	1
MASC	RT	2	2
Guardian ECM Suite	H	2	1.5
Void-Signature System	*	7	0

*The Void-Signature System occupies 1 slot in every location except the Head.

TRG-1N TARGE

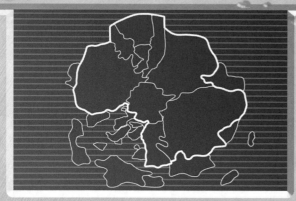

Mass: 40 tons
Chassis: Norse Medium SE5-3c
Power Plant: Pitban 320 Light
Cruising Speed: 86 kph
Maximum Speed: 129 kph, 172 kph with MASC
Jump Jets: None
Jump Capacity: None
Armor: Valiant Lamellor Special Heavy Ferro-Fibrous with CASE
Armament:
1 Shigunga MRM 10 Launcher
3 Diverse Optics Extended Range Small Lasers
Manufacturer: Cosara Weaponries
Primary Factory: Northwind
Communications System: O/P AIR500
Targeting and Tracking System: DLK Type Phased Array Sensor System

Overview

With the end of the Jihad, Northwind joined the Republic of the Sphere and Cosara Weaponries looked to add a new 'Mech to the fledgling RAF's arsenal and to their own profit margin. The strategic research team analyzed what the Coalition had, what was needed as the RAF grew, and what Cosara could sell. The rather strict guidelines called for a medium 'Mech that could exceed 160 kph for short bursts, carried a missile system

and supporting lasers. The designers set about making a 'Mech that fit those needs, resulting in the *Targe*, named after the shield that was the primary means of defense for the Scottish Highlanders of Terra. Cosara had a long history of building the venerable *Crab*, and had even updated the design when new production was restarted in the 3050s. Their *Crab* and *Black Watch* were solid, if unspectacular designs and the *Targe* was their plan to change that.

Capabilities

The *Targe* is fast for its weight, similar to the *Cicada*. While an extralight engine would allow for a greater payload, the expense and vulnerability made the design team choose to go with a slightly heavier light fusion engine. Mating that to a strong chassis and MASC allowed the design to exceed the speed requirements. When it came to payload, however, they had some serious decisions to make. They wanted to give it a large multi-missile launcher, but in doing so they would leave the *Targe* with the armor of a light 'Mech even before the lasers were factored in. They instead settled for a system they were familiar with from the *Black Watch*, a Shigunga medium-range missile system. A trio of small lasers was added for close range support. While medium lasers might have been more useful, they too would reduce the armor load significantly.

Left with five tons, the design team requested ferro-fibrous armor to give the *Targe* its best chance of survival should speed not be enough. In this the purchasing department exceeded expectations, landing a contract with Valiant to purchase their new heavy ferro-fibrous armor. The build team gladly installed it, along with a CASE system surrounding the missile launcher and ammunition bin. With the design complete, Cosara presented the prototype. Cosara's strategic research team was thrilled, the RAF quartermasters less so. Despite limited firepower and range, testing showed it very capable of hunting smaller opponents, even those seen as fast themselves. While the *Targe* is a part of the RAF arsenal, its sales are not what Cosara hoped for.

Deployment

The *Targe* is found more frequently in Northwind Highlander units than other RAF forces. Generally used for scouting and counter-recon, the *Targe* can occasionally be found bolstering RAF cavalry units. Pilots often try to use the 'Mech to strafe: they will approach their targets at a high rate of speed, close to around 100 meters, fire and then activate their MASC to get out of the enemy's line of fire. While this has been generally successful in the simulator and on the practice field, the *Targe* has yet to see live fire in combat.

Variants

With lackluster sales, Cosara has allowed the design team to tinker with the design. They have slowed the 'Mech down some in order to increase the payload. This allowed them to mount a multi-missile system like they initially wanted to. They were also able to upgrade two of the lasers to mediums and place the ammunition in the better armored legs. Additional armor replaces the CASE. This has worked well in simulations and dry runs, but some *Targe* pilots are concerned that MASC failure could result in sudden electrical discharges threatening the ammunition. Cosara has dismissed these concerns but the Quartermaster's office is performing a full investigation prior to making any purchases of the new variant.

Type: **Targe**
Technology Base: Inner Sphere
Tonnage: 40
Battle Value: 813

Equipment		Mass
Internal Structure:		4
Engine:	320 Light	17
Walking MP:	8	
Running MP:	12 (16)	
Jumping MP:	0	
Heat Sinks:	10 [20]	0
Gyro:		4
Cockpit (Small):		2
Armor Factor (Heavy Ferro):	99	5

	Internal Structure	Armor Value
Head	3	8
Center Torso	12	15
Center Torso (rear)		4
R/L Torso	10	10
R/L Torso (rear)		4
R/L Arm	6	7
R/L Leg	10	15

Weapons and Ammo	Location	Critical	Tonnage
MRM 10	RT	2	3
Ammo (MRM) 24	RT	1	1
CASE	RT	1	.5
ER Small Laser	RT	1	.5
ER Small Laser	CT	1	.5
ER Small Laser	LT	1	.5
MASC	LT	2	2

EFT-7X EISENFAUST

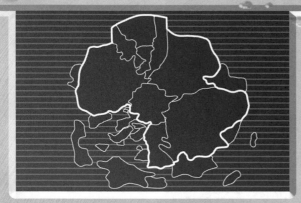

Mass: 45 tons
Chassis: Chariot Type II-B
Power Plant: Edasich Motors 180 XL
Cruising Speed: 43 kph
Maximum Speed: 64 kph
Jump Jets: None
   Jump Capacity: None
Armor: Durallex Medium
Armament:
   1 Defiance NovaShot Model 2 Plasma Rifle
   1 Defiance Model 6 Extended Range Large Laser
   2 Defiance P5M Medium Pulse Lasers
   1 Diverse Optics Extended Range Small Laser
Manufacturer: Defiance Industries
   Primary Factory: Hesperus II
Communications System: Neil 6000-G
Targeting and Tracking System: RCA Instatrac Mark XXII

Overview

The revitalization of the Lyran Commonwealth's military production lines allowed a number of previously discarded or rejected concepts to be revisited. Designs that featured components which could be produced in large numbers or were already in ample supply came to the forefront as the basis for an entirely new Lyran military arsenal. One of the designs resurrected by this new policy was the *Eisenfaust* (literally, iron fist).

In the earliest days of BattleMech production, the Lyrans had attempted to create a specialized medium-class 'Mech geared for siege duty. While initial field tests prompted an optimistic view of the design, in the end the *Eisenfaust* was too slow for practical battlefield use. Its plodding, lumbering speed and relatively small size meant that faster BattleMechs could exploit weaknesses in the *Eisenfaust* with ease.

Since then, new technologies have become available. Extralight engines coupled with advanced chassis and armor components meant that the *Eisenfaust* was not only a viable, but, in fact, a desirable design. After an expedited redesign and review process, the *Eisenfaust* became one of the first units to enter production in the wake of the Word of Blake's assault against the Lyran Alliance.

Capabilities

Envisioned as a siege specialist, the *Eisenfaust* was always designed to pack a serious punch for its size. The search for a powerful yet compact main weapon system saw many iterations before finally settling on the ultra-modern plasma rifle. In the plasma rifle, the design team found a weapon that rivaled the venerated particle projection cannon for damage potential but at less weight and without the need for field inhibitors.

The complementary weapon systems shaped around the plasma rifle focused on two major factors. First and foremost the weapons needed to defend the *Eisenfaust* from hit and run attacks by smaller, faster machines. The secondary concern was to keep the *Eisenfaust* as free as possible from a constant need to reload. An array of energy weapons were chosen that could fulfill both roles. The Defiance extended-range large laser provided additional long-range firepower while the twin medium pulse lasers kept smaller, faster units at bay.

Perhaps the single most relevant factor in the resurrection of the *Eisenfaust* was the upgrade of the *Hatchetman* BattleMech from the Edasich 180 extralight engine. The engine was produced in such large numbers that even in the wake of the Jihad they were readily available. Designers quickly adapted the *Eisenfaust* to utilize the engine. Not only would this assist with production efforts, it would also increase the 'Mech's speed by thirty-three percent. The weight saved by utilizing the Edasich 180 XL engine also allowed enough additional heat sinks to help dissipate the considerable heat of design's weapon systems.

Deployment

First produced at the Defiance Tharkad facility, the Seventh Donegal Guards have received most of this original production run of the *Eisenfaust*. Other Lyran units including Royal Guard and Lyran Regulars regiments have received small numbers of the 'Mech as well, though most of these are from Hesperus, where all production now occurs.

The Republic has also exercised our option to purchase production runs of the *Eisenfaust*. It will be used primarily to fill out our defensive formations, freeing higher-end units for premiere formations.

Variants

A handful of original EFT-4J *Eisenfaust*s were created in order to allow BattleMech design engineers to adapt modern technologies to the frame. Some of these basic technology designs still remain in use and are occasionally utilized to produce "concept" versions.

Another variant, the EFT-8X, was created to showcase the blazer cannon as a viable battlefield technology. The EFT-8X removes the plasma rifle and ER large laser in order to install the experimental cannon and copies of the Word of Blake's medium variable-speed pulse lasers. While the raw damage potential of the blazer cannon is promising, it remains to be seen if the *Eisenfaust* can handle the extreme heat generated by the weapon.

EFT-7X EISENFAUST

Type: **Eisenfaust**
Technology Base: Inner Sphere
Tonnage: 45
Battle Value: 1,203

Equipment		Mass
Internal Structure:		4.5
Engine:	180 XL	3.5
Walking MP:	4	
Running MP:	6	
Jumping MP:	0	
Heat Sinks:	15 [30]	5
Gyro:		2
Cockpit:		3
Armor Factor:	152	9.5

	Internal Structure	Armor Value
Head	3	9
Center Torso	14	20
Center Torso (rear)		7
R/L Torso	11	16
R/L Torso (rear)		6
R/L Arm	7	14
R/L Leg	11	22

Weapons and Ammo	Location	Critical	Tonnage
2 Medium Pulse Lasers	CT	2	4
Plasma Rifle	LT	2	6
Ammo (Plasma) 20	LT	2	2
ER Large Laser	LA	2	5
ER Small Laser	LA	1	.5

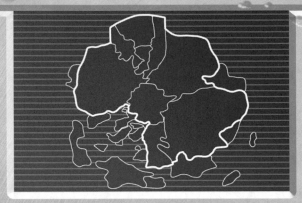

Mass: 45 tons
Chassis: Chariot Type II
Power Plant: Edasich Motors 225 Light
Cruising Speed: 54 kph
Maximum Speed: 86 kph
Jump Jets: Luxor 2/Q
　　Jump Capacity: 150 meters
Armor: Durallex Super Medium Ferro-Fibrous with CASE
Armament:
　　1 Helga Series 9-Tube Multi-Missile Launcher
　　2 Defiance Model XII Extended Range Medium Lasers
Manufacturer: Defiance Industries, Johnston Industries
　　Primary Factory: Hesperus II (Defiance),
　　　　New Syrtis (Johnston - Offline)
Communications System: TharHes Thalia HM-22
　　with Guardian ECM
Targeting and Tracking System: TharHes Ares-8a

Overview

Faced with mixed feedback for their *Hatchetman* design, Defiance Industries began planning an upgrade for the innovative BattleMech. Building on improvements introduced in the HCT-6S model, engineering teams began evaluating some of the new technology to emerge from the bloodbath into which the Blakists had plunged the Inner Sphere. With Johnston's New Syrtis plant rendered temporarily unusable, Johnston approached Defiance to assist them with their redesign. Johnston successfully brokered its R&D staff & development funds to Defiance in exchange for royalties & a license for future use.

Months of simulations and prototyping followed, until Johnston settled on the radical idea of replacing the BattleMechs' primary ballistic armament with the multi-missile launcher technology invented by the ill-fated Battle Magic mercenary company.

Capabilities

Though conceived of as an urban combat specialist when it was introduced in 3023, the *Hatchetman* was all too often pressed into service as a general purpose BattleMech. This trend continued as Inner Sphere weapons manufacturers began upgrading their wares with recovered Star League technology, often with mixed results. Though it incorporated a number of innovative features, the *Hatchetman* was too slow, too vulnerable and lacking the kind of long-range firepower needed on the battlefield in the latter half of the thirty-first century.

The HCT-6S that entered service late in the FedCom Civil War attempted to address the issue of survivability by replacing the vulnerable XL fusion engine of the HCT-5S with a modern light fusion power plant. Using that as their starting point, the engineering team at Defiance Industries increased the engine's rating to boost ground speed by twenty-five percent. The installation of double efficiency heat sinks and an additional jump jet required several structural changes and some significant redesign of the BattleMech's torso. Other design changes also served to alter the *Hatchetman*'s appearance, culminating in the decision to copy other BattleMech manufacturers and restyle the whole chassis.

Meanwhile, the Johnston team concentrated on weapons systems and electronics. With C³ systems becoming increasingly common, the inclusion of powerful electronic countermeasures in a design intended to close with the enemy was an obvious upgrade. Installation of the latest extended-range lasers from Defiance as the BattleMech's secondary armament also was something of a no-brainer. It was the radical move to replace the ballistic weaponry around which the original *Hatchetman* had been designed that came as the big surprise. Originating in an attempt to duplicate the Clans' advanced tactical missile system using Inner Sphere technology, the multi-missile launcher lacks the sophistication of the Clan weapon. Nevertheless it has proven an effective and flexible weapon in its own right. The inclusion of a generous three-ton magazine enables the *Hatchetman* to carry a wide range of munitions and get the most out of the new weapon.

Deployment

The Royal Guards were given the honor of field-testing the revitalized *Hatchetman*, and the LCAF continues to make widespread use of the design. Next in supply priority, the Lyran Guards have received several shipments. The 'Mechs of Reid's Company from the Third Lyran Guards—equipped with four of the new HCT-7S models—performed admirably, smashing the pirates that landed on Odessa in June of 3084 looking to pick over the Word of Blake's leavings.

The new *Hatchetman* has become a firm favorite with Davion units as well. The Seventh Crucis Lancers made use of its ECM systems to infiltrate the fortress of Parron Benton on Parma and put down the rebellious nobleman's forces.

After delivering the first production runs to the LCAF, Defiance Industries has made the design available for general purchase. The Republic of the Sphere and several mercenary commands took advantage of the opportunity to purchase cutting-edge technology to replace shambling wrecks of battlefield salvage.

A number of HCT-5S *Hatchetman* BattleMechs fell into the Free Worlds League's possession during the early phases of the Jihad. Many of these have been refitted to create the HCT-6M variant. The Duchy of Oriente and the Principality of Regulus both employed the design in their most recent clashes.

Variants

With a number of heavily damaged HCT-5S captured from Lyran forces, the Free Worlds League developed a refit program to return them to service. The heat sinks were replaced with double efficiency models and the old autocannon has been swapped out for a heavy PPC. The medium pulse lasers were retained and a Beagle active probe added.

Type: **Hatchetman**
Technology Base: Inner Sphere
Tonnage: 45
Battle Value: 1,243

Equipment		Mass
Internal Structure:		4.5
Engine:	225 Light	7.5
Walking MP:	5	
Running MP:	8	
Jumping MP:	5	
Heat Sinks:	10 [20]	0
Gyro:		3
Cockpit:		3
Armor Factor (Ferro):	152	8.5

	Internal Structure	Armor Value
Head	3	9
Center Torso	14	21
Center Torso (rear)		6
R/L Torso	11	16
R/L Torso (rear)		6
R/L Arm	7	14
R/L Leg	11	22

Weapons and Ammo	Location	Critical	Tonnage
ER Medium Laser	RA	1	1
Hatchet	RA	3	3
MML 9	RT	5	6
Ammo (MML) 39/33	RT	3	3
CASE	RT	1	.5
Guardian ECM Suite	LT	2	1.5
ER Medium Laser	LA	1	1
Jump Jets	RL	2	1
Jump Jet	CT	1	.5
Jump Jets	LL	2	1

Note: If playing under Advanced Rules, treat head as having a Full-Head Ejection System.

GST-10 GHOST

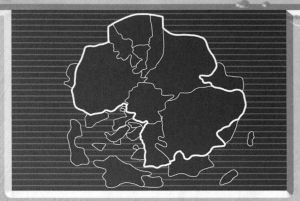

Mass: 50 tons
Chassis: Enran TXS2A Standard
Power Plant: GM 300 XL
Cruising Speed: 64 kph
Maximum Speed: 97 kph
Jump Jets: None
 Jump Capacity: None
Armor: Starshield Ultra-Tech Stealth
Armament:
 2 Defiance 1002 Light Particle Projector Cannons
 1 BlazeFire Longshot ER Medium Laser
 2 Helga Series Multiple Missile Launcher 3-Packs
Manufacturer: Defiance Industries, Earthwerks-FWL, Inc.
 Primary Factory: Hesperus II (Defiance),
 Calloway VI (Earthwerks)
Communications System: Nashan Comm-i U-284 with ECM
Targeting and Tracking System: Nashan Trac V-102
 with Active Probe

Overview

Electronic warfare underwent a technical revolution with the arrival of the Clans. BattleMech sensor capabilities once again rivaled, and often surpassed, those of the best BattleMech units found in the SLDF during the Golden Age. While several new designs featured various EW components, dedicated stealth designs were unheard of outside of a handful of Blakist & Liao units.

The changing battlefields of the thirty-first century made reconnaissance and stealth far more important both tactically and strategically. In the wake of the liberation of Hesperus II from the Word of Blake, the Lyran Alliance made the development of a dedicated EW recon unit a priority. Utilizing several of the most cutting-edge detection and anti-detection technologies, Lyran engineers created the *Ghost*.

The process was arduous and a logistical nightmare. In order to corral and assemble the components that the *Ghost* would require, the Lyrans needed assistance with transportation and the repairs to make Defiance Industries operational once more. Help came from an unlikely quarter when the Duchy of Oriente's Earthwerks Incorporated reached out to offer aid. In return for the rights to produce the *Ghost* in their own factories, Earthwerks helped the Lyran Alliance acquire and ship the needed parts and labor to finish both the prototype of the *Ghost* and the main Defiance facilities on Hesperus II. In fact, as of this writing, all of the Earthwerks-manufactured *Ghosts* feature Lyran power plants. This symbiotic relationship is likely to continue for the foreseeable future as BattleMech production throughout the Inner Sphere continues at a trickle of its formerly robust pace.

Capabilities

The *Ghost* is designed around its stealth armor capabilities. Many of these were pioneered with the *Mongoose II* design, from which the *Ghost* borrowed heavily. For example, the sophisticated stealth armor, active probe and ECM suite were all directly borrowed from the *Mongoose II*.

On top of the most sophisticated electronics package of any mass-produced Inner Sphere unit to date, the *Ghost* is designed to survive. It has a top speed nearing 100 kph that keeps it on par with all but the lightest and fastest reconnaissance units. The protection offered by this speed is augmented by a hefty ten and a half tons of stealth armor. When coupled with the ECM suite and detection capabilities of the Beagle active probe, the *Ghost* is hard to detect and nearly impossible to corner or trap.

Offensively, the design features cutting-edge weaponry that allows for a wide range of combat roles. The multiple-missile launcher systems provide the 'Mech with long- and short-range firepower. Tandem light particle cannons give it a main weapon system capable of causing solid damage at respectable ranges. Finally, an extended-range medium laser serves as a versatile auxiliary weapon. While the *Ghost* may not feature overwhelming firepower, it certainly can cause enough damage to make it a fearsome deep penetration raider.

Deployment

Ready and waiting for the first *Ghosts* to roll of the assembly line were the Royal Guards regiments of the LCAF. The *Ghost* has quickly become a favorite of Lyran commanders for its ability to disrupt enemy supply lines and command structures. In the Oriente Protectorate, the *Ghost* has been assigned to elite reconnaissance companies in the Fusiliers regiments. Technological limitations surrounding the construction of the stealth armor and an expected but ugly legal battle with manufacturers in the Capellan Confederation have kept production runs relatively small.

With production levels so low, the *Ghost* is unlikely to see widespread service anytime soon. However, in an effort to offset the high cost of *Ghost* production, Earthwerks and the Lyran Commonwealth have made the design available for purchase. While only a handful of *Ghosts* are available each year, the design has begun to crop up in military units throughout the Inner Sphere. Rumors abound that select mercenary units have ordered the *Ghost* as well, but to date no mercenary unit has been recorded fielding one within its ranks.

Variants

In an effort to increase production numbers, the GST-11 sheds the stealth armor for conventional armor. This model is seeing heavy purchase by mercenary units.

Type: **Ghost**
Technology Base: Inner Sphere
Tonnage: 50
Battle Value: 1,353

Equipment			Mass
Internal Structure:			5
Engine:	300 XL		9.5
Walking MP:	6		
Running MP:	9		
Jumping MP:	0		
Heat Sinks:	14 [28]		4
Gyro:			3
Cockpit:			3
Armor Factor (Stealth):	168		10.5

	Internal Structure	Armor Value
Head	3	9
Center Torso	16	21
Center Torso (rear)		10
R/L Torso	12	17
R/L Torso (rear)		7
R/L Arm	8	16
R/L Leg	12	24

Weapons and Ammo	Location	Critical	Tonnage
ER Medium Laser	RA	1	1
Guardian ECM Suite	RA	2	1.5
Light PPC	RT	2	3
MML 3	RT	2	1.5
Ammo (MML) 40/33	RT	1	1
Light PPC	LT	2	3
MML 3	LT	2	1.5
Ammo (MML) 40/33	LT	1	1
Beagle Active Probe	LA	2	1.5

SKW-2F SHOCKWAVE

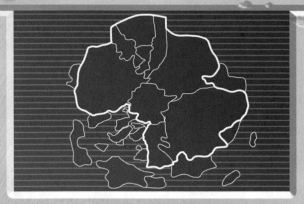

Mass: 50 tons
Chassis: Corean-II Delux Endo Steel
Power Plant: Hermes 250 XL
Cruising Speed: 54 kph
Maximum Speed: 86 kph
Jump Jets: None
   Jump Capacity: None
Armor: Starshield
Armament:
   1 Martell Extended Range Large Laser
   1 Zeus LRM 10
   1 Imperator Rotary Autocannon/5
Manufacturer: Earthwerks-FWL, Inc.
   Primary Factory: Keystone
Communications System: Corean Transband-J9
Targeting and Tracking System: Corean B-Tech
   with Artemis IV Fire Control

Overview

While the Word of Blake caused unprecedented havoc and destruction during their campaign to punish the Inner Sphere for destroying the Star League, their aggressive program of BattleMech production and development drastically heightened the technology base and production facilities of factories under their occupation. Many of these facilities were sabotaged during the Word of Blake's retreat, but the net effect of the Blakist occupation was to spread technological advances across international borders. What might have taken years or decades to accomplish through diplomacy and negotiation, the Word of Blake achieved through terror and aggression.

The Jihad also left countless worlds battered and broken in the fallout of the battles required to liberate them from the Word's grasp. For some worlds, the damage was so severe it is unlikely they will ever rebuild to their former status. However, the road to recovery has been much swifter for worlds possessing military production facilities. Militaries throughout the Inner Sphere were forced to rebuild their ranks through any means available, which made the restoration of production facilities to operational status a national priority.

In the Free Worlds League, the Jihad not only wrought havoc, it also splintered a once-proud nation into fragments. When worlds formerly part of the Free Worlds League emerged from the shadow of Blakist occupation, they were forced to rebuild on their own. For the burgeoning Marik-Stewart Commonwealth and the world of Keystone, the reconstruction effort centered on the Earthwerks-FWL Inc. facility. Once a robust and capable factory, the facility was revamped by the Word of Blake and then heavily damaged in the Jihad.

With few other viable exports, the leaders of Keystone turned to BattleMech production as a method of acquiring the monies necessary to rebuild their shattered cities. In addition to previously successful designs such as the *Bloodhound*, the Earthwerks factory contained suitable development facilities to create entirely new designs. The first of these post-Jihad designs to be produced for international export was the *Shockwave*.

Capabilities

The *Shockwave* is designed for one purpose: combat. It has respectable speed, a heavily armored frame and a weapons package that balances range, destructive capability and heat dissipation. The design features little in the way of specialized components or advanced electronics. Instead, it relies on a toolset compatible with modern BattleMech tactics.

At the heart of the design lies the Hermes 250 extralight engine. This reliable power plant enables the *Shockwave* to attain a top speed in line with modern battlefield tactics. An impressive ten tons of Starshield armor is draped over the lightweight endo steel frame in order to make the *Shockwave* capable of taking considerable damage while remaining combat effective. This combination of speed and durability serves as the basis for a capable frontline medium BattleMech.

The weapons package is designed for a battle, not a campaign. The ammunition-dependent Imperator Rotary autocannon gives the *Shockwave* an impressive primary weapon, while the Zeus long-range missile system coupled with the improved Corean-B Tech targeting and tracking system grants the *Shockwave* range. Finally, the Martell extended-range large laser augments both long- and short-range engagements. In all, the *Shockwave*'s arsenal delivers large quantities of damage in a short period of time.

Deployment

Sales of the *Shockwave* have been brisk. To date, every major Inner Sphere nation except the Lyran Commonwealth has ordered the design and deployed it within their ranks. Obviously, a portion of *Shockwave* production is set aside every year to bolster the defenses of the Marik-Stewart Commonwealth.

The Capellan Confederation and the Republic of the Sphere are the largest importers of the *Shockwave*. Both nations are aggressively expanding and reforming their military structures, and the willingness of Earthwerks to sell to anyone who will meet their price makes the *Shockwave* easy to acquire. Increasing orders for new *Shockwaves* indicate that commanders around the Inner Sphere view the 'Mech as a capable design. It is only a matter of time before *Shockwaves* face off against one another on the battlefield.

Variants

To date, only one variant of the *Shockwave* has been noted. The *Shockwave* 4G removes a heat sink and the Artemis system in order to upgrade the extended-range large laser to an experimental large X-pulse laser. This variant has seen limited use, as the laser requires extensive maintenance to keep operational.

Type: **Shockwave**
Technology Base: Inner Sphere
Tonnage: 50
Battle Value: 1,453

Equipment			Mass
Internal Structure:	Endo Steel		2.5
Engine:	250 XL		6.5
Walking MP:	5		
Running MP:	8		
Jumping MP:	0		
Heat Sinks:	11 [22]		1
Gyro:			3
Cockpit:			3
Armor Factor:	160		10

	Internal Structure	Armor Value
Head	3	9
Center Torso	16	22
Center Torso (rear)		9
R/L Torso	12	17
R/L Torso (rear)		6
R/L Arm	8	15
R/L Leg	12	22

Weapons and Ammo	Location	Critical	Tonnage
Rotary AC/5	RT	6	10
Ammo (RAC) 40	CT	2	2
LRM 10	RT	2	5
Artemis IV FCS	RT	1	1
ER Large Laser	LT	2	5
Ammo (LRM) 12	LT	1	1

OSP-26 OSPREY

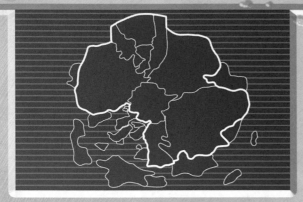

Mass: 55 tons
Chassis: Hollis Mk II Endo Steel
Power Plant: DAV 220 XL
Cruising Speed: 43 kph
Maximum Speed: 64 kph
Jump Jets: Anderson Propulsion 25
    Jump Capacity: 120 meters
Armor: Durallex Heavy with CASE
Armament:
    1 M-7 Gauss Rifle
    1 Holly MML 7 Rack
    2 Diverse Optics ER Medium Lasers
    1 Diverse Optics ER Small Laser
Manufacturer: Skobel MechWorks, Hollis Incorporated,
    Achernar BattleMechs
    Primary Factory: Terra (Skobel), Corey (Hollis),
        Achernar (Achernar- Destroyed)
Communications System: O/P COM-211
Targeting and Tracking System: O/P 1078 with
    Beagle Active Probe

Overview

The original *Osprey* OSP-15 was a limited-use unit in SLDF Royal Units. Answering a quartermaster's bid for a mobile, medium-weight fire support unit, Hollis Incorporated created the *Osprey*. They lost the SLDF bid to Blue Shot Weapons' *Lynx*, relegating the *Osprey* to a limited contract in an urban fire support role. Desperate for durable, high-firepower machines with which to equip their Protectorate Militias, the Word of Blake resurrected the *Osprey* in the early 3070s and thrust it into its most prominent role ever.

Capabilities

Using ancient plans and a museum-piece *Osprey*, the Word of Blake commissioned Skobel MechWorks to replicate the original design. The first test units were a minor upgrade of the Star League-era OSP-15, visually indistinguishable from the original. After an accelerated field trial, Skobel went back to design boards and created the updated OSP-26. Sporting new technologies, this design also received a physical upgrade that allowed for easier maintenance and transformed the OSP-26 into a more visually intimidating machine.

The core of the *Osprey*'s firepower is built around the M-7 Gauss rifle. Identical to the one used on the *Highlander*, the M-7 is an extremely reliable system that delivers severe damage with pinpoint accuracy. A modern MML system supplements the M-7's long-range firepower and offers a greatly improved short-range punch. Two Diverse Optics ER medium lasers and a single ER small laser round out the offensive armament. Built chiefly for urban combat, the OSP-26 has an average ground speed but backs this up with 120-meter jump jet ability. Further improving on the original *Osprey*, the OSP-26 mounts a Beagle active probe to allow better tracking of hostiles in the urban jungles it favors. As part of the physical makeover, the probe was fashioned to look like a laser system and the ER small was placed in a larger housing, giving the *Osprey* the appearance of four arm lasers of the same size.

Deployment

During the Star League era, the *Osprey* was deployed in limited numbers. Assigned to urban specialist units and Special Forces, less than a thousand were manufactured before the Star League collapsed. Few of these units survived the Exodus and subsequent Succession Wars. Only two have been documented in recent years, one discovered by a FedCom mercenary unit in the 3020s and the other being the museum piece used as the prototype for the Word's revival of the design.

Once the Word began new production, it turned out the simple upgrade OSP-25 and OSP-26 redesign in significant numbers at the Skobel plant on Terran and on Achernar, where the old IndustrialMech lines were upgraded to produce the design. Images of a company of white *Ospreys* firing en masse to destroy a Wolf-in-Exile *Daishi* remain a lasting symbol of the brutal battle to capture the Achernar complex. Though the factory was completely destroyed, the Coalition recovered several lances of *Ospreys*.

The nascent Republic was impressed with the *Osprey*'s durability and effectiveness in urban environments, and so Victor Steiner-Davion designated the surviving Skobel *Osprey* line as a priority to repair. In the intervening years, a small but steady stream of *Ospreys* has continued to march off the line and into RAF front-line units.

Seeing the renewed success of the *Osprey*, Hollis Incorporated, the original manufacturer of the 'Mech, retooled one of their *Catapult* lines to produce the OSP-15E. Functionally identical to the OSP-25, this *Osprey* was quickly accepted by the Confederation Strategios. When paired with the *Catapult*, the two units were found to make an effective fire support team. The advantage of the newer OSP-26's MML system was proven in a brief clash on Shipka, where two *Ospreys* from the Eighth Hastati Sentinels encountered a mixed Capellan *Osprey/Catapult* lance in broken terrain. Using the added short-range firepower of their MMLs, the two Hastati *Ospreys* destroyed the *Catapults* and one of the Capellan *Ospreys* in a cat-and-mouse battle through the hills and gullies.

Variants

No known Star League-era variants are known to have been produced, as the compact chassis complicated anything but the most basic refits. The original OSP-15 lacked the Beagle probe, mounted an LRM 10 in place of the MML and carried three standard Martell medium lasers instead of the ER models on the OSP-26. When the Word of Blake first began fielding the recovered *Osprey*, they created the OSP-25, a simple upgrade of the OSP-15 that exchanged the Martell lasers for three extended-range versions.

Type: **Osprey**
Technology Base: Inner Sphere
Tonnage: 55
Battle Value: 1,541

Equipment			Mass
Internal Structure:	Endo Steel		3
Engine:	220 XL		5
Walking MP:	4		
Running MP:	6		
Jumping MP:	4		
Heat Sinks:	10 [20]		0
Gyro:			3
Cockpit:			3
Armor Factor:	176		11

	Internal Structure	Armor Value
Head	3	9
Center Torso	18	30
Center Torso (rear)		5
R/L Torso	13	22
R/L Torso (rear)		4
R/L Arm	9	16
R/L Leg	13	24

Weapons and Ammo	Location	Critical	Tonnage
ER Medium Laser	RA	1	1
Beagle Active Probe	RA	2	1.5
Gauss Rifle	RT	7	15
Ammo (Gauss) 8	RT	1	1
Ammo (Gauss) 8	LT	1	1
MML 7	LT	4	4.5
Ammo (MML) 34/28	LT	2	2
ER Medium Laser	LA	1	1
ER Small Laser	LA	1	.5
CASE	LT	1	.5
Jump Jets	CT	2	1
Jump Jet	RT	1	.5
Jump Jet	LT	1	.5

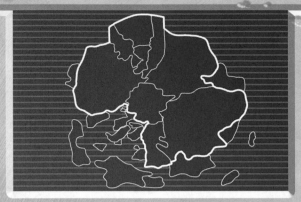

Mass: 55 tons
Chassis: Hessen Rook Mk II
Power Plant: DAV 220
Cruising Speed: 43 kph
Maximum Speed: 64 kph
Jump Jets: Rawlings 45i Improved Jump Jets
    Jump Capacity: 180 meters
Armor: New Hessen Laminar Weave
Armament:
    1 Tiegart Maximum ER PPC
    1 Sutel Precision Line Small Pulse Laser
    4 Hellion-V Medium Lasers
Manufacturer: New Hessen WorkMechs
    Primary Factory: New Hessen
Communications System: Neil 6000
Targeting and Tracking System: Octagon Tartrac System C

Overview

Among the nigh-legendary performances of the New Hessen WorkMechs personnel was not only the development and initial commissioning of the NH-1A *Rook* during the Jihad, but also the design and construction of its successor. This upgrade replaced the primitive technology of the NH-1A with more modern and effective equipment and was christened the NH-2 *Rook*. While the NH-1A was a primary factor in defending New Hessen from the Blakist invasion of 3076, it was the NH-2, albeit in limited numbers, that saw action in allied service during the final thrust to Terra. Though less well-known, the NH-3X *Rook* has incorporated more advanced technology than either of the other variants. If the NH-3X succeeds in its trials, it will become a welcome component in nearly any BattleMech force.

Capabilities

The NH-1A was constructed using several pieces of antiquated technology. This RetroMech packed a powerful array of lasers to back up a PPC, creating a fearsome opponent on the battlefield. However, the NH-1A's outdated engine technology only allowed it a top speed of fifty-four kph. While the primitive technology of its construction allowed the New Hessen WorkMechs factory to produce the 'Mech with ease, the slow NH-1A was clearly outclassed by other 'Mechs of the same weight class. This was alleviated when Devlin Stone delivered advanced engines and specifications to General Pat Hampton in thanks for Hampton's permission to use New Hessen as a staging ground against the Blakists. The result was the NH-2, a 'Mech which, while still slow for its weight class, is better able to compete with enemy forces.

The top speed of the NH-2 is limited in part by Hampton's refusal to reduce the firepower of the *Rook*. Feeling that the *Rook*'s primary role was the defense of his homeworld, Hampton directed the WorkMech factory engineers to concentrate less on the 'Mech's speed than on its weaponry. Sacrificing only the rear-firing lasers of the NH-1A, the NH-2 keeps the same number of lasers but upgrades the PPC to an extended-range model. The head-mounted small laser was replaced with a pulse version to aid in anti-infantry activity. The use of double heat sinks greatly increases the usefulness of the *Rook*'s complement of energy weapons.

While Hampton constrained their efforts to install a larger engine for a higher top speed, the engineers were able to convince the general to install improved jump jets. This system, along with the modern engine, provides the NH-2 with a jump capability twice that of its predecessor. This implementation was only successful after the engineers replaced the gyro with a compact version, which enabled proper balancing of the jump jet array across the entirety of the *Rook*'s rear torso. The network of thrusters had given the engineers nothing but headaches during the development of the NH-2 until this innovative gyroscope was used.

Deployment

Though introduced just a few years ago the *Rook* was constructed in great haste using the full complement of the New Hessen WorkMechs' labor force. Thus, over 100 of these 'Mechs were constructed and in the field to repel the Blakists in 3076. Used almost exclusively on defense, the slow NH-1A was quite successfully deployed as a supplementary component of combined-arms units in the New Hessen Defense Force. Given how widespread the NH-1A was in the New Hessen forces, some were captured by insurgent Blakist forces during their guerrilla campaign in late 3076. With the presence of so many Coalition forces in New Hessen staging centers able to take part in repelling the Blakist invasion, some *Rook*s have found their way into the RAF and AFFS.

Variants

A prototype *Rook*, the NH-3X, sports a supercharger in addition to a new 330 XL engine, giving it a standard top speed of ninety-seven kph (129 kph with the supercharger). Though the jump jets were downgraded to the locally-produced Hessen Heavy Boosters of the NH-1A, the NH-3X is able to retain the 180-meter jump range of the NH-2. The NH-2's ER PPC is replaced with a blazer cannon at the expense of two heat sinks. The head-mounted small pulse laser is replaced with the NH-1A's standard small laser.

There are still a number of the primitive *Rook*s serving in the field, using its primitive engine to obtain a top speed of fifty-four kph and a jumping range of only ninety meters. Its standard heat sinks, only fourteen of them, force the MechWarrior to keep a careful eye on the engine temperature while firing the PPC and complement of lasers.

Type: **Rook**
Technology Base: Inner Sphere
Tonnage: 55
Battle Value: 1,525

Equipment			Mass
Internal Structure:			5.5
Engine:	220		10
Walking MP:	4		
Running MP:	6		
Jumping MP:	6		
Heat Sinks:	12 [24]		2
Gyro (Compact):			4.5
Cockpit:			3
Armor Factor:	185		12

	Internal Structure	Armor Value
Head	3	9
Center Torso	18	27
Center Torso (rear)		9
R/L Torso	13	20
R/L Torso (rear)		6
R/L Arm	9	18
R/L Leg	13	26

Weapons and Ammo	Location	Critical	Tonnage
Medium Laser	RA	1	1
ER PPC	RT	3	7
Medium Laser	RT	1	1
Small Pulse Laser	H	1	1
Medium Laser	LT	1	1
Medium Laser	LA	1	1
Improved Jump Jet	RL	2	1
Improved Jump Jet	RT	2	1
Improved Jump Jets	CT	4	2
Improved Jump Jet	LT	2	1
Improved Jump Jet	LL	2	1

TFT-A9 THUNDER FOX

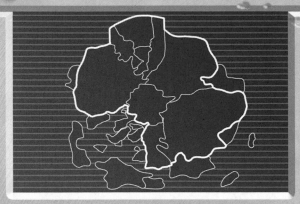

Mass: 55 tons
Chassis: Dennenbach-Mitchell Series 8 - Modified
Power Plant: DAV 220
Cruising Speed: 43 kph
Maximum Speed: 64 kph
Jump Jets: Rawlings 60
   Jump Capacity: 90 meters
Armor: Krupp 205 Light Ferro-Fibrous with CASE
Armament:
   1 Corean Light Gauss Rifle
   1 Diverse Optics Sunbeam Extended Range Large Laser
   1 Guided Technologies 2nd Gen Streak SRM 4
   1 Diverse Optics ER Small Laser
Manufacturer: Skobel 'Mech Works, Defiance Industries, Luthien Armor Works
   Primary Factory: Terra (Skobel),
      Hesperus II (Defiance), New Samarkand (LAW)
Communications System: Skobel Wave 13
Targeting and Tracking System: Matabushi Sentinel

Overview

With the collapse of the Word of Blake Protectorate most corporations lost stable sales. Some came through the events scarred but functional, while others saw their facilities destroyed during the Jihad. Amidst the destruction and against the odds, some prospered. Skobel 'Mech Works was one of the lucky few thanks to Lara Harman (an upper-level design engineer) who defected from Mitchell Vehicles and joined Skobel in 3075. Republic Intelligence later uncovered that Harman used her position in Mitchell to siphon off trade secret data on the *Blue Flame* BattleMech and may have been on Skobel's payroll all along.

Harman correctly predicted that most of the Blake designs, regardless of their battlefield reputation, would inherit a stigma at the end of the Jihad. Sales plummeted as the Protectorate shrank, and companies like Mitchell scrambled to reposition their product lines. By 3076, Harman had been using her position and connections within the Word to repurpose equipment for her project.

Hidden under layers of bureaucracy, the *Thunder Fox* was the 'Mech that didn't exist. Virtually every component on the *Thunder Fox* was "borrowed" from other Blake designs. *Vanquisher* production lost some light Gauss rifles, redirected shipments meant for the *Legacy* provided the Streak SRM 4, and the *Blue Flame* provided the chassis and Sunbeam ER Large Lasers. Even the light ferro-fibrous armor and fusion engine were acquired through Harman's efforts.

Her gamble paid off, and the *Thunder Fox* has become a popular design in The Republic, though it would ultimately not benefit Harman, who was indicted for war crimes and profiteering.

Capabilities

With average performance for a 'Mech mounting a standard fusion engine, many analysts blame the public spectacle of Harman's indictment for the commercial success of the *Thunder Fox*. Built from a heavily modified *Blue Flame* chassis, the *Thunder Fox* adds ten tons to the design, sacrifices its light engine and some mobility.

The *Thunder Fox* has a sixty-four kph top speed and is meant for sniping and skirmishing. Its Sunbeam ER Large Laser and Corean Light Gauss Rifle give it effective striking power at over 600 meters. In close engagements, the *Thunder Fox* is often outgunned, adding only a Streak SRM 4 and ER small laser as secondary weaponry. Nine tons of light ferro-fibrous armor provide acceptable protection, allowing the *Thunder Fox* to withstand a heavy PPC strike without suffering penetration except when caught from behind. A unique, center-mounted jump jet system provides a surprising amount of lift, while two rear-leg mounted jets provide directional control.

Deployment

The TFT-A9 is currently deployed to the Principes Guards in The Republic. Lyran units stationed along the border have been receiving limited quantities for the last five years, and Combine deployments began in 3083. Both Houses are also testing variants that are expected to see deployment in early '86.

Variants

The Combine TFT-C3 design sacrifices the light Gauss rifle, adding a cockpit command console and C³ master computer while upgrading to a light fusion engine. Designed to coordinate lances of C³ slave-enabled scouts, the Combine variant is ideal for command-training junior officers, giving them battlefield experience without the distraction of piloting and engaging targets at the same time. The spacious command console—essentially a second cockpit—leaves the officer free to concentrate on C³ data, troop movements, and tactical decisions. Currently in field trials, the Combine has already placed initial orders with Luthien Armor Works for several of this model. In an attempt to provide a smoother (and less distracting) ride for the command officer the TFT-C3 trades in jump jets for experimental mechanical jump boosters in each leg, extending jumping range by 30 meters.

The Lyran TFT-L8 variant more closely resembles the *Blue Flame* than the standard model. Equipped with a 275 XL engine, top speed is boosted to 86 kph. Jumping movement is similarly increased with the L8's capacity sitting at a comfortable 150 meters. Two snub-nose PPCs and an LB-10X give the variant a decent punch at all ranges.

Type: **Thunder Fox**
Technology Base: Inner Sphere
Tonnage: 55
Battle Value: 1,325

Equipment		Mass
Internal Structure:		5.5
Engine:	220	10
Walking MP:	4	
Running MP:	6	
Jumping MP:	3	
Heat Sinks:	10 [20]	0
Gyro:		3
Cockpit:		3
Armor Factor (Light Ferro):	152	9

	Internal Structure	Armor Value
Head	3	9
Center Torso	18	21
Center Torso (rear)		6
R/L Torso	13	20
R/L Torso (rear)		4
R/L Front Leg	13	17
R/L Rear Leg	13	17

Weapons and Ammo	Location	Critical	Tonnage
Light Gauss Rifle	RT	6	12
Ammo (Light Gauss) 16	RT	1	1
Streak SRM 4	LT	2	3
Ammo (Streak) 25	RT	1	1
CASE	RT	1	.5
ER Large Laser	LT	2	5
ER Small Laser	LT	1	.5
Jump Jet	RRL	1	.5
Jump Jet	CT	1	.5
Jump Jet	LRL	1	.5

BRM-5A BRAHMA

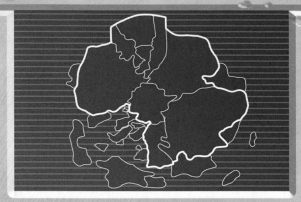

Mass: 60 tons
Chassis: TTI MK VI
Power Plant: VOX 300 XL
Cruising Speed: 54 kph
Maximum Speed: 86 kph
Jump Jets: Rawlings 54
    Jump Capacity: 90 meters
Armor: Durallex Heavy with CASE
Armament:
    1 Pontiac Ultralight Light AC/5
    3 Diverse Optics Extended Range Medium Lasers
    1 Flameshot Flamer
    1 Hovertec Streak SRM 6 Launcher
    1 McArthur Mk.II Anti-Missile System
Manufacturer: Taurus Territorial Industries
    Primary Factory: Taurus
Communications System: Neil 9000-C
Targeting and Tracking System: Octagon AccuTrak
    with Enhanced Targeting

Overview

When the dust cleared from the Jihad in the Taurian Concordat, two things were abundantly clear. First, the Concordat was nowhere near as prepared for invasion as it had believed and, second, its production capabilities were all but non-existent. The Taurians had believed their pre-Jihad expansion of production sites would greatly increase their ability to defend their realm and even prosecute their war with the Federated Suns. However, when they clashed with cutting-edge Inner Sphere militaries all of their venerable tanks and BattleMechs failed to rise to the occasion.

From those ashes, Marshal Victor Sharpe and CEO Matthias Commager hatched a plan to retool and re-design the Taurian military complex. Never again would they be forced to sit helpless while the cutting-edge war machines of mercenaries and foreign nations tore their realm asunder. They would drag Taurian industry into the modern age by any means at their disposal.

The project began by hiring a top flight team of technicians and engineers. This design team was tasked with providing a blueprint for a single advanced BattleMech design and encouraged to utilize or develop components with Taurus Territorial Industries. They were assured that if any of the facilities needed to be retooled to produce more advanced versions of those components that no expense would be spared to do so.

The next phase required daring and courage of a different kind. Leveraging their personal fortunes, heavily indebting TTI, and using their considerable political capital to divert some of the national reconstruction funding, Sharpe and Commager managed to completely fund the project from both a development and construction standpoint. Much was riding on the success of the project that the design team dubbed the *Brahma*.

Capabilities

Facing such a critical task, the designers hired by TTI decided to base their efforts on one of the most successful BattleMech groups ever fielded. Through every major historical confrontation fifty-five ton BattleMechs served with distinction in a broad variety of mission roles. *Shadow Hawk*s, *Wolverine*s, and *Griffin*s were the backbone of every Great House and Periphery nation's military.

Seizing key elements from these successful designs, the engineers soon found that in order to fulfill all of the specifications they were tasked with the new 'Mech would need a slight increase in mass. This major change set off a ripple of design issues, but the engineers remained confident that the end package warranted the radical overhaul of the production facilities on Taurus.

The eventual result would be the *Brahma*, a completely Taurian-inspired and Taurian-constructed BattleMech, replete with advanced electronics, defensive systems and weapons. The *Brahma* retained the speed and mobility that had made its predecessors so capable while increasing both its armor protection and firepower.

An ultra-modern class-5 light autocannon and advanced targeting computer were the primary weapons of the *Brahma*. These were further enhanced by a trio of reliable extended-range medium lasers and the highly efficient Hovertec Streak SRM 6 launcher. A flamer was added for urban warfare and anti-infantry missions. The final key system was an anti-missile system designed to improve the 'Mech's defenses, which already included a solid twelve-and-half tons of Durallex Heavy armor. Whether raiding, keeping the peace or entering frontline combat duty, the *Brahma* is built to excel.

Deployment

The *Brahma* was rushed into service in an effort to rebuild the Taurian Guards and Taurian Lancers to full strength. To date production levels are still nowhere near sufficient to resupply both units. This was further exacerbated by the need to recoup the significant manufacturing investments. To increase revenue, Taurians are reluctantly making a portion of *Brahma*s available to various mercenary commands.

A *Brahma* piloted by a member of the Battle Corps Legion faced off against a mixed lance of pirates on the world of Payvand. Using his jump jets in broken terrain, further confusing the pirates with smoke from fires made by the *Brahma*'s flamer, the pilot was able to put down a pirate *Centurion* and *Rifleman* before Legion reinforcements arrived to drive off the remaining pirates.

Variants

In order to carry a more impressive main weapon the Taurians have begun to construct a small number of experimental BRM-5B *Brahma* variants. The 5B replaces the Light Autocannon 5 with a large X-pulse laser. The exchange of weapons also removes the anti-missile system and reduces the Streak to a standard SRM launcher.

BRM-5A BRAHMA

Type: **Brahma**
Technology Base: Inner Sphere
Tonnage: 60
Battle Value: 1,572

Equipment			Mass
Internal Structure:			6
Engine:	300 XL		9.5
Walking MP:	5		
Running MP:	8		
Jumping MP:	3		
Heat Sinks:	13 [26]		3
Gyro:			3
Cockpit:			3
Armor Factor:	200		12.5

	Internal Structure	Armor Value
Head	3	9
Center Torso	20	29
Center Torso (rear)		10
R/L Torso	14	20
R/L Torso (rear)		8
R/L Arm	10	20
R/L Leg	14	28

Weapons and Ammo	Location	Critical	Tonnage
3 ER Medium Lasers	RA	3	3
Flamer	LA	1	1
Light AC/5	RT	2	5
Ammo (Light AC) 20	RT	1	1
CASE	RT	1	.5
Streak SRM 6	LT	2	4.5
Ammo (Streak) 15	LT	1	1
Targeting Computer	LT	2	2
CASE	RT	1	.5
Anti-Missile System	H	1	.5
Ammo (AMS) 12	CT	1	1
Jump Jet	RT	1	1
Jump Jet	CT	1	1
Jump Jet	LT	1	1

OWR-3M OSTWAR

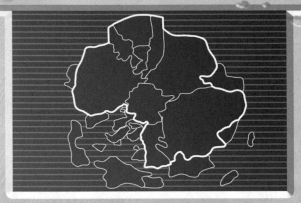

Mass: 65 tons
Chassis: Ost-I
Power Plant: Hermes 260
Cruising Speed: 43 kph
Maximum Speed: 64 kph
Jump Jets: None
    Jump Capacity: None
Armor: Kallon FWL Special Light Ferro-Fibrous with CASE
Armament:
    2 Shannon Sh-47 Streak SRM 4 Launchers
    1 Doombud Long Range Missile 20-Rack
    2 Diverse Optics Extended Range Medium Lasers
Manufacturer: Ronin Incorporated
    Primary Factory: Wallis
Communications System: Barret Party Line-200
    with Guardian ECM Suite
Targeting and Tracking System: Wasat Watchdog W100
    with Artemis IV FCS

Overview

Almost forgotten in modern times, the *Ostwar* was the first of the "walkerpods" pioneered by Ostmann Industries. Produced in limited numbers from 2470, full-scale production was delayed until 2500 due to Ostmann's limited resources. By that time, the Terran Hegemony Armed Forces considered the design obsolete and orders began to dry up. Faced with financial ruin, company director Ernst Ostmann looked beyond the borders of the Hegemony for places where the primitive design could still find a market. The *Ostwar* went on to enjoy limited success until it was

eclipsed by more modern equipment, bringing production to a halt at the start of the Reunification War.

By 3075, the Principality of Regulus had suffered grievous losses to its BattleMech forces. Even at the best of times, Regulus would have been hard pressed to replace so much equipment and materiel. Ronin Inc. on Wallis, one of the Principality's bigger weapons manufacturers, could not come close to meeting demand. With supplies of critical components drying up, Ronin's executives rushed the ancient *Ostwar* back into production as a stopgap measure at Harmony MetalWorks. Since then, Ronin has built a new assembly line to produce the upgraded OWR-3M *Ostwar*.

Capabilities

The original *Ostwar* turned in a solid performance on the bloody battlefields of the Age of War. Well armored and armed, the BattleMech's only significant flaw was its relatively slow ground speed. To modernize the design, Ronin replaced the basic armor with more than eleven tons of light ferro-fibrous material and added CASE, an advanced ECM system and double heat sinks. The designers improved short-range firepower by upgrading the SRMs to Streak racks and replacing the standard medium lasers with extended-range models. Similarly, the Doombud LRM system was enhanced by the addition of an Artemis IV fire control system. Finally, the underpowered power plant was replaced by a modern Hermes 260 unit that addressed the *Ostwar*'s subpar ground speed. The result is exactly what Regulus needs—an inexpensive and robust BattleMech design that can be produced in quantity to bolster its BattleMech forces.

One flaw the upgrade failed to address was the *Ostwar*'s lack of hand actuators. The arm-mounted missile launchers and medium lasers are an effective weapons mix at short range, but when fighting becomes a point-blank affair, this BattleMech can find itself at a disadvantage.

Deployment

Titus Cameron-Jones has deployed the improved *Ostwar* throughout his forces, using it as a replacement for heavy and assault BattleMechs lost in the ongoing conflict with the Duchy of Oriente. A jack-of-all-trades heavy design,

the walkerpod serves equally well in the line of battle and as part of a fire lance alongside *Archers* and *Trebuchets*. On Jouques, the *Ostwars* of the Regulan Hussars fought a rearguard action against the Fusiliers of Oriente's Second Brigade, buying precious time for the raiders to fall back to their DropShips.

Many of the primitive OWR-2M *Ostwars* remain in service, and some have fallen into the hands of the other states that comprise the fragmented Free Worlds League. Chronic equipment shortages and the ease with which this primitive technology can be maintained and repaired is keeping them in service.

Variants

Constructed with technology considered primitive even by the standards of the Succession Wars, the OWR-2M *Ostwar* is powered by a Hermes 235 fusion plant. Underpowered by modern standards, this engine limits top speed to 54 kph. Though it mounts more than seventeen tons of armor, the protection granted by the antiquated material is average at best. Weaponry is similar to the upgraded OWR-3M, but the energy weapons are standard Martel medium lasers that lack the reach of the newer Diverse Optics models. Likewise, the missile weapons lack advanced fire control systems, and modern CASE and ECM are also absent from the older design.

Many of the sub-assemblies and components used by the *Ostwar* were reused in Ostmann's later *Ostsol* and *Ostroc* designs. During the Succession Wars, it was not uncommon to see these newer BattleMechs sporting limbs salvaged from their ancient cousins.

Notable MechWarriors

Lieutenant SG Miles Block: Commander of the Fire Lance in Gold Company of the Third Regulan Hussars, Block fought the rearguard action on Jouques in November 3084. Armed with a variety of munitions for their LRM launchers, his *Ostwars* held back more than a company of Oriente troops while the rest of the raider force boarded their DropShips. Rumor has it that Block will be promoted to command a Regulan company.

OWR-3M OSTWAR

Type: **Ostwar**
Technology Base: Inner Sphere
Tonnage: 65
Battle Value: 1,557

Equipment		Mass
Internal Structure:		6.5
Engine:	260	13.5
Walking MP:	4	
Running MP:	6	
Jumping MP:	0	
Heat Sinks:	12 [24]	2
Gyro:		3
Cockpit:		3
Armor Factor (Light Ferro):	195	11.5

	Internal Structure	Armor Value
Head	3	9
Center Torso	21	30
Center Torso (rear)		10
R/L Torso	15	22
R/L Torso (rear)		7
R/L Arm	10	20
R/L Leg	15	24

Weapons and Ammo	Location	Critical	Tonnage
Streak SRM 4	RA	1	3
LRM 20	RT	5	10
Artemis IV FCS	RT	1	1
Ammo (LRM) 18	RT	3	3
CASE	RT	1	.5
Guardian ECM Suite	CT	2	1.5
2 ER Medium Lasers	LT	2	2
Ammo (Streak) 25	LT	1	1
CASE	LT	1	.5
Streak SRM 4	LA	1	3

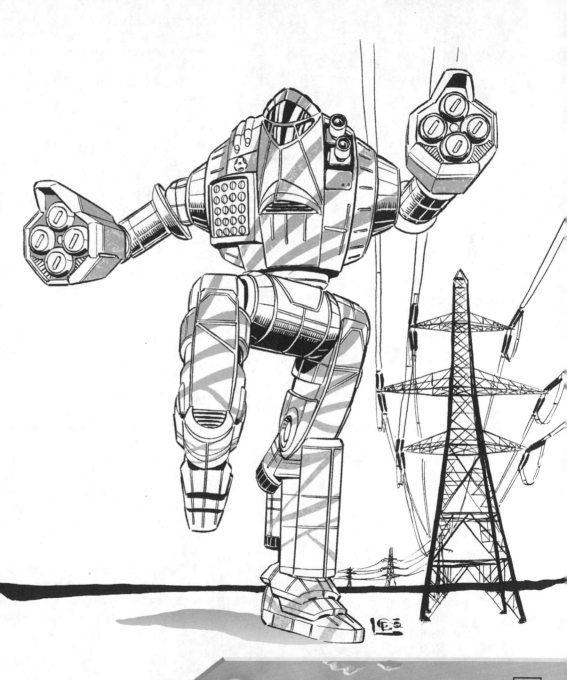

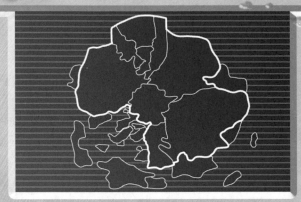

Mass: 65 tons
Chassis: Earthwerks SYI
Power Plant: Hermes 260 XL
Cruising Speed: 43 kph
Maximum Speed: 64 kph
Jump Jets: None
  Jump Capacity: None
Armor: Hellespont Lite Stealth
Armament:
  1 Firmir UltraLase ER Large Laser
  2 Sian/Ceres Puma MRM 20 Launchers
  2 Firmir High-Frequency Medium Pulse lasers
Manufacturer: Hellespont BattleMech Works
  Primary Factory: Sian
Communications System: Ceres Metals Model 666
  with Guardian ECM Suite
Targeting and Tracking System: Radcom TXXI

Overview

The Capellan Confederation has pursued stealth-equipped BattleMechs more aggressively than any other nation. Since the development of the *Raven* in the days preceding the Fourth Succession War, the CCAF has been fielding cutting-edge stealth technologies in a search for the perfect reconnaissance unit. The next major evolution was the *Men Shen,* which perfected the electronic warfare components first explored by the *Raven.* The advent of the *Sha Yu* in the mid-3060s made the stealth armor concept a reality. By 3070, the Capellans had an entire arsenal of stealth options waiting to be utilized by future designs.

The Jihad stalled Capellan efforts to field all-new stealth BattleMechs. In fact, eschewing the mutual support of Devlin Stone's Coalition came close to destroying the Capellan nation entirely. The Confederation fought back against the Word of Blake, but at great expense in equipment and personnel. The CCAF liberated not only their own worlds, but those of the Magistracy of Canopus as well, all at the cost of stagnated development and new designs.

Though battered and bloodied, the CCAF remained a viable combat force in the wake of their battles with the Word of Blake. They faced the same effort to rebuild as the militaries of every nation in the Inner Sphere, but also had a chance at last to resume fielding their stealth technologies. Where they once saw stealth as a reconnaissance tool, the Capellans turned it to front-line combat units, enabling them to strike at their foes with an enormous advantage. The *Pillager* offered a hint of this doctrine, while the *Shen Yi* is the realization of that vision.

Capabilities

The *Shen Yi* features the stealth armor perfected in the Sha Yu design. Entwined with the reliable Guardian ECM suite, the stealth armor deters accurate targeting by the *Shen Yi*'s foes. However, where other, lighter designs sought to use this advantage in an effort to complete objectives and retreat unseen, the *Shen Yi* is built to exploit the advantage in sustained combat. The fact that the design employs thirteen tons of stealth armor indicates that the Capellans expect the 'Mech to see heavy combat use.

The weapons employed by the *Shen Yi* also speak to its role as a front-line combat unit. The Firmir extended-range large laser is a reliable weapon capable of dealing significant damage at range. A pair of Firmir medium pulse lasers provides the *Shen Yi* with brawling capacity as well as the ability to strike lighter, faster 'Mechs that attempt to harass it.

The bulk of the *Shen Yi*'s firepower, however, comes from a primitive weapon perfected by the Draconis Combine. The Combine's success with the medium-range missile system convinced Capellan engineers to examine a similar system of their own. They found a relatively lightweight weapon system capable of rapidly showering damage on enemy units. Though starkly unsophisticated in comparison with the electronics and armor employed by the *Shen Yi*, the medium-range missile systems give the 'Mech a well-rounded arsenal.

Deployment

The *Shen Yi* is still finishing its final field trials. When the design becomes operational, it is slated for deployment first to the elite Warrior Houses as well as to the various regiments of McCarron's Armored Cavalry. If the *Shen Yi* performs as its early tests indicate, it will be the first of many new stealth-equipped combat units deployed by the CCAF. Despite this pressure to succeed, the *Shen Yi*'s performance to date has encouraged CCAF commanders at every level.

Variants

To date, no variants of the *Shen Yi* have been reported, likely because the 'Mech has yet to fully enter production. However, leading military theorists suggest that an all-energy weapon variation is a likely extension of the stealth combat concept that the Capellans seek to employ.

SHY-3B SHEN YI

Type: **Shen Yi**
Technology Base: Inner Sphere
Tonnage: 65
Battle Value: 1,561

Equipment		Mass
Internal Structure:		6.5
Engine:	260 XL	7
Walking MP:	4	
Running MP:	6	
Jumping MP:	0	
Heat Sinks:	14 [28]	4
Gyro:		3
Cockpit:		3
Armor Factor (Stealth):	208	13

	Internal Structure	Armor Value
Head	3	9
Center Torso	21	30
Center Torso (rear)		11
R/L Torso	15	22
R/L Torso (rear)		8
R/L Arm	10	19
R/L Leg	15	30

Weapons and Ammo	Location	Critical	Tonnage
ER Large Laser	RA	2	5
2 Medium Pulse Lasers	RA	2	4
MRM 20	RT	3	7
Ammo (MRM) 12	RT	1	1
Ammo (MRM) 24	CT	2	2
MRM 20	LT	3	7
Ammo (MRM) 12	LT	1	1
Guardian ECM Suite	LA	2	1.5

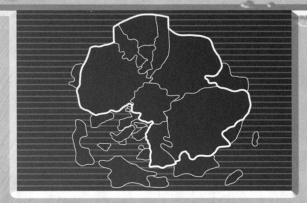

Mass: 70 tons
Chassis: Skobel 250-RB
Power Plant: GTEM 210 XL
Cruising Speed: 32 kph
Maximum Speed: 54 kph
Jump Jets: Waterly Heavy Lifters
    Jump Capacity: 150 meters
Armor: Pribak 9000
Armament:
    2 Tronel XIII Large Pulse Lasers
    1 Skobel Drotnik MRM 20
    1 Hovertec Streak SRM 2
    1 Zippo Flamer
Manufacturer: Skobel MechWorks
    Primary Factory: Terra
Communications System: Skobel Wave VI Comm
Targeting and Tracking System: Falcon 15 Watcher

Overview

Like Stefan Amaris centuries before, the Word of Blake turned to desperate and sometimes fanatical strategies in their attempt to hold on to Terra. Unlike Amaris, however, the Word of Blake showed a sociopathic efficiency that made their tactics far more effective and far less predictable. They even unleashed weapons of mass destruction on Terra itself in quantities far beyond the scant nuclear strikes launched by the Usurper.

One of the less bizarre tactics employed during the defense of Terra was to rush nearly completed BattleMech designs into production in an effort to quickly bolster their defenses in the face of the impending invasion. These BattleMechs, often lacking components such as proper engine shielding or ejection seats, swelled the ranks of the Word of Blake to levels that the best reconnaissance by Stone's Coalition never discovered before battle. Unfortunately, they were often as dangerous to their own MechWarriors as they were to the enemy.

During the initial Coalition recovery efforts after their hard-won victory, many of these haphazardly built 'Mechs were discarded. Others showed promise as effective battlefield units; these were set aside for continued examination and perhaps continued production. The *Gallant,* produced in Moscow's historical Skobel MechWorks facility, was one of the designs The Republic chose to refine and continue producing.

The design specifications were also exported to the Federated Suns and Lyran Commonwealth as a gesture of thanks for their extensive support of the Coalition and the forming Republic. The exchange of recovered technology has been part of the initial Coalition agreement. It was also a calculated diplomatic decision in hopes of easing the sting of losing worlds to the Republic of the Sphere.

Capabilities

The *Gallant* was originally conceived as a broken-terrain cavalry platform utilizing improved jump jets. The increased mobility was seen as a potential boon in any tightly packed terrain such as urban settings or remote mountains. When the Coalition attacked Terra, the design was entering its initial field tests. The Word of Blake scrapped the field tests and rushed the design into production at breakneck speed.

One major design change made at the eleventh hour was its weapons package. It originally carried a fairly standard deployment of energy and missile weapons, but the combined-arms nature of Devlin's Stone assault force initiated a radical overhaul of the 'Mech's weapons. A pair of large pulse lasers was installed to provide accurate firepower even for novice MechWarriors. The medium-range missiles were inexpensive and easy to install. The Streak missile launcher and a flamer were added to give the *Gallant* a terrifying capacity to wipe out enemy infantry or armor wholesale. While this hand-tailored payload proved too little, too late to stop the Coalition's advance, it did wreak havoc and earn the *Gallant* a reputation among Coalition soldiers.

Once the Coalition's technical personnel could take the time to go over the Skobel facility in Moscow, they discovered detailed plans for the *Gallant* as well as its ad hoc assembly line. They also had the time to put it through abbreviated field trials to judge its readiness. With the need for BattleMechs so dire throughout the Inner Sphere, a nearly completed heavy 'Mech was a significant and valuable find. Rather than re-tool the entire facility for another design, the decision was made to fully develop the assembly facility and put the BattleMech into a more finished and polished production run.

Deployment

The *Gallant* has deployed with many of the units serving on or around Terra. It has also begun production in the Lyran Commonwealth and the Federated Suns, which use the design as replacements for their Lyran Guards and Heavy Guards regiments, respectively. All three nations have also made the design available for purchase and it has quickly spread into general service throughout the Inner Sphere.

Variants

Federated Suns engineers worked to re-create the weapons package as originally conceived for the *Gallant*. Once finished with their research, they updated the weapons with newer, more advanced components. This 8-0 variant sheds all the production variant's weaponry in order to mount a pair of Thunderbolt 10 launchers and four medium X-pulse lasers. The 8-0 also protects the Thunderbolt ammunition with CASE.

GLT-7-0 GALLANT

Type: **Gallant**
Technology Base: Inner Sphere
Tonnage: 70
Battle Value:1,436

Equipment		Mass
Internal Structure:		7
Engine:	210 XL	4.5
Walking MP:	3	
Running MP:	5	
Jumping MP:	5	
Heat Sinks:	14 [28]	4
Gyro:		3
Cockpit:		3
Armor Factor:	208	13

	Internal Structure	Armor Value
Head	3	9
Center Torso	22	28
Center Torso (rear)		13
R/L Torso	15	20
R/L Torso (rear)		10
R/L Arm	11	20
R/L Leg	15	29

Weapons and Ammo	Location	Critical	Tonnage
2 Large Pulse Lasers	RA	4	14
Streak SRM 2	RT	1	1.5
Ammo (Streak) 50	RT	1	1
Flamer	H	1	1
MRM 20	LT	3	7
Ammo (MRM) 12	LT	1	1
Improved Jump Jet	RL	2	2
Improved Jump Jet	RT	2	2
Improved Jump Jet	CT	2	2
Improved Jump Jet	LT	2	2
Improved Jump Jet	LL	2	2

MNL-3L MANGONEL

Mass: 70 tons
Chassis: AR-7b Endo-Steel
Power Plant: Magna 350 Light
Cruising Speed: 54 kph
Maximum Speed: 86 kph
Jump Jets: None
   Jump Capacity: None
Armor: Royal-7 Ferro-Fibrous
Armament:
   2 Corean Light Gauss Rifles
   4 Diverse Optics Extended Range Medium Lasers
Manufacturer: Arc-Royal MechWorks
   Primary Factory: Arc-Royal
Communications System: K9 Comms System
Targeting and Tracking System: Type V Bloodhound
   T&T System

Overview

Faced with dwindling stockpiles of Clan technology, Khan Phelan Kell sponsored several programs to adapt more readily available Inner Sphere equipment to the needs of his Wolves. Among the outcomes of these initiatives was the creation of the MNL-3L *Mangonel*. Rumored to be the result of a collaborative effort between Sergi Ivanovich (Chief Tech for the Tooth of Ymir and the mastermind behind *Schwerer Gustav*) and the Kell Hounds' Chief Tech, Daniel Holstein, the unusual design entered production in 3078. Arc-Royal MechWorks continues to produce the design in limited quantities for Wolf MechWarriors.

Capabilities

Envisioned as a heavy cavalry unit, the controversial *Mangonel* is reminiscent of designs such as the first Star League's *Excalibur* or the WiE *Arctic Wolf*. Emphasis is placed on speed and firepower over heavy armor protection and endurance. The BattleMech is literally built around the massive weapons bay that occupies almost the entire right side of its torso. Housed therein are twin Gauss weapons—exceptionally accurate Corean light Gauss rifles. The *Mangonel*'s MechWarrior uses the superior speed imparted by the Magna 350 power plant to dance around larger and better-armored opponents and pick them apart with ranged fire. Against lighter foes, a more direct approach is common, and at medium and short range the quartet of arm-mounted Diverse Optics extended-range medium lasers is just as deadly as the Gauss weapons.

However, this speed and firepower come at a price. The Royal-7 ferro-fibrous armor offers excellent protection by weight, but the *Mangonel* doesn't carry enough of it and the Gauss weapons lack CASE to protect against coil detonation. Likewise, the magazine for the primary armament is barely adequate. A MechWarrior must choose his shots with care lest his primary armament be reduced to dead weight. At this point, the quartet of lasers appears to make the *Mangonel* a respectable battler, and the MechWarrior's thoughts may turn to closing with an opponent. Statistically, however, only an exceptionally skilled MechWarrior can survive such a maneuver more than a handful of times.

The first *Mangonel*s off the production line soon developed issues from excessive wear to the leg actuators. Arc-Royal MechWorks isolated the problem and took corrective measures, but techs working on the BattleMech still complain about having to spend much more time on preventative maintenance even though the manufacturer claims the problem has been addressed.

Deployment

The Wolves-in-Exile use the Inner Sphere-built *Mangonel* to pad out their ravaged BattleMech forces. Typically, the *Mangonel* replaces OmniMechs like the *Loki* or *Linebacker*. Inevitably, the largest concentration can be found in the WiE second-line Omega Galaxy fighting alongside the *Pack Hunter* and *Arctic Wolf*. A handful of upgraded MNL-3W models have entered service with front-line commands. These units place great emphasis on mobility and surprise—tactics well suited to the quirky *Mangonel* in the fighting along the frontier with the Clan Occupation Zone.

With this BattleMech being manufactured on Arc-Royal, it is no surprise that the Kell Hounds have incorporated it into their ranks. At least three *Mangonel*s have been sighted sporting Hounds colors.

Several examples of the design have found their way into the hands of the Republic of the Sphere. Many WiE MechWarriors fought as part of Devlin Stone's coalition against the Word of Blake. Following the Blakist defeat, some chose to join the newly created Republic and brought the *Mangonel* into service with the newest Inner Sphere power.

Variants

Though classified as a variant of the MNL-3L *Mangonel*, the MNL-3W *Mangonel* is actually a different machine. What started as an attempt to upgrade some of the Inner Sphere technology resulted in a complete rebuild with Clan technology. Built on a Clan endo steel internal structure and powered by a Clan 350 XL power plant, the MNL-3W is armed with two Clan Gauss rifles. The bulkier weapons proved impossible to shoehorn into the right torso weapons bay, and extensive modifications were required to install one of the big guns in the left torso instead. One advantage of this redistribution was that it freed up space to carry more ammunition, and each weapon has a dedicated sixteen-round magazine. Two additional heat sinks and an upgrade with Clan extended-range medium lasers complete the internal changes.

Armor protection is increased somewhat with more than ten tons of Clan ferro-fibrous armor—a modification that also adds Clan CASE to protect against damage from a detonating Gauss weapon.

MNL-3L MANGONEL

Type: **Mangonel**
Technology Base: Inner Sphere
Tonnage: 70
Battle Value: 1,552

Equipment		Mass
Internal Structure:	Endo Steel	3.5
Engine:	350 Light	22.5
Walking MP:	5	
Running MP:	8	
Jumping MP:	0	
Heat Sinks:	10 [20]	0
Gyro:		4
Cockpit:		3
Armor Factor (Ferro):	143	8

	Internal Structure	Armor Value
Head	3	9
Center Torso	22	20
Center Torso (rear)		6
R/L Torso	15	20
R/L Torso (rear)		7
R/L Arm	11	11
R/L Leg	15	16

Weapons and Ammo	Location	Critical	Tonnage
2 ER Medium Lasers	RA	2	2
2 Light Gauss Rifles	RT	10	24
Ammo (Light Gauss) 16	LT	1	1
2 ER Medium Lasers	LA	2	2

PEN-2H PENTHESILEA

Mass: 75 tons
Chassis: Dynastic 75-P
Power Plant: Vlar 300
Cruising Speed: 43 kph
Maximum Speed: 64 kph
Jump Jets: Nike Doublejet 9s
    Jump Capacity: 90 meters
Armor: Maximillian 42F Ferro-Fibrous with CASE
Armament:
    1 Majesty Metals Royal Flush Extended Range
        Particle Gun
    1 Majesty Metals Deuce Light Particle Gun
    1 Imperator Code Red LB-10X Autocannon
    3 Diverse Optics Type II ER Medium Lasers
Manufacturer: Majesty Metals and Manufacturing
    Primary Factory: Dunianshire
Communications System: FoxxCom 75
Targeting and Tracking System: FoxxFire 190

Overview

That nearly all of the Magistracy's weapons of war were being made on Detroit put the Magestrix under political assault from two groups. Reactionaries were wary of relying on a planet under tenuous Magistracy control, while Majesty Metals and Manufacturing wanted to produce (and profit from) the advanced technology that has helped transform the Magistracy Armed Forces. With the fragile peace that followed the end of the Jihad, the Magestrix acquiesced, gaining political capital while strengthening her realm. The same design team that started the work on the *Eyleuka* was tasked with creating the heaviest unit the Magistracy had ever built. Named after an Amazon queen who fought to protect Troy, the 75-ton design was completed in early 3083.

Capabilities

The *Penthesilea* balances offensive and defensive capabilities well. A complex endo steel frame and twelve tons of ferro-fibrous armor provide a solid base, while a compact gyro nestled next to a standard fusion engine provides endurance even after the armor fails. Its 64 kph top speed isn't much for a heavy 'Mech on the modern battlefield, but is still acceptable. A trio of jump jets gives the pilot more options, though some aren't impressed with a jump capacity of less than one hundred meters.

When it comes to engaging the enemy, the *Penthesilea* is a sniper and a brawler. An extended-range particle cannon gives it reach, with a heavy autocannon and light PPC supporting it. When the enemy closes, a trio of extended-range medium lasers can be added, though the machine lacks the capacity to keep up with the heat produced by all the energy weapons. The autocannon's ability to switch over to cluster shot allows it to find the weak points that the other weapons have opened up. The ammo placement is right next to the autocannon to reduce jamming issues. Designers still installed CASE in the right torso, in the event that an explosion reaches it. However simulations have shown that the ammunition is 20 percent less likely to be detonated in the arm than in the accompanying torso.

Deployment

The first few *Penthesilea*s produced were sold to Zeus' Thunderbolts for field testing. Despite their ridiculous reflective paint scheme making their units blindingly apparent, the tests showed that the *Penthesilea* was an effective fighter, whose long-range fire forced the enemy to close to where a spray of shorter-range fire could finish the job. The jump jets, thought by some to be tactically questionable, proved a strategic advantage; the Thunderbolts were able to position their new 'Mechs quickly in sniping positions and cross small waterways.

Once full production started, half the lot was assigned to the usual units, the Royal Guard and Chasseurs á Cheval regiments. In an interesting side effect of this assignment, the machines replaced in both groups went to the Chasseurs. Rumors are floating around that Colonel deSummersVille might be padding his units' rosters to build up enough troops to replace the long-missing fourth regiment. Meanwhile, the other half of the *Penthesilea* output is being sold to other Periphery nations and loyal mercenaries. While only the Taurian Concordat has been approved for shipments to date, a few other realms are likely to follow. Protector Boris Tharn has rushed Taurian *Penthesilea*s to Concordat units in Federated Suns space, where the heavy 'Mech is expected to form the backbone of TDF fire support lances.

Variants

The designers at Majesty have done some tinkering for a heavier-hitting version. They upgraded the autocannon to a larger model, the light PPC to an ER large laser and removed two of the other lasers. The remaining one was moved to the head as an extralight gyro replaced the compact model. Gone were the jump jets in favor of another heat sink, and protection was increased despite the use of light instead of standard ferro-fibrous armor.

Type: **Penthesilea**
Technology Base: Inner Sphere
Tonnage: 75
Battle Value: 1,899

Equipment		Mass
Internal Structure:	Endo Steel	4
Engine:	300	19
Walking MP:	4	
Running MP:	6	
Jumping MP:	3	
Heat Sinks:	13 [26]	3
Gyro (Compact):		4.5
Cockpit:		3
Armor Factor (Ferro):	215	12

	Internal Structure	Armor Value
Head	3	9
Center Torso	23	30
Center Torso (rear)		10
R/L Torso	16	20
R/L Torso (rear)		10
R/L Arm	12	23
R/L Leg	16	30

Weapons and Ammo	Location	Critical	Tonnage
LB 10-X AC	RA	6	11
Ammo (LB-X) 20	RA	2	2
CASE	RT	1	.5
ER PPC	LA	3	7
Light PPC	LA	2	3
3 ER Medium Lasers	CT	3	3
Jump Jet	RL	1	1
Jump Jet	CT	1	1
Jump Jet	LL	1	1

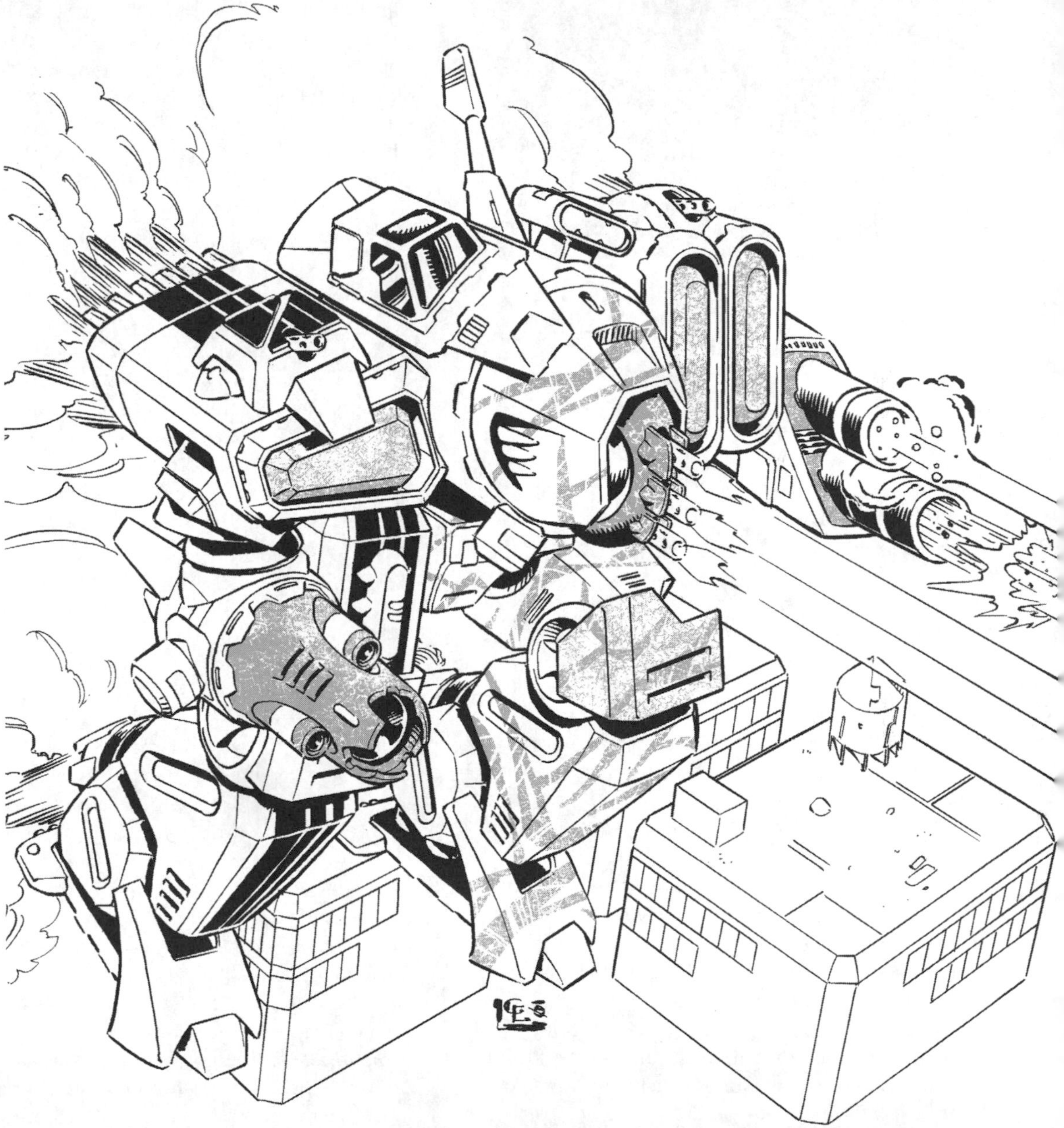

PRF-1R PREFECT

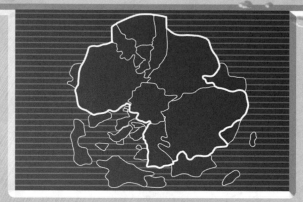

Mass: 75 tons
Chassis: Crucis-III Deluxe Endo Steel
Power Plant: PlasmaStar 375 Light
Cruising Speed: 54 kph
Maximum Speed: 86 kph
Jump Jets: None
Jump Capacity: None
Armor: Durallex Ferro-Fibrous
Armament:
1 Lord's Light 3 Heavy Particle Projector Cannon
1 Lord's Light 5 Snub-Nose Particle Projector Cannon
2 Diverse Optics ER Medium Lasers
Manufacturer: Irian BattleMechs Unlimited
Primary Factory: Irian
Communications System: Irian Technologies HMR-35s
Targeting and Tracking System: Omnicron TrackerKeeper

Overview

As Devlin Stone planned his campaign of swords-to-plowshares, he was pragmatic enough to know such work often requires a big hammer. At the same time, the horrific end of the Jihad had left far too many worlds (and their factories) in smoking ruins.

Also, in late 3082, Stone's information network learned that several corporations were in secret talks to file lawsuits that would interrupt military production. That information would come to fruition when Krupp Armaments sued a host of entities—including Stone and the Republic of the Sphere—in 3084 over lost profits stemming from the systematic destruction and looting of their Budapest facility during the Terran invasion. (The pressure tactics used by this interstellar conglomerate—and others that joined the suit—would result by 3085 in a slowdown of advanced military production across numerous fronts, creating major recessions across large portions of The Republic as it struggled to take its first faltering steps as a new interstellar empire.)

To create jobs, strengthen his military position (as he was still engaged in active combat on several fronts) and try to stave off the worst of what would come of such lawsuits, Stone commissioned a new BattleMech. Taking lessons from his years of guerrilla-style warfare at the start of the Jihad—when he fought his way out of the re-education camp on Kittery—Devlin mandated a simple design, completely ammunition-independent, heat efficient and able to move quickly while withstanding heavy punishment. This would be a 'Mech designed for dropping behind enemy lines in long-term solo deployments. While the *Prefect* meets most of those requirements, Stone made several concessions along the way to help win over the military-industrial complex, such as the inclusion of a light engine, endo steel, ferro-fibrous armor and perhaps the greatest concession, an XL gyro.

Capabilities

As Irian hosted the largest military manufacturing center other than Terra within the boundaries of the newly formed Republic of the Sphere, Stone took an immediate interest in Irian Technologies. Long weeks behind closed doors resulted in an undisclosed agreement that led Irian to start production in 3083. Irian took the GLT-5M *Guillotine* chassis and modified it for a slightly heavier design while utilizing many of the same systems to shorten development time.

The majority of equipment stems from Irian Technologies, but several items were drawn from other companies. From Independence Weaponry on Quentin came the Durallex ferro-fibrous armor. In one of Stone's most effective coups, he successfully negotiated to acquire the full design specifications for the relatively new PPC variants from a Luthien Armor Works mobile factory (the details of the deal are sealed). While boosting economies on any world within the Republic of the Sphere was important, jump-starting reconstruction on Terra itself was paramount. Money was poured into Holly Industries (a subsidiary of StarCorps) in Kuala Lumpur, resulting in the creation of much-needed jobs (not to mention the accompanying positive public relations). A direct result of this cash infusion was a heavy modification of the PlasmaStar 375 extralight power plant—mounted on StarCorps' *Thanatos*—into a "light" version. Finally, the XL gyro deal was brokered with Krupp Armaments (in hindsight, an obvious attempt to stave off the coming lawsuits). When Krupp filed the lawsuits despite the behind-closed-doors deal with Stone, it was a personal betrayal; the likely reason why no middle ground has yet been found between The Republic, Stone and Krupp.

Ultimately, the *Prefect* is under-armed for a 75-ton BattleMech. However, very few Inner Sphere 'Mechs of the same tonnage can match its movement profile. In its element as a heavy striker/guerrilla unit, it is quickly proving almost unmatched.

Deployment

Few *Prefect*s have been produced to date, with most deployed to The Republic's Triarii Protectors. While it is true that the numbers of those produced and those deployed to the Triarii don't match, there is no credence to the rumors that Exarch Stone has formed a shadow force to perform whatever black ops are necessary to keep our enemies and allies alike in check.

Variants

The only known variant, currently undergoing live-fire testing, trades out the heavy PPC and twin extended-range medium lasers for another snub-nose PPC and a pair of light PPCs.

Type: **Prefect**
Technology Base: Inner Sphere
Tonnage: 75
Battle Value: 1,847

Equipment		Mass
Internal Structure:	Endo Steel	4
Engine:	375 Light	29
Walking MP:	5	
Running MP:	8	
Jumping MP:	0	
Heat Sinks:	17 [34]	7
Gyro (XL):		2
Cockpit:		3
Armor Factor (Ferro):	215	12

	Internal Structure	Armor Value
Head	3	9
Center Torso	23	35
Center Torso (rear)		9
R/L Torso	16	24
R/L Torso (rear)		7
R/L Arm	12	22
R/L Leg	16	28

Weapons and Ammo	Location	Critical	Tonnage
Snub-Nose PPC	RA	2	6
Heavy PPC	LA	4	10
ER Medium Laser	LT	1	1
ER Medium Laser	RT	1	1

OR-21 OROCHI

Mass: 90 tons
Chassis: Alshain Class 98c
Power Plant: Hermes 360 XL
Cruising Speed: 43 kph
Maximum Speed: 64 kph
Jump Jets: None
    Jump Capacity: None
Armor: Starshield A
Armament:
    2 Telos ThunderShot Thunderbolt 20 Launchers
    2 Telos TargetLok-4 Streak SRM 4
    1 Victory 12E Extended Range Small Laser
Manufacturer: Victory Industries
    Primary Factory: Marduk
Communications System: Sipher CommSys 4b
Targeting and Tracking System: Matabushi Sentinel

Overview

The cession of worlds to Devlin Stone's Republic of the Sphere cost the Draconis Combine some of its most productive military facilities. Quentin alone cost the DCMS several of its modern and highly prized designs. However, the loss of industry was not unanticipated. Even before the agreement was signed, the DCMS high command had begun implementing plans to shift production to other worlds. Marduk and Victory Industries figured prominently in those plans.

Marduk already had a considerable number of assembly plants. It had long served as the source of various *Griffin* and *Wolverine* variants, as well as components that shipped all across the DCMS for other designs. Now those facilities would require expansion and upgrading in order to pick up the slack of worlds lost in the formation of The Republic. Vast sums of money and labor were sent to Marduk to make the necessary improvements.

The revitalization effort was put to the test when the DCMS launched a series of new BattleMechs that would lead the way in the national effort to recover from the Word of Blake's Jihad. Concepts that had been laid to rest in the chaos of the Jihad were dusted off and put back into production. The *Orochi*, a long-desired update of the antiquated *Longbow*, was one of the first projects assigned to the new and improved Victory factories. Armed with an array of new capabilities, the engineers at Victory took to the task with zeal. They intended to prove that Marduk could indeed replace Quentin, or at least shoulder much of the burden that loss had created.

Capabilities

The *Longbow* struggled through the Succession Wars, with MechWarriors and commanders alike finding many fatal flaws in the LGB-OW design. The 7V variant gave the 'Mech a much-needed facelift. Soon it was serving in mainline units across the Inner Sphere. The Draconis Combine, which had acquired small numbers of *Longbows* over the years, coveted this foreign design for its massive indirect and volley-fire capabilities.

Advancing technology made possible an even more powerful design. The Combine enjoyed success with both the *Naginata* and the *O-Bakemono*. Over and over, DCMS design teams utilized the fire support concept to create highly successful BattleMechs with incredible long-range firepower. Looking to Solaris and Thunderbolt missile systems for inspiration, the High Command became eager to see the practical battlefield application of this weapon.

That union of curiosity and opportunity created the core concept of the *Orochi*. The ancient *Longbow* frame was stretched to ninety tons and the 'Mech was equipped with a larger version of the shoulder actuators that allow the *Rifleman's* infamous "arm-flipping"

technique. Massive Thunderbolt 20 launcher systems were housed in each arm, along with three tons of missiles. Outside the center-mounted Thunderbolt, a Streak SRM 4 was positioned for close combat. The *Orochi* moved from concept to field testing of prototypes in a scant seven months.

While the Thunderbolt launchers reduce the range of the *Orochi* compared to the *Longbow*, they more than make up for that loss with damage potential. More compact by far than Arrow IV artillery systems, the Thunderbolt 20 launchers allow the *Orochi* to penetrate even the heaviest armor at ranges typical of the scrubbing fire of LRMs. The Streak launchers serve as a perfect complementary weapon system that can exploit holes punched in armor by the heavier Thunderbolt missiles.

The *Orochi* is more of a direct combatant than its predecessors. While this was not the original vision of the design, it has pleasantly surprised officers in the highest echelons of the DCMS. Now approved for production runs, it is likely the *Orochi* will see deployment across the far reaches of the Combine as a fire support machine, though the high maintenance needs of the Thunderbolt launcher will likely limit overall production numbers and thus the number encountered in the field.

Deployment

With many elite DCMS units shattered between the Black Dragon rebellion and the wholesale destruction of the Jihad, the need for replacement BattleMechs is at an all-time high. The Sword of Light regiments and other loyal elite forces will likely be the first to field the *Orochi*. As more become available, it will find its way to other units such as the Dieron Regulars or Arkab legions.

Variants

The *Orochi* has yet to inspire or require any variants.

Type: **Orochi**
Technology Base: Inner Sphere (Advanced)
Tonnage: 90
Battle Value: 2,077

Equipment			Mass
Internal Structure:	Endo-Steel		4.5
Engine:	360 XL		16.5
Walking MP:	4		
Running MP:	6		
Jumping MP:	0		
Heat Sinks:	10 [20]		0
Gyro:			4
Cockpit:			3
Armor Factor:	279		17.5

	Internal Structure	Armor Value
Head	3	9
Center Torso	29	44
Center Torso (rear)		14
R/L Torso	19	28
R/L Torso (rear)		10
R/L Arm	15	30
R/L Leg	19	38

Weapons and Ammo	Location	Critical	Tonnage
Thunderbolt 20	RA	5	15
Ammo (Thunderbolt) 9	RA	3	3
Streak SRM 4	RA	1	3
Ammo (Streak) 25	RA	1	1
ER Small Laser	H	1	.5
Thunderbolt 20	LA	5	15
Ammo (Thunderbolt) 9	LA	3	3
Streak SRM 4	LA	1	3
Ammo (Streak) 25	LA	1	1

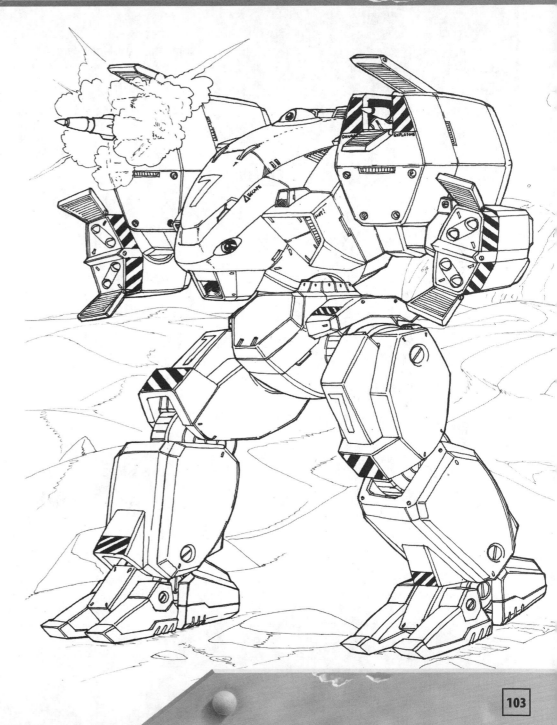

PKP-1A PEACEKEEPER

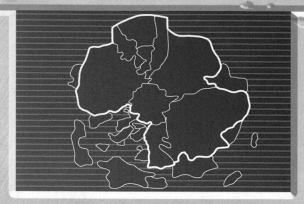

Mass: 95 tons
Chassis: Combine-Republic Peacekeeper Superheavy
Power Plant: GM 380XL
Cruising Speed: 43 kph
Maximum Speed: 65 kph (86 kph with TSM)
Jump Jets: Lexington Ltd. Lifters
    Jump Capacity: 90 meters
Armor: Valiant Lamellor Armor
Armament:
    1 Lord's Light 3 Heavy Particle Projection Cannons
    1 Lord's Light 2 ER PPC
    1 Victory Blast Furnace Plasma Rifle
    1 Victory Nickel Alloy ER Large Laser
    1 Guided Technologies 2 SRM-2
Manufacturer: Independence Weaponry,
    Luthien Armor Works
    Primary Factory: Quentin (Independence),
      New Samarkand (LAW)
Communications System: Voice of Peace with C³
Targeting and Tracking System: Keeper of the Peace

Overview

In a gesture of trust between the newly-formed Republic of the Sphere and the Draconis Combine, a joint BattleMech development effort was undertaken. To reassure the nervous Combine leadership that their concession of worlds was not an error to be redressed, field testing of the prototype has progressed as though the Jihad were still raging. Intended for independent construction by both realms, a lack of proprietary technology was mandated.

The name of the new 'Mech became a serious point of contention, with the Combine insisting on naming rights and Republic officials feeling the name should signify the cooperative origin of the design. When the names suggested by each side continually met with disapproval by the other, the lead engineer for the project, Neal Corcovilos, stormed out of the conference room, shouting that he wanted "no part in playing *peacekeeper* for a bunch of squabbling children!" When the delegates considered the new 'Mech's intended role, they realized that his outburst had solved the problem he wanted no part in remedying. Thus was born the *Peacekeeper*.

Capabilities

The negotiators decided that the new design should be a very large 'Mech capable of staying in the field for extended periods without resupply and able to put down insurgencies, rebellions, or raids without significant upkeep costs. Thus, ammo-based weaponry was to be minimized.

At ninety-five tons, the *Peacekeeper* is among the heaviest of 'Mechs, though its sixty-four-kph top speed is faster than many assault 'Mechs. To attain this speed and leave sufficient free tonnage for a suitable range of weapons, a new 380 XL engine was designed and constructed on Terra with the specs given to the Combine for their own construction efforts. A trio of powerful jump jets gives the PKP-1A a ninety-meter jump radius.

Mounting a pair of PPCs, the *Peacekeeper* is a deadly threat at long ranges. Though no match for Clan extended-range PPCs, MechWarriors have a healthy respect for the long-range killing power of these Combine-developed weapons. The short-range inaccuracy of the heavy PPC called for backup weaponry to put down enemies that close with the *Peacekeeper*. An extended-range large laser contributes further long-range capacity and some short-range firepower. A plasma rifle, though ammunition-dependent, provides the final component of the PKP-1A's armament. In addition to inflicting significant damage, the plasma rifle substantially heats its targets, which should further convince enemies to avoid the *Peacekeeper*. Almost as an afterthought, an SRM 2 was installed in a covered launcher on the right shoulder. Intended as an anti-infantry weapon, it typically will carry fragmentation rounds.

18 tons of standard armor protect the massive frame, while a CASE system partially protects the chassis from ammunition explosions.

Deployment

The *Peacekeeper* is still undergoing field trials and will not go into full production until the proving period is over. Five mercenary units were commissioned to perform the field testing. The units were chosen for their assignments in various active combat zones, especially those retained for pirate hunting duties. Their reports have been mostly positive, leaving them happy with their new 'Mechs as compensation for their services. Production at the newly-retooled factories is expected to begin in mid-to-late 3086 in both The Republic and the Combine.

Variants

Though the *Peacekeeper* is still under initial qualification testing, input from the field trials has refined the design. Despite its construction being not yet complete, the engineers decided to drop the SRM, its ammo, and the CASE system, allocating that tonnage to upgrade the ER PPC to another Heavy PPC, hopefully easing some of the strain on the firing computer. Despite the weight savings of its endo-steel skeleton, the *Peacekeeper*'s weapons array is so heavy that the standard armor is being replaced with light ferro-fibrous. Though it turns the *Peacekeeper*'s interior into something of a cramped nightmare for techs, it provides the same degree of protection with one half-ton of weight savings.

PKP-1A PEACEKEEPER

Type: **Peacekeeper**
Technology Base: Inner Sphere
Tonnage: 95
Battle Value: 2,824

Equipment		Mass
Internal Structure:	Endo Steel	5
Engine:	380 XL	20.5
Walking MP:	4 (5)	
Running MP:	6 (8)	
Jumping MP:	3	
Heat Sinks:	15 [30]	5
Gyro:		4
Cockpit:		3
Armor Factor:	288	18

	Internal Structure	Armor Value
Head	3	9
Center Torso	30	45
Center Torso (rear)		14
R/L Torso	20	30
R/L Torso (rear)		10
R/L Arm	16	30
R/L Leg	20	40

Weapons and Ammo	Location	Critical	Tonnage
Heavy PPC	RA	4	10
Plasma Rifle	RT	2	6
SRM 2	RT	1	1
Ammo (SRM) 50	RT	1	1
CASE	RT	1	.5
Ammo (Plasma) 20	RT	2	2
C³ Slave	H	1	1
ER Large Laser	LT	2	5
ER PPC	LA	3	7
Triple-Strength Myomer	RA/LA/RL/LL	2/2/1/1	0
Jump Jet	RL	1	2
Jump Jet	CT	1	2
Jump Jet	LL	1	2

jsm10

TR-XB TREBARUNA

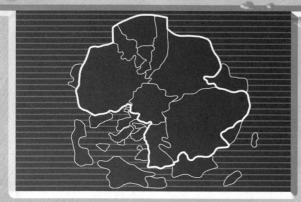

Mass: 95 tons
Chassis: NOS Rev 7-ETS Quad
Power Plant: Pitban 285
Cruising Speed: 32 kph
Maximum Speed: 54 kph
Jump Jets: Chilton 950 Improved Jump Jets
Jump Capacity: 120 meters
Armor: Durallex Heavy with CASE
Armament:
    1 Imperator Dragon's Fire Gauss Rifle
    3 Moscovia Light Particle Projector Cannons
Manufacturer: J. B. BattleMechs, Inc.,
    Earthwerks-FWL Incorporated, Ceres Metals
    Primary Factory: New Earth (JB),
        Keystone (Earthwerks), St. Ives (Ceres)
Communications System: Hartford JEQ-5
Targeting and Tracking System: Orion Suretrak XVII
    with Targeting Computer

Overview

Plans for the *Trebaruna* were discovered in Blakist databases seized during the assault on Terra. Partially decrypted information suggests the 'Mech was developed from stolen Free Rasalhague Republic drafts, but that is uncorroborated. The Blakists apparently planned to begin production in 3078, but scrapped the project as Stone began closing the noose around Terra and instead focused on strategic weaponry. Though much of the captured Blakist data was available to the Coalition, the Federated Suns, Draconis Combine and Lyran Commonwealth have so far chosen not to develop the *Trebaruna*. Given the Steiner fondness for quad designs, analysts predict a Lyran variant will appear within the decade. Based on their independent fielding of the *Trebaruna*, it is apparent that the Capellan Confederation has also managed to obtain some or all of the Blakist database.

The *Trebaruna* takes its name from an ancient goddess. Exact details have been lost to the ages but she is believed to be related to battles, protection and death. Given the capabilities of this potent 'Mech, it seems a fitting moniker. The RAF was the first to field the design, followed closely by the Marik-Stewart Commonwealth and the Capellan Confederation. All three debuted their variants in 3081.

Capabilities

The *Trebaruna* is an incredibly resilient design. Sixteen tons of armor protect the Pitban standard fusion engine at its heart. Forgoing an extralight engine not only saves precious space in the cramped confines of a quadruped chassis, but provides excellent survivability in the event of side torso destruction. Where many modern 'Mechs are rendered functional kills after losing a side torso, the *Trebaruna* can fight on.

Firepower is modest for an assault-class 'Mech. The Imperator Dragon's Fire has a solid record on the *Atlas* and *Orion* as a reliable, low-maintenance weapon, and is an excellent choice for the *Trebaruna*'s primary armament. Two tons of ammunition are stored in a rapid-feed magazine below the breach. Backing up the Norse-Storm is a trio of Moscovia particle cannons. The Moscovia output is only half that of the popular Donal or Hellstar models, but when combined with the Gauss rifle, they give the TR-XB more long-range firepower than any *Hauptmann* variant. Combined with generous heat dissipation and CASE to protect the chassis from a Gauss rifle explosion, the *Trebaruna* can continue striking long after more weapon-heavy designs have shut down. An Orion Suretrak—one of the most accurate targeting computers ever produced—significantly enhances the value of these armaments.

Every centimeter of the TR-XB is used to the utmost benefit. Some weight savings are achieved by the use of an XL gyro, and designers considered a small cockpit, but ultimately opted for the standard model. Each of the well-armored legs houses a Chilton 950 improved jump jet, giving the *Trebaruna* a 120-meter jump range—nearly unheard of in a ninety-five ton 'Mech. The Hartford JEQ-5 communications system is simple to operate and includes all the standard features expected in a battalion or regimental command 'Mech.

Deployment

In the RAF, the TR-XB is deployed to the Hastati Sentinels and Principes Guards. Various forces in the Marik-Stewart Commonwealth field the TR-XJ variant; where amenable relations permit, the TR-XJ is being sold to other former Free Worlds League forces. House Liao fields the largest number of TR-XLs in the St. Ives Armored Cavalry, and that variant appears in the forces of multiple Warrior Houses.

Variants

Manufactured in the Marik-Stewart Commonwealth, the TR-XJ replaces the trio of Moscovias with a brace of snub-nose PPCs and adds a double-strength heat sink. This reconfiguration replaces the Orion Suretrak with a Spillman Multitrack 8. The Spillman is a solid piece of technology, but lacks the Suretrak's enhanced targeting modes. Removing the targeting computer allows for two extra tons of armor and an upgrade to light ferro-fibrous technology.

The most significant changes to the *Trebaruna* appear in the Ceres Metals variant, the TR-XL. This Capellan 'Mech trades the Gauss rifle for a Shengli LB-20X autocannon. This devastating close-range weapon is augmented by a pair of Confederation-made plasma rifles. Three tons of autocannon ammo and two tons of plasma rifle ammo are all housed in the left torso and protected by CASE. One additional ton of plasma rifle ammo is stored in the center torso. This variant mounts seventeen and a half tons of standard armor. A light fusion engine frees up the necessary weight for these modifications.

TR-XB TREBARUNA

Type: **Trebaruna**
Technology Base: Inner Sphere
Tonnage: 95
Battle Value: 2,223

Equipment		Mass
Internal Structure:		9.5
Engine:	285	16.5
Walking MP:	3	
Running MP:	5	
Jumping MP:	4	
Heat Sinks:	10 [20]	0
Gyro (XL):		1.5
Cockpit:		3
Armor Factor:	256	16

	Internal Structure	Armor Value
Head	3	9
Center Torso	30	41
Center Torso (rear)		10
R/L Torso	20	30
R/L Torso (rear)		8
R/L Front Leg	20	30
R/L Rear Leg	20	30

Weapons and Ammo	Location	Critical	Tonnage
Gauss Rifle	RT	7	15
Ammo (Gauss) 16	RT	2	2
CASE	RT	1	.5
3 Light PPCs	LT	6	9
Targeting Computer	LT	6	6
Improved Jump Jet	RFL	2	4
Improved Jump Jet	LFL	2	4
Improved Jump Jet	RRL	2	4
Improved Jump Jet	LRL	2	4

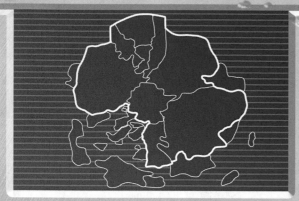

Mass: 100 tons
Chassis: Foundation Type 10X
Power Plant: Vlar 400 XL
Cruising Speed: 43 kph
Maximum Speed: 64 kph
Jump Jets: None
 Jump Capacity: None
Armor: Durallex Special Heavy with CASE
Armament:
 1 Imperator Dragon's Fire Gauss Rifle
 2 Victory Nickel Alloy/Defiance Model 6
  Extended Range Large Lasers
 2 Guided Technologies Second Generation
  Streak SRM 6
Manufacturer: Defiance Industries, Yori MechWorks
 Primary Factory: Furillo, Hesperus II (Defiance),
  Al Na'ir (Yori)
Communications System: Angst Discom with Guardian ECM
Targeting and Tracking System: Angst Accuracy

Overview

The loss of Hesperus II to Word of Blake forces prompted Defiance Industries to create an *Atlas* design that could be produced at its other manufacturing plants. The Furillo lines were unable to support full production of assault 'Mechs, but Defiance could produce prototype models. By the time Hesperus was freed, Defiance was ready to produce a limited run of the new variant on the liberated production lines. Enthusiastic reports from the field prompted Defiance to expand production of the new variant, and they continue to produce this model alongside the *Atlas II* on Hesperus II. In the past year, Yori MechWorks has licensed the rights to produce the variant in The Republic.

Capabilities

Faced with loss of access to the forms used to forge the distinctive armor of the original *Atlas*, the engineers on Furillo elected to switch to ferro-fibrous armor. The result was a BattleMech markedly different in appearance from the classic "Death's Head" originally created by designers during the First Star League. While not quite as well protected as previous variants, this version makes up for it through the installation of CASE and the inclusion of a powerful ECM suite.

Similarly, the limited availability of weapons and equipment required a rethink of the loadout that Defiance had previously used on its AS7-S variant. Inspired by the Combine's design work on the AS7-K, Defiance created what became known as the AS7-K2 *Atlas*. Though it retains the primary weapons array of arm-mounted lasers and a Gauss rifle on the right hip, all secondary weapons have been stripped out and replaced with a pair of Guided Technologies advanced Streak launchers.

For all the exterior changes, the most significant alteration was the replacement of the Vlar 300 power plant with a more powerful 400-rated unit. The additional speed and agility imparted by the new power plant frequently catches an opponent by surprise. MechWarriors often deliberately hold down their speed to lull the unwary into misjudging the BattleMech's capabilities.

Deployment

Lyran officers greeted the faster *Atlas* with enthusiasm following its arrival in 3082. After the Blakists' final defeat, Hauptmann-General Thomas Hogarth (newly promoted to head of procurement) personally requested that Defiance Industries expand production; as of 3085, some twenty percent of the *Atlas* BattleMechs in service with the LCAF are of this new type. Most of these are concentrated on the frontiers facing the Clans and the increasingly unstable Free Worlds League.

Having filled its orders from the Lyran military, Defiance Industries began selling their new *Atlas* to all comers. The BattleMech can now be found in service across the Inner Sphere, and some have even shown up in the Periphery.

In The Republic, the AS7-K2 has become a popular choice as a command vehicle. Several of Devlin Stone's Paladins have adopted the 'Mech as their personal ride. On Kervil, the Fulton family resisted the Military Materiel Redemption Program and refused to hand over their privately owned BattleMechs. Paladin David McKinnon attempted to defuse the situation, but the Fultons rebuffed all attempts to reach a peaceful solution and launched an attack on The Republic representatives. McKinnon met the charge by a lance of Succession Wars antiques in his new *Atlas*. The Fultons proved no match in skill or technology for the Paladin. First to fall was a *Dragon*, cut in half by a volley of Gauss rifle and laser fire. Next, the Fultons' *Panther* went down with its legs sheared off and their *Jenner* dissolved under a hail of Streak missiles. The fight then became a one-on-one match between Hohiro Fulton's *Awesome* and Paladin McKinnon's *Atlas*. McKinnon used his superior speed and weapons reach to hammer the aging assault 'Mech.

Clan Diamond Shark purchased the bulk of one production run from Defiance Industries in 3084. Recent reports of the AS7-K2 in the Clan Occupation Zone support rumors that some of this consignment was delivered to the Clans and not resold to Inner Sphere interests.

Variants

Defiance Industries has produced the AS7-K3 in limited numbers. This model drops one missile launcher from the left torso and downgrades the one in the right torso to four tubes. This modification frees up space to mount jump jets, allowing this version of the *Atlas* to jump up to 90 meters at a time. An extra ton of armor is added, bringing protection up to the maximum the chassis can handle. The Federated Suns recently put their AS8-D into limited production as well. Using particle cannons, multi-missile launchers and a rotary autocannon allows a wide array of firepower until the triple-strength myomers can get this *Atlas* into brawling range.

Struggling for front line units, the Lyran armed forces pulled older model *Atlas*es from planetary militias. The AS7-Dr replaces the Defiance autocannon with a heavy PPC. The weight savings allows an upgrade of the SRM and installation of ECM, C³ and two additional heat sinks.

Notable MechWarriors

Hauptmann Rüdiger Steiner: Initially best known for his lineage as the son of Reinhardt Steiner, Rüdiger Steiner's fame increased following the public drama that surrounded his sister Claudia's kidnapping. Some blame him for interfering and allowing the pirates to commit the crime, while others believe his Lyran Irregulars saved her life. None can deny that Rüdiger is a formidable pilot, using his *Atlas* AS7-K2 to take down two pirate *Goliath*s and a *Marauder* during the rescue.

AS7-K2 ATLAS

Type: **Atlas**
Technology Base: Inner Sphere
Tonnage: 100
Battle Value: 2,160

Equipment			Mass
Internal Structure:			10
Engine:	400 XL		26.5
Walking MP:	4		
Running MP:	6		
Jumping MP:	0		
Heat Sinks:	10 [20]		0
Gyro:			4
Cockpit:			3
Armor Factor (Ferro):	295		16.5

	Internal Structure	Armor Value
Head	3	9
Center Torso	31	42
Center Torso (rear)		14
R/L Torso	21	31
R/L Torso (rear)		10
R/L Arm	17	33
R/L Leg	21	41

Weapons and Ammo	Location	Critical	Tonnage
ER Large Laser	RA	2	5
Streak SRM 6	RT	2	4.5
Ammo (Streak) 30	RT	2	2
Ammo (Gauss) 16	RT	2	2
CASE	RT	1	.5
Guardian ECM Suite	CT	2	1.5
Gauss Rifle	LT	7	15
Streak SRM 6	LT	2	4.5
ER Large Laser	LA	2	5

Mass: 100 tons
Chassis: Curtiss Diomede
Power Plant: Nissan 200 Fusion Engine
Cruising Speed: 22 kph
Maximum Speed: 32 kph
Jump Jets: None
  Jump Capacity: None
Armor: Kallon FWL Heavy Industrial with CASE
Equipment:
  1 ThruSteel Heavy Duty Pile Driver
  2 Aeneas Lift Hoists
  2 SperryBrowning-Civ Rivet Guns
  2 Curtiss Expert Sprayers
  2 Doombud MML 7 Tube Systems
Manufacturer: Curtiss Hydroponics
  (Power Systems Division)
  Primary Factory: Silver
Communications System: CurtissComm Mk III
  Heavy Industrial
Targeting and Tracking System: Dynatec 256/
  MissileTrac V Advanced

Overview

The Word of Blake Jihad saw destruction on a scale not seen since the Second Succession War—and the wave of violence that engulfed all factions did not halt at the military sector. As in all wars, the Inner Sphere civilian population bore the brunt of the atrocities. The lesson that the defenseless are too often left to their own devices is an old one, painfully relearned during the Jihad.

Now the time of reconstruction has begun, and with it the exponential growth of the civilian sector. The design of IndustrialMechs bears witness to a paradigm shift: It is becoming increasingly important for an IndustrialMech to guarantee at least token protection to its users, elevating its advantage over other conventional tools above the purely psychological. One of the new IndustrialMechs that showcases this change is the D-M3D-3 *Diomede*, manufactured by Curtiss Hydroponics (Power Systems Division) in partnership with Curtiss MiliTech on Silver.

Capabilities

Best described as a cross between a heavy ConstructionMech and a SecurityMech, the *Diomede* was designed to act as a mobile crane and industrial drill, while also serving as a deterrent to individuals with hostile intent.

The *Diomede* stands taller and sleeker than any other IndustrialMech to date and its dual lift hoists can carry up to 100 tons, thus fulfilling its primary function as a crane. The 'Mech's core houses the highly reliable Nissan 200 fusion engine, providing the same power and fuel-free endurance found in a BattleMech. To aid it when working in urban areas, the 'Mech also sports tracks. With treads affixed to its lower legs, the long legs can bend at the knee to create a more stable tank-like lower chassis on which the *Diomede* rests, which allows impressive mobility even when fully burdened.

The limbs serve to increase versatility. The right arm sports a fully articulated hand, an uncommon feature among ConstructionMechs. This hand actuator is so dexterous that experienced *Diomede* pilots claim to have been able to hold a girder in place with it while using the wrist-mounted rivet guns on the same arm to secure the load. The *Diomede*'s left arm sports a huge pile driver generally used for digging trenches to house various landlines and other installations. An added dimension of this lance-like tool is the humanoid *Diomede*'s resemblance to its namesake from ancient mythology.

Like the mythological hero whose name it bears, it can harm the real gods of the battlefield with its twin large MML launchers hidden below a fairing on either torso. The launchers were officially installed to assist in heavy demolition work, though their potential military application has not gone unnoticed. This IndustrialMech's cockpit features an ejection seat as well as advanced fire control systems otherwise reserved for BattleMechs, and its heavily armored carapace is likewise an unusual feature. Officially, all this only serves to enable the *Diomede* to clear building areas of rubble or even unexploded ordnance, but The Republic has imposed stiff licensing requirements for civilian sale.

Deployment

The *Diomede*'s sales debut in the fall of 3084 has been very promising. Currently, Curtiss is set on retaining neutrality, fulfilling orders from all governments of the former Free Worlds League. All independent companies or mercenary military commands can also place orders, though why the latter would be interested is currently unknown and should be carefully monitored.

Variants

Curtiss Hydroponics offers a second version, the D-M3D-4, that is of more use in demolition sites. It replaces the pile driver with a rock cutter and sports a cutting torch on its right arm. As this DemolitionMech lacks hands and cannot guarantee the same versatility and safety as the D-M3D-3, Curtiss has made it a policy to sell this unit only to prior purchasers of their base model. That the D-M3D-4 has nevertheless seen good sales is a testament to the *Diomede*'s general popularity.

D-M3D-3 DIOMEDE CONSTRUCTIONMECH

Type: **Diomede**
Technology Base: Inner Sphere
Tonnage: 100
Battle Value: 1,228

Equipment		Mass
Internal Structure:	IndustrialMech	20
Engine:	200 (Fusion)	8.5
Walking MP:	2	
Running MP:	3	
Jumping MP:	0	
Heat Sinks:	10	0
Gyro:		2
Cockpit (Industrial):	3	
Armor Factor (Heavy Industrial): 304		19

	Internal Structure	Armor Value
Head	3	9
Center Torso	31	45
Center Torso (rear)		16
R/L Torso	21	30
R/L Torso (rear)		12
R/L Arm	17	33
R/L Leg	21	42

Weapons and Ammo	Location	Critical	Tonnage
Heavy-Duty Pile Driver	LA	8	10
MML 7	LT	4	4.5
Ammo (MML) 34/28	LT	2	2
Sprayer	LT	1	.5
Lift Hoist	LT/R	3	3
Searchlight	LT	1	.5
CASE	LT	1	.5
Liquid Cargo Storage	CT	2	2
MML 7	RT	4	4.5
Ammo (MML) 34/28	RT	2	2
Sprayer	RT	1	.5
Lift Hoist	RT/R	3	3
Searchlight	RT	1	.5
CASE	RT	1	.5
2 Rivet Guns	RA	2	1
Ammo (Rivets) 600	RA	2	2
Ejection Seat	H	1	.5
Tracks	LL/RL	1/1	10

Note: The D-M3D-3 has advanced targeting.

PGD-Y3 POIGNARD

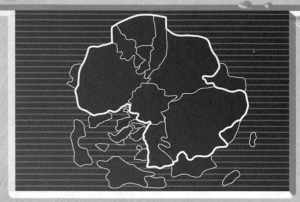

Mass: 35 tons
Chassis: Aeroframe XSR
Power Plant: Magna 245 XL
Armor: Kallon AeroWeave II Ferro-Aluminum
Armament:
    1 Imperator Napoleon Light AC/5
    1 Martell Small Pulse Laser
    4 Magna Mk VI ER Medium Lasers
Manufacturer: Kallon Industries
    Primary Factory: Loyalty (M-SC), Asuncion (RotS)
Communications System: SecureComm 867
Targeting and Tracking System: Kallon Victory
    Tracker Delta

Overview

The *Poignard* is the first aerospace fighter built by Kallon Industries. However, the company is no stranger to aerospace manufacturing. They produce the *Kuan-Ti* and *Vengeance*-class DropShips in orbital yards in the Loyalty system. With the neighboring SelaSys WarShip facility receiving the majority of hostile attentions, the Kallon facilities made it through the Jihad relatively unscathed, positioning them well for post-Jihad reconstruction.

In addition to fortifying their DropShip yards in the mid-3070s, Kallon expanded their surface-based fabrication plant to incorporate an aerospace fighter production line. Intel gathered prior to the breakup of the Free Worlds League suggests that Kallon may have considered adding a second aerospace or conventional fighter production line to the facility.

Following the successful launch of the *Poignard* in the Marik-Stewart Commonwealth in 3083, Kallon approached Stone with an offer to manufacture it for The Republic. Negotiations were described as amicable by both sides. At the beginning of 3085, Kallon expanded its factory on Asuncion with a new line and *Poignard*s began shipping to RAF units.

Capabilities

Designed to combat craft like the Blakist *Shade* OmniFighter, the *Poignard*'s Magna extralight engine delivers a sustained 4.5 Gs of acceleration. Maximum combat power allows for 7 Gs of acceleration, though pilots are strictly warned to keep the throttle below sixty-five percent, as exceeding that setting can potentially damage the structural integrity of the airframe. A full 7-G burn is almost certain to damage the fighter and may injure even the toughest aerojock.

The *Poignard*'s primary model is a light, multi-role fighter with space-based engagement ranges of approximately 200 km, lasers suited for strafing, and ample bomb capacity. A nose-mounted Imperator Napoleon light autocannon is the fighter's sole ballistic weapon, though a full ton of ammunition gives it twenty bursts, enough for most dogfights. Owing to the proliferation of capital missiles during the Jihad, the *Poignard* is equipped with a single Martell small pulse laser for point-defense purposes. The nose mount limits the efficacy of this weapon to head-to-head engagements, but given the number of WarShips destroyed by nuclear missiles during the Jihad, point defense may well become part of tactical fighter doctrine. A quartet of Magna extended-range medium lasers delivers the *Poignard*'s true offensive punch. Split evenly between each wing, the lasers are fitted in underwing pods and are easily mistaken for external stores in a visual inspection.

The Victory Tracker fire control system seamlessly coordinates all five weapons while automatically managing the Martel in point-defense mode and working with the *Poignard*'s eleven double-strength freezers to maintain a comfortable heat curve. A total of five firing modes may be programmed into the Victory Tracker and enabled by toggles on the control stick. Approach vector, armor status, velocity and other useful information is summoned through inputs on the throttle.

Deployment

The *Poignard* appears with various units in the Marik-Stewart Commonwealth. Sales to other former Free Worlds League factions are in negotiations, though no confirmed deals had been made as of this briefing.

In the RAF, the first *Poignard* production run is being shipped to Stone's Lament. Future production runs will be deployed to the Triarii Protectors and Hastati Sentinels.

Variants

Kallon produces two variants of the *Poignard*. The L3 is built for long-range engagements, with a pair of ER large lasers and an additional double heat sink replacing the armaments of the standard Y3 version. A more radical design, the R3, has been developed with two primary roles in mind. The R3 drops one Magna Mk VI and the light autocannon, adding five additional Martell small pulse lasers and two freezers in their place. With an all-laser armament and a significant portion of its firepower coming from pulse lasers, the R3 is adept at strafing attacks, particularly against conventional infantry forces. The other intended role is the relatively new concept of missile defense escort. With more and more Q-ships appearing in lieu of new WarShips, Kallon may be at the forefront of a new combat niche—and marketing campaign.

PGD-Y3 POIGNARD

Type: **Poignard**
Technology Base: Inner Sphere
Tonnage: 35
Battle Value: 1,310

Equipment		Mass
Engine:	245 XL	6
Safe Thrust:	9	
Maximum Thrust:	14	
Structural Integrity:	9	
Heat Sinks:	11 [22]	1
Fuel:	320	4
Cockpit:		3
Armor Factor (Heavy Ferro):	198	10
	Armor Value	
Nose	70	
Wings	50/50	
Aft	28	

Weapons and Ammo	Location	Tonnage	Heat	SRV	MRV	LRV	ERV
Light AC/5	Nose	5	1	5	5	—	—
Ammo (Light AC) 20	—	1					
Small Pulse Laser	Nose	1	2	3	—	—	—
2 ER Medium Lasers	RW	2	5	5	5	—	—
2 ER Medium Lasers	LW	2	5	5	5	—	—

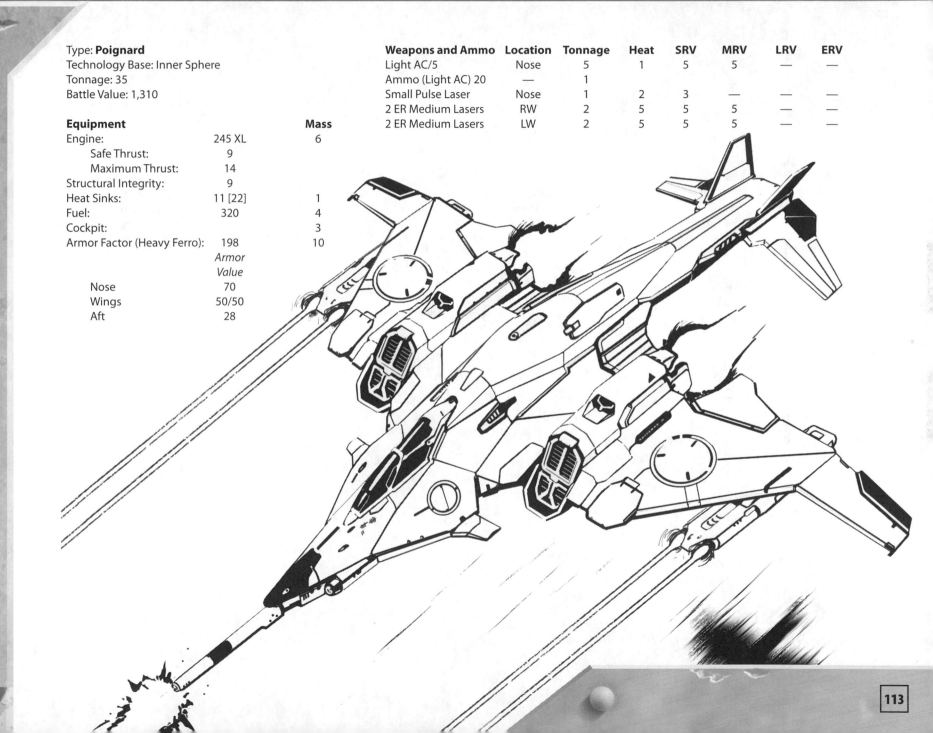

SGT-2R SAGITTARII

Mass: 45 tons
Chassis: Shipil 35B
Power Plant: PlasmaStar 270 XL
Armor: Fiber 15 Heavy Ferro-Aluminum
Armament:
    1 Donal Snub-Nose PPC
    2 Holly MML 7 Racks
Manufacturer: Boeing Interstellar
    Primary Factory: Terra
Communications System: Lassitor FibroLink
Targeting and Tracking System: BANDAR 9

Overview

Even four years after the liberation of Terra, the units that made up the newly formed RAF were a mishmash of technology and readiness. In the ground forces this variety became something of an asset, but in the burgeoning Republic aerospace forces it proved a liability. Fighter squadrons rely heavily on mutual support and maneuver. With units from across the Inner Sphere, with capabilities ranging from the Star League era to modern times, it quickly became a logistical and strategic nightmare. Purchasing contracts from key allies helped resolve these issues, but a large gap persisted in the mid-weight range, and so one of the RAF's first requisition orders was for a strong multi-role medium fighter. In response, Boeing Interstellar launched the *Sagittarii* in 3084.

Capabilities

Boeing chose Wangker Aerospace's reliable *Tomahawk* airframe as the starting point for their new fighter (having acquired Wangker's surviving facilities after the Jihad). Calling on Wangker's component suppliers, the *Sagittarii* shares many components with the *Tomahawk*. PlasmaStar Engines had launched a new extralight version of their 270-series engine in the final days of the Jihad, and this system gave the *Sagittarii* the same thrust profile as the *Tomahawk* at half the weight. Heavy ferro-fibrous armor encases the hull, enabling the *Sagitarii* to withstand significant punishment and even shrug off many weapons. Ten double heat sinks provide more than enough heat dissipation, and the four-ton fuel reserve is sufficient for the short engagements this fighter is most often expected to encounter.

The *Sagittarii* can generate six gees of thrust, and its armament is understandably lighter than equivalent medium weight designs. A nose-mounted snub-nose PPC gives the craft a reasonable energy weapon while keeping weight and heat loads down. Wing-mounted MML 7s, each with a two-ton ammo bin, give the fighter flexibility to engage in long-range sniping or to close in on slower opponents and pepper them with massed SRM volleys.

Deployment

Only in production since late 3084, the *Sagittarii* is just starting to appear in significant numbers and has yet to see major combat operations. Boeing is selling the design only to the RAF, which is purchasing all available models, and has been forced to turn down repeated requests by the Federated Suns to purchase the unit.

In January of 3085, the RAF and AFFS conducted a joint war game on the world of New Hessen. A lance of *Dagger* Primes dropped out of the sun on the first two *Sagittarii* to be deployed to a combat unit. Used to being the fastest medium fighters around, the *Dagger* pilots were surprised by the speed and agility of the *Sagittarii*. Out-turning the Davion fighters, the *Sagittarii* managed to stay behind the *Daggers* and wear away their thick armor with repeated PPC and SRM barrages. This standout engagement is one reason the AFFS Quartermaster's office has issued purchase requests to Boeing every month since the war games. Despite these repeated requests and The Republic's good relations with the Federated Suns, there are no plans to allow Boeing Interstellar to sell *Sagittarii* to the AFFS.

Variants

Boeing has released a new variant, now undergoing RAF field trials. The SGT-3R replaces the snub-nosed PPC with a newly developed Donal heavy PPC. The mass increase necessitated a downgrade in the Hollys to five-tube launchers and three tons of ammunition. The 3R loses little in overall firepower, exchanging the spread of PPC and MML damage for the single heavy penetration of the heavy PPC. Testing has so far shown it to be a viable design, but it should be supported by other craft to allow it to close to PPC range.

SGT-2R SAGITTARII

Type: **Sagittarii**
Technology Base: Inner Sphere
Tonnage: 45
Battle Value: 1,293

Equipment		Mass
Engine:	270 XL	7.5
Safe Thrust:	8	
Maximum Thrust:	12	
Structural Integrity:	8	
Heat Sinks:	10 [20]	0
Fuel:	320	4
Cockpit:		3
Armor Factor (Heavy Ferro):	228	11.5
	Armor Value	
Nose	67	
Wings	55/55	
Aft	51	

Weapons and Ammo	Location	Tonnage	Heat	SRV	MRV	LRV	ERV
Snub-Nose PPC	Nose	6	10	10	8	—	—
MML 7	RW	4.5	4	8	4	4	—
MML 7	LW	4.5	4	8	4	4	—
Ammo (MML) 68/56	—	4					

MR-1S MORGENSTERN

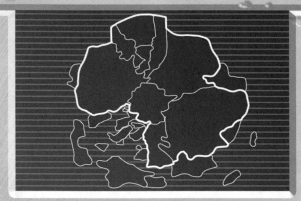

Mass: 70 tons
Chassis: Lockheed/CBM 300
Power Plant: WAS 280
Armor: Donegal Omni-Sheath Ferro-Aluminum
Armament:
31 tons of pod space available
Manufacturer: Lockheed/CBM
Primary Factory: Tharkad
Communications System: Lockheed/CBM COMSET 300
Targeting and Tracking System: Lockheed/CBM TarSet 75

Overview

Lockheed released a terrible airframe to the Lyran military over half a millennium ago. Despite the problems with the *Lucifer*, the design has remained in service only by necessity. With the technological renaissance of the latter half of the 31st Century there was a push to replace the *Lucifer* with a newer, better design. Finally the Jihad came and the Word of Blake severely damaged the Lockheed/CBM plants on Tharkad that were producing the *Lightning* and *Hellcat* designs. Noting that both designs had similar weights and components, designers proposed that instead of rebuilding both the lines they could replace both with an OmniFighter. Thus the *Morgenstern* was approved, with engineers working hard to make a design to eventually replace all three fighters.

Capabilities

The *Morgenstern* has moderate thrust for its size, matching that of the three designs it replaces. While initial plans called for a light fusion engine this was denied, not for survivability issues but rather to keep costs down. With so many aging *Lucifer*s, *Hellcat*s and *Lightning*s in the LCAF, replacement will be expensive. Following the lead of the *Eisensturm*, the fighter's delta frame was covered in a thick shield of ferro-aluminum armor. Designers were also tasked with making it able to handle atmospheric conditions well, an area where the *Lucifer* performed poorly. *Lucifer* pilots will be very pleased to know that the fighter has a working ejection system.

With thirty-one tons for payload, almost forty-five percent of the craft is devoted to weapons and equipment. One drawback is an integral fuel capacity of only four tons, something critics have complained about. However, as an OmniFighter, the designers wanted to leave plenty of room for extra weapons on shorter missions.

The most common version refines the *Lucifer* payload. The rarely-used wing lasers are gone, with most of the weapons located in the nose. A pair of extended-range large lasers provide punch at a distance, while a pair of multi-missile launchers add to firepower at all ranges. Both launchers have Artemis IV guidance systems to increase accuracy and punch. An aft-mounted laser is common throughout the designs, as is heat sink capacity to salvo the primary weapons load.

The A configuration is meant for aerospace superiority and ground attacks. An ER PPC and twin plasma rifles are able to maul even the toughest armor. The *Lightning* clone, configuration B, is focused on the improved heavy Gauss rifle. Studying the *Hellcat*'s performance, it was found that many of the weapons weren't used because of the immense heat requirements. Configuration C was thus modified to upgrade one large laser to a pulse version and put a medium pulse in the rear. Finally, the missile-heavy configuration D is a consummate support craft.

Deployment

The design is still in the final trials and is expected to first be issued in 3086 to replace aging fighters. So far only a general procurement announcement has gone out, rather than specific assignments. The Lyran Commonwealth will be getting the lion's share of the production, with Clan Wolf-in-Exile having the option to purchase some of the output.

Type: Morgenstern
Technology Base: Inner Sphere
Tonnage: 70
Battle Value: 1,640

Equipment			Mass
Engine:	280		16
Safe Thrust:	6		
Maximum Thrust:	9		
Structural Integrity:	7		
Heat Sinks:	10 [20]		0
Fuel:	320		4
Cockpit:			3
Armor Factor (Ferro):	286		16
	Armor Value	Free Space	
Nose	93	5	
Wings	71/71	4/4	
Aft	51	5	

Weapons and Ammo	Location	Tonnage	Heat	SRV	MRV	LRV	ERV
Primary Weapons Configuration							
2 ER Large Lasers	Nose	10	12	8	8	8	—
2 MML 7+Artemis	Nose	11	4	12	6	6	—
Ammo (MML) 34/28	—	2					
ER Medium Laser	Aft	1	5	5	5	—	—
7 Double Heat Sinks	—	7					
Alternate Configuration A							
ER PPC	Nose	7	15	10	10	10	—
2 Plasma Rifles	Nose	12	10	10	10	—	—
Ammo (Plasma) 30	—	3					
ER Medium Laser	Aft	1	5	5	5	—	—
8 Double Heat Sinks	—	8					
Battle Value: 2,012							
Alternate Configuration B — Experimental							
Improved Heavy Gauss Rifle	Nose	20	2	22	22	22	—
Ammo (iHeavy Gauss) 12	—	3					
MML 5	Nose	3	3	6	3	3	—
Ammo (MML) 48/40	—	2					
ER Medium Laser	RW	1	5	5	5	—	—
ER Medium Laser	LW	1	5	5	5	—	—
ER Medium Laser	Aft	1	5	5	5	—	—
Battle Value: 1,949							

Weapons and Ammo	Location	Tonnage	Heat	SRV	MRV	LRV	ERV
Alternate Configuration C							
2 ER Large Lasers	Nose	10	12	8	8	8	—
2 ER Medium Lasers	Nose	2	5	5	5	—	—
Large Pulse Laser	Nose	7	10	9	9	—	—
ER Medium Laser	RW	1	5	5	5	—	—
ER Medium Laser	LW	1	5	5	5	—	—
ER Medium Laser	Aft	1	5	5	5	—	—
Medium Pulse Laser	Aft	2	4	6	—	—	—
7 Double Heat Sinks	—	7					
Battle Value: 1,816							
Alternate Configuration D							
ER Large Laser	Nose	5	12	8	8	8	—
ER Medium Laser	Nose	1	5	5	5	—	—
MML 7+Artemis	Nose	5.5	4	12	6	6	—
Ammo (MML) 68/56	—	4					
MML 7+Artemis	RW	5.5	4	12	6	6	—
MML 7+Artemis	LW	5.5	4	12	6	6	—
ER Medium Laser	Aft	1	5	5	5	—	—
Small Laser	Aft	.5	1	3	—	—	—
Targeting Computer	—	2					
Double Heat Sink	—	1					
Battle Value: 1,704							

M▌▌G-8L MĚNGQÍ

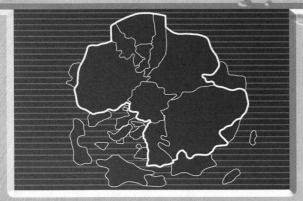

Mass: 95 tons
Chassis: Owens L118A7
Power Plant: Pitban 285
Armor: Detroit Ferro-Aluminum Special
Armament:
　2 Ceres Arms Crusher Plasma Rifles
　3 Sian/Ceres Cougar SRM 6 Racks
　2 Delta Dart LRM 15
　4 Ceres Arms ER Medium Lasers
　2 Diverse Optics Type 2 ER Medium Lasers
　1 Magna 200p Pulse Laser
Manufacturer: Rashpur-Owens, Inc., Detroit
　Consolidated Aerospace
　Primary Factory: Capella (Rasphur), Detroit (DCA)
Communications System: Ceres MaserCom B-33
Targeting and Tracking System: Brightstar Model III

Overview

As military action wound down following the successful Coalition assault on Terra, many corporations looked at their balance sheets and saw the looming specter of bankruptcy. Rashpur-Owens was no stranger to that threat, having clawed their way back from near-insolvency several times during the Succession Wars and finally establishing strong financial footing in the 3050s. While it had solid DropShip sales booked through 3082, Rashpur-Owens began investigating alternative markets in the late 3070s ahead of the anticipated end of the Jihad.

Aerospace fighter design seemed only natural for a company that had produced assault DropShips for hundreds of years, but bringing the *Měngqín* to market was

more of a struggle than Lord Riley Doh could have likely imagined. Design requirements and functional specs were six months late. Contract negotiations with Ceres Arms took much longer than expected and looked as though they would fall through entirely. When the deal with Ceres was finally inked, alternative deals for extended-range medium lasers had accidentally been executed leaving Rashpur-Owens no choice but to include two different models of the weapon on the fighter. After the last domestic challenge was finally conquered in 3078 and the prototype construction under way, Rashpur-Owens began marketing the design to firms in the Confederation, Magistracy and, with permission from Sian, the Taurian Concordat. Expecting a quick sale, Rashpur-Owens was instead surprised: the Taurians refused to even evaluate the fighter, and it took several months to reach acceptable terms with the Magistracy, who insisted the fighter also be built under license at Detroit Consolidated Aerospace.

With all the setbacks from prototype to production model, analysts predict that Rashpur-Owens will not recoup their investment in the *Měngqín* until after the last unit of the 3088 production run is shipped. Whether they will explore variants or develop additional aerospace fighters remains unknown.

Capabilities

The cost-effective design and proven technology have earned Rashpur-Owens and Detroit Consolidated Aerospace brisk sales in the last four years. Although the design is not available to the RAF, analysts have been able to tour the factory on Detroit and, combined with observations from within the Confederation, an accurate picture of this new powerhouse can be sketched.

Much like the *Chippewa*, it's difficult to classify the *Měngqín*'s main armament. Two nose-mounted Ceres Arms Crusher Plasma Rifles offer good weight-to-damage ratios and solid medium-range firepower. The wing-mounted Delta Dart missile launchers have a slightly worse weight-to-damage ratio but give the fighter long-range options. Short-range firepower is provided by a trio of Cougar short-range missile racks, which deliver solid armor-defeating damage. Wing-mounted pairs of ER medium lasers boil off ferro-aluminum armor with the efficacy of particle cannons. The designers even included two aft-mounted

Diverse Optics lasers to discourage tailing fighters and a nose-mounted Martell small pulse laser for point defense. All of that was combined with a Brightstar targeting and tracking system.

The *Měngqín* is a fighter of careful choices. A full salvo greatly exceeds the heat dissipation capability of seventeen double heat sinks and forces a reactor shutdown. With a real chance of ammunition explosions and pilot injury only the most insane aerojock would use this attack profile.

Five tons of fuel and a class-standard two-and-a-half Gs of acceleration combine for average battlefield endurance, but the ammunition supplies for all of the ammo-dependent weapon systems just barely meet minimum recommended requirements. The *Měngqín* is far more likely to run out of ammo than fuel. Fourteen and a half tons of ferro aluminum armor ensure most pilots have ample opportunity to do both.

Deployment

Rashpur-Owens, Inc. has an exclusive contract with the CCAF, where the *Měngqín* has been positively received by most Confederation forces. A disturbing number of the craft have been spotted along the border with Prefectures V and VI, but analysts so far attribute this to Capellan posturing and none have been spotted amid the "pirate" forces discovered on Republic border worlds.

In the Periphery Detroit Consolidated Aerospace offers the fighter throughout the Magistracy. Initial production runs have gone to the Canopian Fusiliers, with future production runs sold out through 3087. Detroit also exports the fighter to the Inner Sphere mercenary market through various points of sale in the Confederation, Republic, former Free Worlds League, and Federated Suns.

Variants

No variants of the *Měngqín* have been produced to date.

MNG-8L MĚNGQÍN

Type: **Měngqín**
Technology Base: Inner Sphere
Tonnage: 95
Battle Value: 2,301

Equipment		Mass
Engine:	285	16.5
Safe Thrust:	5	
Maximum Thrust:	8	
Structural Integrity:	9	
Heat Sinks:	17 [34]	7
Fuel:	400	5
Cockpit:		3
Armor Factor (Ferro):	259	14.5
	Armor Value	
Nose	80	
Wings	70/70	
Aft	39	

Weapons and Ammo	Location	Tonnage	Heat	SRV	MRV	LRV	ERV
2 Plasma Rifles	Nose	12	10	10	10	0	0
Ammo (Plasma) 20	—	2					
SRM 6	Nose	3	3	8	—	—	—
Ammo (SRM) 30	—	2					
Small Pulse Laser	Nose	1	2	3	—	—	—
2 ER Medium Lasers	RW	2	5	5	5	—	—
SRM 6	RW	3	3	8	—	—	—
LRM 15	RW	7	5	9	9	9	—
2 ER Medium Lasers	LW	2	5	5	5	—	—
SRM 6	LW	3	3	8	—	—	—
LRM 15	LW	7	5	9	9	9	—
Ammo (LRM) 24	—	3					
2 ER Medium Lasers	Aft	2	5	5	5	—	—

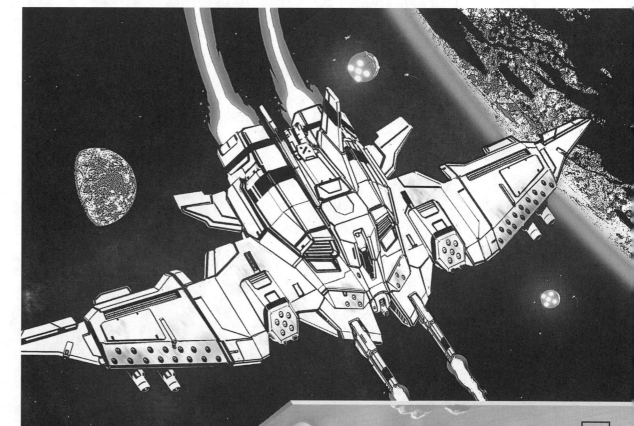

ARES MARK IX (ATTACK CRAFT)

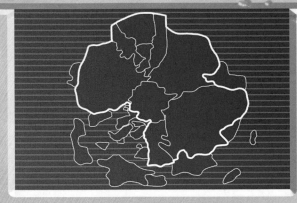

What is now typically referred to as the "Mark series" of small craft began as the *Ares* small craft series. The *Ares* Mark 1 long-range landing craft debuted in the mid-2400s, named for the Ares Conventions signed earlier in that century. From this first craft, a series of three, all built on the same base hull, came to be synonymous with space travel. The long-range landing craft (LRLC)—best known for its most-produced version, the MK VII—has long been the most recognizable of the three, with the close attack landing craft (CALC) and the combat-oriented *Ares* attack craft (AAC) often mistaken for their more common cousin. After the fall of the Star League, the original manufacturer—IncStar Dymanics—dropped the *Ares* name in an effort to distance itself from the then-shattered Ares Conventions. IncStar did not survive the Succession Wars, but other firms across the Inner Sphere continued to build the Mark series craft.

The *Ares* was out of production for nearly a century until Universal Air (now merged with Federated Boeing) restarted production of the *Ares* attack craft in 3066. The resurgence of WarShips and the increasing size of the Federated Suns Naval DropShip fleet once more called for a close escort craft. The *Ares* attack craft is a radical departure from the landing craft series. Heavily armored, one of the AAC's most striking differences from the original landing craft models is the dual engine nacelles that replace the lander's single-nacelle design. The added engine gives the AAC a maximum thrust nearly double that of the LRLC series. With only a marginal increase in firepower, the AAC's primary use is in electronic warfare defense, deployed to screen DropShips or WarShips in deep space combat.

The updated AAC Mark IX takes advantage of recovered technologies to heavily upgrade the craft's offensive firepower. The AAC Mark VII carried sixteen standard heat sinks to support three large lasers and four medium lasers, all forward-facing. The Mark IX uses fifteen heat sinks, upgraded to freezer models. It loses one large laser, but the remaining two are an extended-range and pulse model for long-range sniping and accurate short-range fire. The four medium lasers are all upgraded to pulse models as well. Finally, a Beagle active probe was added. This last modification allows the AAC Mark IX to support aerospace fighters, using the probe to punch a hole through hostile ECM fields.

In the final battle for Terra, Federated Suns *Arondight*s deployed *Ares* Mark IXs to devastating effect. Using their ECCM and active probes, the Mark IXs cleared the path for Coalition ships to destroy one of the *Naga* CASPAR II Drone control ships.

Federated Boeing has since licensed the *Ares* Mark IX to Lyran, Republic and Combine manufacturers and is in talks with Andurien AeroTech.

ARES ATTACK CRAFT (MARK IX)

Type: Military Aerodyne
Use: Deep Space Escort
Tech: Inner Sphere
Introduced: 3077
Mass: 200 tons
Battle Value: 2,064

Dimensions
   Length: 21.4 meters
   Width: 20 meters

Fuel: 10 tons (800)
Safe Thrust: 7
Maximum Thrust: 11
Heat Sinks: 15 (30)
Structural Integrity: 11

Armor
   Nose: 159
   Sides: 118
   Aft: 81

Cargo:
   Bay 1: Cargo (3 tons)   0 Door

Ammunition: None

Crew: 3 Enlisted, 1 Gunner

Note: All crew quarters assigned as Steerage-class (5 tons per crewman). Mounts 27 tons of standard armor.

Weapons and Ammo	Location	Tonnage	Heat	SRV	MRV	LRV	ERV
Large Pulse Laser	Nose	7	10	9	9	—	—
ER Large Laser	Nose	5	12	8	8	8	—
2 Medium Pulse Lasers	RW	4	4	6	—	—	—
2 Medium Pulse Lasers	LW	4	4	6	—	—	—
Beagle Active Probe	—	1.5					

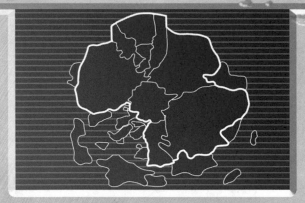

After the Jihad, many Word of Blake combat units fell into disfavor. Regardless of the effectiveness of the Blakist Celestial OmniMechs, few could envision piloting them, so strong was their connection to the horrors of their Manei Domini MechWarriors. Other designs, such as the *Gallant* and the *Trajan,* carried far less baggage and easily found a place in the armies of the new Republic and its Coalition allies. On rare occasions, a Blakist design closely associated with the horrors of the Jihad was deemed so vital as to continue in service post-Jihad. The *Interdictor* Pocket WarShip is one such craft.

Though outnumbered by the Q-Ship PWS vessels, the *Interdictor* was the Word's most prolific single class of front-line assault ship. From its first sighting over Gallery to the final space battle in Terran orbit, the *Interdictor* was present in every major battle, turning the tide of the fight in the Blakists' favor on more than one occasion. Given this impressive track record, it was a natural choice to continue production under The Republic's banner. With WarShip assets so depleted, Pocket WarShips have become the backbone of Republic defensive fleets, with the upgraded *Interdictor* serving in a prominent role.

Taking its cue from the Federated Suns *Arondight* refit, The Republic *Interdictor* removes all its capital missiles in favor of batteries of sub-capital cannons. Two nose-mounted medium SCCs provide the primary offensive punch, while wing-mounted sub capital lasers give the DropShip long-distance striking range. The standard weapons load takes advantage of the space freed up by the removal of the capital missiles. All the MML bays are now triple bays with sufficient ammunition for a protracted engagement. Additional heavy PPCs were placed in the forward wing mounts. The cargo bay was reduced, but the thirty-six battle armored marines now have standard living quarters, allowing for longer deployments. With unchanged armor, the SCC *Interdictor* is an improvement over an already deadly ship.

The majority of Republic *Interdictor*s are stationed with the home fleet and so have not seen action. One was dispatched to Holt in August of 3084. Reports of well-equipped pirate raiders sparked the deployment of one SCC-equipped version, along with a *Leopard CV* with a mixed fighter squadron. Believing they had caught the raiders' *Triumph* in the act of boarding a disabled *Mammoth* DropShip, the *Leopard* moved in to provide close air support while the *Interdictor's* marines used battle taxis to counter-board. As the *Leopard* closed, a second pirate DropShip, an *Achilles,* broke out of the *Mammoth*'s sensor shadow and destroyed the *Leopard* with a single concentrated salvo. The commander of the *Interdictor* reacted quickly, opening fire with her light sub-capital cannons while closing to medium range. The would-be ambushers were quickly overwhelmed, and the pirate *Achilles* soon shared the fate of the *Leopard*.

INTERDICTOR SCC-CLASS "POCKET WARSHIP" DROPSHIP

Type: Military Aerodyne
Use: Pocket WarShip
Tech: Inner Sphere (Advanced)
Introduced: 3078
Mass: 9,400 tons
Battle Value: 23,727

Dimensions
   Length: 175 meters
   Width: 125 meters
   Height: 53 meters

Fuel: 400 tons (12,000 points)
Tons/Burn-day: 1.84
Safe Thrust: 7
Maximum Thrust: 11
Heat Sinks: 244 (488)
Structural Integrity: 25

Armor
   Nose: 685
   Sides: 513
   Aft: 342

Cargo
   Bay 1: Small Craft Cubicle (2)   2 Doors
   Bay 2: Cargo (385 Tons)   2 Doors

Life Boats: 6
Escape Pods: 0
Crew: 5 officers, 9 enlisted/non-rated, 13 gunners, 10 bay personnel, 36 Battle Armor marines

Ammunition: 30 rounds Medium SCC ammunition (30 tons), between 429 and 507 rounds MML ammo depending on composition (39 tons), 240 rounds Anti-Missile ammunition (20 tons)

Notes: Equipped with 112.5 tons of Heavy Ferro-Aluminum armor.

Weapons:	Capital Attack Values (Standard)				
Arc (Heat) Type	Short	Medium	Long	Extreme	Class
Nose (150 Heat)					
2 Medium Sub-Capital Cannons (30 Rounds)	10 (100)	10 (100)	—	—	Capital AC
3 Heavy PPCs	5 (45)	5 (45)	—	—	PPC
3 MML 9 +Artemis IV (52/44 rounds)	4 (42)	2 (21)	2 (21)	—	MML
3 Large VSP Lasers	3 (33)	3 (27)	—	—	Laser
2 AMS (48 rounds)	1 (6)†	—	—	—	AMS
FL/FR (132 Heat)					
1 Sub-Capital Laser	1 (10)	1 (10)	1 (10)	—	Capital Laser
3 Heavy PPCs	5 (45)	5 (45)	—	—	PPC
3 MML 9 +Artemis IV (52/44 rounds)	4 (42)	2 (21)	2 (21)	—	MML
3 Large VSP Lasers	3 (33)	3 (27)	—	—	Laser
2 ER PPCs	2 (20)	2 (20)	2 (20)	—	PPC
2 AMS (48 rounds)	1 (6)†	—	—	—	AMS
AL/AR Aft (55 Heat)					
1 Heavy PPC	2 (15)	2 (15)	—	—	PPC
4 Large VSP Lasers	4 (44)	3 (28)	—	—	Laser
1 AMS (36 rounds)	0 (3)†	—	—	—	AMS
Aft (75 Heat)					
2 Heavy PPCs	3 (30)	3 (30)	—	—	PPC
3 MML 9 +Artemis IV (52/44 rounds)	4 (42)	2 (21)	2 (21)	—	MML
3 Large VSP Lasers	3 (33)	3 (27)	—	—	Laser
1 AMS (24 rounds)	0 (3)†	—	—	—	AMS

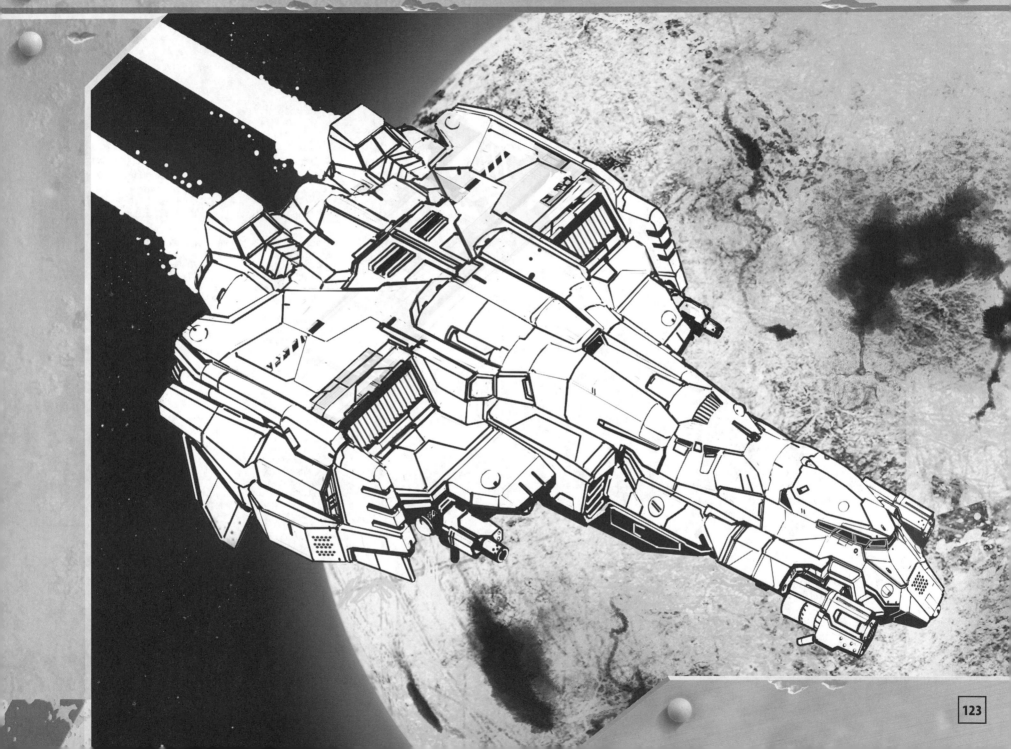

The Federated Suns' confidence in, and reliance on, capital missiles went through a trial by fire in the early days of the Protectorate campaign. Arguably the backbone of their naval defense strategies, the Suns had made heavy use of capital missiles technology both in their WarShips and their emerging Pocket WarShip class of vessels. Even the cancelled *Durandel*-class destroyer project was said to be focused on massed AR-10 batteries.

As early as 3069 FSN strategists knew the face of naval warfare was undergoing another fundamental shift. The Word of Blake's heavy use of nuclear-tipped capital missiles had resulted in a slew of emergency refits to both attack and transport DropShips to install heavy AMS batteries. They knew it was only a matter of time before the Blakists began to do the same. But even after reverse engineering the Word of Blake's capital cannon designs, the Federated Suns chose to build their newest Pocket WarShip around capital and sub-capital missiles. Produced in even greater numbers than the *Overlord* and *Excalibur* PWS, the *Arondight* would be a key part of the Federated Suns' naval offense against the Word of Blake Protectorate.

At the battle of Hean in May of 3077 the *Arondight*'s reliance on missiles would end in disaster. Still damaged from the liberation of Towne, the FSS *Indefatigable* was totally destroyed by two *Tiamat* Pocket WarShips. The six heavy sub-capital cannons massed in the nose of each *Tiamat* were able to easily blast through the *Fox* corvette's light armor. The five *Arondight*s supporting the *Indefatigable* found their missile attacks all but useless against the *Tiamats*' heavy anti-missile systems. While ultimately victorious, the FedSuns victory was more attributed to the arrival of the NCS *Path of Honor* than to the prowess of the Suns' own forces.

Showing a remarkable adaptability and willingness to change tactics on the fly the Davion High Command ordered Federated-Boeing to set up an emergency refit yard over Tikonov and began a crash refit program of all *Arondight*s in service. Fed-Boeing engineers gutted the existing Kraken and AR-10 weapons bays. In the nose they fitted three heavy sub-capital cannons, providing the DropShip with its primary capital fire. The AR-10 bays were replaced with four light sub-cap cannons, allowing the DropShip to engage targets at ranges close to its old capital missile ranges. The changes greatly increased the *Arondight*'s throw weight.

The first SCC refits saw action over Ingress in November 3077. The Protectorate's naval defense consisted primarily of *Achilles* assault DropShips upgraded with laser AMS and a single *Interdictor* Pocket WarShip. Expecting their opponents to use capital missiles, the Word quickly closed the range. The refitted *Arondight*s quickly cut through the unprepared Word DropShips and earned the Coalition an unmolested drop onto Ingress.

The redesign was not without some problems. Using the existing Kraken weapon bay required packing the heavy sub-capital cannons tightly together. This led to ongoing fire control and ammo feed issues and requires very high levels of maintenance. These issues were addressed in keel-up construction but the Tikonov refits continue to have problems. After an *Arondight* SCC exploded during routine gunnery practice in 3082, Federated-Boeing issued a recall for all SCC refits done over Tikonov. These refits had two heavy SCCs removed and the original Kraken launcher put back in.

ARONDIGHT SCC-CLASS "POCKET WARSHIP" DROPSHIP

Type: Military Spheroid
Use: Pocket WarShip
Tech: Inner Sphere (Advanced)
Introduced: 3077
Mass: 12,000 tons
Battle Value: 29,120

Dimensions
    Length: 120 meters
    Width: 117 meters
    Height: 137 meters

Fuel: 250 tons (7,500 points)
Tons/Burn-day: 1.84
Safe Thrust: 5
Maximum Thrust: 8
Heat Sinks: 200 [400]
Structural Integrity: 20

Armor
    Nose: 352
    Sides: 322
    Aft: 301

Cargo
    Bay 1: Small Craft Cubicle (2)   2 Doors
    Bay 2: Cargo (370 Tons)   2 Doors

Life Boats: 7
Escape Pods: 4
Crew: 6 officers, 8 enlisted/non-rated, 24 gunners, 10 bay personnel, 24 marines

Ammunition: 60 rounds Heavy SCC ammunition (120 tons), 160 rounds Light SCC ammunition (160 tons), 20 Piranhas (400 tons), 64 rounds Gauss rifle ammunition (8 tons), 480 rounds Rotary AC/5 ammunition (48 tons), 384 rounds Anti-Missile ammunition (32 tons).

Notes: Equipped with 68 tons of Ferro-Aluminum armor.

Weapons: Arc (Heat) Type	Capital Attack Values (Standard)				
	Short	Medium	Long	Extreme	Class
Nose (148 Heat)					
3 Heavy Sub-Capital Cannon (60 rounds)	21 (210)	21 (210)	—	—	Capital AC
2 Gauss Rifles (32 rounds)	2 (15)	2 (15)	2 (15)	—	Gauss
4 ER Medium Lasers	2 (20)	2 (20)	—	—	Laser
3 AMS (72 rounds)	1 (9)†	—	—	—	AMS
FL/FR (88 Heat)					
2 Piranha (20 Missiles)	6	6	6	—	Capital Missile
4 Light Sub-Capital Cannon (80 rounds)	8 (80)	8 (80)	8 (80)	—	Capital AC
2 Rotary AC/5 (120 rounds)	4 (40)	4 (40)	—	—	Autocannon
2 ER Medium Lasers	1 (10)	1 (10)	—	—	Laser
2 AMS (48 rounds)	1 (6)†	—	—	—	AMS
AL/AR (45 Heat)					
2 Piranha (20 Missiles)	6	6	6	—	Capital Missile
2 Rotary AC/5 (120 rounds)	4 (40)	4 (40)	—	—	Autocannon
3 ER Medium Lasers	2 (15)	3 (15)	—	—	Laser
3 AMS (72 rounds)	1 (9)†	—	—	—	AMS
Aft (22 Heat)					
Screen Launcher (10 rounds)	—	—	—	—	Screen
2 Gauss Rifles (32 rounds)	2 (15)	2 (15)	2 (15)	—	Gauss
4 ER Medium Lasers	2 (20)	2 (20)	—	—	Laser
3 AMS (72 rounds)	1 (9)†	—	—	—	AMS

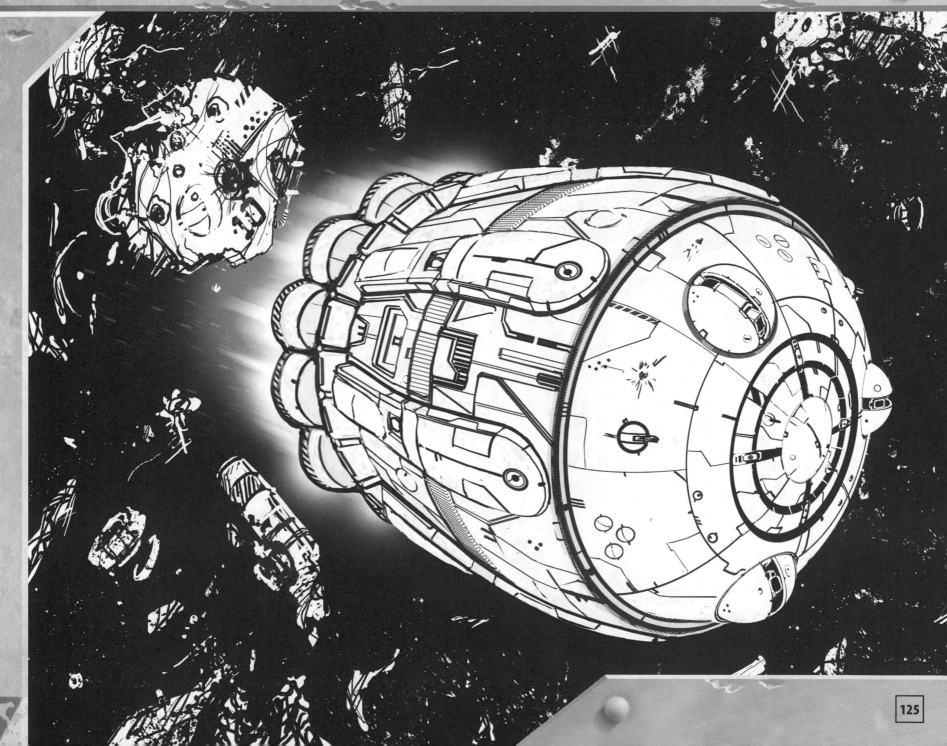

TAIHOU ASSAULT DROPSHIP

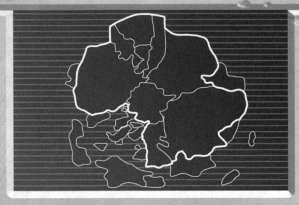

The Jihad was a trying time for the Draconis Combine Admiralty. With the Black Dragons and Word of Blake shutting down or redirecting production at Dieron, Luthien, and Altair, Draconis naval production ground to a halt. When the threat receded in the late 3070s, thoughts turned to how to rebuild the navy. Funding and infrastructure for more WarShips was unlikely so the Admiralty decided to base the new navy on DropShips utilizing the naval C³ system to overcome their limited firepower.

BBP Industries, with its extensive array of modern DropShip designs, would get the majority of funds to revamp its lines. But the damage to Luthien meant that it would take decades for all of BBP's lines to receive upgrades. Instead Hinsdale Elec was selected to develop a new assault ship that would take into account all of the lessons of the Jihad. Honored though they were, Hinsdale was not sophisticated enough to complete the project on their own. Technicians from Midway Warship Yard were transferred to assist with the capital weapons while Nirasaki Computer Collective was brought in to handle the linkup with their naval C³ system. The prototype *Taihou* launched in 3077 and mass production started in 3078.

Using a smaller, stronger hull than the *Nekohono'o*, the *Taihou* is covered in heavy ferro-aluminum armor, making it a tough nut to crack. Its wings are lined with Lord's Light Heavy PPCs and computer-guided MRMs. The main firepower comes from a battery of Imperator sub-capital autocannons. These hundred-ton weapons allow the *Taihou* to batter other DropShips into submission with a degree of accuracy unavailable to most DropShips, but the real heart of the *Taihou* is the Nirasaki C³ system. This allows the

Taihou to use targeting data from other fleet units for even more accurate fire. As the system is rolled out to the rest of the fleet it's expected that BBP's *Nekohono'o* will be one of the first to benefit and will serve as fire support for the *Taihou*s. The *Taihou* is rounded out with a useful complement of battle armor and shuttles.

In typical DCA fashion the first production runs were disasters. Under political pressure to have a strike force ready for the Liberation of Terra, the first *Taihou*s had major faults in their advanced electronics systems. This is known to have left one *Taihou* at Terra operating without weapons at all. When they functioned correctly the *Taihou*s proved devastating, able to smash well-armored ships like *Interdictor*s with ease. After Terra's liberation Hinsdale was able to reinstate proper quality control with a corresponding reduction in faults. *Taihou*s are typically deployed with *Nekohono'o*s, *Achilles*, and *Okinawa*s in naval support squadrons. The *Taihou*'s heavier armor means they end up as the point units for the squadron's C³ system. So far, fully integrated squadrons are rare but the DCA hopes to have its fleet assets refitted by the turn of the century.

TAIHOU CLASS ASSAULT DROPSHIP

Type: Military Aerodyne
Use: Assault DropShip
Tech: Inner Sphere (Advanced)
Introduced: 3079
Mass: 12,000
Battle Value: 25,417

Dimensions
    Length: 200 meters
    Width: 90 meters
    Height: 30 meters

Fuel: 400 tons (12,000 points)
Tons/Burn-day: 1.84
Safe Thrust: 6
Maximum Thrust: 9
Heat Sinks: 250 [500]
Structural Integrity: 30

Armor
    Nose: 601
    Sides: 451
    Aft: 328

Cargo
    Bay 1: Cargo (472 tons)   2 Doors
    Bay 2: Small Craft (2)   1 Doors

Life Boats: 5
Escape Pods: 5
Crew: 4 Officers, 10 Enlisted/Non-rated, 9 Gunners, 36 Battle Armor Marines, 10 Bay personnel

Ammunition: 120 rounds Heavy Sub Capital Cannon ammunition (120 tons), 504 rounds MRM 40 Ammunition (28 tons), 288 rounds Anti Missile System Ammunition (24 tons), 10 rounds Screen Launcher ammunition (100 tons)

Notes: Carries 115 tons Heavy Ferro Aluminum armor, 120 tons Naval C³.

Weapons:	Capital Attack Values (Standard)				
Arc (Heat) Type	Short	Medium	Long	Extreme	Class
Nose (349 Heat)					
4 Heavy Sub-Capital Cannons (60 rounds)	28 (280)	28 (280)	—	—	Capital AC
3 Heavy PPC	5 (45)	5 (45)	—	—	PPC
3 MRM 40 +Apollo (42 rounds)	7 (72)	7 (72)	—	—	MRM
1 Screen Launcher (10 rounds)	—	—	—	—	Screen
LW/RW (84 Heat)					
3 Heavy PPC	5 (45)	5 (45)	—	—	PPC
3 MRM 40 +Apollo (42 rounds)	7 (72)	7 (72)	—	—	MRM
3 AMS (72 rounds)	1 (9)	—	—	—	AMS
LW/RW Aft (3 Heat)					
3 AMS (72 rounds)	1 (9)	—	—	—	AMS
Aft (81 Heat)					
3 Heavy PPC	5 (45)	5 (45)	—	—	PPC
3 MRM 40 +Apollo (42 rounds)	7 (72)	7 (72)	—	—	MRM

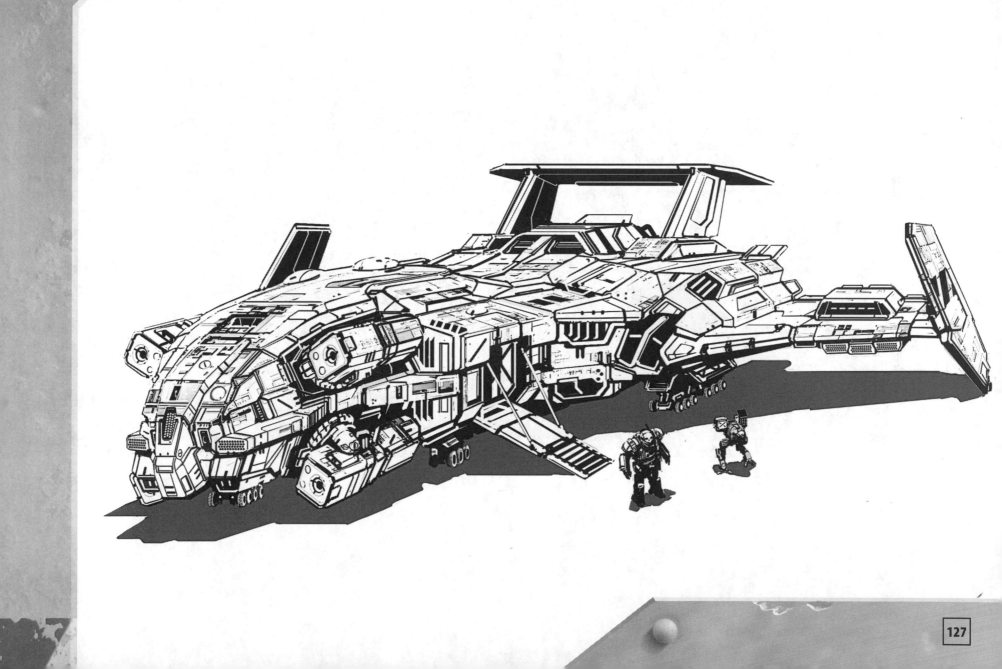

THE CLANS

Thirteen years have passed since any verifiable contact with the Clan Homeworlds. While we have entered a new era of uneasy peace with the Clans of the Inner Sphere, neither that peace nor our new alliances have allowed us to pierce the veil of silence that surrounds Clan space. All attempts to discover what has happened on their homeworlds have been rebuffed, and our best intelligence experts theorize that the Clans themselves may not fully understand the situation.

The complete cessation of supply from the Homeworlds has noticeably affected the Sphere Clans' ability to support their military infrastructure. Forced to rely on their Inner Sphere holdings, several archetypal Clan designs are now beyond their ability to manufacture. No new *Masakari* OmniMechs have appeared among Clan forces in more than a decade, the Wolves nearly lost their ability to manufacture their signature *Mad Cat* and only the Falcons appear to have production capacity for the *Thor* heavy OmniMech. The seven Inner Sphere Clans have been forced to adapt or die. For better or worse, they have all risen to the challenge in one way or another.

Blurring the lines between Clan and Inner Sphere, the Bears and Ravens have slowly begun to integrate with their Inner Sphere allies. The Diamond Sharks rely more and more on their mobile facilities and extensive trade networks, while the Falcons and Wolves have created armed worlds akin to Hesperus to protect their vital production interests. Even as the Clans work to rebuild their industrial base, they continue to adapt and innovate.

As the march to Terra began, the Clans were bringing new weapons to bear. Using the Protectorate campaign as a live-fire proving ground, they introduced more than a dozen new designs and major updates. The Ghost Bears conducted the first ever prototype trials of their *Ostrogoth* OmniFighter in an active naval battle. The Jade Falcons' *Flamberge* Standard B configuration was an outgrowth of experimentation during combat against the Blakists on Phecda. These field trials have given way to new designs and new make-ups of all the Clan toumans. In many cases, these newer units have virtually replaced the original sixteen OmniMech designs that stormed into the Inner Sphere thirty-five years ago.

Necessity may be the mother of invention for most, but for the Clans, the mother of invention is warfare.

—Lt. Col. Jake Crow
Assistant Director, Clan Affairs
Department of Military Intelligence

IRONHOLD ASSAULT BATTLE ARMOR

The Ironhold assault battle armor is Clan Jade Falcon's answer to the myriad other assault suits that have proliferated since the mid-3050s. Designed by the scientist caste in close cooperation with Elementals from Gamma Galaxy, it went through a furious development process during the early 3070s. That the Jade Falcons are ostensibly twenty years late in deploying heavy battle armor can be explained by their preference for mobility over brute strength. Early attempts to combine attributes of assault units with standard battle armor mobility resulted in negligible firepower.

The introduction of the high-powered and lightweight anti-personnel Gauss rifle in 3069 finally offered a solution to this problem. By mounting two of the weapons the technicians found they could finally supply firepower befitting a high-end suit. Soon afterward, an Elemental Trinary of the Third Falcon Talon Cluster was detached by order of Gamma Galaxy Commander Amelia Icaza to actively participate in the development of a new suit, codenamed Project Ferrum. This military influence guaranteed a speedy design phase. Lyran intelligence showed that program was warrior-driven with complete autonomy of the team toward all other castes.

Mounting jump jets that propel it an impressive sixty meters, the suit utilized standard armor molded to ensure safe jumps. Despite lacking the almost-trademark fire-resistant armor of other Falcon specialty suits, its defenses were impressive. The Gauss weapons offered excellent tactical range compared to other direct-fire weapons and good endurance compared to missiles. Their firepower was deemed respectable against armored targets and extremely deadly against infantry. Thus was born a suit that for the first time balanced all three parameters of Jade Falcon battle armor design.

As soon as Project Ferrum was ready for trial deployment, it was renamed Ironhold. Choosing their homeworld as the name for the new suit, at a time when Clan space appears to again be isolated from the Inner Sphere, symbolized the iron will with which the Jade Falcons pursued greatness. Within a short time, the Third Falcon Talon Cluster Elemental Trinary tested the suit in the Periphery to great effect. Though intelligence of the action remains sketchy, it has to be assumed that the Ironhold excelled, as the Trinary was quickly re-deployed to the Inner Sphere. In conflicts against the Inner Sphere, Elementals have demonstrated that their Ironholds could replace ProtoMechs in combat.

Despite being immediately slated for full-scale production, it took until 3077 for the manufacturing line on Sudeten to achieve active status. The delay happened due to the various conflicts the Jade Falcons were involved in that demanded an increasing flow of current armor designs. Nevertheless, the development was swift in comparison to many Inner Sphere design efforts of the same complexity.

It would not take long for these mass-produced Ironholds to be put to the test. In June of 3077 the Lyran thrust of the Coalition advance hit Shiloh. Believing the world to be better defended than intelligence indicated, Duke Kelswa-Steiner used two of his combat groups, including the Falcon Alpha and Wolf Delta Galaxies, to execute an assault on a key Shiloh military base. Once taken, the base had to be held in the face of determined Blakist efforts to dislodge them. In the tight confines of the base, the Ironholds' jump jets and thick armor made them brutally effective against lighter Blakist battle armor and light tank forces.

The Ironhold found an enthusiastic reception amongst warriors. Falcon Elementals, previously on the defensive against the conventional assault units of Clan Hell's Horses and Word of Blake, could now match or exceed their enemies' capabilities. The suit could be produced faster than any other assault armor due to its simple construction. Today, it has spread to almost all Galaxies of Clan Jade Falcon. The Trinary who first used the Ironhold has taken the suit to the Third Falcon Talon Cluster, now unique for equipping all their Elementals with it. This extensive deployment of the Ironhold has led to the predominance of the hitherto relatively obscure Jade Falcon Bang-Chu Elemental Bloodname, which dominates the Cluster.

Once production started on Sudeten, the responsible technicians were tasked to further develop the suit's full potential. Satisfied with its flexibility, further parameters included up-gunning the suit and utilizing fire-resistant armor that had become the norm for Jade Falcon armor. The bulk of the fireproof armor meant the Ironhold could no longer be safely controlled when jumping, so the jets were removed. The lack of mobility was offset by adding two additional AP Gauss rifles to the body of the suit. The fire suit, filling the traditional role of a pure assault armor, has again met with enthusiastic support from its operators.

Type: Ironhold
Manufacturer: Olivetti Weaponry
    Primary Factory: Sudeten

Tech Base: Clan
Chassis Type: Humanoid
Weight Class: Assault
Maximum Weight: 2,000 kg
Battle Value:
    77 (Standard)
    108 (Fire)
Swarm/Leg Attack/Mechanized/AP: No/No/No/No
Notes: None

Equipment		Slots	Mass
Chassis:			700 kg
Motive System (Standard):			
Ground MP:	1		0 kg
Jump MP:	2		500 kg
Motive System (Fire):			
Ground MP:	1		0 kg
Jump MP:	0		0 kg
Manipulators:			
Left Arm:	Basic Manipulator		0 kg
Right Arm:	Basic Manipulator		0 kg
Armor (Standard):	Standard		400 kg
Armor Value: 16 + 1 (Trooper)			
Armor (Fire):	Fire-Resistant	5	480 kg
Armor Value: 16 + 1 (Trooper)			

Weapons and Equipment	Location	Slots (Capacity)	Tonnage
Standard			
AP Gauss Rifle (20)	RA	2	200 kg
AP Gauss Rifle (20)	LA	2	200 kg
Fire			
AP Gauss Rifle (20)	RA	2	200 kg
AP Gauss Rifle (20)	LA	2	200 kg
2 AP Gauss Rifles (20 x2)	Body	4	400 kg

BALAC STRIKE VTOL

Mass: 25 tons
Movement Type: VTOL
Power Plant: Consolidated 135 XL
Cruising Speed: 119 kph
Flank Speed: 184 kph
Armor: Forging AM15 Ferro-Fibrous
Armament:
    2 Type 6 ATM-6
    1 Mk.3 ER Medium Laser
Manufacturer: New York Vehicle Y2 Facility
    Primary Factory: Trondheim
Communications System: Neil 9000 Comm System
Targeting and Tracking System: RCA Econotrac

Overview

The Diamond Sharks expected the Inner Sphere and Clan militaries would invest heavily to restore their forces to pre-Jihad strength. With their lower production complexities, this reconstruction was expected to initially focus on vehicle acquisition, so the Sharks examined a fast-to-market VTOL design.

It appears as if the Balac's design is not derivative of any established designs such as the Donar or Anhur. Another interesting aspect is that the Diamond Sharks seemingly spared no expense, supplying the craft with an XL fusion engine and top-of-the-line ATM 6 launchers. Despite the inclusion of these expensive technologies, the Balac is still one of the more affordable means to bring ATMs to the battlefield, and at a speed not easily rivaled by other VTOL craft.

Capabilities

Intended as anti-vehicle support, the Balac is ideally suited to the task, courtesy of its paired ATMs. The weapons allow the craft to engage hostile vehicles from beyond the range of their weapons, and its substantial ammunition bay grants the Balac extended durability in the field. For additional firepower, and in case it runs out of ATMs, the Balac can rely on an ER medium laser.

One disadvantage of the Balac is its armor protection, which allows the craft to survive incidental strikes from all but the heaviest of weapons but is insufficient to survive a sustained salvo. Since the majority of Balac operators prefer to fire at their targets while hovering, giving them a more stable firing platform, there have been numerous incidents of Balacs being surprised by a hostile 'Mech or vehicle in close proximity. As a result, most Balacs only hover and fire over terrain that has been vetted by friendly forces. Otherwise they typically orbit the enemy formation while close to their top speed.

Deployment

Despite a price tag noticeably above the norm for VTOLs the Balac found an eager market both among the Clans and the Inner Sphere until Exarch Stone's swords-to-plowshares philosophy became widespread enough to slow sales. It is still a sought-after asset among mercenary units and continues to be common in most standing militaries, being preferred over many other designs that are being phased out.

Variants

The inherent flexibility of the ATM has reduced the need for variant craft, although the Diamond Sharks do produce a version that reduces the ammunition supply to mount an ECM suite and active probe. This version also swaps the ER medium laser out for TAG.

A "budget" version of the Balac exists as well, using a standard fusion engine and downgrading the ATM 6s to LRM 15s. The ammunition supply is curtailed to compensate for the heavier engine.

Notable Crews

Point Commander Caleb: A warrior in the Hell's Horses Clan, Caleb is an ancient soldier even by Inner Sphere standards, having been born in the last year of the 30th Century. He has managed to survive to this day through a combination of fierce battlefield prowess and his relatively inoffensive manners. Being assigned to a solahma unit for the better part of four decades has not crushed his spirit as it is wont to do. Caleb continues to gleefully assault any and all of his Clan's enemies, and his extensive career has given him the distinction of having killed the most combat vehicles of any other VTOL pilot we are aware of.

Kommandant Samantha Thomlinson: As a member of the Lyran Guards, Thomlinson has been assigned to the majority of the brigade's component units. She has become known for her "triad" attack maneuver, where she utilizes speed to place her VTOL company, including Balacs, at 120-degree angles to the intended target formation. One of the three prongs then attacks, causing the target to expose itself to receiving rear shots from one of the other two prongs if they pursue. Turning to retreat is nigh-impossible for ground based forces.

In one instance, Thomlinson was able to harry a battalion of tracked armor in this fashion over the course of three days while stopping frequently for rest and ammunition reloads in an unpredictable pattern. Despite having lost only eight tanks the commander of the battalion surrendered at dawn on the fourth day.

BALAC STRIKE VTOL

Type: **Balac**
Technology Base: Clan
Movement Type: VTOL
Tonnage: 25
Battle Value: 1,271

Equipment		Mass
Internal Structure:		2.5
Engine:	135	4
Type:	XL Fusion	
Cruising MP:	11	
Flank MP:	17	
Heat Sinks:	10	0
Control Equipment:		1.5
Lift Equipment:		2.5
Power Amplifier:		0

Equipment		Mass
Turret:		0
Armor Factor (Ferro):	48	2.5
	Armor Value	
Front	15	
R/L Side	12/12	
Rear	7	
Rotor	2	

Weapons and Ammo	Location	Tonnage
2 ATM 6	Front	7
Ammo (ATM) 40	Body	4
ER Medium Laser	Front	1

David White

ZEPHYROS INFANTRY SUPPORT VEHICLE

Mass: 25 tons
Movement Type: Wheeled
Power Plant: Fusion 180
Cruising Speed: 86 kph
Flank Speed: 129 kph
Armor: "Magnum" Ferro-Fibrous Composite
Armament:
2 Series 2b Extended Range Medium Lasers
2 Series HL-II Light Machine Guns
Manufacturer: Swedenborg Heavy Industries
Primary Factory: Kirchbach
Communications System: Build 1685 Tacticom with ECM
Targeting and Tracking System: Series VI Integrated TTS

Overview

(Editor's Note: Recent intelligence out of Hell's Horse space shows that the Horses are continuing to establish themselves in the Inner Sphere. – JC) Cut off from their Home World production centers, the vehicle heavy Hell's Horses has taken this as an opportunity and not a weakness. Lacking production capacity for many of their infantry support units, such as the Odin, Mithras and Indra, they chose to forge a new design. Taking lessons learned from the last three decades of warfare, the Horses have just completed field trials of their new ISV, the Zephyros.

Capabilities

Named for the Greek god of the West-Wind who, in the shape of a horse, drew the chariot of Zeus, the mandate for the Zephyros was rapid response infantry support unit. Focused on this mission, it does not try and be a multi-role unit, leaving recon to hover or VTOL units and heavier guns to main line tanks. A standard fusion engine drives it at a cruise speed of 86 kph, matching the speed of the older Odin and out pacing the Mithras. The rugged dune-buggy style chassis and oversized wheels give it greater ground clearance than the ground hugging Odin, while being more durable the hover skirted Svantovit.

One of the greatest lessons learned by the Horses, is that of battlefield sustainability. On their return to the Inner Sphere, they observed how the Bears were using "lesser" Kungsarme vehicles that carried the armor to stand up to the thin skinned Clan tanks and tough out the longer battle. As a result, over a fifth of the Zephyros's mass is dedicated to ferro fibrous armor and an ECM suite offers some protection from advanced missile munitions. Able to withstand fire from even the largest battlefield weapons the Zephyros is able to withdraw from battle where a thinner skinned Odin would be a smoking wreck of burnt rubber and armor shreds.

To carry out its support mission the Zephyros mounts a simple yet elegantly effective weapons payload. Primary firepower comes from a pair of medium extended-range lasers. These clan model weapons can threaten most lighter tanks, Clan or Inner Sphere, and are equally effective at bringing down battle armor units. The dual light machine guns, with their own dedicated gunner, are capable of suppressing or outright wiping out conventional infantry formations.

Deployment

Rolling off newly finished production lines at the Swedenborg complex on Kirchbach, the Zephyros is expected to see wide spread deployment among the Horses Touman. Simple and fast to produce, with its success in field trials has made the Zephyros a sought after tank by front and second line infantry commanders. Iota Galaxy is experimenting with battle armor binaries that use Anhurs for transport and Zephyross for direct ground support of the Elementals.

On the borders of the Inner Sphere, the Hell's Horses did not have long to wait before experiencing the age old scourge of piracy. Toland, having suffered repeated pirate attacks, had a Trinary of Iota Galaxy's infantry heavy Sixty-Seventh BattleMech cluster stationed to it in 3085. In April the pirate band Gort's Hounds struck the world, hoping to make off with some of the worlds rare minerals. A Star of Zephyross, supporting the Sixty-Seventh's heavy Solahma infantry, were in the path of the pirate band's advance. Using the Trinary's cavalry points and Anhur VTOL for reconnaissance and herding, the Zephyross laid in wait for the advancing pirate force. When the pirate band, a mixture of mostly conventional forces backed by a handful of BattleMechs, paused under the fire of the entrenched heavy infantry, the Star of Zephyross cut through the pirate formation targeting two of the BattleMechs. Their heavy armor allowed them to survive return fire and massed extended-range laser fire brought down one of the 'Mechs and crippled the other. Turning about the light tanks dove into the enemy formation again and again. By the close of the battle, half the Zephyross were destroyed and most others barely operational but the larger sized pirate force had been completely wiped out.

Variants

The Horses are experimenting with making the pintle mounted machine guns a free floating turret, thus allowing the machine gunner to fire independently of the extended-range lasers as opposed to the standard model which limits the machine guns to a limited arc on either side of the lasers. To make room for the turret structure, a half ton of ammunition is being removed. Prototypes are currently experimenting with armor layout, to properly protect the more exposed turret ring of the LMG turret.

CLAN

ZEPHYROS INFANTRY SUPPORT VEHICLE

Type: **Zephyros**
Technology Base: Clan
Movement Type: Wheeled
Tonnage: 25
Battle Value: 840

Equipment		Mass
Internal Structure:		2.5
Engine:	180	10.5
Type:	Fusion	
Cruising MP:	8	
Flank MP:	12	
Heat Sinks:	10	0
Control Equipment:		1.5
Turret:		.5
Armor Factor (Ferro):	105	5.5

	Armor Value
Front	31
R/L Side	18/18
Rear	18
Turret	20

Weapons and Ammo	Location	Tonnage
2 ER Medium Lasers	Turret	2
2 Light Machine Guns	Turret	.5
Ammo (LMG) 200	Body	1
ECM Suite	Body	1

JOUST BE700 MEDIUM TANK

Mass: 40 tons
Movement Type: Tracked
Power Plant: 200 XL Fusion
Cruising Speed: 54 kph
Flank Speed: 86 kph
Armor: Advanced Compound Beta
Armament:
    1 Series 7NC ER Large Laser
    1 Type 9 Series 1 ATM 9 Rack
    4 Series 2c Light Machine Guns
Manufacturer: Barcella Beta
 Primary Factory: Irece
Communications System: Build 1685/6 Tacticom
Targeting and Tracking System: Series XXVIII IWS

Overview

The battlefield and commercial success of the SM1 tank destroyer encouraged Clan Nova Cat's scientists and merchants to bring another combat vehicle to market as quickly as possible. Unfortunately for them, "as quickly as possible" was hampered by the Jihad, and it wasn't until 3077 that they succeeded in getting their new Joust medium tank into the Clan's touman.

Capabilities

Though its light mass barely qualifies the Joust for inclusion in the medium weight class, the tank is by no means weak on either armament or armor. Almost ten tons of Compound Beta ferro-fibrous armor encases the Joust's sensitive innards with protection equal to that of many heavy tanks. An extended-range large laser provides the Joust's primary offensive armament, a threatening weapon to even the heaviest assault BattleMech. A nine-tube advanced tactical missile system—liberally provided with three separate ammunition magazines to offer a mix of munitions—sits beside the laser and allows the Joust's gunner to engage at any range. For close-in support, four light machine guns are spread across the turret in a deadly phalanx.

The Joust is slower than many vehicles of comparable mass, but it is fast enough to move with the heavier assault elements it is designed to accompany. In fact, when placed with Mars or Ishtar Starmates it can act as heavy cavalry, given that it is normally much faster than the rest of its Star. When placed against swifter enemies, the solution is simple: trust in the thick armor, the big laser and the gunner's skill.

Rumors have gathered around the Joust in recent months based on reports from the Triarii that the ER large laser misfires without being triggered. As the Triarii Protectors are the least-experienced units in the Republic Armed Forces, most observers put these reports down to inexperience, but in the past two months similar reports have been made in the Draconis Combine. If they prove true, it would be the first time quality complaints have been lodged against an Irece manufacturer since the Nova Cats took over.

Deployment

The Irece manufactory has been in full production since the first Joust tracked off the assembly line, and Stars of this tank have been shipped to every Nova Cat second-line Cluster and many front-line formations as well. A number have also been sighted in Draconis Combine formations.

Many of the Nova Cats who remained inside The Republic with Devlin Stone brought Jousts with them, and the RAF has been negotiating with the Nova Cat merchant caste to acquire a steady supply of the tank. A number of the Hastati and Triarii are clamoring for this powerful tank after seeing it in action on the Capellan border.

Variants

Only one variant of the Joust has appeared, which replaces the advanced tactical missile system with a ten-tube long-range missile battery. The savings in mass allows the tank to add another four light machine guns, greatly increasing its anti-infantry ability and utility in urban combat. Though the first BE701s are still undergoing testing on Irece, a number of pundits have speculated that the Nova Cats intend to sell this version of the Joust to Inner Sphere buyers, who might not have a logistical system able to procure the expensive advanced tactical missiles. Reinforcing this supposition is the replacement of the expensive XL engine with a cheaper standard engine, easily procurable away from Clan production facilities.

JOUST BE700 MEDIUM TANK

Type: **Joust**
Technology Base: Clan
Movement Type: Tracked
Tonnage: 40
Battle Value: 1,307

Equipment		Mass
Internal Structure:		4
Engine:	200	7
Type:	XL Fusion	
Cruising MP:	5	
Flank MP:	8	
Heat Sinks:	12	2
Control Equipment:		2
Lift Equipment:		0
Power Amplifier:		0

Equipment		Mass
Turret:		1
Armor Factor (Ferro):	180	9.5
	Armor Value	
Front	46	
R/L Side	38/38	
Rear	28	
Turret	30	

Weapons and Ammo	Location	Tonnage
ER Large Laser	Turret	4
ATM 9	Turret	5
Ammo (ATM) 21	Body	3
4 Light Machine Guns	Turret	1
Light Active Probe	Front	.5
Ammo (Light MG) 200	Body	1

David White

137

ELDINGAR HOVER SLED

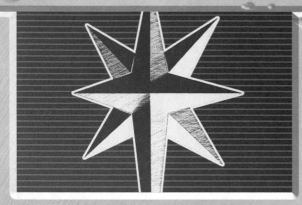

Mass: 50 tons
Movement Type: Hover
Power Plant: Type 215 XL Fusion
Cruising Speed: 97 kph
Flank Speed: 151 kph
Armor: Compound 2110 Ferro Fibrous
Armament:
    1 CC-9 Series Advanced Tactical Missile Systems
    3 Pattern J2 Streak 2 SRM Launchers
Manufacturer: Gorton, Kingsley & Thorpe Enterprises
    Primary Factory: Rasalhague
Communications System: Consolidated BMR 6 with ECM
Targeting and Tracking System: TRTTS Mark II

Overview

Peace is a relative term in the Inner Sphere. While the Jihad that engulfed every nation has burnt out most passion for war, embers still flicker to life. The symbiotic nation made up of the Ghost Bears and Free Rasalhague Republic is currently very vulnerable. Over half the Ghost Bear Touman was destroyed in their single-minded drive to eradicate the Blakists. They also lack complete faith in their Inner Sphere citizens, limiting how far they can rely on the natives of their worlds. In an effort to cover the holes in their defense, they have turned to many different options, including vehicles such as the Eldingar to build up their second line forces. The original frame was designed by a local company and assigned the name for lightning in their native Icelandic. Since Ghost Bear leadership expected it to be utilized mainly by natives and sub-par warriors, they didn't bother changing the name when they completed the design.

Capabilities

Possessing capable speed for a hovercraft the Eldingar can engage and disengage quickly, making it an ideal reaction vehicle, especially against raiders. By mounting an advanced tactical missile launcher, this hovercraft can provide fire support outside the range of most return fire. Should they need to move in close, the power of the weapons will increase as more powerful missiles come into range. Additionally, a trio of Streak SRM launchers can add their punch around 350 meters. The open sled design allows incredibly fast deployment of its battle armor support.

One of the most useful pieces of equipment isn't a powerful or reliable weapon, but an ECM suite. Not terribly common in the Clan arsenal, the Ghost Bears find themselves in greater need of ECM coverage with the C3 and other targeting/communications gear used increasingly by their neighbors. The standard doctrine for forces including an Eldingar is to concentrate on disrupting these systems over actual combat. In many cases, the vulnerable hovercraft will try to find cover that blocks enemy fire but still allows the ECM to affect them. The manufacturer included more than seven tons of ferro-fibrous armor for when they can't find such cover.

Deployment

The Eldingar has an uneven deployment among the Ghost Bear and FRR forces. When distributed to Clan forces, it is considered a vehicle for mediocre armor crews, primarily a rear-echelon player to assist the BattleMechs and Battle Amor. Amongst Free Rasalhague Republic forces in the Ghost Bear Dominion, the Eldingar is an advanced machine reserved for commanders and the best crews with the best special infantry available. This dichotomy has given the Eldingar an interesting reputation in the Dominion and led to more than a few drunken brawls. Additionally, raiders who have encountered it before might misjudge the hovercraft based on earlier experiences with different forces.

Dominion forces actually used this to their advantage against a pirate incursion on Porthos. Two companies of 'Mechs with an attached armor battalion landed with their forces split on either end of the Sienne Valley. The defenders were a mix of Ghost Bears and Rasalhague militia. The militia forces met the northernmost raiders while the Clan forces protected their rear. Six Eldingars were amongst the first forces to hit the invaders and destroyed three vehicles and a 'Mech in the initial engagement. The commander noticed that they recoiled when the Eldingars came around to re-engage. He had the Ghost Bear Eldingars dispatched to join the battle while the militia crews were sent to delay the southern attack. Despite the less effective soldiers piloting the Eldingars, the northern prong still pulled back when they came to attack. Boxing them in, the militia was able to destroy the northern forces and join the Clan forces in sending the remaining raiders off planet.

Variants

Ghost Bear forces are experimenting with a new version of the Eldingar. Rather than using the ATM system it mounts two Streak launchers firing LRMs instead of SRMs. While lacking the range of the ATM ER missiles, they guarantee that all their missiles will hit, providing a heftier punch at longer ranges. In addition, the ECM system was upgraded to an advanced version for even more electronic warfare capability. The infantry bay has been filled by this larger turret. These new fire support Eldingars have only been seen piloted by the best Clan Eldingar crews.

ELDINGAR HOVER SLED

Type: **Eldingar Hover Sled**
Technology Base: Clan
Movement Type: Hover
Tonnage: 50
Battle Value: 1,402

Equipment		Mass
Internal Structure:		5
Engine:	215	10
Type:	XL Fusion	
Cruising MP:	9	
Flank MP:	14	
Heat Sinks:	10	0
Control Equipment:		2.5
Lift Equipment:		5

Equipment		Mass
Turret:		1
Armor Factor (Ferro):	144	7.5
	Armor Value	
Front	38	
R/L Side	28/28	
Rear	24	
Turret	26	

Weapons and Ammo	Location	Tonnage
ATM 9	Turret	5
Ammo (ATM) 28	Body	4
3 Streak SRM 2	Turret	3
Ammo (Streak) 50	Body	1
ECM Suite	Body	1
Infantry Transport Bay	Body	5

CARNIVORE ASSAULT TANK

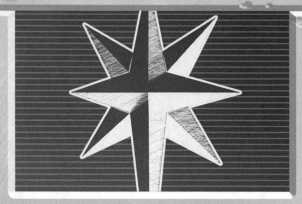

Mass: 80 tons
Movement Type: Tracked
Power Plant: 320 XL
Cruising Speed: 43 kph
Flank Speed: 64 kph
Armor: Advanced/3
Armament:
    2 Series II Gauss Rifles
    2 Series 2d ER Medium Lasers
    2 Series XIV Heavy Machine Guns
Manufacturer: W-7 Facilities
    Primary Factory: Weingarten
Communications System: 2SH C3 with ECM Suite
Targeting and Tracking System: Build 4 JVJ TTS

Overview

The Carnivore was produced in a crash program to help rebuild the Wolf Touman after the liberation of Terra. Despite the unity against the Blakist threat and the damage Coalition armed forces suffered, the Wolves remained as concerned about defense as anyone else. While armored vehicles weren't granted the same respect as 'Mechs, battle armor or aerospace fighters by the warriors of Clan Wolf, they were easier and cheaper to build—just what the Clan needed. The scientists involved were ordered to reuse as many existing components as possible but still make an effective combat machine. The early reviews seem to indicate that they met both challenges.

Capabilities

Utilizing an extralight fusion engine, the Carnivore packs a good amount of armor and weaponry. The simple Advanced/3 armor may not provide as much protection as ferro-fibrous armor, but it is cheaper, easier to manufacture and imposes fewer space constraints. A CASE system is included, providing a better chance of recovering both tank and crew in the event of catastrophic explosions. The modest sixty-four kph speed of the tank will not win any records but it is better than many of the tanks of its size.

The Carnivore isn't built for the short-range combat of many assault tanks. Twin Gauss rifles give it plenty of range with which to abuse an opponent, though with only thirty-two rounds the gunners should make the most of their ammunition. The rifles are the same model being used on the *Sun Cobra*. Backing up those is a pair of extended-range medium lasers. They are excellent middle-range weapons and provide the Carnivore with combat endurance. Finally, a pair of heavy machine guns provide a nasty surprise for any infantry unwise enough to close with the Carnivore. While they are effective against other units, one salvo can easily destroy a platoon out in the open or even cripple one in cover. For communications and targeting, both systems were lifted straight off the Ares that has served the Wolves well in a second-line role. For additional protection an ECM suite was added, a necessity in combating the increase of electronic warfare on the modern battlefield.

Deployment

Released in mid-3082, the Carnivore has been assigned to temporarily shore up frontline units. The tank has also found its way to the open marketplace, though mainly as variants. A few of the second-line versions have found their way into, appropriately, second-line units, though minimally—second-line forces did not take significant damage after the cease-fire with the Horses. Commanders prefer that if a force has a significant amount of Carnivores that one or two HAG versions be included, as the spread on the HAG allows it to act as a clean-up unit with the big holes the Gausses inflict. The additional defensive equipment might also be a factor, though few would ever admit it.

Variants

With the success of the basic chassis a version was made to trade with the Falcons, who had a larger 'Mech-producing industrial base. The Gauss rifles were removed and replaced with a massive HAG while the lasers were replaced with pulse versions. The machine guns were dropped and in their place dual AP Gausses reside. For additional protection, a pair of anti-missile systems was added to the turret.

With the success of the HAG version the Wolves ordered a more stripped-down version be made and sold to a wider customer base. So far the Lyrans and Wolves-in-Exile have purchased some of these, though some would argue there is little difference between the two these days. The second-line version lacks the extralight engine and reduces the weaponry significantly. A single class-10 LB-X cannon replaces the Gauss weapons, while the machine guns are downgraded to light versions. As with the HAG variant, the lasers are changed to pulse versions.

CLAN

CARNIVORE ASSAULT TANK

Type: Carnivore
Technology Base: Clan
Movement Type: Tracked
Tonnage: 80
Battle Value: 1,997

Equipment		Mass
Internal Structure:		8
Engine:	320	17.5
Type:	XL Fusion	
Cruising MP:	4	
Flank MP:	6	
Heat Sinks:	10	0
Control Equipment:		4
Turret:		2.5
Armor Factor:	248	15.5

	Armor Value
Front	62
R/L Side	46/46
Rear	42
Turret	52

Weapons and Ammo	Location	Tonnage
2 Gauss Rifles	Turret	24
Ammo (Gauss) 32	Body	4
2 ER Medium Lasers	Front	2
Heavy Machine Gun	Right	.5
Heavy Machine Gun	Left	.5
Ammo (Heavy MG) 50	Body	.5
ECM Suite	Body	1

141

ARBALEST

Mass: 25 tons
Chassis: Star League NCX
Power Plant: Vlar 125
Cruising Speed: 54 kph
Maximum Speed: 86 kph
Jump Jets: None
    Jump Capacity: None
Armor: Irece Standard
Armament:
    2 Series 2a Mk. 5 Extended Range Medium Lasers
    2 Mk. 46 Type II LRM 10 Launchers
Manufacturer: Irece Alpha
    Primary Factory: Irece
Communications System: Raldon R1 with ECM
Targeting and Tracking System: Dalban Hirez II

Overview

Like the *Ocelot* before it the Nova Cats developed the *Arbalest* as part of the program to build up their second-line forces. Unveiled in 3077, the design emphasized reducing the drain on the Nova Cats' limited supply of Clan technology—thus minimizing the strain on their limited production facilities.

Capabilities

Quite slow for a light BattleMech, the *Arbalest's* design places emphasis on weaponry, which is also where its Clan technology is concentrated. Two compact Mk. 46 Type II LRM launchers provide respectable long-range firepower, and two arm-mounted extended-range medium lasers effectively double the *Arbalest's* throw weight at shorter

ranges. To counter the spread of sophisticated C³ systems—especially in Blakist forces—the 'Mech is equipped with a powerful ECM module. *Arbalest*s can forge ahead and disrupt enemy fire control networks, transforming a battle into something more akin to the single combats with which Clan MechWarriors are more comfortable.

Carrying all this weaponry and equipment comes at a price; the *Arbalest's* paltry three and a half tons of armor places the BattleMech at a distinct disadvantage in prolonged engagements. The need to adopt hit-and-run tactics sits poorly with many Clan MechWarriors.

Another advantage of the *Arbalest's* minimalist design philosophy is the ease with which it can be maintained and repaired. While still a far cry from the sophistication of Omni technology, the limited maintenance resources available to many second-line formations makes this new design popular with the technician caste members who must work on it.

Deployment

Faced with the fall of the second Star League and the Word of Blake's ferocious response, the Nova Cats began to strengthen Omicron Galaxy by promoting it from its status as a provisional formation to a fully operational second-line Galaxy. Intended to be quick and inexpensive to build, the *Arbalest* was perfect for this project. Since its introduction the 'Mech has also made its way into other second-line (and even on occasion frontline) Clusters.

The *Arbalest's* combat debut came in early 3077 fighting alongside *Pack Hunter*s and *Ha Otoko*s. Nova Cat MechWarriors used their *Arbalest*s' ECM systems to disrupt the C³ networks employed by their Blakist foes. Many of the new 'Mechs were destroyed but their sacrifice disrupted the Word of Blake's cohesion and ensured a victory for the Clansmen.

In late 3077 *Arbalest*s of the Nova Cats' Delta Galaxy tangled with Word of Blake forces on Sheratan. In the hard fight for this world the *Arbalest* demonstrated its effectiveness in neutralizing enemy C³ networks. In 3078, Delta clashed with elements of the Blakist Protectorate Militia on Epsilon Eridani. Learning from their previous encounters, the Blakists deployed fast hovercraft and battle armor to hunt down the *Arbalest*s and other ECM-equipped units early in the battle. Victory cost the Nova Cats far heavier casualties.

Ever vigilant for the deal, Clan Diamond Shark has traded the Nova Cats much-needed Clan technology for the output of several limited production runs. These *Arbalest*s were subsequently sold to mercenary commands and the Republic of the Sphere. Hired to protect mining facilities on Cammal, the mercenary command Covenant's Commandos employed a pair of *Arbalest*s to harass a combined-arms force of pirates. The mercenary BattleMechs sprung a series of ambushes on the raiders, buying Captain Matthew Covenant time to redeploy the rest of his company and catch the pirates in a vice from which none would escape.

Variants

Two major variants of the *Arbalest* have been introduced by the Nova Cats. The first, the *Arbalest* 2, addresses the frailty of the original by increasing armor protection to the maximum the light chassis will carry. Ground speed is boosted by the installation of MASC. In order to accommodate these changes, the left-torso missile launcher and magazine have been removed.

The *Arbalest* 3 is better suited to close-range battles and to fighting battle armor. It improves protection by switching to ferro-fibrous armor, which is further improved by replacing the ECM system with an additional ton of armor. Each arm-mounted laser is replaced with two extended-range small lasers.

ARBALEST

Type: **Arbalest**
Technology Base: Clan
Tonnage: 25
Battle Value: 1,029

Equipment		Mass
Internal Structure:		2.5
Engine:	125	4
Walking MP:	5	
Running MP:	8	
Jumping MP:	0	
Heat Sinks:	10 [20]	0
Gyro:		2
Cockpit:		3
Armor Factor:	56	3.5

	Internal Structure	Armor Value
Head	3	8
Center Torso	8	8
Center Torso (rear)		2
R/L Torso	6	5
R/L Torso (rear)		2
R/L Arm	4	5
R/L Leg	6	7

Weapons and Ammo	Location	Critical	Tonnage
ER Medium Laser	RA	1	1
LRM 10	RT	1	2.5
Ammo (LRM) 12	RT	1	1
ECM Suite	H	1	1
LRM 10	LT	1	2.5
Ammo (LRM) 12	LT	1	1
ER Medium Laser	LA	1	1

David White

PACK HUNTER II

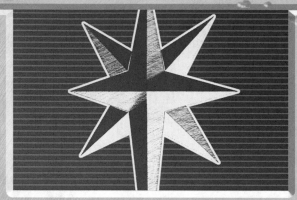

Mass: 30 tons
Chassis: Type AR1 Endo Steel
Power Plant: Light Force (ExtraLight) 210
Cruising Speed: 75 kph
Maximum Speed: 118 kph
Jump Jets: Leaper Model, L5
    Jump Capacity: 210 meters
Armor: Royal-7a Ferro-Fibrous
Armament:
    1 Ripper Series A1 Extended Range PPC
    2 Series 2b Extended Range Medium Laser
    2 Delta X B-Pods
Manufacturer: WC Site 3
    Primary Factory: Arc-Royal
Communications System: Trueborn Ultra 945B
Targeting and Tracking System: Hunter 5 Dedicated TTS

Overview

A proof-of-concept of the Wolf-in-Exile Clan's manufacturing capability on Arc-Royal, the *Pack Hunter* was slated for obsolescence from the very start, its line to be retooled to build OmniMechs. Matters changed when Arc-Royal was attacked in force by the Word of Blake in March of 3072. Efforts to produce the OmniMech successor of the *Pack Hunter* were ceased and the design work was used to generate a comprehensive update of the BattleMech. First deployment of the *Pack Hunter II* did not occur until 3077. It was delayed by Exile assistance in the efforts to begin production of the *Mongoose II* at Arc-Royal MechWorks,

and further delayed when an opportunity for collaboration with the Hell's Horses arose, which ultimately resulted in the *Cygnus*.

Work on the *Pack Hunter II* was complicated by repeated attempts by the Wolves to incorporate some of their cutting-edge technologies, such as endo-composite structure, modular armor and actuator enhancement systems. While all these technologies failed to meet the requirements of mass-production, the extralight engine necessary to free up mass for their installation was retained. Instead, the *Pack Hunter II*'s arsenal was expanded. Its armor protection was also enhanced to about eighty percent of the total possible on a thirty-ton frame by using ferro-fibrous armor. Another enhancement, perhaps inspired by Khan Kell's own experience, was the installation of a full-head ejection system. Finally, the *Pack Hunter II* is one of the first Wolf 'Mechs to receive B-pods.

Capabilities

A substantial improvement of the original design, the *Pack Hunter II* benefits from a pair of ER medium lasers. Operationally, *Pack Hunter* pilots continue to get the most out of their machines when they use their outstanding mobility to keep their quarry at arm's length. Small groups of *Pack Hunters* peck mercilessly at their foe until they swarm in for the kill. Clan Wolf MechWarriors have taken to the *Hunter*'s ejection system, considering it a tool that reduces waste in the warrior caste. The B-pods have also proven their worth. Apparently an afterthought installed when the Clan failed to deploy either modular armor or AES in the legs, they have been instrumental in allowing *Pack Hunters* to survive battle armor ambushes on several worlds.

Deployment

Since completing construction the Wolves have been supplying the *Pack Hunter II* to their allies, which explains how some have made their way to the Hell's Horses as well as the Combine. Their existence among mercenary ranks is likewise unsurprising as Stone's Coalition was another recipient of the capable design, as has been The Republic since its formation.

Variants

Only months after full-scale production of the *Pack Hunter II* had begun, production of the XL engine was temporarily halted by sabotage action by a group of anti-Clan insurgents on Arc-Royal. The Wolves managed to acquire a supply of light fusion engines to continue *Pack Hunter II* production, but the heavier engine forced technicians to remove the ER medium lasers and to downgrade the B-pods to A-pods. On the other hand, they were able to increase armor protection by half a ton.

A more recent variant drops the lasers and B-Pods in order to add an array of improved jump jets. Expanding the jump range to an amazing 300 meters, this *Pack Hunter II* lacks a ton of armor and installs an extralight gyro to allow the design to retain its Ripper Series A1.

Notable MechWarriors

Star Captain Harlan: Born on Arc-Royal as Harlan Jacovi, Harlan is one of several Spheroids who have endeavored to join the Wolf Clan based on their merits. Joining at the relatively old age of thirty-three, Harlan won his first Trial of Position only two years later. He has proven himself an extremely capable MechWarrior, and many consider him to be one of the Clan's most competent warriors. He has managed to prove himself a capable commander on the battlefield several times during the Jihad. The only impairment of his career stems from his lack of a Bloodname. As he lacks a maternal line to the Clan Founders, a movement has started within the Exiles for Phelan Kell to create a new Bloodname. The issue is polarizing even with a Clan as progressive as that of Khan Kell.

Type: **Pack Hunter II**
Technology Base: Clan
Tonnage: 30
Battle Value: 1,797

Equipment		Mass
Internal Structure:	Endo Steel	1.5
Engine:	210 XL	4.5
Walking MP:	7	
Running MP:	11	
Jumping MP:	7	
Heat Sinks:	10 [20]	0
Gyro:		3
Cockpit:		3
Armor Factor:	86	4.5

	Internal Structure	Armor Value
Head	3	7
Center Torso	10	12
Center Torso (rear)		3
R/L Torso	7	11
R/L Torso (rear)		2
R/L Arm	5	9
R/L Leg	7	10

Weapons and Ammo	Location	Critical	Tonnage
ER Medium Laser	RA	1	1
ER PPC	RT	2	6
ER Medium Laser	LA	1	1
B-Pod	RL	1	1
B-Pod	LL	1	1
Jump Jets	RT	3	1.5
Jump Jet	CT	1	.5
Jump Jets	LT	3	1.5

Note: If playing under Advanced Rules, treat head as having a Full-Head Ejection System.

MORRIGAN

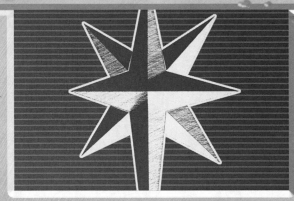

Mass: 35 tons
Chassis: NCIS Endo Steel Type L
Power Plant: Consolidated 280 XL
Cruising Speed: 86 kph
Maximum Speed: 129 kph
Jump Jets: None
    Jump Capacity: None
Armor: Alpha Composite Ferro-Fibrous
Armament:
    1 Model X Heavy Large Laser
    3 Type 3 Series ATM 3s
Manufacturer: Mualang Alpha
    Primary Factory: Coudoux
Communications System: Sipher CommSys 5
Targeting and Tracking System: Cat's Eyes 7

Overview

Clan Nova Cat had a need for a new scout 'Mech and the Draconis Combine was willing to help them in order to gain access to Clan technology for their elite units. The Combine provided resources and manpower while the Nova Cats provided technical expertise. The resulting design is not one of great flexibility but appears effective. While the design has been built and well-received, politics are still impairing the design's deployment. The Nova Cats want to limit the number provided to the Combine and in turn the Combine is shorting raw material shipments until they receive what they believe is a fair share of the number produced.

Capabilities

The *Morrigan* possess a good amount of speed for a machine of its size, able to keep up with the Combine's *Owens* or the Nova Cats' *Dragonfly*. The active probe improves the scouting abilities of the design immensely, helping the pilot find hidden units that would otherwise be missed. The armor is decent, though pilots always demand more. The DCMS pilots are very appreciative of the integral CASE on each torso and that the engine is smaller than a comparable Inner Sphere extralight engine. The best of the design, however, is in the weapons array.

Three advanced tactical missile racks, each with three tubes and sharing three tons of ammunition, make one wonder if someone favored the number three. With the incredible range of the weapons' extended-range missiles, the *Morrigan* can chew up enemy armor before it can return fire. When the enemy can fire back, the pilot can then use the design's speed to close. There the high explosive missiles combined with the heavy hitting power of the heavy large laser can finish off the enemy. When engaging larger opponents, the pilot of a *Morrigan* should never slow down, as its armor cannot take the pounding that designs twice its size can. Luckily an advanced targeting computer can help mitigate the heavy laser's inherent inaccuracy, which, combined with a design that should be kept at high speeds, is severely detrimental. Additionally, the heat build-up from the laser practically eliminates the ability to fire the missiles until it has abated.

Deployment

Illustrating the difference between the two fighting forces, the Nova Cats have dispatched the *Morrigan* mainly to second-line units while the Combine has only distributed the 'Mech to its best-equipped units. Some frontline Nova Cat units in need of replacements have also been issued the *Morrigan*, though the pilots grumble at not having proper OmniMechs. Among Combine units, the *Morrigan* is mainly distributed to the Sword of Light, Ryuken and Genyosha. DEST has also been given access to the design.

Variants

With less than regular access to the advanced missile munitions, the Combine design team lobbied for an energy-based variant. By removing the missile systems and the probe, four laser systems could be added in each torso. A pair of extended-range medium lasers would augment the heavy while four smaller versions would add punch up close, though at better ranges than the Inner Sphere pilots were used to.

A pair of small pulse lasers allows incredible accuracy up close and provide anti-personnel support. The targeting computer was enhanced to handle the additional weaponry and another heat sink was added to prevent the heat burden from rising too high. Designers also added additional armor, which, when combined with removing the ammunition, increased the survivability of the design significantly.

The Combine has further modified several of these variants for their special operations units, removing the heavy laser and targeting computer to install a 'Mech Taser.

MORRIGAN

Type: **Morrigan**
Technology Base: Clan
Tonnage: 35
Battle Value: 1,523

Equipment		Mass
Internal Structure:	Endo Steel	2
Engine:	280 XL	8
Walking MP:	8	
Running MP:	12	
Jumping MP:	0	
Heat Sinks:	10 [20]	0
Gyro:		3
Cockpit:		3
Armor Factor (Ferro):	105	5.5

	Internal Structure	Armor Value
Head	3	9
Center Torso	11	15
Center Torso (rear)		7
R/L Torso	8	10
R/L Torso (rear)		5
R/L Arm	6	8
R/L Leg	8	14

Weapons and Ammo	Location	Critical	Tonnage
Heavy Large Laser	RA	3	4
ATM 3	RT	2	1.5
Ammo (ATM) 40	RT	2	2
Targeting Computer	RT	1	1
ATM 3	CT	2	1.5
ATM 3	LT	2	1.5
Ammo (ATM) 20	LT	1	1
Active Probe	LT	1	1

PARASH

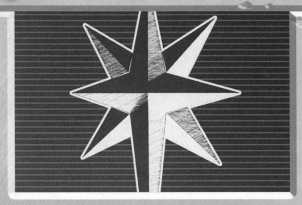

Mass: 35 tons
Chassis: Model MH-26
Power Plant: Magna 245 XL
Cruising Speed: 75 kph
Maximum Speed: 118 kph
Jump Jets: Model KT Boosters
    Jump Capacity: 210 meters
Armor: Compound 12A1 Standard
Armament:
    1 Series 44h Large Pulse Laser
Manufacturer: Manufacturing Site #3
    Primary Factory: New Oslo
Communications System: CH2 Series Integrated
    with ECM Suite
Targeting and Tracking System: Version Gamma-V

Overview

It is a sad fact of modern warfare that scouts—be they on foot, in vehicles, or piloting BattleMechs—have one of the shortest battlefield lifespans of any combat units. This is especially true among the Clans, where the drive for personal glory leads to altogether too many scout 'Mechs being destroyed in the face of overwhelming firepower.

By the early 3080s Clan Hell's Horses faced a dire situation: they were running dangerously low on light BattleMechs. The Clan's leadership had hoped that encouraging the use of support configurations such as the *Dasher* C would preserve their unique capabilities but casualties mounted regardless. Finally, the decision was made to procure a new light scout BattleMech.

Capabilities

The *Parash* is an all-new chassis that drew inspiration from several other machines in its weight class. From the *Pack Hunter* and *Hussar* came the idea of using a single large energy weapon for maximum firepower and endurance, in this case an arm-mounted pulse laser. The *Dasher* provided the concept of maximum speed for survivability, combined with the *Spider*'s vast jumping capability (though the *Parash* is slightly slower than that ancient design). Finally, the *Raven* showed that concentrating a force's electronic warfare capability in a single unit still provided a great deal of tactical ability while freeing up firepower on the scout's mates.

The visual design and name of this BattleMech have led to some debate among Republic analysts. Even for a light 'Mech it is unusually short and squat, with a rather baroque armor design. Indeed, the first pictures smuggled out of the Horses occupation zone lacked a proper sense of scale, leading some to hypothesize that it was a ProtoMech. While this has been disproven, its name—Hebrew for cavalryman—has been a hot topic of discussion. Combined with the Jihad-era Svantovit IFV variant named Masada, it would appear that the "tank Clan" has taken to Jewish history and language. The why of this trend is as of yet unclear.

Interestingly, while the *Parash* is a rather derivative 'Mech, its usage is unique among the Clans, and indeed among most Inner Sphere forces: it's meant to provide scouting ability not to 'Mech formations, but for conventional combat vehicles. Although this would be a major morale disaster among the other Clans, reports indicate that this has actually had the opposite effect among Hell's Horses MechWarriors. The Clan's armored forces appreciate the support, the traditionalist MechWarriors are freed up to pilot line combat units, and warriors who might have been forced to test down or even join the lower castes have the opportunity to pilot a 'Mech.

Deployment

As the Hell's Horses have only claimed their current occupation zone for a little over a decade—as opposed to over 30 years for their neighboring Clans—the development and deployment of the *Parash* has followed in a similar fashion to the invading Clan designs of the early 3060s. Production has been somewhat limited due to the difficulty in building and converting proper factories, but as of this writing a *Parash* has been seen in every frontline Cluster.

It is unclear at this time exactly how the Hell's Horses came to lose quite so many scout 'Mechs since reappearing in the Inner Sphere. While their actions against Clans Wolf and Jade Falcon have been heated, none have been bloody enough to explain such amazing losses. There have been rumors that the Horses suffered some degree of internal conflict, much like the other Inner Sphere Clans during the Jihad, but nothing has been confirmed. Given the Orwellian nature of the Clans and the length of time that has passed, it is unlikely that any such reports can be properly confirmed or debunked.

Variants

A single variant has been spotted. It is externally almost identical to the standard *Parash* but detailed analysis has shown some differences. First, it appears that the large pulse laser has been replaced with an experimental extended-range pulse model. More interestingly, it seems that the Hell's Horses have finally gotten their hands on some of the old Smoke Jaguar Watchdog CEWS units and combined it with a light TAG. It is unclear exactly how the Clan has utilized the extra tonnage freed up by mounting this suite; further surveillance is required.

PARASH

Type: Parash
Technology Base: Clan
Tonnage: 35
Battle Value: 1,300

Equipment		Mass
Internal Structure:		3.5
Engine:	245 XL	6
Walking MP:	7	
Running MP:	11	
Jumping MP:	7	
Heat Sinks:	10 [20]	0
Gyro:		3
Cockpit:		3
Armor Factor:	112	7

	Internal Structure	Armor Value
Head	3	9
Center Torso	11	16
Center Torso (rear)		5
R/L Torso	8	10
R/L Torso (rear)		3
R/L Arm	6	12
R/L Leg	8	16

Weapons and Ammo	Location	Critical	Tonnage
Large Pulse Laser	RA	2	6
Active Probe	RT	1	1
ECM Suite	LT	1	1
TAG	LA	1	1
Jump Jets	RL	2	1
Jump Jet	RT	1	.5
Jump Jet	CT	1	.5
Jump Jet	LT	1	.5
Jump Jets	LL	2	1

DASHER II

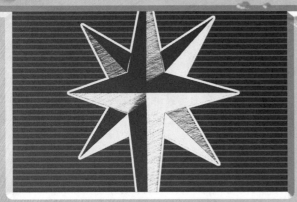

Mass: 40 tons
Chassis: Dominator Medium-Alpha 01
Power Plant: Type 79 400 XL
Cruising Speed: 108 kph
Maximum Speed: 162 kph
Jump Jets: None
   Jump Capacity: None
Armor: Compound 6F Ferro Fibrous
Armament:
   6 Mustang 4.5 Extended Range Micro Lasers
Manufacturer: Manufacturing Plant DSF-IT1,
   Auxiliary Production Site #4
   Primary Factory: Itabaiana, DSS *Poseidon* Mobile
      Production Facility
Communications System: Comset 1
Targeting and Tracking System: J-Track 52

Overview

[Editor's Note: While the existence of this design has been confirmed, only now have we had an agent manage to get any detailed data. While this account takes a lot of editorial liberty, it draws some frightening conclusions regarding Clan Diamond Shark's motives. –JC]

By the Unfinished Book, the Sharks' mercantile acumen is terrifying. My cover as a buyer for the AFFS got me an invite to their showcase on Itabaiana where seeing Industrialplex-C was like seeing the elephant all over again. I've been to Talon—before it was destroyed—and this mobile factory could give it a run for its money. The

Sharks are tight-lipped about production capacity, but Deathstrike Galaxy has more than a Cluster of shiny new 'Mechs on-planet and my sources confirm regular exports to the Wolves, Falcons, Combine, and Suns.

Until recently the *Dasher II* has been an enigma, one that—as Republic Intelligence's Shark expert—it's been my job to figure out. I'll start with the obvious: given the Sharks' reputation for selling quality equipment, why build the *Dasher II*? Clearly it's meant for Inner Sphere consumption, an upgrade of the *Dasher* (Clan designation *Fire Moth*) in the way the old CDA-2A *Cicada* was an upgrade of the LCT-1V *Locust*: twice the weight and price for roughly the same performance.

Unlike its namesake, the *Dasher II* is not an Omni, but if the Sharks' goal was merely a non-Omni analogue for the *Dasher* they needed look no further than the solahma-friendly *Piranha* that they've been producing since the '50s. Creating Mk II versions of popular units is now in vogue. Thumb through Chandrasekhar Kurita's 3075 publication and you'll see what I mean, but if the Sharks were hoping to capitalize on this fad why build such an outclassed 'Mech? The biggest mystery, however, is not the *Dasher II*'s specs, but where it's produced. Why are the Sharks building a mediocre, lower-tech unit at Itabaiana which is not only Omni-central, but their primary R&D facility?

Capabilities

As an upgrade of the *Dasher,* the *Dasher II* fails miserably. Three tons of ferro-fibrous armor provide the only advantage over its namesake. In all other categories the *Dasher* is an equal or superior design. Shark scientists gave the *Dasher II* six Mustang 4.5 ER micro lasers. Although this gives the 'Mech modest firepower for its role as a scout, an engagement range of 120 meters nullifies the Clans' chief advantage over Inner Sphere technology. Matching its predecessor's base speed of 108 kph comes with an incredible price—a massive, Type 79 extralight engine that weighs more than a *Dasher*.

Deployment

When the first *Dasher II*s rolled off the lines in '77 the Sharks inexplicably offered it to House militaries

and Inner Sphere Clans below cost. Stone's Coalition procured a number prior to invading the Word of Blake Protectorate in '77 and the design remains in service with the RAF today. Despite more cost-effective alternatives, the *Dasher II* is readily available and limited quantities of have made their way into the AFFS, LCAF, and DCMS. Of the Sharks' peers, only the Bears, Cats, and Ravens field the 'Mech.

Variants

I've struggled for eight years to explain the *Dasher II* and the showcase I attended earlier this year finally gave me the answer in the form of the *Dasher II* 2. The Sharks' wily merchant caste sold the *Dasher II* at a loss to accelerate funding and development of the Model 53b XXL engine. This experimental engine alone costs nearly three times as much as the *Dasher II*, but the weight saved allows for much-needed upgrades. The *Dasher II* 2 adds two and a half tons of armor, MASC, and upgrades its ER micro lasers to ER medium lasers. Although it costs more than many assault 'Mechs initial sales to the Bears and Ravens have been brisk and, if sustained, I anticipate the *Dasher II* 2 will outnumber the base model within a decade.

Of more immediate concern, the Type 79 engine is a popular choice in Shark manufacturing with XL versions used in multiple *Phoenix Hawk IIC* variants, and the new *Warhammer IIC* 8. I suspect the *Dasher II* 2's true purpose is a test bed for the Model 53b and we can expect new variants of the *Phoenix Hawk IIC* and *Warhammer IIC* with nine additional tons of equipment in the near future.

Type: **Dasher II**
Technology Base: Clan
Tonnage: 40
Battle Value: 522

Equipment		Mass
Internal Structure:	Endo Steel	2
Engine:	400 XL	26.5
Walking MP:	10	
Running MP:	15	
Jumping MP:	0	
Heat Sinks:	10 [20]	0
Gyro:		4
Cockpit:		3
Armor Factor (Ferro):	57	3

	Internal Structure	Armor Value
Head	3	6
Center Torso	12	7
Center Torso (rear)		2
R/L Torso	10	7
R/L Torso (rear)		2
R/L Arm	6	5
R/L Leg	10	7

Weapons and Ammo	Location	Critical	Tonnage
3 ER Micro Lasers	RA	3	0.75
3 ER Micro Lasers	LA	3	0.75

David White

GOSHAWK II

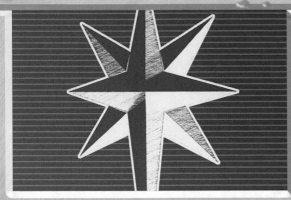

Mass: 45 tons
Chassis: GS-2E
Power Plant: Extralight 315 Fusion
Cruising Speed: 75 kph
Maximum Speed: 118 kph
Jump Jets: SR Starlifter 45
    Jump Capacity: 210 meters
Armor: Raven Comp A
Armament:
    1 Series 6b ER Large Laser
    6 Series 3c Micro Pulse Lasers
    2 Series 4c Small Pulse Lasers
Manufacturer: Industrial Complex Alpha
    Primary Factory: Dante
Communications System: SR Com 6 with ECM
Targeting and Tracking System: Type 13e
    with Targeting Computer

Overview

The *Goshawk II* is not a machine for the impetuous. A lighter, faster version of the original *Goshawk*, the Snow Ravens commissioned the design to fill holes in their second-line forces as they settle into their marriage with the Outworlds Alliance. Despite the intermingling of second-line Ghost Bear machines in frontline FRR units, this is not the case in the Snow Raven/OA alliance. The *Goshawk II* is a Clan 'Mech meant for Clan warriors.

Capabilities

Many of the basics of the *Goshawk* have been transferred to the *Goshawk II*. It is lighter and faster than the original, boasting a top speed of nearly 120 kph with over 200 meters of jump range. This speed allows for excellent positioning, a must for this machine. Even with nine tons of armor the battlefield can be deadly to a medium 'Mech in the open. To help against the newer electronics, especially the C³ systems the Raven's neighbors have become used to, ECM is included both to protect the 'Mech as well as allowing the 'Mech to help protect its unit.

When attacking, the *Goshawk II* requires patience. Enhanced by the complex targeting computer concept of its forebear, an extended-range large laser makes an excellent sniping weapon. As accurate as it is, one weapon isn't enough to go charging at most enemies, allowing them to bring their weapons to bear. Rather, the laser should be used to open up holes in the enemy's armor first. Only then should the rest of the weaponry of the *Goshawk II* be brought into play. With a pair of small pulse lasers and half a dozen micro pulse lasers, it needs to close with the enemy—and close fast.

Given the intriguing weapons on the 'Mech it will be interesting to see what sort of role that the Ravens will use it in. It could be good in the hands of the older pilots, who have the skill and patience to use it effectively. It could also be a tool for testing the aptitude of newer warriors, to see which will be able to learn quickly enough to both survive and be effective. Finally, with such a large array of pulse weapons, it could be used to focus on an anti-personnel role, using a wide number of weapons to compensate for the speed it will use to close and avoid being hit by their targets.

Deployment

There are currently only a dozen or so *Goshawk II*s, all being field-tested, primarily against pirates. The simulators and test runs have shown the design is solid and meets the Snow Ravens' needs. All that is left is to look for the small issues that might pop up under stress.

Variants

In tune with some of the other 'Mechs the Snow Ravens manufacture, a version of the *Goshawk II* has been optimized for space combat support. The micro pulse lasers have been removed and the small pulse lasers upgraded to mediums. The ECM has been removed as well, proving less useful in the vast distances of space-to-space combat. With the weight saved from the removal of the pulse lasers the cockpit was armored to give the pilot increased protection. This model is still in the prototype stage, with field testing due in a few months.

[Editor's note: Image pictured here is that of the Goshawk II 2 variant. - JC]

GOSHAWK II

Type: **Goshawk II**
Technology Base: Clan
Tonnage: 45
Battle Value: 1,849

Equipment			Mass
Internal Structure:	Endo Steel		2.5
Engine:	315 XL		11
Walking MP:	7		
Running MP:	11		
Jumping MP:	7		
Heat Sinks:	10 [20]		0
Gyro:			4
Cockpit:			3
Armor Factor:	144		9

	Internal Structure	Armor Value
Head	3	9
Center Torso	14	20
Center Torso (rear)		7
R/L Torso	11	16
R/L Torso (rear)		6
R/L Arm	7	12
R/L Leg	11	20

Weapons and Ammo	Location	Critical	Tonnage
ER Large Laser	RA	1	4
2 Micro Pulse Lasers	RA	2	1
ECM Suite	RT	1	1
Micro Pulse Laser	H	1	.5
Small Pulse Laser	LT	1	1
Targeting Computer	LT	2	2
Small Pulse Laser	LA	1	1
3 Micro Pulse Lasers	LA	3	1.5
Jump Jets	RT	3	1.5
Jump Jet	CT	1	.5
Jump Jets	LT	3	1.5

David White

URSUS II

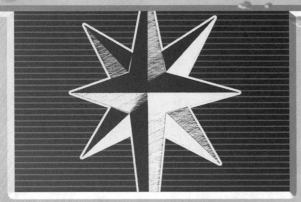

Mass: 50 tons
Chassis: Bergan XIV Endo Steel
Power Plant: Firebox 200 XL
Cruising Speed: 43 kph
Maximum Speed: 65 kph
Jump Jets: Leaper Model, L5 Improved
   Jump Capacity: 180 meters
Armor: Royal-7 Standard
Armament:
   1 Series 7K Extended Range Large Laser
   2 Series 1g Extended Range Small Lasers
   2 Kolibri Delta Series Medium Pulse Lasers
   1 Type X LRM 10 Launcher
   1 Smartshot Mk. VI Streak SRM 6
Manufacturer: Arc-Royal MechWorks, Bergan Industries
   Primary Factory: Arc-Royal, Alshain
Communications System: Garret T10B with ECM Suite
Targeting and Tracking System: RCA Instatrac Mark VI
   with Artemis IV FCS

Overview

Clan Ghost Bear and Clan Wolf-in-Exile have much in common and by all rights should get on, but so far they have not. To a certain degree it comes back to Clan Ghost Bear's general dislike of Clan Wolf, but ever since the Exiles arrived in Lyran space they have continually bumped heads with the Dominion. So it came as a surprise when Arc-Royal MechWorks announced it would be producing a brand new 'Mech based on the *Ursus* with funding from Bergan Industries.

Over the following months some details have emerged. Flush with funds, Bergan had been looking to expand its influence by investing in companies outside the Ghost Bear Dominion. Arc-Royal MechWorks is virtually the private 'Mech factory of the Kell family but historically has been locked out of Clan technology production due to Clan Wolf-in-Exile's unwillingness to share. Bergan's offer allowed Arc-Royal MechWorks to circumvent the Exiles' restrictions. From Bergan's point of view Arc-Royal MechWorks is a secure site to produce advanced technology with a ready Clan market on hand. It's unclear what Khan Kell and the Clan Ghost Bear Council think of this, though they must have approved it. This deal represents a degree of independence in a company most likely neither Clan would have accepted was it not for the desperate needs of post-Jihad rebuilding.

Capabilities

The *Ursus II* is a major rethink of the *Ursus*. Previous *Ursus* variants utilized large XL engines to improve the 'Mech's mobility but proved too expensive for a garrison 'Mech. Designers utilized a mid-weight XL engine to provide a new degree of mobility without dragging costs up to an unreasonable level. When combined with a lightened chassis, the XL engine frees up enough mass to install six improved jump jets, which gives the blocky 'Mech a surprising amount of mobility.

The major changes to the *Ursus*' internal structure made some changes to the weapons necessary. Heat sinks had to be removed to fit the bulky jump jets, which meant the laser systems had to be scaled back. The missiles are enhanced to compensate. Despite this, the effect on the *Ursus II*'s ability to fight was minimal. The *Ursus II* remains a well-balanced brawler and has gained a much-improved ability to respond to off-axis threats. The main fault relates back to the vulnerability of the XL engine, which has resulted in a slightly higher loss rate despite the enhanced maneuverability.

Deployment

Produced on both Alshain and Arc-Royal, a large number of *Ursus II*s have been built since 3078. Because of the small size of the Wolf-in-Exile Touman, Arc-Royal *Ursus II*s serve in both front and second-line forces. Usually positioned as bodyguard units for assault 'Mechs, they have proven hard for traditional, fast-moving headhunter 'Mechs to outmaneuver. Arriving too late for the Chara debacle, *Ursus II*s took part in the remaining battles of the Terran campaign where their ECM capabilities proved invaluable for shutting down Blakist electronics networks. Exile *Ursus II*s have also had success serving as anchors for Stars of fast-moving 'Mechs like *Pack Hunters* and *Arctic Wolf*s, providing much-needed toughness without slowing the Star too much.

Built alongside the old *Ursus*, the Alshain *Ursus II*s have largely gone to KungsArmé and garrison forces. Deemed too slow for the front line, *Ursus II*s have instead been used to replace old Inner Sphere designs. Here they serve as a link 'Mech between fast-movers like the *Arcas* or *Karhu* and less maneuverable 'Mechs like the *Kodiak*. These *Ursus II*s have largely found themselves facing raiders probing the Dominion's defenses and hunting down what remains of the Word of Blake. As an "expendable" asset, *Ursus II*s invariably find themselves on point, drawing out enemies to be disposed of by heavier 'Mechs like the *Karhu*. Understandably, warriors assigned to this duty tend to be twitchy and prone to use their jump jets to leap backwards at even the slightest sign of trouble.

Given the loyal following the *Ursus* has developed over the years, a debate has sprung up as to which *Ursus* is superior. With large cutbacks to military spending expected in the near future, it is likely the results of this debate will decide the fates of both these 'Mechs.

Variants

There are no known variants of the *Ursus II*.

URSUS II

Type: **Ursus II**
Technology Base: Clan
Tonnage: 50
Battle Value: 2,069

Equipment			Mass
Internal Structure:	Endo Steel		2.5
Engine:	200 XL		4.5
Walking MP:	4		
Running MP:	6		
Jumping MP:	6		
Heat Sinks:	13 [26]		3
Gyro:			2
Cockpit:			3
Armor Factor:	168		10.5

	Internal Structure	Armor Value
Head	3	9
Center Torso	16	24
Center Torso (rear)		7
R/L Torso	12	20
R/L Torso (rear)		4
R/L Arm	8	16
R/L Leg	12	24

Weapons and Ammo	Location	Critical	Tonnage
ER Large Laser	RA	1	4
2 Medium Pulse Lasers	RA	2	4
ER Small Laser	RT	1	.5
Streak SRM 6	CT	2	3
Ammo (Streak) 15	LT	1	1
ER Small Laser	LT	1	.5
LRM 10	LA	1	2.5
Artemis IV FCS	LA	1	1
Ammo (LRM) 12	LT	1	1
ECM Suite	RT	1	1
Improved Jump Jets	RT	4	2
Improved Jump Jets	LT	4	2
Improved Jump Jet	RL	2	1
Improved Jump Jet	LL	2	1

DARK CROW

Mass: 55 tons
Chassis: SR3084/b Endo Steel
Power Plant: Fusion 330 Extralight
Cruising Speed: 64 kph
Maximum Speed: 97 kph
Jump Jets: None
   Jump Capacity: None
Armor: Forging C629/j
Armament:
   2 Type 31 Ultra AC/5
   1 Series 6b Extended Range Large Laser
   1 Mk 22 SRM 6
Manufacturer: Industrial Complex Alpha
   Primary Factory: Dante
Communications System: GBX Series Integrated
Targeting and Tracking System: Tokasha B4-T&T

Overview

When one thinks of the Clans, innovative is not often a word that springs to mind. While their culture is relatively unique, their technology and combat philosophies are mere incremental improvements and/or modifications on that which existed in the first Star League.

This stereotype may be changing, however. One of the strongest examples of truly new concepts being developed by the Clans is the Snow Ravens' *Dark Crow*, a high-end medium BattleMech with a unique and effective layout.

Capabilities

The dark crow (*Corvus subsolaneus dantis*) is a strange predator found only in several large caves on the world of Dante. Unlike most avian analogues, it is a true troglodyte, perfectly adapted for its subterranean environment. The creature is notable for having a six-limbed body structure, with two powerful legs for running and climbing, two stubby arms to aid in navigation and grip prey, and two oddly-shaped wings that allow the dark crow to fly in the largest of the caverns. It is a fierce predator, though too small to be much threat to humans.

The *Dark Crow* BattleMech is built very similarly to its namesake. It is very fast for its mass, easily able to reach speeds approaching 100 kilometers per hour. Its side torsos feature stubby "wings" that act as stand-off armor, giving it above-average protection for its thick torso. Its most interesting features are its low-mounted arms. Where most 'Mechs have their arms protruding from their shoulders, the *Dark Crow*'s are much lower on the torso, near what would be the 'Mech's abdomen. This gives this machine a superior field of fire when in confined spaces.

The actual weapons carried by the *Dark Crow* are simple and proven models. Its primary firepower comes from a pair of medium-class Ultra autocannons, with two tons of ammunition for each. These are mounted in the 'Mech's arms, allowing it to easily and effectively rake fire along the ground, and provide enough punch and rate of fire to threaten nearly any battlefield unit. In the right torso is a six-tube short-range missile system, chosen for its light weight yet high power inside the autocannons' dead zone. Finally, an ER large laser in the left torso provides long-range sniping capability, as well as acting as an effective backup weapon when the 'Mech runs out of ammunition.

It should be noted that the *Dark Crow* is somewhat under-armored when compared to other 'Mechs in its weight class. However, the Ravens seem to accept this as a natural and unavoidable side-effect of the 'Mech's mission role.

Also, oddly, when compared to its other Snow Raven contemporaries, the *Dark Crow*'s base model lacks any jump capability.

Deployment

The *Dark Crow* has proven fairly popular among Clan Snow Raven's second-line forces, though most pilots will still choose an OmniMech if given the option. The Clan has not shared this design with the Outworlds Alliance, but this may simply be because the Periphery power has little interest in new BattleMechs of any sort.

The base model and anti-aircraft versions of this 'Mech have yet to see combat, but the advanced space combat model has proven very effective in anti-piracy operations.

Variants

One basic variation on the *Dark Crow* simply replaces the Ultra autocannon with LB-5X models and the SRM 6 with a targeting computer and an ER small laser. This model is considered an excellent anti-aircraft and sniper machine. There has been some talk that future variants may replace the standard armor of the base *Dark Crow* with ferro-fibrous, but at this time this remains just a theory.

Another configuration has been seen quite often among the Snow Ravens' new "S-Teams." This model mounts an astonishing array of advanced technologies, modifying nearly every aspect of the basic machine, from Clan-spec rotary autocannon and improved heavy lasers through an endo-composite structure and XXL engine, to laser heat sinks and ferro-lamellor armor. This version also mounts jump jets and a partial wing system, along with fuel tanks for space operations, making it a truly terrifying—if fragile—opponent and a fitting tribute to its namesake creature.

DARK CROW

Type: **Dark Crow**
Technology Base: Clan
Tonnage: 55
Battle Value: 1,594

Equipment		Mass
Internal Structure:	Endo Steel	3
Engine:	330 XL	12.5
Walking MP:	6	
Running MP:	9	
Jumping MP:	0	
Heat Sinks:	10 [20]	0
Gyro:		4
Cockpit:		3
Armor Factor:	128	8

	Internal Structure	Armor Value
Head	3	8
Center Torso	18	20
Center Torso (rear)		4
R/L Torso	13	17
R/L Torso (rear)		4
R/L Arm	9	11
R/L Leg	13	16

Weapons and Ammo	Location	Critical	Tonnage
Ultra AC/5	RA	3	7
Ultra AC/5	LA	3	7
SRM 6	RT	1	1.5
Ammo (SRM) 15	RT	1	1
Ammo (Ultra) 40	RT	2	2
ER Large Laser	LT	1	4
Ammo (Ultra) 40	LT	2	2

David White

KUMA

Mass: 60 tons
Chassis: Clan Series Heavy KMX
Power Plant: 360 Type II XL
Cruising Speed: 64 kph
Maximum Speed: 97 kph
Jump Jets: Clan Series Type 4 Heavy Improved Jump Jets
Jump Capacity: 240 meters
Armor: Arcadia Compound Delta VII Ferro-Fibrous Armor
Armament:
  1 Series 4D-2 Heavy Large Laser
  2 Series 2f Extended Medium Lasers
Manufacturer: Alshain Battleworx
Primary Factory: Alshain
Communications System: Garret GBX-2 Amalgamated
Targeting and Tracking System: RCA Instatrac Version 8

Overview

As Clan Ghost Bear has tightened its hold on the former Free Rasalhague Republic, traditionalists within the Clan have expressed sometimes-violent distrust of the former KungsArmé. To these trueborn—and even Clan freeborn—warriors, the Sphere-born soldiers are simply not worthy of inclusion in the Clan's ranks. That most of these supposedly "inferior Spheroids" have actually been born in the Dominion since Operation REVIVAL is a detail rarely mentioned. Still, the Bears' Khans have sought to avoid the internal problems that had plagued the other invading Clans.

To try and unite its warriors, the Khans took the almost-unprecedented step of asking Clan and KungsArmé warriors to collaborate on a new 'Mech design. Almost unanimously both sides wanted a heavy design with good ground speed, well-armored and free from ammunition concerns. Actual firepower was a secondary concern, as the Clan already fielded several chassis that were weapon-heavy. The new BattleMech—named rather predictably the *Kuma*, from the Japanese word for bear—would be a fast scout and cavalry raider.

Capabilities

The *Kuma* may be the most mobile heavy 'Mech ever produced. It is as fast on the ground as the forty-five ton *Phoenix Hawk* and jumps as far and as high as the diminutive *Spider*. This is all due to its enormous 360 Type II engine, an extralight engine more typical for lighter designs like the *Fenris* and *Pouncer*. This allows the *Kuma* to speed along at nearly 100 kilometers per hour, providing a heavy cornerstone to light Stars.

Of course, this kind of speed from such a large machine has its downside. The *Kuma*, though impressively styled, carries an almost anemic array of energy weapons. While its ammunition independence is considered an asset, the simple fact is that its firepower can be compared to 3025-vintage Inner Sphere medium 'Mechs. It also has a rather steep heat curve due to its mix of heavy and ER lasers, but its impressive jumping capability means that it can easily break contact when overheating, and of course it never needs to worry about ammunition explosions.

Deployment

While prototypes were fielded during the Jihad, none saw actual combat and full-scale production didn't begin until after the war was over. The *Kuma*, as a symbol of Inner Sphere-Clan unity, has spread throughout the Dominion, being awarded to trueborns and freeborns alike. While numbers are limited, even after three years, its rather specialist role seems to indicate this is deliberate rather than a result of poor production capability. Reception has been quite positive, though a few warriors have dismissed the *Kuma* as a "*Charger* IIC"—a not-wholly-unfair comparison, given its devotion to speed and armor over actual striking power.

Variants

A second version has also been spotted, which is almost conservative compared to its more mobile cousin. While it retains the 360 XL engine of the base model, the *Kuma* 2 replaces the advanced jump jets with enough standard models to leap only 180 meters. The tonnage saved has been used to upgrade its weapons complement to one based around a plasma cannon and an advanced tactical missile launcher. This model is still very maneuverable, but now strikes with firepower commiserate with its mass, though it gains a vulnerability to ammunition explosions.

Unbelievably, there is an even faster prototype of the *Kuma*. Though it strips armor to the bare minimum and removes all built-in weaponry, the *Kuma* 3 is perfectly capable of outrunning many hovercraft and even some VTOLs and has a jumping profile that's best compared to Land-Air BattleMechs. The tradeoff is a fusion power plant that nearly fills the torso completely and the aforementioned weak armor and weapons; indeed, it carries its only weapon in an external gun pod. It should be noted that this model is just a proof of concept and is not intended for actual combat. The Clan's own development notes state that the Bears wanted to add a partial wing and another jump jet to boost its mobility even further, but simply couldn't find enough room in the chassis to shoehorn them in.

KUMA

Type: **Kuma**
Technology Base: Clan
Tonnage: 60
Battle Value: 1,952

Equipment		Mass
Internal Structure:	Endo Steel	3
Engine:	360 XL	16.5
Walking MP:	6	
Running MP:	9	
Jumping MP:	8	
Heat Sinks:	11 [22]	1
Gyro:		4
Cockpit:		3
Armor Factor (Ferro):	201	10.5

	Internal Structure	Armor Value
Head	3	9
Center Torso	20	30
Center Torso (rear)		10
R/L Torso	14	20
R/L Torso (rear)		8
R/L Arm	10	20
R/L Leg	14	28

Weapons and Ammo	Location	Critical	Tonnage
2 ER Medium Lasers	RA	2	2
Heavy Large Laser	LA	3	4
Improved Jump Jet	RL	2	2
Improved Jump Jets	RT	6	6
Improved Jump Jets	LT	6	6
Improved Jump Jet	LL	2	2

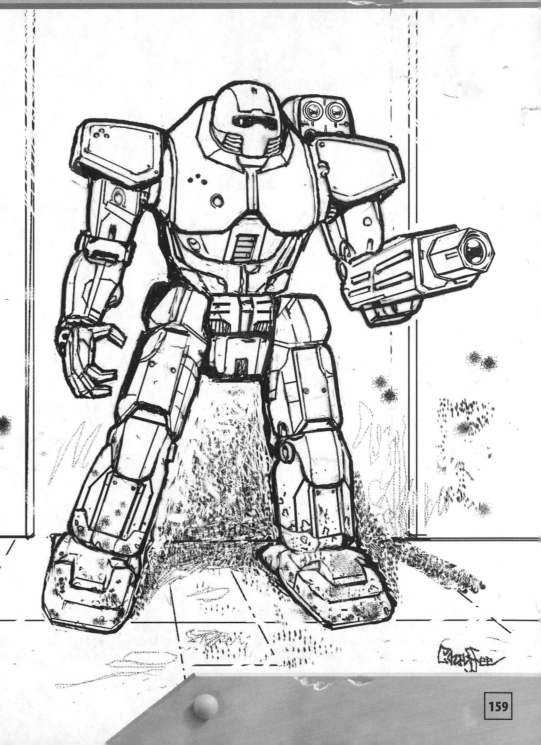

Mass: 60 tons
Chassis: Type 79-60 Endo Steel
Power Plant: Type 79 360 XL
Cruising Speed: 64 kph
Maximum Speed: 97 kph
Jump Jets: Clan Standard Type A1
   Jump Capacity: 180 meters
Armor: Compound H17 Ferro-Fibrous
Armament:
   1 Type 0 Hyper-Assault Gauss 20
   2 Type X Short Bow LRM 10s
   1 Series 7Ja ER Medium Laser
Manufacturer: Olivetti Weaponry
   Primary Factory: Sudeten
Communications System: JNE Integrated
Targeting and Tracking System: Build 3Z CAT TTS

Overview

In the waning years of the Jihad, Jade Falcon technicians delivered many new 'Mechs for their Clan's Touman. The crisis created many opportunities to innovate and many new designs emerged as a result of the Sphere-wide conflict, but some felt that improving on existing technology was the more effective approach. A merchant named Daniel championed this tactic. Brought to the attention of Khan Clees by continually exceeding expectations for the Olivetti production facility, Daniel proposed significant manufacturing changes. One of these was the creation of the *Shadow Cat II*. At a time when many Falcons called for a new heavy 'Mech design, Daniel's plan ultimately won out on three points: cost-efficiency, ease of development, and a significantly shortened delivery time.

Republic agents report that the original plans for the upgraded *Shadow Cat II* called for keeping the Gauss rifle from its prime configuration, but with the Falcons winning rights to HAG technology, the Gauss was dropped in favor of the newer weapon. Although Daniel was the conceptual mind behind the *Shadow Cat II*, he was not the principal architect of the design. It's unclear if the design was completed by scientists in the Inner Sphere or in the Clan Homeworlds. There are several contradictory rumors (possibly a deliberate misinformation campaign) that place the initial development in the homeworlds. All efforts to gain additional insight have been unsuccessful. As one of our agents put it, "It's almost like the Falcons are going out of their way to hide something."

The original prototype *Shadow Cat II*—with the Gauss rifle—never made it off the drawing board. No prototypes were produced, though it would be simple enough to create one. The Falcons are apparently more interested in experimenting with the HAG.

Capabilities

The *Shadow Cat II*'s primary weapon is a Type 0 Hyper-Assault Gauss HAG-20. A pair of Type X Short Bow LRM launchers augment its damage curve up to 630 meters. The potential damage delivered by the three systems is enough to chew through almost two full tons of standard armor. Where other fire support 'Mechs focus this kind of firepower into a narrow region—often punching through in a volley or two—the *Shadow Cat II*'s payload creates a shotgun-like effect. This configuration excels at exploiting targets that have already been softened up, but it has a much more difficult time against undamaged units. A right torso-mounted ER medium laser is almost an afterthought, and the tonnage may have been better spent on additional ammunition for the HAG.

Seven and a half tons of ferro-fibrous armor provide the *Shadow Cat II* with slightly more armor than its predecessor. A top speed of 97 kph and jumping capacity of 180 meters gives the 'Mech excellent mobility for its weight class. Ten double-strength heat sinks provide a reportedly comfortable cockpit even with continual weapons fire.

Deployment

Since the end of the Jihad, the *Shadow Cat II* has been deployed exclusively with the Jade Falcons. No other Inner Sphere Clan has yet held a Trial of Possession for the design, and Republic Intelligence believes the Falcons are unlikely to offer it, though it has been confirmed that the Diamond Sharks have tried—and failed—to acquire the design through trade agreements.

Variants

After the initial production run of *Shadow Cat II*s were complete, Falcon scientists appropriated several to test more experimental weaponry. The *Shadow Cat II* 2—currently in limited trials—mounts an ER large pulse and ER medium pulse laser in place of the HAG. Additionally, both of these beam weapons have been fitted with laser insulators. The laser insulator shields the 'Mech from the heat generated by the lasers, allowing for a smoother heat curve at the expense of a higher rate of laser failure. Falcons scientists are continuing experiments from the *Winged Cougar*, fitting this variant with a 'Mech-scale partial wing to give it increased jumping range in standard atmospheres.

Type: **Shadow Cat II**
Technology Base: Clan
Tonnage: 60
Battle Value: 2,064

Equipment		Mass
Internal Structure:	Endo Steel	3
Engine:	360 XL	16.5
Walking MP:	6	
Running MP:	9	
Jumping MP:	6	
Heat Sinks:	10 [20]	0
Gyro:		4
Cockpit:		3
Armor Factor (Ferro):	144	7.5

	Internal Structure	Armor Value
Head	3	9
Center Torso	20	20
Center Torso (rear)		7
R/L Torso	14	15
R/L Torso (rear)		5
R/L Arm	10	14
R/L Leg	14	20

Weapons and Ammo	Location	Critical	Tonnage
HAG 20	RA	6	10
Ammo (HAG) 12	RT	2	2
LRM 10	RT	1	2.5
LRM 10	LT	1	2.5
Ammo (LRM) 24	LT	2	2
ER Medium Laser	RT	1	1
Jump Jets	RT	2	2
Jump Jets	CT	2	2
Jump Jets	LT	2	2

KARHU

Mass: 65 tons
Chassis: Beowulf 4 Enhanced
Power Plant: Pitban 325 XL
Cruising Speed: 54 kph
Maximum Speed: 86 kph
Jump Jets: None
   Jump Capacity: None
Armor: Compound A2F Ferro-Fibrous
Armament:
   30 tons of pod space available
Manufacturer: Odin Manufacturing
   Primary Factory: Orestes
Communications System: Dash-2 Standard
Targeting and Tracking System: Blade 12

Overview

For the executives of Odin Manufacturing, the merger of the Free Rasalhague Republic and the Ghost Bear Dominion was cause for excitement. They could gain Dominion funding for their Orestes plant, which had been damaged by Word of Blake raids in the late 3060s, and re-tool using Clan technology. Progress was typically slow as the needs of the Jihad forced Odin to continue manufacturing its existing designs, but by 3077 they were ready to build their first Clantech 'Mech.

Identifying Bergan Industries as their primary competitor, Odin set out to challenge Bergan directly by bidding for a new heavy OmniMech design. Two years of design work resulted in a 65-ton OmniMech using the latest technology available. To back this up, Odin launched a massive sales campaign based around Rasalhaguian nationalism

and aimed at KungsArmé officers in the Dominion touman. To the surprise of many observers, Odin's OmniMech proved superior to Bergan's effort and won the contract.

Capabilities

The *Karhu* is technologically superior to Bergan's similar *Arcas*, employing advanced armor and Omni technology. The chassis is sculptured with a fearsome *Ursus*-like skull motif and a huge claw over its right hand intended to inspire fear and appeal to the KungsArmé's love of physical combat.

Most *Karhu* variants combine high mobility and heavy armor. A heavy weapon is normally mounted in the left arm, a claw-like array of lasers or an actual claw in the right arm. The design routinely carries advanced electronics as well.

Unfortunately, a series of faults has demonstrated Odin's inexperience with Clan technology. Odin reused the *Beowulf's* proven targeting and communications suite to save time and money. However, in combat the *Karhu* has been plagued by intermittent electronics glitches. Technicians blame the problem on a fundamental incompatibility, citing similar failings on *Beowulf*s retrofitted with Clan gear, but Odin denies any culpability.

Deployment

First deployed in 3079, the *Karhu* was rushed to the front line but missed out on service in the Protectorate campaign. After being paired with the *Ursus II* in the closing stages of the Jihad, the *Karhu* earned a reputation as a cavalry 'Mech, flanking opponents while the *Ursus II* drew fire at close range. *Karhu*s are now concentrated in frontline clusters alongside *Vultures* and other OmniMechs. During the Jihad, the Dominion had to make extensive use of standard BattleMechs, but with the return of peace they hope to restore the former balance. However, the Dominion's 'Mech manufacturers make more money from customized BattleMechs than from generic Omnis and are lobbying accordingly.

Competition between Odin and Bergan has taken a distinctly nasty turn, with Odin officials referring to Bergan as "that Capellan company with their Combine workers." Requests for Orestes-built 'Mechs are noticeably higher among Rasalhaguian warriors as a result. Not used to capitalism at its most ruthless, the Ghost Bear Council is concerned by this infighting and has requested that its merchant caste

representatives in both companies rein things in. Reports that the merchants are fully engaged in the fighting may make this harder than the Council thinks.

Type: **Karhu**
Technology Base: Clan
Tonnage: 65
Battle Value: 2,488

Equipment			Mass
Internal Structure:		Endo Steel	3.5
Engine:		325 XL	12
Walking MP:		5	
Running MP:		8	
Jumping MP:		0	
Heat Sinks:		12 [24]	2
Gyro:			4
Cockpit:			3
Armor Factor (Ferro):		201	10.5
		Internal	Armor
		Structure	Value
Head		3	9
Center Torso		21	30
Center Torso (rear)			10
R/L Torso		15	23
R/L Torso (rear)			7
R/L Arm		10	20
R/L Leg		15	26

Weight and Space Allocation

Location	Fixed	Spaces Remaining
Head	1 Ferro-Fibrous	0
Center Torso	None	2
Right Torso	2 XL Engine	7
	3 Ferro-Fibrous	
Left Torso	2 XL Engine	7
	3 Ferro-Fibrous	
Right Arm	1 Endo Steel	7
Left Arm	2 Endo Steel	6
Right Leg	2 Endo Steel	0
Left Leg	2 Endo Steel	0

Weapons and Ammo	Location	Critical	Tonnage
Primary Weapons Configuration			
Retractable Blade	RA	5	4
Plasma Cannon	RA	1	3
Ammo (Plasma) 10	RA	1	1
ECM Suite	RT	1	1
ER PPC	LA	2	6
ER Medium Laser	LA	1	1
Improved Jump Jets	RT	6	6
Improved Jump Jet	CT	2	2
Improved Jump Jets	LT	6	6

KARHU

Weapons and Ammo	Location	Critical	Tonnage
Weapons Configuration A			
Large Pulse Laser	RA	2	6
ER Medium Laser	RA	1	1
Micro Pulse Laser	RA	1	.5
LRM 10	LT	1	2.5
Ammo (LRM) 12	LT	1	1
Ammo (Gauss) 16	LT	2	2
Gauss Rifle	LA	6	12
Jump Jet	CT	1	1
Jump Jets	LT	2	2
Jump Jets	RT	2	2
Battle Value: 2,560			
Weapons Configuration B			
3 ER Medium Lasers	RA	3	3
2 Double Heat Sinks	RA	4	2
Targeting Computer	RT	3	3
ECM Suite	RT	1	1
Ammo (Ultra) 20	LT	4	4
Ultra AC/20	LA	8	12
Jump Jets	RT	2	2
Jump Jet	CT	1	1
Jump Jets	LT	2	2
Battle Value: 2,787			
Weapons Configuration C			
Retractable Blade	RA	5	4
Ultra AC/5	RT	3	7
Ammo (Ultra) 20	RT	1	1
Ultra AC/5	LT	3	7
Ammo (Ultra) 20	LT	1	1
ER Large Laser	LA	1	4
ER Medium Laser	LA	1	1
Jump Jets	RT	2	2
Jump Jet	CT	1	1
Jump Jets	LT	2	2
Battle Value: 2,092			
Weapons Configuration D			
3 ER Medium Lasers	RA	3	3
Double Heat Sink	RA	2	1
Targeting Computer	RT	3	3
Active Probe	RT	1	1
ECM Suite	RT	1	1
Double Heat Sink	RT	2	1
Anti-Missile System	CT	1	.5
Streak SRM 6	LT	2	3
Ammo (Streak) 15	LT	1	1
Anti-Missile System	LT	1	.5
Ammo (AMS) 24	LT	1	1
Double Heat Sink	LT	2	1
2 ER PPCs	LA	4	12
Double Heat Sink	LA	2	1
Battle Value: 3,118			

David White

BLOOD REAPER

Mass: 70 tons
Chassis: Type W4 Endo Steel
Power Plant: 280 Fusion XL
Cruising Speed: 43 kph
Maximum Speed: 64 kph
Jump Jets: BMP Series XV
    Jump Capacity: 120 meters
Armor: Advanced/3
Armament:
    2 Type 22 Extended Range PPCs
    2 General Systems Heavy Medium Lasers
    2 CC 6-Rack Advanced Tactical Missile Launchers
Manufacturer: W-7 Facilities
    Primary Factory: Weingarten
Communications System: Build 1685 Tacticom
Targeting and Tracking System: Build 2 CAT TTS

Overview

The latest BattleMech from Clan Wolf marks an interesting shift in the way these Crusaders view their future. Cunning, wits and determination have long characterized the Wolves' tactical approach to warfare, but even the most cunning must ultimately pay the price of war. Khan Vlad Ward has expertly proven the value of using symbols to direct his Clan. While Clan Wolf has proven their ability in bloodlines and machines, the purist Ward was concerned with the number of non-Wolf designs in the touman. Though he knew that a superior warrior in an inferior machine will still be victorious, he viewed assigning even the lowliest Wolf warrior to an unworthy machine as an insult to the Clan's heritage, and so was determined to cull anything that weakened the heirs of Kerensky's legacy.

In a typical bold stroke, Ward issued a challenge to the ranking members of his scientist caste to forge a symbolic weapon that the Wolves could rally around. The Khan vowed that if their efforts were unacceptable, he would personally put them in the cockpit of those inadequate machines and destroy them on the battlefield. As this challenge came from the man who had crushed the life out of an ilKhan with his foot on the floor of the Grand Council, the scientists took it seriously. Their efforts did not disappoint.

Capabilities

The rallying cry for this particular design was most unusual––and this new unit has the guns to back it up. Much like the iconic *Tundra Wolf* design, the *Blood Reaper* is a straightforward second-line 'Mech. The design parameters stressed survivability, impact, cost and proven technology. By drawing on the best elements of several highly successful designs, this new machine pays tribute to the Clan's history in a way the *Tundra Wolf* did not.

Given the Wolves' historic success with the *Mad Cat,* the design team drew heavily from its chassis and structural design. They also chose to reference several complementary elements from the proven structure of the *Black Hawk.* Multi-range firepower flexibility comes from a pair of ATM launchers, while ER PPCs were chosen for their raw hitting power. This threat is backed up by two heavy medium lasers for close-range punch. Though relatively slow compared to a frontline Clan Omni, the standard version has jump jets to increase flexibility.

Ward was satisfied that the *Blood Reaper* met his strict requirement of "the flexibility to prove his cunning, the teeth to draw the enemy's blood, and the hide to withstand the savagery of battle." His warriors took this typical Clan posturing as a challenge to see if they could win despite being hobbled by a second-line machine.

Deployment

In 3079, the first Star of *Blood Reaper*s saw their trial by fire against a Trinary of Hell's Horses who believed a flanking maneuver through untested prototypes would allow them to avoid the main Wolf force. The Horses failed to realize they had been led into the *Blood Reaper*s, and fell into the trap. The *Blood Reaper*s savaged the mostly light and medium Horse machines, leaving only two Horse 'Mechs to flee the battle.

At a Wolf Grand Council meeting two weeks later, Vlad Ward outlined his plans to forge a touman worthy of Kerensky's chosen, and showed footage from the Horse battle. His reported words were: "Even in the weakest Wolf machine, our warriors are superior to our enemies." He followed this claim by stating that the spirit of the Wolf would welcome any who sought a little more challenge with their victories. Ward's call to action prompted requisitions from every Galaxy Commander, and the Khan offered to supply *Blood Reaper*s as replacements for any units the commanders deemed "unworthy of the Wolf." In remarkably short order, the *Blood Reaper* was being produced in record numbers.

The warriors of Alpha Galaxy received the first shipments of the new 'Mechs, which were predominantly assigned to Bloodnamed warriors. The *Blood Reaper* is quickly joining the *Mad Cat* and *Tundra Wolf* as one of the Wolves' iconic machines.

Variants

A second variant released within a year of the first *Reaper* drops the four jump jets in favor of two arm-mounted medium pulse lasers. Capable of heavier fire, it must be doubly careful about overheating. Its firepower has made it popular in dueling and Trials of Position, seeing as much, if not more, production than the standard version.

BLOOD REAPER

Type: **Blood Reaper**
Technology Base: Clan
Tonnage: 70
Battle Value: 2,665

Equipment		Mass
Internal Structure:	Endo Steel	3.5
Engine:	280 XL	8
Walking MP:	4	
Running MP:	6	
Jumping MP:	4	
Heat Sinks:	18 [36]	8
Gyro:		3
Cockpit:		3
Armor Factor:	216	13.5

	Internal Structure	Armor Value
Head	3	9
Center Torso	22	34
Center Torso (rear)		9
R/L Torso	15	22
R/L Torso (rear)		8
R/L Arm	11	22
R/L Leg	15	30

Weapons and Ammo	Location	Critical	Tonnage
ER PPC	RA	2	6
Heavy Medium Laser	RA	2	1
ATM 6	RT	3	3.5
Ammo (ATM) 30	RT	3	3
ER PPC	LA	2	6
Heavy Medium Laser	LA	2	1
ATM 6	LT	3	3.5
Ammo (ATM) 30	LT	3	3
Jump Jets	RL	2	2
Jump Jets	LL	2	2

FLAMBERGE

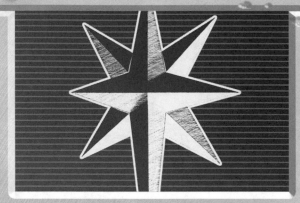

Mass: 70 tons
Chassis: JF 7 Light Endo Steel
Power Plant: 280 XL Fusion
Cruising Speed: 43 kph
Maximum Speed: 65 kph
Jump Jets: None
    Jump Capacity: None
Armor: JF Standard
Armament:
    2 Pattern J7 SRM 6 Racks
    35 tons of pod space available
Manufacturer: Olivetti Weaponry
    Primary Factory: Sudeten
Communications System: JF Integrated
Targeting and Tracking System: JFIX/Olivetti
    Pinpoint Advanced

Overview

In the 3060s, Falcon scientists combined the partial wing design of the Kage battle armor with the shoulder baffles from the *Goshawk*, resulting in a successful debut on an experimental *Cougar* chassis. Their attempt to transplant this success to a new design kept encountering problems and was shelved. However, in 3074, Khan Pryde and Merchant Factor Daniel tasked what remained of Falcon design teams to use what was in the pipeline to rebuild the touman. By removing much of the partial wing hardware, the *Flamberge* was left with just an imposing cosmetic appearance. This new design was intended as a heavy hitter to work with the *Loki* and *Thor*.

Capabilities

Despite slower ground speed compared to its contemporaries, the *Flamberge* was designed with mobility in mind.

While most configurations use jump jets, designers left them off the base model for flexibility. The structure of the upper wing meant the prototype's shoulder-mounted SRMs could not be removed without significant alteration, and so they were kept in the base version. Fortunately, the 'Mech's advantages outweigh its disadvantages. Thirteen and a half tons of armor protect the *Flamberge*, while compact construction materials grant thirty-five tons of pod space, allowing it to emulate the sword that is its namesake and destroy the enemy's weapons.

The primary configuration uses improved jump jets for greater mobility. A pair of advanced tactical missiles provides multi-range fire, while quad pulse lasers provide accurate fire up close. The standard SRMs can be used to exploit holes made by the other weapons. The alpha configuration emulates the version that Quinn Kerensky has used since piloting the machine, similar to what she used on her *Thor*. A large pulse laser and extended-range particle cannon tied to a targeting computer give it a ranged punch, while more than a score of SRMs can clean up once the warrior closes in on the target. Five improved jump jets give it the same aerial reach as the *Thor*.

The beta configuration is a harasser, whose three plasma cannons can wreak havoc on enemy 'Mechs and ravage other units. Large and dual medium extended-range lasers provide more of a bite. The fourth configuration is unusual, sporting the Arrow IV artillery launcher for support, but with an array of lasers tied into a targeting computer to allow the warrior to still pose a threat.

Deployment

The *Flamberge* has been assigned to premier Falcon units, such as Epsilon's Fifth Battle Cluster and the First Falcon Strikers. Many *ristars* and prominent warriors have been assigned the new design. Galaxy Commander Kerensky was assigned one after she destroyed her third *Thor* in five years with her aggressive tactics, and shortly thereafter Gamma Galaxy requested as many of the machines as they could get.

On Phecda, a former Smoke Jaguar warrior in his *Masakari* was terrorizing Falcon warriors. Ingrid Pryde had her techs outfit her 'Mech in the B configuration and engaged him. By randomly firing her plasma cannons and infernos, she dampened his return fire while she cut his 'Mech up with her lasers and SRMs. As a last desperate tactic, he fired all his weapons and savaged the *Flamberge*, but overheated his 'Mech. An aimed shot to the cockpit ended his service with the Blakists. Ingrid Pryde's exploits have made the *Flamberge* an acceptable choice to traditionalists in the Clan.

Variants

With the recent influx of scientists from Clan Wolf, the problem with the partial wing was finally solved and the remaining prototypes are in testing. Accompanied by a bevy of pulse lasers, six improved jump jets with even greater range due to the wing allow this new model to practically never touch ground, shredding opponents in test runs so far. It is unknown if these will prompt a restart of the initial program or if these prototypes will be just that.

Type: Flamberge
Technology Base: Clan
Tonnage: 70
Battle Value: 2,266

Equipment			Mass
Internal Structure:		Endo Steel	3.5
Engine:		280 XL	8
Walking MP:		4	
Running MP:		6	
Jumping MP:		0	
Heat Sinks:		11 [22]	1
Gyro:			3
Cockpit:			3
Armor Factor:		216	13.5
		Internal Structure	Armor Value
Head		3	9
Center Torso		22	31
Center Torso (rear)			12
R/L Torso		15	20
R/L Torso (rear)			10
R/L Arm		11	22
R/L Leg		15	30

Weight and Space Allocation		
Location	Fixed	Spaces Remaining
Head	1 Endo Steel	0
Center Torso	None	2
Right Torso	2 XL Engine	8
	2 Endo Steel	
Left Torso	2 XL Engine	10
Right Arm	SRM 6	5
	2 Endo Steel	
Left Arm	SRM 6	5
	2 Endo Steel	
Right Leg	None	2
Left Leg	None	2

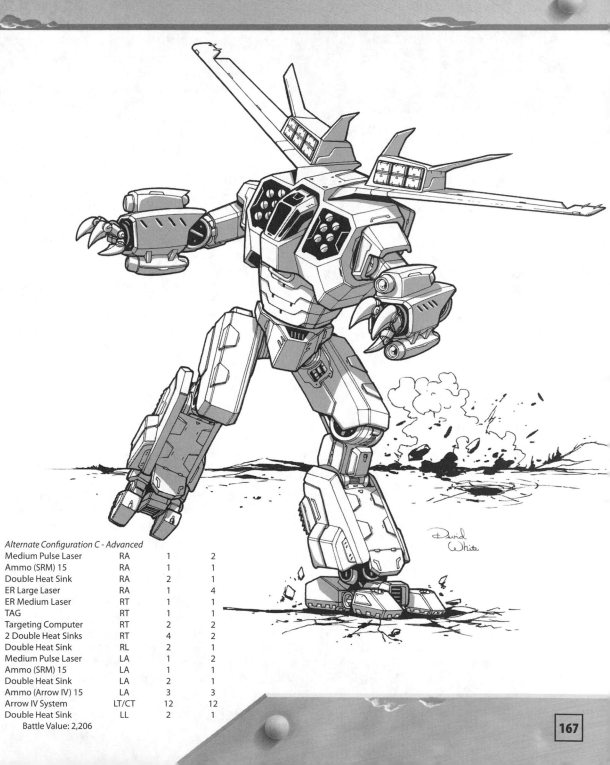

Weapons and Ammo	Location	Critical	Tonnage
Primary Weapons Configuration			
2 Medium Pulse Lasers	RA	2	4
Ammo (SRM) 15	RA	1	1
Double Heat Sink	RA	2	1
ATM 6	RT	3	3.5
Ammo (ATM) 10	RT	1	1
Improved Jump Jets	RT	4	4
Improved Jump Jet	RL	2	2
2 Medium Pulse Lasers	LA	2	4
Ammo (SRM) 15	LA	1	1
Double Heat Sink	LA	2	1
ATM 6	LT	3	3.5
Ammo (ATM) 10	LT	1	1
Improved Jump Jets	LT	4	4
Double Heat Sink	LT	2	1
Improved Jump Jet	LL	2	2
Double Heat Sink	CT	2	1
Alternate Configuration A			
ER PPC	RA	2	6
Ammo (SRM) 15	RA	1	1
Double Heat Sink	RA	2	1
SRM 6	RT	1	1.5
Improved Jump Jets	RT	4	4
Targeting Computer	RT	3	3
Double Heat Sink	RL	2	1
Large Pulse Laser	LA	2	6
Ammo (SRM) 30	LA	2	2
Double Heat Sink	LA	2	1
SRM 6	LT	1	1.5
Improved Jump Jets	LT	4	4
Double Heat Sink	LL	2	1
Improved Jump Jet	CT	2	2
Battle Value: 2,575			
Alternate Configuration B			
Plasma Cannon	RA	1	3
Ammo (Plasma) 10	RA	1	1
ER Medium Laser	RA	1	1
Ammo (SRM) 15	RA	1	1
Double Heat Sink	RA	2	1
ER Large Laser	RT	1	4
Ammo (Plasma) 10	RT	1	1
Jump Jets	RT	2	2
Double Heat Sink	RL	2	1
Plasma Cannon	LA	1	3
Ammo (Plasma) 10	LA	1	1
ER Medium Laser	LA	1	1
Ammo (SRM) 15	LA	1	1
Double Heat Sink	LA	2	1
Targeting Computer	LT	3	3
Ammo (Plasma) 10	LT	1	1
2 Double Heat Sinks	LT	4	2
Jump Jets	LT	2	2
Double Heat Sink	LL	2	1
Plasma Cannon	CT	1	3
Ammo (Plasma) 10	CT	1	1
Battle Value: 2,750			

Alternate Configuration C – Advanced			
Medium Pulse Laser	RA	1	2
Ammo (SRM) 15	RA	1	1
Double Heat Sink	RA	2	1
ER Large Laser	RA	1	4
ER Medium Laser	RT	1	1
TAG	RT	1	1
Targeting Computer	RT	2	2
2 Double Heat Sinks	RT	4	2
Double Heat Sink	RL	2	1
Medium Pulse Laser	LA	1	2
Ammo (SRM) 15	LA	1	1
Double Heat Sink	LA	2	1
Ammo (Arrow IV) 15	LA	3	3
Arrow IV System	LT/CT	12	12
Double Heat Sink	LL	2	1
Battle Value: 2,206			

David White

SPHINX

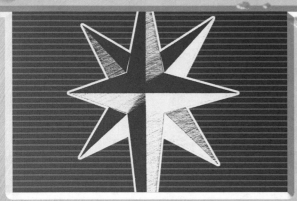

Mass: 75 tons
Chassis: Bergan Version 6.2 Endo Steel
Power Plant: Starfire 375 XL
Cruising Speed: 54 kph
Maximum Speed: 86 kph
Jump Jets: None
    Jump Capacity: None
Armor: Compound 12A2
Armament:
    2 Series 6b Extended Range Large Lasers
    10 Series 2f Extended Range Medium Lasers
Manufacturer: Avon Alpha
    Primary Factory: Avon
Communications System: Raldon R1
Targeting and Tracking System: Dalban Hirez II

Overview

Learning from their experience against the Word of Blake, Clan Nova Cat developed the *Sphinx* as a heavy cavalry design with extended endurance and minimal dependence on supply lines. Rushed into service in 3078, this is a conventional BattleMech, not an OmniMech as had been intended during its early design phases.

Capabilities

Envisioned as a companion to designs such as the *Black Hawk*, the *Sphinx* is intended to operate as a fast-strike unit with an impressive all-energy weapon loadout. The arm-mounted Series 6b lasers allow the Clan MechWarrior to reach out and touch an opponent. Using the power of the Starfire 375 XL engine to close the range, a battery of ten Series 2f lasers can shred BattleMech and vehicle armor. Their effect on battle armor is equally impressive. However, the massed laser fire comes with a heavy heat burden. Though the *Sphinx* mounts a staggering twenty-three double efficiency heat sinks, an inexperienced MechWarrior can easily push the BattleMech into shutdown in seconds.

Rushed into production, the *Sphinx* lacks the elegance and polish of many modern designs, but only an unwise MechWarrior dismisses the blocky and ungainly-looking BattleMech out of hand. Rough and unfinished-looking it may be, but the Clan technicians created a simple and rugged chassis (reminiscent of the *Highlander* assault 'Mech), well protected by more than thirteen tons of armor. Low maintenance requirements and an all-laser armament have produced a 'Mech whose endurance is limited only by that of the MechWarrior in the cockpit. An unintended bonus comes from the legacy of the design starting life as an OmniMech. Many of the primary assemblies and components retain modular features that make replacement and repair an easy task.

The only problem Clan Nova Cat has experienced with their new BattleMech design is production hampered by shortages in supply of the Starfire 375 XL, which remains in great demand for repairs to the redoubtable *Mad Cat*.

Deployment

Originally content to deploy the *Sphinx* in its intended role, the Nova Cats have been so impressed with the BattleMech's success in vicious fighting with the Word of Blake that they have increased production and the *Sphinx* is now appearing in front-line commands.

In 3084, Clan Nova Cat dispatched their 246th Battle Cluster to aid the First Sword of Light against the elements of the Ghost Bear Dominion's Ninth PGC on Mualang. The open terrain favored fast BattleMechs with superior ranged armament, and the 246th's *Sphinx* Star performed magnificently against the *Kodiak*, *Arcas* and *Grizzly* BattleMechs fielded by the Bears. In the end it was not fighting prowess that decided the battle, but the collapse of the Bears' logistical tail. By the end of November it was all over; the Ninth abandoned Mualang and returned to Dominion territory.

The *Sphinx* is also well suited to the Clan tradition of dueling and has become a firm favorite with *ristars* looking to secure a Bloodname. In an epic confrontation, Star Commander Ramon and MechWarrior Sadig faced off in identical *Sphinx* BattleMechs in the final round of a Trial of Bloodright for a Rosse Bloodname. The pair stalked each other through the ruins of LexaTech's production line. The battle was long and fierce and the pair appeared evenly matched as their tough BattleMechs absorbed hit after hit from their opponent's lasers. Finally it appeared as if Sadig had gained the upper hand when Ramon's *Sphinx* lost power to its right arm laser. Sensing an opening, Sadig closed from his opponent's right, only to see Ramon bring up his *Sphinx*'s right arm and fire the still-operational laser into Sadig's cockpit.

Variants

An interesting variant of the *Sphinx* surfaced in 3080 among the ranks of the Nova Cats who participated in operations against the Word of Blake Protectorate. This model drops a heat sink and the extended-range medium lasers. The arm-mounted, extended-range large lasers have been moved to the center torso, and extended-range small lasers are installed—five in the left and five in the right torso. The *Sphinx* 2 is equipped with an advanced targeting computer in the right torso and MASC in the left torso. This modification to the weapons mix makes the crippling heat problems of the original more manageable, while the targeting computer allows the MechWarrior to make precision strikes against opponents after using the MASC to close rapidly.

SPHINX

Type: **Sphinx**
Technology Base: Clan
Tonnage: 75
Battle Value: 2,883

Equipment		Mass
Internal Structure:	Endo Steel	4
Engine:	375 XL	19.5
Walking MP:	5	
Running MP:	8	
Jumping MP:	0	
Heat Sinks:	23 [46]	13
Gyro:		4
Cockpit:		3
Armor Factor:	216	13.5

	Internal Structure	Armor Value
Head	3	9
Center Torso	23	34
Center Torso (rear)		11
R/L Torso	16	23
R/L Torso (rear)		8
R/L Arm	12	20
R/L Leg	16	30

Weapons and Ammo	Location	Critical	Tonnage
ER Large Laser	RA	1	4
4 ER Medium Lasers	RT	4	4
2 ER Medium Lasers	CT	2	2
4 ER Medium Lasers	LT	4	4
ER Large Laser	LA	1	4

TUNDRA WOLF 4

Mass: 75 tons
Chassis: TW-2 Heavy Endo Steel
Power Plant: Starfire 300 XL
Cruising Speed: 43 kph
Maximum Speed: 64 kph, 86 kph with MASC
Jump Jets: BMP Series XV
   Jump Capacity: 120 meters
Armor: Beta Compound (Standard)
Armament:
   1 Type 9 Series Advanced Tactical Missile Systems
   2 Series 2b ER Medium Lasers
   2 Tau-II Anti-personnel Gauss Rifles
   2 Delta Series Large Pulse Lasers
Manufacturer: W-7 Facilities
   Primary Factory: Tamar
Communications System: Khan Series (Type 3a)
   with ECM Suite
Targeting and Tracking System: Build 4 MadCat TTS

Overview

The *Tundra Wolf* 4 is clearly the product of a revised combat doctrine that emerged during the Jihad. An emphasis is placed on accuracy and efficiency with several "contingency systems" that would have been un-Clanlike twenty years ago. Under different circumstances, the warrior who oversees this configuration might well have found himself in a Circle of Equals defending his honor. Instead, the design has been heralded as a welcome companion on the battlefield. Emerging just twelve months after the debut of the first three variants, the *Tundra Wolf* 4 quickly outpaced them in deployment within Clan Wolf.

Capabilities

The *Tundra Wolf* 4 is a heat-friendly brawler prepared for any battlefield contingency. MASC gives it short bursts of speed nearing ninety kph. Fourteen and a half tons of standard armor outfits a robust chassis with the maximum available protection, though analysis of battleROM footage suggests that the shoulder and elbow joints are particularly vulnerable to damage.

A pair of torso-mounted Delta Series lasers gives it an ammo-independent punch and the ability to operate for extended periods without re-supply. Retaining the left arm-mounted ATM 9 and three tons of ammunition serves up tactical flexibility without compromise. For close-range support, the *Tundra Wolf* 4 mounts a brace of Series 2b lasers alongside a pair of AP Gauss rifles; a clear nod to the threat posed by conventional infantry forces that would be surprising outside of Clan Hell's Horses if not for the Jihad. A ton of Gauss ammo offers the reserves to fire for effect. The Series 2b lasers are excellent secondary weapons, effective in dropping some Blakist battle armor designs with a single shot and efficiently chewing through armor on harder targets.

An ECM suite rounds out the design. Installed specifically to foul Blakist C³i computers, the compact electronics showcase robust Clan engineering.

Deployment

Appearing near the high-water mark of the Jihad, the *Tundra Wolf* became a symbol to Clan Wolf. The 'Mech appears in many Stars throughout the Clan's touman, and piloting one has become a symbol of honor among Wolf MechWarriors. During the fierce fighting to shatter the Blake Protectorate, the Wolves allowed Stone's Coalition to salvage and repair a number of the 'Mechs, and it still appears in modest numbers within the RAF. The Wolves have offered spare parts and other supplies to the RAF to maintain their supply of *Tundra Wolf* 'Mechs, but have not yet agreed to sell complete 'Mechs.

Clan Wolf-in-Exile also fields some of the design, though whether they were acquired in Trials against Clan Wolf or through other means remains unclear.

Variants

Since its inception in 3076, the Wolves have built three variants of the *Tundra Wolf*. The original features two additional Series 2b lasers in place of the AP Gauss rifles. A Long Bow twenty-tube missile rack and a four-tube Smartshot Streak replace one of the large pulse lasers, while the other is swapped for an extended-range version. This variant also features maximum armor protection for its weight, but mounts two fewer heat sinks.

The *Tundra Wolf* 2 is equipped with a total of six Series 2b lasers, a Series 7K ER large laser, and an ER particle cannon all tied to a targeting computer. An LRM 15 rides in the right torso as an afterthought. Even with nineteen double-strength heat sinks, the *Tundra Wolf* 2 is capable of exceeding its heat dissipation capacity by fifty percent. Fortunately, the armament selection allows a MechWarrior to shift between long-range and close-range weaponry as the engagement scenario dictates, and the 'Mech's heat sinks adequately handle either firing option.

With a pair of ER particle cannons, backed by a Series 7K ER large laser and LRM 15, the *Tundra Wolf* 3 is destined for long-range engagements. The *Tundra Wolf* 3 also carries a quartet of Series 2b lasers backed by a four-tube Streak launcher. As with the *Tundra Wolf* 2 and 4, the *Tundra Wolf* 3 relies on nineteen double-strength sinks to shed its significant waste heat. The *Tundra Wolf* 3's primary long-range arsenal alone generates nearly twenty-five percent more heat than the 'Mech can immediately shed. Despite the heat problems, this variant quickly became a favorite among more traditional Wolves who favor *zellbrigen*.

TUNDRA WOLF 4

Type: **Tundra Wolf 4**
Technology Base: Clan
Tonnage: 75
Battle Value: 2,873

Equipment		Mass
Internal Structure:	Endo Steel	4
Engine:	300 XL	9.5
Walking MP:	4	
Running MP:	6 (8)	
Jumping MP:	4	
Heat Sinks:	19 [38]	9
Gyro:		3
Cockpit:		3
Armor Factor:	231	14.5

	Internal Structure	Armor Value
Head	3	9
Center Torso	23	34
Center Torso (rear)		12
R/L Torso	16	24
R/L Torso (rear)		8
R/L Arm	12	24
R/L Leg	16	32

Weapons and Ammo	Location	Critical	Tonnage
2 ER Medium Lasers	RA	2	2
2 AP Gauss Rifles	RA	2	1
Ammo (AP Gauss) 40	RA	1	1
Large Pulse Laser	RT	2	6
ECM Suite	CT	1	1
Large Pulse Laser	LT	2	6
ATM 9	LA	3	5
Ammo (ATM) 21	LA	3	3
MASC	LT	3	3
Jump Jets	RL	2	2
Jump Jets	LL	2	2

David White

BRUIN

Mass: 80 tons
Chassis: Bergan Version 8.4 Standard
Power Plant: 320 Light Force XL
Cruising Speed: 43 kph
Maximum Speed: 64 kph
Jump Jets: Clan Standard Type A3
    Jump Capacity: 120 meters
Armor: Compound 12A1 Standard
Armament:
    1 Kolibri Delta Series Large Pulse Laser
    1 Omega 12-coil Gauss Rifle
    2 Series 2f Extended Range Medium Lasers
    1 Type X "Short Bow" LRM 10 Launcher
    2 Smartshot Mark V Streak SRM 4 Launchers
Manufacturer: Bergan Industries C-Division
    Primary Factory: Alshain
Communications System: Garret L30
Targeting and Tracking System: RCA Instatrac Mark XII

Overview

In 3059, Khan Bjorn Jorgensson's vision of Inner Sphere-produced Clan BattleMechs became a reality with the release of the *Ursus* design. The production of the *Ursus* helped revive several sectors of the economy within the shattered and conquered area of the Inner Sphere once known as the Free Rasalhague Republic. In addition, the inclusion of engineering and military leaders from Rasalhague's population made enormous strides in changing attitudes about the Ghost Bears. No longer seen as invading overlords, the Ghost Bears became the future leaders for billions of former Rasalhaguians.

That military industrial growth continued throughout the 3060s. The *Arcas* became the second successful BattleMech design, with its release in 3061. If not for the chaos of the FedCom Civil War and the terrible destruction of the Jihad, Bergen Industries' C-Division would likely have already produced an entire range of Clan BattleMechs for use by Ghost Bear warriors and the absorbed Royal KungsArmé.

As the widespread destruction of the Jihad wound down, the factories of the Ghost Bear Dominion were once again gearing up to produce BattleMechs. The Ghost Bears could once again focus on their long-term plans, which included a wide array of civic and martial projects—among them the continuation of the Bergan C-Division BattleMech line. The *Bruin* was the next design scheduled for completion and soon became the re-launch project for the factories on Alshain.

Capabilities

Production levels are unlikely to approach their previously prolific pitch for years or even decades to come. However, BattleMechs are still a wanted and needed commodity. Assault 'Mechs have long stood as both extensions and symbols of power. The sheer firepower of a Clan-technology assault BattleMech is horrifying and captivating to behold. Retaining the *Arcas'* concept of high mobility, the Bergen-C team created the *Bruin* with excellent mobility for its hefty 80-ton weight. While its top speed is average, the inclusion of jump jets enables the *Bruin* to move in the most difficult terrain.

The choice of weapons was a source of evaluation and intense analysis. The evolution of battlefield tactics dictated that an assault 'Mech carry both long-range firepower and an arsenal capable of dispatching foes quickly at shorter ranges. Utilizing the reliable Gauss rifle and large pulse laser weapon systems, the *Bruin* has ample long-range firepower. As ranges decrease, its firepower becomes lethal with the addition of a battery of classic Clan extended-range medium lasers and a pair of Streak short-range missile launchers. Both systems, while old by Clan standards, have an infamous history on battlefields in Clan space and the Inner Sphere. The long-range missile system, while also venerable, is one of the most compact yet reliable in the Clan arsenal.

The *Bruin* weapon package may be simple, but it is effective. In addition to the comprehensive weapon systems, fifteen tons of Compound 12A1 standard armor sheathes the *Bruin* in a protective shell. With ample tonnage devoted to survivability and firepower, the *Bruin* is designed to give and take a solid punch.

Deployment

The *Bruin* is already being dispersed among second-line units throughout the Dominion. While not as rapidly produced as the earlier *Arcas* or *Ursus* designs, the Ghost Bears hope to have a substantial run of *Bruins* in the field by 3086. Initial responses from assigned warriors are extremely positive.

The sheer size and menace of the *Bruin* has served the defense of the Dominion nearly as well as its firepower and combat abilities. Raiding units that encounter Stars of pristine Ghost Bear assault 'Mechs are quick to abandon their plans and retreat. Even in an age where wholesale destruction can rain from the skies, the psychological impact of enormous BattleMechs towering over the battlefield cannot be underestimated.

Variants

In the aftermath of Terra's liberation, the need for a BattleMech designed to combat armor and infantry heavy opponents spawned the *Bruin* 2 variant. The Gauss rifle and medium lasers were shed in order to give the *Bruin* a *Rifleman*-like foursome of over-under large pulse lasers and Ultra-5 autocannons. An SRM 2 was mounted in order to give the *Bruin* inferno capabilities, and machine guns were added to handle infantry threats.

BRUIN

Type: **Bruin**
Technology Base: Clan
Tonnage: 80
Battle Value: 2,630

Equipment		Mass
Internal Structure:		8
Engine:	320 XL	11.5
Walking MP:	4	
Running MP:	6	
Jumping MP:	4	
Heat Sinks:	14 [28]	4
Gyro:		4
Cockpit:		3
Armor Factor:	240	15

	Internal Structure	Armor Value
Head	3	9
Center Torso	25	35
Center Torso (rear)		14
R/L Torso	17	24
R/L Torso (rear)		10
R/L Arm	13	25
R/L Leg	17	32

Weapons and Ammo	Location	Critical	Tonnage
Gauss Rifle	RA	6	12
Ammo (Gauss) 16	RA	2	2
ER Medium Laser	RA	1	1
Streak SRM 4	RT	1	2
LRM 10	CT	1	2.5
Ammo (LRM) 12	CT	1	1
Streak SRM 4	LT	1	2
Ammo (Streak) 25	LT	1	1
Large Pulse Laser	LA	2	6
ER Medium Laser	LA	1	1
Jump Jets	RL	2	2
Jump Jets	LL	2	2

NIGHT WOLF

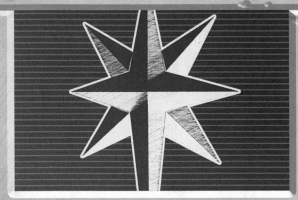

Mass: 90 tons
Chassis: DSAM Endo 4
Power Plant: Light Force 360 (XL) Fusion
Cruising Speed: 43 kph
Maximum Speed: 64 kph
Jump Jets: Grandthrust Mk. 5
    Jump Capacity: 120 meters
Armor: Compound 12B2 Standard
Armament:
    1 Series 4D-2 Heavy Large Laser
    1 Zeta-series X Plasma Cannon
    1 Series 2b Extended-Range Medium Laser
    2 Type 9 Series 1 Advanced Tactical Missile Launchers
    1 Shield 3A Anti-Missile System
Manufacturer: W-7 Facilities
    Primary Factory: Weingarten
Communications System: TJ6 "Bell" Mark II with ECM
Targeting and Tracking System: Mars System 9 (Build 2)
    with Targeting Computer

Overview

Clan Wolf may be one of the strongest Clans politically, and one of the most effective militarily, but it became clear during the Jihad that their sense of logistics and grand strategy remained sub-par. In an effort to minimize predations by neighbor Clans, Inner Sphere raiders, and local insurgents, the Wolves left many of their more advanced military industries in the homeworlds, content to replenish their materiel losses through a year-long supply line. The Word of Blake Jihad, combined with the upheavals in the Kerensky Cluster, severed this lifeline, forcing the bastion of the Crusader movement to hastily upgrade facilities they had long ignored.

More than that, however, the combined-arms philosophies of the Wolves' enemies—most notably the Word of Blake and the returning Hell's Horses—challenged the Wolves' combat philosophies, increasing the need for a more flexible response in the battlefield. The *Night Wolf*, an assault-class standard BattleMech, was one answer the Clan developed to the dual crises of their lost supply lines and the sheer variety of combined arms warfare.

Capabilities

For a Clan-made assault 'Mech, the *Night Wolf* appears somewhat unremarkable. Its mobility, firepower, and armor are generalized, neither particularly impressive, nor particularly lacking. While the combination of a 360 extralight engine and jump jets do offer maneuverability common to many heavy 'Mechs made by the Inner Sphere (or assault 'Mechs in the various Clan toumans), their primary purpose seems to be transporting a rather eclectic mix of firepower across built-up terrain.

The *Night Wolf*'s weapons load includes twin nine-tube ATM launchers, a heavy large laser, and a plasma cannon, backed up by a medium laser and an anti-missile system. This gives the BattleMech the ability to contend with a variety of threats, but in a "jack-of-all-trades" fashion, with no overwhelming firepower directed against any one opponent type. A targeting computer for enhanced direct-fire capability, and an ECM suite to counter hostile electronics support this collection of armaments and attest to the lessons learned during the Jihad.

The armor is standard, as much a concession to cost as it is to the lack of space. Because of this, the *Night Wolf* carries twenty percent less protection than it would have using a comparable amount of ferro-fibrous armor. Even so, the armor remains thick enough to absorb blasts from some of the heaviest conventional weapons in production today.

Deployment

Clan Wolf has been using the *Night Wolf* mainly to replenish losses in its second-line assault formations, where it is gradually replacing some more venerable second-line machines the Clan cannot presently acquire (like the *Highlander IIC* and the *Supernova*). Many of these BattleMechs have appeared among forces arrayed along the Wolves' shared border with the Hell's Horses, where they would logically form a key part of a defense line against future inter-Clan fighting.

Variants

There are no known variants of the *Night Wolf*.

NIGHT WOLF

Type: **Night Wolf**
Technology Base: Clan
Tonnage: 90
Battle Value: 2,878

Equipment		Mass
Internal Structure:	Endo Steel	4.5
Engine:	360 XL	16.5
Walking MP:	4	
Running MP:	6	
Jumping MP:	4	
Heat Sinks:	18 [36]	8
Gyro:		4
Cockpit:		3
Armor Factor:	248	15.5

	Internal Structure	Armor Value
Head	3	9
Center Torso	29	37
Center Torso (rear)		12
R/L Torso	19	28
R/L Torso (rear)		10
R/L Arm	15	25
R/L Leg	19	32

Weapons and Ammo	Location	Critical	Tonnage
ER Medium Laser	RA	1	1
ATM 9	RA	4	5
Ammo (ATM) 21	RA	3	3
Heavy Large Laser	RT	3	4
Targeting Computer	RT	2	2
Anti-Missile System	H	1	.5
Ammo (AMS) 24	CT	1	1
ECM Suite	CT	1	1
Ammo (Plasma) 20	LT	2	2
Plasma Cannon	LA	1	3
ATM 9	LA	4	5
Ammo (ATM) 21	LA	3	3
Jump Jets	RL	2	4
Jump Jets	LL	2	4

ONAGER

Mass: 90 tons
Chassis: ONG-90
Power Plant: Consolidated Fusion 270
Cruising Speed: 32 kph
Maximum Speed: 54 kph
Jump Jets: JF Improved Jump Jets
    Jump Capacity: 150 meters
Armor: Forging MD4 Ferro-Fibrous
Armament:
    1 Type 0 Hyper Velocity Assault Gun 30
    2 Series 14a Medium Pulse Lasers
    2 Pattern J7 SRM 6
    2 Raid Micro Pulse Lasers
    1 Chi Series Small Pulse Laser
Manufacturer: Red Devil Industries
    Primary Factory: Pandora
Communications System: Angst 2400
Targeting and Tracking System: Omicron XX

Overview

With an enormous losses over the past decade, the Jade Falcons needed to rebuild their forces, especially their defensive units. To this end, Khan Clees ordered the team that had just finished developing the *Flamberge* to develop a heavier unit that was easy and cheap to manufacture. Given these requirements, they built an effective new design named after a medieval siege engine. The most controversial decision in the creation of the *Onager* was to upgrade and expand the facilities on Pandora to build the 'Mech. Apparently Merchant Factor Daniel's segregation of different plants is starting to fade.

Capabilities

Built around a sturdy endo steel frame, the *Onager* is protected by fifteen tons of ferro-fibrous armor. It lacks an extralight engine, making it inexpensive and highly durable. It is primarily built around a medium hyper-assault Gauss rifle. Nestled in the left arm, it provides all of the long-range firepower of the *Onager*. Upon closing, it can bring the rest of its weaponry into play. Dual SRM six-tube launchers can exploit the holes that the HAG has opened up, while a bevy of pulse lasers—currently imported from the Diamond Sharks—provide ammo-independent firepower. The medium lasers can help cover medium-range engagements while the other three can be used at point blank-range, though they are primarily installed for anti-personnel defense.

The final asset of the *Onager* is mobility. Five improved jump jets give the 'Mech the jump capability of lighter 'Mechs. Standard procedure for *Onager* pilots is to slowly approach the enemy under cover of HAG fire. Then, when in close, use the jump capability of the machine with the accuracy of the pulse lasers to finish off opponents. The design has shown promise as an urban fighter, working well in close ranges while the HAG hits harder with more accurate fire inside a quarter-kilometer.

Deployment

Unusual for a second-line design, the first *Onager* was sent to Iota Galaxy. There it has been tested on pirates and other Periphery denizens. Against such inferior opponents it isn't surprising that it has fared well. In the past year the 'Mech has slowly been allocated to fill out second-line units. Many warriors are grateful to replace their Inner Sphere designs with a solid Clan 'Mech, even if it isn't an OmniMech. The older machines are being sent to solahma units in addition to the more loyal militia units that the Clan has allowed to form. Reportedly, Khan Clees has been contemplating sending units out to raid other Clans to test the *Onager* against more capable foes, but nothing has occurred yet.

Variants

There are no factory variants at this time. There have been discussions of replacing the HAG with a pair of heavy-hitting Ultra autocannons and swapping the launchers out for long-range versions. At this time it is an academic proposal, as such a configuration would require massive redesigning of the chassis.

Type: Onager
Technology Base: Clan
Tonnage: 90
Battle Value: 2,732

Equipment		Mass
Internal Structure:	Endo Steel	4.5
Engine:	270	14.5
Walking MP:	3	
Running MP:	5	
Jumping MP:	5	
Heat Sinks:	12 [24]	2
Gyro:		3
Cockpit:		3
Armor Factor (Ferro):	279	15

	Internal Structure	Armor Value
Head	3	9
Center Torso	29	40
Center Torso (rear)		18
R/L Torso	19	25
R/L Torso (rear)		13
R/L Arm	15	30
R/L Leg	19	38

Weapons and Ammo	Location	Critical	Tonnage
Medium Pulse Laser	RT	1	2
2 Micro Pulse Lasers	RT	2	1
SRM 6	RT	1	1.5
Small Pulse Laser	H	1	1
Medium Pulse Laser	LT	1	2
SRM 6	LT	1	1.5
Ammo (SRM) 30	LT	2	2
Ammo (HAG) 8	LT	2	2
HAG 30	LA	8	13
Ammo (HAG) 8	LA	2	2
Improved Jump Jets	RT	4	8
Improved Jump Jet	CT	2	4
Improved Jump Jets	LT	4	8

David White

HELLSTAR

Mass: 95 tons
Chassis: Type MA-58 Endo Steel
Power Plant: GM 380 XL
Cruising Speed: 43 kph
Maximum Speed: 64 kph
Jump Jets: None
    Jump Capacity: None
Armor: Royal-7 Standard
Armament:
    4 Ripper Series A1 Extended-Range PPCs
Manufacturer: WC Site 1, Csesztreg Industriplex Alpha
    Primary Factory: Arc-Royal (WC Site 1), Csesztreg
Communications System: CH6 Series Integrated
Targeting and Tracking System: Hunter (7a) Dedicated TTS

Overview

Following the success of the *Cygnus*, the *Hellstar* is another joint production effort from Clan Wolf-in-Exile and Clan Hell's Horses that first appeared in 3079. A somewhat unconventional design, the *Hellstar* shares a large number of components with the *Cygnus*. RAF analysts are uncertain why the designers didn't simply create an all-energy version of the *Cygnus*, but given the extensive changes required for a fixed-configuration BattleMech it might have been easier to start from the ground up.

More worryingly, it could mark a possible change in Clan tactics.

Capabilities

While the *Cygnus* was developed in haste, the *Hellstar* represents a more measured approach. As the *Cygnus*

took its inspiration from the *Annihilator*, the *Hellstar* appears to be the big brother of the Exiles' *Pack Hunter*. Built around a massive all-energy arsenal, protected by thick armor, and with good mobility, the *Hellstar* is built for long-running campaigns. This appears to clash with the quick-and-fierce style of Clan warfare, but the adaptable Wolves and Horses seemingly have no problem with this.

Featuring a more-streamlined chassis than the *Cygnus*, the *Hellstar* acts more-or-less like a Clan version of the *Awesome*, but with far more firepower. Lacking any pretense of secondary weapons, the *Hellstar*'s arsenal consists of four Ripper Series A1 Extended-Range PPCs. Able to drop many medium and heavy 'Mechs with a single salvo, the 'Mech utilizes an unprecedented thirty double heat sinks which allow it to maintain this deadly rain of fire indefinitely without heat build-up. Maximum defense is provided by over eighteen tons of Royal-7 Standard armor, should any attacker survive the PPC onslaught to get close enough to challenge the machine.

The weapons are mounted in large reinforced housings in the arms, and deeply in the 'Mech's torsos. Certain theories suggest that the large housings were designed to obscure the 'Mech's weaponry until it fires. BattleROM footage from the bloody final days of the Jihad perhaps offers a different explanation—Wolf-in-Exile 'Mechs were seen using the arm mounts as clubs to savagely finish off downed Blakist 'Mechs. Though the Exiles are no strangers to the use of flexible tactics, even they have previously adhered to the Clan-wide bias against physical combat. What with the Falcons also reportedly testing melee weapons, has a turning point been reached in the Clans' evolution?

Deployment

The *Hellstar* appears equally in the ranks of the Wolves-in-Exile and the Horses, though RAF forces did manage to salvage a few badly-damaged examples from the many battlefields of the Jihad. Polite overtures have been made to Clan Wolf-in-Exile—via the Lyran Commonwealth—regarding the possibility of acquiring more of the 'Mech for the RAF but all have been rebuffed. So far all production appears to have been used to replenish the damaged Toumans of both Clans.

Variants

Only two variants have been documented so far, though, oddly, both appeared alongside the original during the Jihad—almost as if the Exiles and Horses were performing an extended field test. The first, more of a sub-variant really, adds a targeting computer at the expense of five heat sinks. Although now only capable of maintaining a four-three-four barrage without reaching crippling levels of heat, battle reports provide evidence of this model amputating 'Mechs' limbs and coring center torsos with deadly accuracy.

A second variant exchanges the ER PPCs for Series 7Ja ER Large Lasers but retains the targeting computer. What this variant loses in damage it gains in range, becoming more of a mobile sniper—and yet another step away from accepted Clan norms. Two Kolibri Omega Series Medium Pulse Lasers provide backup firepower, and sit almost unnoticed in the 'Mech's center torso. Twenty-eight double heat sinks provide the ability to fire its entire armament without heat build-up. An active probe and an ECM suite round out the package, showing that the Wolves and Horses have learned from their exposure to the "dirty" tactics used by the Word of Blake and Inner Sphere.

HELLSTAR

Type: **Hellstar**
Technology Base: Clan
Tonnage: 95
Battle Value: 3,084

Equipment		Mass
Internal Structure:	Endo Steel	5
Engine:	380 XL	20.5
Walking MP:	4	
Running MP:	6	
Jumping MP:	0	
Heat Sinks:	30 [60]	20
Gyro:		4
Cockpit:		3
Armor Factor:	293	18.5

	Internal Structure	Armor Value
Head	3	9
Center Torso	30	45
Center Torso (rear)		15
R/L Torso	20	30
R/L Torso (rear)		10
R/L Arm	16	32
R/L Leg	20	40

Weapons and Ammo	Location	Critical	Tonnage
ER PPC	RA	2	6
ER PPC	RT	2	6
ER PPC	LT	2	6
ER PPC	LA	2	6

WUSUN

Mass: 55 tons
Chassis: UOC Medium Spec 4
Power Plant: 330 XL Fusion
Armor: Raven Ferro-Aluminum Comp B
Armament:
    24 tons of pod space available
Manufacturer: United Outworlders Corporation
    Primary Factory: Ramora
Communications System: Outworlds Advanced 6ai
Targeting and Tracking System: Multi-platform T12d

Overview

Throughout the 3060s, United Outworlders Corporation maintained a long apprenticeship under the technicians of Clan Snow Raven, producing first the *Corax* OmniFighter and then the advanced *Hellcat*s and *Lightning*s. By the mid-3070s UOC was ready to attempt manufacture of a fighter built from Clan technology. In 3074, Camden Avellar laid a business plan before the Snow Raven Merchant Factor. The extensive document cited the successful amalgamation of Clan merchants and private industry with Joint Equipment Systems and Alshain Weapons. It pointed to the strong support for Clan Snow Raven amongst the population of Ramora and it illustrated the efficiency gains of a surface-based factory over the Raven's mobile factories. Allowing this degree of access to

Clan technology was a step too far for the Raven Council and no decision was made for a year.

That Avellar ultimately got his way was due primarily to economics. Clan Snow Raven needed to rebuild its aerospace infrastructure and United Outworlders Corporation was willing to pay for it. Negotiations were restarted and construction of the new Clantech line began in 3076. Designed around the lessons of a decade of war, the new OmniFighter would be named the *Wusun*—a clear statement that despite Alliance cooperation, this would be a Snow Raven OmniFighter.

Capabilities

Behind its thick skin the *Wusun* combines a high thrust rating with powerful weapon arrays. Eschewing long-range weapons in its standard configurations, the *Wusun* relies on acceleration to close the range and enter a dogfight. At these ranges the *Wusun* can outturn heavier OmniFighters in the atmosphere while outlasting smaller craft. Most variants combine a computer-assisted array of lasers with a missile battery for an effective balance of heat and damage. Following Inner Sphere trends, its armor is unusually heavy, which enables the *Wusun* to weather enemy fire during the closing phase of an engagement.

Deployment

In order to get access to Clan technology, United Outworlders Corporation has been forced to put its new facility under severe restrictions. All staff have to undergo extensive background checks; Clan Snow Raven is the only authorized buyer; and the Clan is the only supplier of key components. Playing a long term game, UOC is willing to accept this with the knowledge that in the future it will be a player on the Clan technology market and there will be inevitable trickle-down effects to its other factories and markets.

For the *Wusun* this means that it is mainly seen in Clan Snow Raven hands with a small number being passed to the most elite Outworld Alliance pilots. Frequently deployed with a pair of air-to-air Arrow missiles under its wings, the *Wusun* is able to gain significant firepower without compromising maneuverability. Simulations have shown this first-strike capability to be very useful against well-armored opponents.

Though the *Wusun* only debuted earlier this year, it has already shown its teeth. In April, a C-variant downed a pirate *Leopard* over Banori single-handedly. Interest is starting to be shown by the other Clans, but so far no Trials have been declared.

Type: **Wusun**
Technology Base: Clan
Tonnage: 55
Battle Value: 2,450

Equipment			Mass
Engine:	330 XL		12.5
Safe Thrust:	8		
Maximum Thrust:	12		
Structural Integrity:	8		
Heat Sinks:	10 [20]		0
Fuel:	400		5
Cockpit:			3
Armor Factor (Ferro):	220		11.5
	Armor Value	Free Space	
Nose	74	5	
Wings	55/55	4/4	
Aft	36	5	

WUSUN

Weapons and Ammo	Location	Tonnage	Heat	SRV	MRV	LRV	ERV
Primary Weapons Configuration							
3 ER Medium Lasers	Nose	3	5	7	7	—	—
2 Streak SRM 6	RW	6	4	12	12		
Ammo (Streak) 30	—	2					
2 Streak SRM 6	LW	6	4	12	12		—
Ammo (Streak) 30	—	2					
Targeting Computer	—	1					
4 Double Heat Sinks	—	4					
Alternate Weapons Configuration A							
3 Medium Pulse Lasers	Nose	6	4	7	7	—	—
LRM 15+Artemis	RW	4.5	5	12	12	12	—
Ammo (LRM) 16	—	2					
LRM 15+Artemis	LW	4.5	5	12	12	12	—
Ammo (LRM) 16	—	2					
Targeting Computer	—	2					
3 Double Heat Sinks	—	3					

Battle Value: 2,369

Weapons and Ammo	Location	Tonnage	Heat	SRV	MRV	LRV	ERV
Alternate Weapons Configuration B							
HAG 40	Nose	16	8	32	24	24	—
Ammo (HAG) 12	—	4					
Targeting Computer	—	4					

Battle Value: 2,450

Weapons and Ammo	Location	Tonnage	Heat	SRV	MRV	LRV	ERV
Alternate Weapons Configuration C							
ER Large Laser	Nose	4	12	10	10	10	10
3 Heavy Medium Lasers	RW	3	7	10	—	—	—
3 Heavy Medium Lasers	LW	3	7	10	—	—	—
Targeting Computer	—	2					
Active Probe	—	1					
11 Double Heat Sinks	—	11					

Battle Value: 2,365

OSTROGOTH

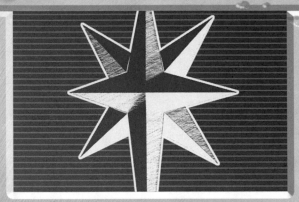

Mass: 75 tons
Chassis: Ursa Major Type VI
Power Plant: GM 375 Fusion Extralight
Armor: Brunin Heavy Ferro-Aluminum
Armament:
    35 tons of pod space available
Manufacturer: Tseng Facility
    Primary Factory: Alshain
Communications System: Vox 91
Targeting and Tracking System: Hunter 62B

Overview

By the mid 3070s, the Ghost Bear Dominion was looking to reorganize its medium OmniFighter forces. In the past it had depended upon the *Visigoth* and more recently the *Jagatai*, but the upheavals of the Jihad made it increasingly difficult to acquire both of these OmniFighters. To make matters worse, combat against the Word of Blake was taking a heavy toll on those few OmniFighters that remained. Production of the low-cost *Ammon* offered a stopgap but its performance was not up to frontline requirements and increased pilot losses to an unacceptable level. Frustrated with the situation, the Ghost Bears began to develop a medium Omnifighter manufactured in an Inner Sphere facility to overcome the problems of performance and supply.

Capabilities

The Dominion was unwilling to give up any of their existing medium OmniFighters' advantages so their response was typical: they increased the mass. This allowed more protection to be worked into the design while a larger engine allowed the fighter to keep the thrust profile the Dominion desired. Technically this made the new OmniFighter a heavy OmniFighter, but the Dominion was intimately familiar with heavy OmniFighter designs and confident in its ability to build the OmniFighter affordably and in numbers.

The result is an impressive weapons platform. Dubbed the *Ostrogoth,* the new fighter combines the acceleration of a medium fighter with the protection of a heavy. Pod space is noticeably less than a *Jagatai* but a number of doctrinal changes minimize the weakness. Fewer fixed heat sinks are installed, while advanced electronics are used to make the most of the weapons carried.

In combat the *Ostrogoth* usually softens up an opponent with its long-range weapons before closing in and unleashing a powerful array of missiles and lasers. Unlike most heavy OmniFighters, *Ostrogoth* configurations excel in a dogfight and many pilots seek close combat. Additionally, the *Ostrogoth* is able to carry a heavy bomb load without compromising its maneuverability, an ability opponents should be wary of in any engagement.

Deployment

Deployed in 3078, the rest of the Inner Sphere first got to see the *Ostrogoth* in the Protectorate campaign. Nearly the same size as the Dominion's *Jengiz*, the *Ostrogoth*'s electronics profile is also nearly identical. This resulted in more than a few Blakist fighters attempting to get behind a slow *Jengiz* only to find themselves being out-turned by an *Ostrogoth*. Limited numbers meant that most *Ostrogoth*s were deployed as shock units in medium Stars where they lived up to expectations and overwhelmed the best the Inner Sphere had to offer.

With the end of the Jihad some external commentators have expressed concern for the future of this OmniFighter, as its massive engine and great size make it far more expensive than other craft assigned to its role. For now the Dominion is continuing production, citing the *Ostrogoth*'s proven war record and, with militaries across the Sphere being reduced in size, a single highly-capable unit offers better economy than several less effective units.

Type: **Ostrogoth**
Technology Base: Clan
Tonnage: 75
Battle Value: 3,720

Equipment			Mass
Engine:	375 XL		19.5
Safe Thrust:	7		
Maximum Thrust:	11		
Structural Integrity:	7		
Heat Sinks:	10 [20]		0
Fuel:	400		5
Cockpit:			3
Armor Factor (Ferro):	240		12.5
	Armor Value	Free Space	
Nose	77	5	
Wings	61/61	4/4	
Aft	41	5	

OSTROGOTH

Weapons and Ammo	Location	Tonnage	Heat	SRV	MRV	LRV	ERV
Primary Weapons Configuration							
ER PPC	Nose	6	15	15	15	15	—
LRM 15+Artemis	RW	4.5	5	12	12	12	—
Ammo (LRM) 16	—	2					
3 ER Medium Lasers	RW	3	5	7	7	—	—
LRM 15+Artemis	LW	4.5	5	12	12	12	—
Ammo (LRM) 16	—	2					
3 ER Medium Lasers	LW	3	5	7	7	—	—
ER Medium Laser	Aft	1	5	7	7	—	—
Targeting Computer	—	3					
ECM Suite	—	1					
5 Double Heat Sinks	—	5					
Alternate Weapons Configuration A							
2 ER PPCs	Nose	12	15	15	15	15	—
Streak SRM 6	RW	3	4	12	12	—	—
Ammo (Streak) 15	—	1					
Streak SRM 6	LW	3	4	12	12	—	—
Ammo (Streak) 15	—	1					
ER Medium Laser	Aft	1	5	7	7	—	—
Targeting Computer	—	3					
Active Probe	—	1					
ECM Suite	—	1					
9 Double Heat Sinks	—	9					
Battle Value: 3,265							
Alternate Weapons Configuration B							
HAG 30	Nose	13	6	24	18	18	—
Ammo (HAG) 12	—	3					
3 ER Medium Lasers	Nose	3	5	7	7	—	—
Streak SRM 6	RW	3	4	12	12	—	—
Ammo (Streak) 15	—	1					
Streak SRM 6	LW	3	4	12	12	—	—
Ammo (Streak) 15	—	1					
Targeting Computer	—	4					
ECM Suite	—	1					
3 Double Heat Sinks	—	3					
Battle Value: 3,171							

Weapons and Ammo	Location	Tonnage	Heat	SRV	MRV	LRV	ERV
Alternate Weapons Configuration C							
LRM 15+Artemis	Nose	4.5	5	12	12	12	—
Ammo (LRM) 16	—	2					
ER Medium Laser	Nose	1	5	5	5	—	—
2 LRM 15+Artemis	RW	9	10	12	12	12	—
Ammo (LRM) 24	—	3					
2 LRM 15+Artemis	LW	9	10	12	12	12	—
Ammo (LRM) 24	—	3					
ER Small Laser	Aft	.5	2	5	—	—	—
ECM Suite	—	1					
2 Double Heat Sinks	—	2					
Battle Value: 2,899							

ISEGRIM ASSAULT DROPSHIP

"Deadly" is how the Tharkad Naval Review described the Clan Wolf-in-Exile's new *Isegrim*-class assault DropShip. "Insubordinate" was how the Commonwealth Navy Command described it. That may be the case, but Clan Wolf-in-Exile has gained a powerful weapons platform and, unfortunately, so has Clan Wolf.

It has been clear for some time that the sundered Wolf Clans have been talking to each other. Lacking their own yards it became commonplace to see Wolf ships undergoing repair in the Arc-Royal yards and it was inevitable warriors and technicians from both Clans would begin comparing notes. In the course of the Jihad, both Clans had been attacked from space by the Word of Blake and needed a way of preventing it happening again. At some time during the late 3070s, this close communication morphed into clandestine plans to design a DropShip that could be produced by both Wolf Clans. The scientist and technicians did not inform their respective Clans that this shared work had been done and both Clans would begin production without knowledge of the other.

Using their own experiences with the formidable Blakist *Interdictor* for inspiration, Clan Wolf-in-Exile proposed a high-thrust interceptor. Using the basic hull form of the *Noruff*, the Wolf technicians increased its mass by a factor of five in order to carry a brace of the Exiles' homegrown sub-capital missiles. A mix of advanced tactical missiles, HAGs, pulse lasers and PPCs provides a whirlwind of fire to exploit gaps opened by the sub-capital weapons. Encased in heavy armor and with more thrust than the Interdictor, this new ship would be able to rapidly close on a target and destroy it. Naming it the *Isegrim*, both groups of technicians went back

to their respective Clans and set in motion plans to construct the DropShip as soon as possible.

Lifting off from the WC Aerospace Annex on Arc-Royal in 3083, the Exile *Isegrim* caused a sensation in Lyran circles, especially as Khan Kell was willing to sell it to the Lyran navy. But within a year, reports from the Clan Wolf Occupation Zone revealed a flotilla of *Isegrim*s in orbit at Tamar and a factory on Dell. Under pressure from the Archon to explain this security leak, Khan Kell launched an investigation to get to the bottom of the mystery. While the answer was found in days, the investigation continued for a further six months in a display of thoroughness that included the execution of three Clan scientists. Ultimately there was nothing that could be done. It had to be accepted that Clan Wolf was also building the *Isegrim*.

After two years of production, useful numbers of *Isegrim*s are spreading throughout the Lyran Commonwealth, operating in assault squadrons. Clan Wolf-in-Exile has established two Stars over Arc-Royal where they serve with Mercers. Clan Wolf has built even more and deploys them in packs, as well as selling a few to Clan Diamond Shark in exchange for HarJel.

ISEGRIM CLASS ASSAULT DROPSHIP

Type: Military Aerodyne
Use: Assault DropShip
Tech: Clan (Advanced)
Introduced: 3083
Mass: 8,500 tons
Battle Value: 37,660

Dimensions
   Length: 170 meters
   Width: 120 meters
   Height: 30 meters

Fuel: 300 tons (9,000 points)
Tons/Burn-day: 1.84
Safe Thrust: 8
Maximum Thrust: 12
Heat Sinks: 210 [420]
Structural Integrity: 21

Armor
   Nose: 671
   Sides: 501
   Aft: 338

Cargo
   Bay 1: Cargo (416 tons)   2 Doors
   Bay 2: Small Craft (1)   1 Doors

Life Boats: 3
Escape Pods: 3
Crew: 5 Officers, 8 Enlisted/Non-rated, 13 Gunners, 10 Battle Armor Marines, 5 Bay personnel

Ammunition: 30 rounds Piranha ammunition (300 tons), 30 rounds Manta Ray Ammunition (540 tons), 180 rounds HAG 40 ammunition (60 tons), 270 rounds ATM 12 ammunition (54 tons), 288 rounds Anti Missile System Ammunition (12 tons)

Notes: Carries 94.5 tons Ferro-Aluminum armor.

Weapons: Arc (Heat) Type	Capital Attack Values (Standard)				
	Short	Medium	Long	Extreme	Class
Nose (165 Heat)					
3 Piranha (30 rounds)	9 (90)	9 (90)	9 (90)	—	Capital Missile
3 Manta Ray (30 rounds)	15 (150)	—	—	—	Capital Missile
3 ER PPCs	5 (45)	5 (45)	5 (45)	—	PPC
3 Large Pulse Lasers	3 (30)	3 (30)	3 (30)	—	Pulse Laser
LW/RW (78 Heat)					
3 HAG 40 (60 rounds)	10 (96)	7 (72)	7 (72)	—	Autocannon
3 Large Pulse Lasers	3 (30)	3 (30)	3 (30)	—	Pulse Laser
3 ATM 12 (90 rounds)	7 (72)	5 (48)	2 (24)	2 (24)	ATM
3 AMS (72 rounds)	1 (9)	—	—	—	AMS
LW/RW Aft (3 Heat)					
3 AMS (72 rounds)	1 (9)	—	—	—	AMS
Aft (123 Heat)					
3 HAG 40 (60 rounds)	10 (96)	7 (72)	7 (72)	—	Autocannon
3 ER PPCs	5 (45)	5 (45)	5 (45)	—	PPC
3 Large Pulse Lasers	3 (30)	3 (30)	3 (30)	—	Pulse Laser
3 ATM 12 (90 rounds)	7 (72)	5 (48)	2 (24)	2 (24)	ATM

AESIR/VANIR ASSAULT DROPSHIPS

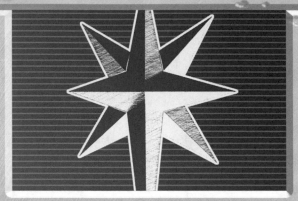

Clan Nova Cat's Trial of Possession in 3067 left the Ghost Bear Dominion lacking the escort ships it needed to properly screen its fleet and logistics network. Looking back to the successful *Titan* class for inspiration, the Dominion sought to build a powerful DropShip to replace its lost destroyers. It took most of a decade to develop the required technologies and establish production lines with the Jihad straining the economy, but the time spent preparing proved worthwhile, with over five Stars of ships built at Alshain and Rasalhague between 3077 and 3081.

Using the same hull and engine, the Bears were able to create two distinct ship classes from the same production facilities. The *Aesir* class combines the aerospace fighters of the *Titan* with a powerful anti-aerospace weapons array. During the design's development it was realized that the demand for additional aerospace fighters would compromise the Leviathan program, so to reduce the impact a derivative class was developed to complement the *Aesir*'s offensive power. Named after the *Vanir*, this secondary class replaced the *Aesir*'s carrier bays with rows of subcapital missiles, making it a formidable defensive platform. Both classes were fitted as command ships with enhanced sensors, control systems and liveability. Lacking aerospace fighters, *Vanir*s are noted for their endurance and carry additional ammunition and supplies.

The Ghost Bear Dominion operates relatively few *Aesir*s, which serve as command ships in their own naval Stars, often with a *Vanir* partner. These Stars generally spent the final months of the Jihad protecting the Dominion's trade lanes and the fleet's logistical tail. The more-numerous *Vanir*s also serve as command ships in escort Stars, but are more famous for acting as screens for the Dominion's battleships. This role thrust them into the thick of the action where their abilities were tested and losses were high.

With the end of the Jihad, both classes have retained their escort duties. Production has continued, at a reduced pace, as the *Aesir* and *Vanir* are seen as a cost effective way to protect the Dominion's merchant fleet. During the recent trouble with the Draconis Combine, the presence of these heavy escorts prevented several attempts at convoy raiding by the Combine and secured the defenses of major Dominion worlds. This freed the fleet's capital units to penetrate the Combine undetected and provide additional political pressure.

Examples of either variant are rare outside of the Ghost Bear Dominion, with Trials and diplomatic gifts being the only way to gain one of these ships. The one exception is Clan Nova Cat. In the lead-up to the Liberation of Terra, it was tasked with escorting the transport elements of the fleet but lacked the screening DropShips required. Devlin Stone met with the Bears and the result of the closed door meeting was the Dominion "gifting" Clan Nova Cat with a mixed binary of *Vanir*s and *Aesir*s. These helped secure the fleet over Terra and most survived the battle. The battleship *Great Bear* gave up its own heavy escorts to meet the needs of Clan Nova Cat and was lost as a result. This is a continuing sore point for the Dominion.

AESIR / VANIR CLASS ASSAULT DROPSHIP

Type: Military Spheroid
Use: Assault DropShip
Tech: Clan (Advanced)
Introduced: 3077
Mass: 18,000 tons
Battle Value: 29,105 / 43,195

Dimensions
   Length: 110 meters
   Width: 100 meters
   Height: 150 meters

Fuel: 1,200 tons (36,000 points)
Tons/Burn-day: 1.84
Safe Thrust: 5
Maximum Thrust: 8
Heat Sinks: 333 [666] / 423 [846]
Structural Integrity: 25

Armor
   Nose: 536
   Sides: 500
   Aft: 400

Cargo (Aesir)
   Bay 1: Cargo (1515 tons)   2 Doors
   Bay 2: Fighters (30) / Small Craft (3) 6 Doors

Cargo (Vanir)
   Bay 1: Cargo (1574 tons)   2 Doors
   Bay 2: Small Craft (3)   2 Doors

Life Boats: 10
Escape Pods: 10
Crew: Aesir (9 Officers, 20 Enlisted/Non-rated, 17 Gunners, 25 Battle Armor Marines, 75 Bay personnel), Vanir (9 Officers, 20 Enlisted/Non-rated, 33 Gunners, 50 Battle Armor Marines, 15 Bay personnel)

Ammunition (Aesir): 120 rounds Piranha ammunition (1200 tons), 360 rounds ATM 12 Ammunition (72 tons), 126 rounds HAG 40 ammunition (42 tons), 1296 rounds Anti Missile System Ammunition (54 tons)

Ammunition (Vanir): 180 rounds Piranha ammunition (1800 tons), 120 rounds Stingray ammunition (1440 tons), 360 rounds ATM 12 Ammunition (72 tons), 126 rounds HAG 40 ammunition (42 tons), 1296 rounds Anti-Missile System Ammunition (54 tons)

Notes: Carries 90 tons of Ferro-Aluminum armor, 100 tons Small NCSS.

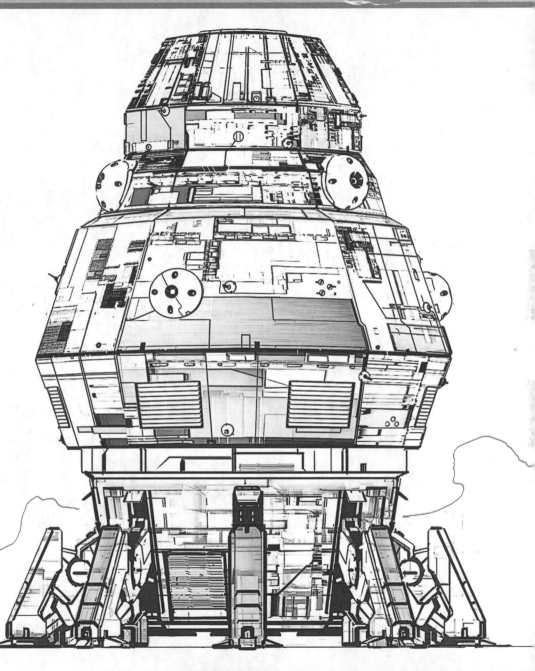

Aesir / Vanir Weapons:

Arc (Heat) Type	Capital Attack Values (Standard)				
	Short	Medium	Long	Extreme	Class
Nose (87 Heat)					
3 ER Large Lasers	3 (30)	3 (30)	3 (30)	3 (30)	Laser
3 Large Pulse Lasers	3 (30)	3 (30)	3 (30)	—	Pulse Laser
2 ATM 12	5 (48)	3 (32)	2 (16)	2 (16)	ATM
(90 rounds)					
5 AMS	2 (15)	—	—	—	AMS
(216 rounds)					
FL/FR (121 Heat-Aesir, 166 Heat-Vanir)					
[Aesir]					
2 Piranha	6 (60)	6 (60)	6 (60)	—	Capital Missile
(30 rounds)					
[Vanir]					
3 Piranha	9 (90)	9 (90)	9 (90)	—	Capital Missile
(45 rounds)					
3 Stingray	11 (105)	11 (105)	—	—	Capital Missile
(30 rounds)					
[Both]					
2 HAG 40	6 (64)	5 (48)	5 (48)	—	Autocannon
(42 rounds)					
3 ER Large Lasers	3 (30)	3 (30)	3 (30)	3 (30)	Laser
3 Large Pulse Lasers	3 (30)	3 (30)	3 (30)	—	Pulse Laser
2 ATM 12	5 (48)	3 (32)	2 (16)	2 (16)	ATM
(90 rounds)					
5 AMS	2 (15)	—	—	—	AMS
(216 rounds)					
AL/AR (105 Heat-Aesir, 150 Heat-Vanir)					
[Aesir]					
2 Piranha	6 (60)	6 (60)	6 (60)	—	Capital Missile
(30 rounds)					
[Vanir]					
3 Piranha	9 (90)	9 (90)	9 (90)	—	Capital Missile
(45 rounds)					
3 Stingray	11 (105)	11 (105)	—	—	Capital Missile
(30 rounds)					
[Both]					
3 ER Large Lasers	3 (30)	3 (30)	3 (30)	3 (30)	Laser
3 Large Pulse Lasers	3 (30)	3 (30)	3 (30)	—	Pulse Laser
2 ATM 12	5 (48)	3 (32)	2 (16)	2 (16)	ATM
(90 rounds)					
5 AMS	2 (15)	—	—	—	AMS
(216 rounds)					
Aft (67 Heat)					
2 HAG 40	6 (64)	5 (48)	5 (48)	—	Autocannon
(42 rounds)					
3 Large Pulse Lasers	3 (30)	3 (30)	3 (30)	—	Pulse Laser
2 ATM 12	5 (48)	3 (32)	2 (16)	2 (16)	ATM
(90 rounds)					
5 AMS	2 (15)	—	—	—	AMS
(216 rounds)					

OLD IS THE NEW NEW

While cutting-edge technologies will always get considerable attention, a proper intelligence briefing would be remiss not to cover the changes in the most common battlefield units. The Jihad was a war that tested the limits of soldiers, equipment, supplies and ingenuity. With manufacturing bases crippled and governments struggling to survive, it was often the innovative field technician that made the greatest impact in fighting. The simple removal of a pulse laser in order to fit an ECM system, allowing the Sword of Light to disrupt a Word C³i network; the replacement of an Iron Guard *Centurion*'s century-old autocannon with a heavy PPC to increase range and damage; or the sealing of an Ajax MBT's hull so that it could make an amphibious assault on the Word's Sydney Castle Brian; these are just three examples of such tide-turning battlefield innovations.

Some of these field refits had limited applications and life spans. For example, there is little call for BattleMechs equipped to fight amid active lava flows, as occurred on Devil's Rock, and so the special ablative plating used was never replicated. At the other end of the spectrum are modifications so practical that they became standard variants produced by factories. This was the case with the *No-Dachi* NDA-2KC field refit, which removed a rear-firing laser to mount a C³ slave. Cosby BattleMechs now offers this refit to the DCMS as a stock factory variant.

Perhaps the most unusual innovations arose with conventional armor. Long considered secondary to the BattleMech, conventional fighting vehicles have made a powerful resurgence as a force to be reckoned with. Combining modern technologies, new tactics and the determined attitude of their crews, these vehicles have reclaimed a place half a step behind the kings of the battlefield, ever ready to remind them that nothing lasts forever. The Word of Blake's willingness to use weapons of mass destruction and terror drove the most common refit, the environmental sealing of combat tanks. During the Jihad it became commonplace to see tanks in hostile environments that had traditionally been the sole domain of the BattleMech. The Coalition used this new flexibility to mount effective surprise assaults on many a Blakist stronghold. With their success in war, many of these designs continue to see use in the post-Word era, in The Republic and other nations.

—Colonel Martin Overstreet
Director of Technology
Department of Military Intelligence

FROM FIELD TO FACTORY

Necessity is the mother of invention and the battlefield is the home of necessity. These variants all began as battlefield refits, whether a simple swapping of an SRM launcher for a ECM gear and a smaller rack done in the brief hours between battles on Al Na`ir, or the ground-up rebuild of a *Hermes* in one of Alys Rousset's mobile repair DropShips. They all went on to become popular and many became standard factory-built variants. Whether a full factory variant or just a simple field refit (as designated by a lower case r after the variant name), these are weapons you can expect to find on the battlefield even today.

Battle Armor

Asterion (Upgrade): Upgrading to advanced armor allows this variant to support a vibro claw and machine gun for swarm attacks.

Fa Shih (Support): This support version removes all the mine equipment to free enough space to mount either a plasma rifle or King David Gauss rifle.

Infiltrator Mk. II (Magnetic): Designed for the active battlefield, the parafoil and AP mount are removed to make way for magnetic clamps.

Longinus (Magnetic): To improve battlefield mobility the missile launcher pack was replaced with magnetic clamps. A standard machine gun and heavy machine gun give it a hefty short-range punch.

Raiden (Anti-Infantry): Both flamer and machine gun support the upgraded vibro claw for close-quarters city fighting.

Rottweiler (Firedrake): With increased armor the anti-infantry version mounts four Firedrake needlers and poses a threat even to BattleMechs.

Theseus (Support): A heavy, single-shot punch from nine rocket tubes is backed up by a grenade launcher for sustained fighting.

Clan Medium "Rache": Clan Wolf version with better armor, and dual SRM3 OS to support the arm-mounted machine gun.

Elemental (Fire): The Jade Falcons' continued experimentation with flame-resistant armor requires the removal of the SRM reload and AP mount.

Gnome (LRM): Clan Hell's Horses created this open-field modification with an LRM 4 and an AP Gauss rifle.

Golem (Support): The Ghost Bears created this urban support version with a six-reload SRM 6 and dual AP weapon mounts.

Vehicles

Scorpion (LAC): One of the most common tanks in service, the Scorpion has spawned many upgrades. The LAC model replaces the autocannon with two light autocannons of the same power.

Yellow Jacket (PPC): A light fusion engine grants a top speed of 151 kph. A C³ system compensates for the loss of firepower, making the ER PPC more accurate.

Scimitar (C3): Working from the common TAG variant, the weapons are all replaced by a rotary autocannon and C³ system. The thin armor is thickened using heavy ferro-fibrous.

Chapparal Missile Tank (CASE): A simple Word refit, with upgraded ferro-fibrous armor and CASE.

Fulcrum III Heavy Hovertank: Alphard Trading's field refit kit upgrades the firepower with a snub-nose PPC and MML 7, its teamwork with a C³ slave, and its survivability with heavy ferro-fibrous armor.

Vedette (Cell): This Protectorate Militia upgrade uses an efficient fuel cell engine. The autocannon is upgraded to an LB-10X with an SRM 2 added to the turret and the rear for close support. CASE and an anti-missile system for defense, along with a C³ slave, was also added.

Manticore (HPPC): A factory upgrade, it uses a light fusion engine to support a targeting computer-backed heavy PPC. All missile armament is exchanged for an MML 7 and defense was improved with an anti-missile system.

Brutus (HPPC): A heavy PPC replaces the energy armament, saving enough mass to add a C³ slave.

Zhukov Heavy Tank (LB-X): Upgrading the autocannons to LB-10X models and reducing the SRM to a 4-tube allows the installation of C³i and CASE. A Capellan copy uses C³ and a Guardian ECM.

Schrek PPC Carrier (Armor): This venerable machine is encased in new heavy ferro-fibrous armor to increase its battlefield longevity.

Ontos Heavy Tank (MML): Two MML 7s replace one of the light Gauss rifles. The hull is reinforced with CASE.

Demolisher II (MML): Removing the autocannons in favor of four Artemis-guided MML 9 racks creates a powerful barrage platform. Guardian ECM gives it additional protection.

BattleMechs

Fireball ALM-10D: For light 'Mechs speed is life. A MASC system and upgrading to heavy ferro-fibrous give the *Fireball* even more life. ER lasers replace the older load out.

Commando COM-2Dr: The 2Dr strips all weapons for an MML 7 with CASE and an ER medium laser.

Dart DRT-6T: A sniper/harasser with a targeting computer and a light PPC, its construction is limited by the expensive light fusion engine.

Mongoose MON-86: A 225 XL engine boosts top speed to 150 kph and a light PPC gives it a reach similar to the Royal *Mongoose* of the Star League era.

Hitman HM-1r: An MML 7 and dual ER medium lasers replace the offensive armament. Durability is reduced with the XL gyro but offset by firepower.

Spider SDR-7Kr: One of the pulse lasers is swapped for an Angel ECM suite.

UrbanMech UM-R80: An electronic warfare city fighter with a snub-nose PPC and TAG in the right arm and a Beagle Active Probe and Guardian ECM in the torsos. Improved jets give a 90-meter jump range.

Raven RVN-4Lr: Using an Artemis-backed MML 7 in place of the Narc and SRM, a third laser is added to make this recon 'Mech a hunter.

Talon TLN-6W: Structural and armor changes allow the 6W to trade range for firepower with a heavy PPC.

Hermes II HER-5Sr: The Ultra autocannon is replaced with a heavy PPC while an XL gyro frees tonnage for a Guardian ECM suite.

Vulcan VT-5Sr: A plasma rifle and two additional heat sinks make for a terrifying anti-infantry machine.

Snake SNK-2Br: Finally achieving a viable anti-battle armor variant, the dual plasma rifles are unfortunately short on ammunition.

Vindicator VND-3Lr: Improving the original recovered-tech upgrade, the weapons are all replaced with a snub-nose PPC, extended-range laser and MML 5.

Enfield END-6Sr: To take advantage of precision and AP ammunition the LB-10X gives way to two LAC/5s.

Nightsky NGS-6T: Following in the *Berserker's* footsteps, one pulse laser is traded for one extended-range medium and two smalls. Triple-strength myomers replace the musculature.

Bushwacker BSW-S2r: Replaces the ER large laser and one SRM for a plasma rifle and ammunition.

Dervish DV-6Mr: The 6Mr upgrades the heat sinks and replaces the troublesome SRMs with pulse lasers.

Starslayer STY-3Dr: Firepower is concentrated into a single heavy PPC. An ECM is added to allow it to disrupt C³ when it closes to use its triple-strength myomer.

Dragon DRG-5Nr: Returning the design to its roots, an LAC/5 allows the replacement of the original model's rear laser as well as adding another arm-mounted laser and a C³ system.

Quickdraw QKD-5Mr: The one-shot launcher and a heat sink are removed for Guardian ECM, Artemis IV, and a targeting computer. The arm lasers are upgraded to extended-range.

Axman AXM-3Sr: Another in the long series of AFFS RAC upgrades, it also features a C³ slave, a medium pulse laser and one additional heat sink.

Catapult CPLT-C5A: A variant of the CPLT-C5, the original LRM set-up of the Catapult is reinstated. The launchers are upgraded with Artemis IV FCS.

Gallowglas GAL-2GLSA: This hot-running refit drops the Gauss rifle for one heavy and one light PPC. Heat sinks are added but are insufficient for the 'Mech's demands.

No-Dachi NDA-2KC: A simple field refit removed the rear-firing right laser for a C³ computer system and later became a standard factory variant after the Jihad.

Bandersnatch BNDR-01Ar: Reducing its rear defense to a single ER small Laser, the 01A incorporates a Guardian ECM suite in the center torso.

Falconer FLC-9R: Losing some range, the Gauss and ER PPC are replaced with an LB-10X and a heavy PPC, requiring additional heat sinks.

Hammerhands HMH-6E: Dropping the expensive targeting computer allows four tons of ammo and protection from CASE and a Guardian ECM.

Rakshasa MDG-1Ar: Keeping only the medium lasers, the refit uses snub-nose PPCs and MML 7s. CASE protects the ammunition bin.

Charger CGR-3Kr: This sword-wielding refit uses an all-energy weapons complement to support the triple-strength myomer modification.

Hatamoto-Chi HTM-28Tr: A simple refit that downgrades a Streak rack to 4 tubes and fits a Guardian ECM suite under the launcher.

Warlord BLR-2Dr: Dropping one heavy PPC for an ER PPC, the lasers are reconfigured to make better use of triple-strength myomer and C³ is installed for lance coordination.

Longbow LGB-8V: Removing the LRMs and most of the pulse lasers clears the room for two Arrow IV launchers and eight tons of ammunition.

Cyclops CP-11-B: This factory refit downgrades the engine to a 270, making room for a second Gauss rifle, CASE and 13.5 tons of ferro-fibrous armor.

Albatross ALB-3Ur: A Gauss rifle and snub-nose PPC increase range and firepower. An MML 9, in place of both existing launchers, reduces ranged missile power but increases the short-range punch.

Banshee BNC-3Mr: Double heat sinks allow replacing the PPCs and medium lasers with extended-range models

Naginata NG-C3Ar: Gutting the left torso allows this command 'Mech to use a captured large variable-speed pulse laser and an experimental boosted C³ system.

Fafnir FNR-5X: When the Skye Guards hit Moscow they did so with a handful of the rare improved heavy Gauss 5X *Fafnirs*. Removing the pulse laser allows a full twelve rounds per rifle.

King Crab KGC-005r: A heavy PPC replaces the large laser, necessitating the removal of a Streak launcher and a half-ton of armor.

Piranha 4: It was only a matter of time before the *Piranha* was mounted with machine gun arrays. Two quad arrays, one light and one standard, form the main armament while a targeting computer improves the ER medium lasers.

Hunchback IIC 4: An experimental test bed for two Clan rotary autocannons, it also adds an ECM suite and more armor.

Ha Otoko 3: A relatively new design, the 3 splits the middle between the original missile carrier and high tech 2 series. Arm missiles are removed and endo steel used to support Artemis IV, ECM, and ER large and medium lasers.

Highlander IIC 3: A continuation of the HAG upgrades gives the IIC a HAG 20 and an ECM suite.

KING NO LONGER

The Jihad saw every side reaching for whatever they could lay their hands on. With so many 'Mech factories in smoking ruins, conventional vehicles and battle armor moved from supporting to leading roles in the decades-long war. Since the end of the Jihad that trend has continued and seen more and more reliance on conventional assets in frontline armies.

These designs are indicative of three major classes of Jihad-era modifications that came about as a result of the new style of warfare. C³ networks continue to grow in use and the need for C³ master vehicles spawned many refits. Countering this were the new style of "interdictor" units whose primary job was to put their ECM in the way of an enemy C³ network. Finally, environmental sealing, once a rare occurrence, has become more common, with some nations fielding entire units of underwater armor, space-adapted combat teams, or NBC troops to defend the ravaged Jihad battlefields from rogue salvage hunters. Even OmniMechs have seen the use of "U" configurations, quick adaptations to the most extreme battlefield environments.

Battle Armor

Kage (Space): With jump boosters in the wing structure the DCA Kage sports a battle claw and cutting torch to support boarding actions.

Sloth (Interdictor): This field refit placed an ECM suite where the pop-up mine had been and upgraded the lasers to ER models. Limited construction of this new, viable design was begun to fill gaps in AFFS and LCAF battle armor ranks.

Afreet (Interdictor): Designed to counter Word of Blake C³, this Falcon battle armor replaces the AP Gauss with a heavy machine gun to make room for an ECM.

Elemental (Space): This Snow Raven space adaptation saw heavy use in the Jihad. It removes the SRMs for space adaptations, life support and a cutting torch.

Vehicles

Savannah Master (Interdictor): This weaponless variant uses a Guardian ECM Suite to provide ECM and ECCM support on the battlefield. Losing a half-ton of armor is partially offset by the use of heavy ferro-fibrous.

Sprint (Interdictor): Exchanging the Beagle Probe for a Guardian ECM allowed the Sprint to serve as a rapid-response interdictor unit.

Beagle (Sealed): An XL engine and heavy ferro-fibrous armor allow the sealing of the hull. The existing C³i makes it popular to pair with the sealed Hetzer.

Skulker (C3M): On the theory that a command unit is better unseen, the DCMS created the Skulker C³M. Weaponless, with upgraded armor, it carries a C³ master computer.

Pegasus Scout Hover Tank (Sealed): A light fusion engine and heavy ferro-fibrous armor allow the sealing of the hull. Dual MML 3s provide the ability to strike at any range.

Plainsman (Sealed): Designed for operating in heavy seas, the fuel cell engine and sealed flotation hull allow it to cut through not just over the waves. The forward launcher is converted to a torpedo launcher.

Striker Light Tank (Sealed): A fuel cell engine, Guardian ECM, and dual MML 5 launchers are protected by a sealed hull.

Hetzer Wheeled Assault Gun (Sealed): A Word Protectorate refit able to operate under NBC conditions. C³i links the RAC to supporting units.

Goblin (Sealed): Forgoing the infantry compartment and a single machine gun allows this snub-nose PPC variant to operate in the airless environment of the Atrean moon Wendigo.

Drillson Heavy Hover Tank (Sealed): Inspired by the Plainsman naval variant, this Drillson uses a sealed flotation hull and replaces its armament with dual light PPCs and an MML 3.

Rommel (Sealed): Intended for amphibious attacks, a heavy PPC replaces the Gauss with a Streak SRM 6 to back it up. A four-tube short-range torpedo launcher on the front gives additional underwater punch. Heavy ferro-fibrous and Guardian ECM protect the vehicle.

Fortune Wheeled Assault Vehicle (C3M): Seeking to create their own Morningstar command vehicle, the LCAF downgraded one of the cannons to medium-class to allow the installation of a C³ master.

Schrek PPC Carrier (C3M): Downgrading one PPC to a light model allows the Schrek to be converted into a C³ master command vehicle. Guardian ECM and an anti-missile system improve its defenses.

Challenger XIVs MBT: A heavy ferro-fibrous sealed hull allows underwater operations. This necessitates the replacement of the Gauss with an ER large laser and the Artemis LRMs with an MML 7. The forward pulse lasers are replaced with a standard SRM 4 and an SRT 4.

Ontos Heavy Tank (Sealed): Two MML 7s and six medium lasers (two extended, four standard) make up this Ontos' firepower. The drop in firepower allows full pressurization of the hull.

Shamash (Interdictor): The Bears' answer to the Savannah interdictor exchanges the small lasers for a single ER medium laser and an ECM suite.

DropShips

Nekohono'o (SCL): Developed to take advantage of the Naval C³ system, the revised *Nekohono'o* replaces its Kraken missiles with batteries of long-range lasers. The old battery has been standardized around computer assisted MRMs and a few PPCs to save weight and some AMS for protection. A Naval C³ system was wired into the heart of the ship.

CONVENTIONAL INFANTRY

"BattleMechs may win the battle, but infantry wins the war" is a modern take on an old adage that long predates the invention of the BattleMech. With the modernization of warfare in the mid-twentieth century, many military theorists predicted the demise of the infantryman as anything other than a glorified security guard. The hellish fighting of the twenty-first century Soviet Civil War disproved those armchair theories and ensured that the foot soldier would always have a place on the battlefield. The 'Mech replaced the armored tank as the primary weapon of war, and aerospace fighters eventually replaced conventional jets, but the infantryman's role remains uncontested.

The modern foot soldier still has many vital jobs that only he can perform. A BattleMech company might conquer a Succession War-era border world, but it takes follow-up regiments of conventional infantry to hold that territory. Likewise, urban warfare remained one place where the "kings of the battlefield" have to tread lightly. Given the right terrain, a single infantry platoon properly outfitted and trained poses a deadly threat to even the most powerful assault 'Mech. Urban warfare will continue to be the great leveler in modern combat, allowing the "PBI" to threaten even BattleMech supremacy. Finally, no matter how nimble one makes a hand actuator, nothing replaces the ability of the human body to manipulate humans' environment. A BattleMech attempting to clear a mined road is like a bull in a china shop during an earthquake. Specialist missions like mine clearing, sniping, covert reconnaissance and such are best left to the infantryman.

Even the advent of battle armor has not reduced the need for or the versatility of conventional infantry forces. Though battle armor enables infantrymen to stand toe to toe with some of the toughest machines on the modern battlefield, battle-armored troops cannot match the sheer adaptability of conventional infantry. Able to carry out any mission, carry any gear and adapt to almost any environment, the common soldier will remain a staple of warfare for centuries to come.

—Colonel Martin Overstreet
Director of Technology
Department of Military Intelligence

In the era of the BattleMech, the Draconis Combine still places value on conventional infantry. District regulars are often assigned extra infantry in garrison roles, sometimes as much as a full regiment. When regular 'Mech forces are required elsewhere, the responsibility of garrisoning an entire world may be handled by conventional infantry. At the start of the Jihad, both the Dieron and Galedon districts relied heavily on infantry for securing military facilities. This has been a tremendous boon to the RAF as most of the forces ceded by the Successor States are conventional infantry and militia units.

During the Jihad, infantry on Blake-occupied planets became guerrilla warfare specialists. As required by the Greater Quintadocs of the *Dictum Honorium* (the Combine's code of conduct for its citizens), all Combine citizens are expected to use all of their talents and abilities to the benefit of House Kurita and work to destroy all enemies of the Combine. Blakist invaders found a continual resistance on every world they occupied. Some planets still report guerrilla activities by soldiers who have refused to rescind their allegiance to the Dragon. RAF field commanders are advised to contact their planetary legate's office for assistance if necessary.

The core RAF infantry assets in Prefectures I, II, III, and X share a common ancestor in the DCMS garrison forces that preceded them. Many of these seasoned veterans took the opportunity of Republic-paid resettlement and now serve the RAF in other prefectures where they are exposed to a variety of cultures that were often suppressed by the Combine.

SPECIAL INFANTRY

The Draconis Elite Strike Teams are House Kurita's elite commandos. Each member is a highly trained specialist in multiple military occupational specialties. DEST members are equally at home behind the controls of a 'Mech, tank, or JumpShip but they excel at stealth. For instance, a DEST unit acquired the heavily-protected *Mackie* blueprints for the Combine, earning much honor and respect at the expense of the Lyrans. When brute force is required, DEST has at its disposal the best equipment available in the Combine. The heavy response platoon is equipped with powerful Blazer rifles and semi-portable particle projection cannons, making them more than a match for any conventional force. Their ebony DEST infiltration suits provide the maximum mixture of protection and information available to non-battle armor soldiers.

Despite the advent of battle armor in the Inner Sphere, the Combine's Sword of Light units have vehemently resisted the inclusion of battlesuits in their TO&E, including such units as the Seventy-first Mechanized's field artillery battalion. Having been uncorrupted by the Second Sword of Light's betrayal, they were assigned to the Ninth Sword of Light but stubbornly continued to demonstrate both their commitment to conventional infantry and their ability to deliver firepower without battle armor. Each soldier carries a TK assault rifle, and support weapons specialists provide suppressive fire with semi-portable autocannon, but the pride of the unit is its Thumper artillery piece, a traditional weapon that still exceeds battle armor capabilities.

Proserpina is famous for its military academy, but it's a lesser known graduating class that deserves recognition in this summary. Equipped with auto pistols and standard DCMS personal protective gear, the 201st Pesht Assault Team's Recon Battalion doesn't appear to be a threat to combat units on first scan, but few enemies of the Dragon have discounted them twice. Highly skilled combat engineers, the 201st specializes in demolition operations and uses the mobility of personal hovercraft and superior training to rapidly achieves its objectives.

The Coordinator's own personal bodyguard, the Otomo are stylized samurai with vibro-katanas and armor that resembles centuries-old chainmail. A handful of auto-rifles provide fire support for each platoon, though they are rarely needed. Assignment to the Otomo is among the highest honors available to infantry in service (quite literally) of the Dragon.

Heavy Jump Infantry
Notable Unit: DEST Heavy Response Platoon
Tech Base (Rating): Inner Sphere (E/X-E-E)
Transport Weight: 4 tons
Equipment:
    Primary Weapon: 18 Blazer Rifles
    Secondary Weapon: 3 Semi-Portable Particle Cannon
    Armor: DEST Infiltration Suit
Battle Value: 95
Notes: +1 to-hit modifier to attackers if unit does not move. Non-Infantry units suffer a +1/+1/+2 to-hit modifier at short/medium/long ranges.

Platoon Type (Specialty): Jump (None)
    Ground MP: 1
    Jump MP: 3
Platoon Size (Squad/Platoon): 21 (7/3)
Armor Divisor: 1
To-Hit Modifier (Range in Hexes):
    −1 (0 Hex), 0 (1-2 Hexes), +2 (3-4 Hexes),
    +4 (5-6 hexes)
Maximum Weapon Damage (# of Troopers):
    8 (21-20), 7 (19-18), 6 (17-15), 5 (14-12), 4 (11-10),
    3 (9-7), 2 (6-4), 1 (3-2), 0 (1)

Mechanized Field Artillery

Notable Unit: Field Artillery Battalion,
Seventy-first Mechanized, Second Sword of Light
Tech Base (Rating): Inner Sphere (C/X-D-D)
Transport Weight: 40 tons
Equipment:
Primary Weapon: 16 TK Assault Rifles
Secondary Weapon: 8 Semi-Portable Autocannons
Armor: Draconis Combine Standard Infantry Kit
Battle Value: 79
Notes: 1 Thumper Artillery Piece with 20 rounds of
ammunition (requires 15 men to operate). Burst Damage

Platoon Type (Specialty): Mechanized/Wheeled,
Field Artillery (None)
Ground MP: 1
Platoon Size (Squad/Platoon): 24 (6/4)
Armor Divisor: 1
To-Hit Modifier (Range in Hexes):
−1 (0 Hex), 0 (1 Hex), +2 (2 Hexes), +4 (3 hexes)
Maximum Weapon Damage (# of Troopers):
13 (24), 12 (23-22), 11 (21-20), 10 (19-18), 9 (17-16),
8 (15-14), 7 (13), 6 (12-11), 5 (10-9), 4 (8-7), 3 (6-5),
2 (4-3), 1 (2-1)

Recon Infantry

Notable Unit: Recon Battalion, 201st Pesht Assault Team,
3rd Proserpina Hussars
Tech Base (Rating): Inner Sphere (C/C-C-D)
Transport Weight: 11 tons
Equipment:
Primary Weapon: 10 Auto-Pistols
Secondary Weapon: None
Armor: Draconis Combine Standard Infantry Kit
Battle Value: 22
Notes: Equipped with Demolition Gear.

Platoon Type (Specialty): Mechanized/Hover
(Combat Engineers: Demolitions)
Ground MP: 5
Platoon Size (Squad/Platoon): 10 (5/2)
Armor Divisor: 1
To-Hit Modifier (Range in Hexes):
0 (0 Hexes)
Maximum Weapon Damage (# of Troopers):
2 (10-8), 1 (7-3), 0 (2-1)

Ceremonial Guard

Notable Unit: Otomo Guard
Tech Base (Rating): Inner Sphere (E/X-X-D)
Transport Weight: 3 tons
Equipment:
Primary Weapon: 20 Vibro-Katana
Secondary Weapon: 8 Auto-Rifles
Armor: Neo-Chainmail (Neo-Samurai)
Battle Value: 58
Notes: None.

Platoon Type (Specialty): Foot (None)
Ground MP: 1
Platoon Size (Squad/Platoon): 28 (7/4)
Armor Divisor: 1
To-Hit Modifier (Range in Hexes):
−2 (0 Hex), 0 (1 Hex), +2 (2 Hexes), +4 (3 hexes)
Maximum Weapon Damage (# of Troopers):
9 (28-27), 8 (26-24), 7 (23-21), 6 (20-18), 5 (17-15),
4 (14-11), 3 (10-8), 2 (7-5), 1 (4-2), 0 (1)

Perhaps no other nation values their infantry as much as the Federated Suns. The Suns' respect for its military extends right down to the regular private in the Planetary Guard infantry. The AFFS was one of the first modern militaries to reintegrate its infantry into its front-line forces. No longer an afterthought, AFFS infantry trained right alongside the BattleMechs and tanks of the front-line RCTs.

The inclusion of battle armor in the AFFS TO&E has not fundamentally altered the structure of the Davion infantry forces. The basic structure of AFFS infantry formations remains unchanged, with battle armor forces mixed in as heavy support and in stand-alone heavy formations. With such a focus on infantry, it is unsurprising that the AFFS has so many specialized infantry units. Nor is it surprising that the RAF's own infantry corps are borrowing heavily from the Federated Suns model.

SPECIAL INFANTRY

From the benign fire-fighting battalion of the Seventeenth Avalon Hussars to the ultra-elite black ops teams of the Rabid Foxes, the AFFS has a higher percentage of specially trained infantry than any other nation. Many infantry are under direct orders of the AFFS High Command, but the stability of line units has led to the evolution of specialty infantry forces within these front-line formations.

Places exist where BattleMechs cannot tread, such as extremely mountainous terrain. Into these places go the men of the Third Davion Guards, Forty-fifth Cerulean Mountain Regiment. The "Goat Men" train extensively for high altitude and rough terrain operations. Able to set up a command post on a sheer cliff, the Forty-fifth has surprised many an enemy by attacking from what was thought to be a safe approach. Adding re-breathers to their kits, the Forty-fifth can operate at altitudes that conventional aircraft and VTOLs find challenging.

Long ago recognizing that war was not won solely on the battlefield, the AFFS has many infantry units devoted to non-combat operations. Able to fight on the line with the best, these units excel in their given roles. The Twenty-fourth Hellfire Battalion, Eighty-fourth Avalon Light Infantry, of the Seventeenth Avalon Hussars is a prime example of this type of formation. Carrying Thunderstroke II Gauss rifles may seem like overkill, but the guns were chosen for their inability to cause fires rather than for their firepower. Riding in compact all-purpose vehicles, it is more common to see a soldier of the Hellfire battalion with a shovel or portable chemical sprayer than with his Thunderstroke.

The AFFS Frogmen are special operations troops trained extensively in sub-surface warfare. Riding their electric-cell underwater sleds and trained in combat, demolitions and reconnaissance, the blue water marines prove the old adage: never turn your back on the water. Equipped with Federated-Barrett laser rifles, they are a decided threat in or out of the water.

When something absolutely must be extracted overnight, the Federated Suns sends in the Rabid Foxes. Officially known as the MI6 division of AFFS Military Intelligence, the men and women of the Rabid Foxes are some of the best and most dedicated personnel in the FedSuns. MI6 units typically operate in five- to seven-man teams, though on occasion the need for something bigger comes along. When this happens, the Rabid Foxes send in an Extraction Specialist Team. Able to deploy from orbit on personal reentry units, the E-Teams are equipped with the finest stealth suits, portable electronics and best-trained experts. Their job is to drop into a location, find and acquire their target, and then make their way to the extraction point, either avoiding all contact or destroying any obstacle barring their path.

Mountaineer

Notable Unit: Forty-fifth Cerulean Mountain Infantry, Second Davion Guards

Tech Base (Rating): Inner Sphere (D/X-X-D)

Transport Weight: 2 tons

Equipment:

Primary Weapon: 12 Federated-Barrett M42B Assault Rifles

Secondary Weapon: 2 Light SRM Launchers

Armor: Federated Suns Standard Infantry Kit (3030 Issue)

Battle Value: 92

Notes: Mountain climbing equipment. Unit can traverse 3 levels per hex. Unit is immune to the effects of Thin Atmosphere.

Platoon Type (Specialty): Foot (Mountain)

Ground MP: 1

Platoon Size (Squad/Platoon): 14 (7/2)

Armor Divisor: 2

To-Hit Modifier (Range in Hexes):

"-2 (0 Hexes), 0 (1 Hex), +2 (2 Hexes), +4 (3 Hexes)

Maximum Weapon Damage (# of Troopers):

14 (14), 13 (13), 12 (12), 11 (11), 10 (10), 9 (9), 8 (8), 7 (7), 6 (6), 5 (5), 4 (4), 3 (3), 2 (2), 1 (1)

HOUSE DAVION

Firefighter

Notable Unit: Twenty-fourth Hellfire Firefighting
Battalion, 84th Avalon LI, 17th Avalon Hussars
Tech Base (Rating): Inner Sphere (E/X-X-D)
Transport Weight: 5 tons
Equipment:
    Primary Weapon: 14 Thunderstroke II Gauss Rifles
    Secondary Weapon: None
    Armor: Federated Suns Standard Infantry Kit (3067 Issue)
Battle Value: 74
Notes: Firefighting Equipment. Cannot conduct Anti-'Mech or Swarming Attacks.

Platoon Type (Specialty): Motorized
    (Combat Engineers: Firefighting)
    Ground MP: 2
Platoon Size (Squad/Platoon): 14 (7/2)
Armor Divisor: 2
To-Hit Modifier (Range in Hexes):
    -2 (0 Hexes), +0 (1-2 Hexes), +2 (3-4 Hexes), +4 (5-6 Hexes)
Maximum Weapon Damage (# of Troopers):
    7 (14-13), 6 (12-11), 5 (10-9), 4 (8-7), 3 (6-5), 2 (4-3), 1 (2-1)

Frogmen

Notable Unit: Blue Water Marine Response Teams
(Frogmen), Special Operations Command
Tech Base (Rating): Inner Sphere (D/X-X-D)
Transport Weight: 3 tons
Equipment:
    Primary Weapon: 10 Federated-Barrett M61A Laser Rifles
    Secondary Weapon: 2 Heavy Support Lasers
    Armor: Flack Vest
Battle Value: 64
Notes: Weapon range is halved (round down) underwater.

Platoon Type (Specialty): Foot (Motorized SCUBA)
    Ground MP: 1
    Water MP: 2
Platoon Size (Squad/Platoon): 12 (6/2)
Armor Divisor: 1
To-Hit Modifier (Range in Hexes):
    −1 (0 Hex), 0 (1-2 Hexes), +2 (3-4 Hexes), +4 (5-6 Hexes)
Maximum Weapon Damage (# of Troopers):
    9 (12), 8 (11-10), 7 (9), 6 (8), 5 (7-6), 4 (5), 3 (4),
    2 (3-2), 1 (1)

SpecOps Paratrooper

Notable Unit: MI6 Extraction Team
Tech Base (Rating): Inner Sphere (D/X-X-E)
Transport Weight: 4 tons
Equipment:
    Primary Weapon: 18 Federated-Barrett
    M42B Assault Rifles
    Secondary Weapon: 3 Sonic Stunners
    Armor: Sneak Suit (Camo/ECM/IR)
Battle Value: 101
Notes: +3 to-hit modifier to attackers if platoon doesn't move, +2 modifier to attackers if platoon expends 1 MP. Non-infantry units suffer a +1/+1/+2 to-hit modifier at short/medium/long ranges. Invisible to Standard/Light Active Probes. May use Atmospheric Drops rules.

Platoon Type (Specialty): Foot (Paratroopers)
    Ground MP: 1
Platoon Size (Squad/Platoon): 21 (7/3)
Armor Divisor: 1
To-Hit Modifier (Range in Hexes):
    -2 (0 Hexes), 0 (1 Hex), +2 (2 Hexes), +4 (3 Hexes)
Maximum Weapon Damage (# of Troopers):
    20 (21), 19 (20), 18 (19), 17 (18), 16 (17), 15 (16),14 (15),
    13 (14), 12 (13), 11 (12), 10 (11-10), 9 (9), 8 (8), 7 (7),
    6 (6), 5 (5), 4 (4), 3 (3), 2 (2), 1 (1)

The infantryman has always been an integral part of Capellan defense, but the proliferation of battle armor and the general advancement of weapons technology during the Jihad has given Capellan foot soldiers even more dangerous weapons to use against the Confederation's enemies.

Because of the Confederation's historic deficit in heavy military industry, it has been forced by sheer necessity to turn to infantry to supply many of its needs. The one resource the Confederation rarely ran out of during the wasteful centuries of the Succession Wars was people—men and women ready to pick up rockets or rifles or even satchel charges and simple clubs to defend the state against aggressors. The *Xin Sheng* movement of the 3060s revitalized the infantry arm of the Capellan Confederation Armed Forces just as it did every other facet of the state, and the foot soldiers facing our RAF troops along the Tikonov border are just as fanatical as their parents were.

SPECIAL INFANTRY

Specialist infantry doctrine in the Confederation has undergone a renewal in the past fifteen years, with new technologies improving the usefulness of these troops by orders of magnitude. A myriad variety of specialist roles have emerged at the squad and platoon level, in addition to the rapid proliferation of battlesuits. As *Fa Shih* and *Trinity* battle armor companies and battalions take over frontline combat duties, more and more infantry battalions are transitioning to specialist roles.

One of the most deadly of the new infantry squads is the battlefield infiltration unit. These units, grouped administratively into two-squad platoons, are outfitted with high-technology sneak anti-detection suits and low-signature heavy shredder rifles. Their role is to sneak across the battlefield, using the cover of battle to pass through enemy lines and wreak havoc on the enemy's rear areas. Several Republic battalions have had their command structures decapitated when infiltration squads penetrated their command posts and assassinated the commanding officers. Though incapable of standing against conventional infantry, Confederation infiltration squads are deadly additions to the Capellan order of battle.

Since 3067, mine-laying infantry have matured and proven to be dedicated and effective components of Capellan defensive doctrine. Mechanized formations have become adept at spreading minefields in the likely paths of enemy advances, and nearly every Home Guard unit in the Confederation maintains at least a company of mine-laying troops, if not full battalions. Several companies, notably the 117th Field Explosive with the Dynasty Guards, have transitioned into front-line units and often provide the deciding edge in skirmishes.

The elite Warrior Houses of the Confederation are not exempt from this infantry expansion—Warrior House Dai Da Chi has trained an entire squad of elite snipers. Armed with the Minolta 9000 sniper system originally custom-built for the Death Commandos, these squads are deadly marksmen and have fought on several worlds against Republic forces. They are highly skilled at identifying opposing commanders and eliminating them. The deaths of Colonel Wagner and Majors Harm and Ridgeway have all been attributed to Dai Da Chi snipers, and RAF strategists are already rushing counter-snipers to the Capellan front.

The infantry forces of McCarron's Armored Cavalry have tried to keep pace with their brethren in other CCAF units, but the former mercenary troops still have much doctrinal inertia to overcome, even after more than twenty years of integration. The Fifth MAC's Kommando troops have begun training in field artillery, using field-mobile Luxor Mobile Battery artillery missile systems in concert with mechanized transports to provide supporting fire for MAC maneuver units. Though the reloading system is unwieldy and there have been some hiccups adapting the missile artillery to a traditional tube artillery role, the results have more than offset the difficulties.

Commando
Notable Unit: CCAF Battlefield Infiltration Units
Tech Base (Rating): Inner Sphere (D/X-X-E)
Transport Weight: 4 tons
Equipment:
    Primary Weapon: 14 Shredder Heavy Needler Rifles
    Secondary Weapon: None
    Armor: Sneak Suit (Camo/ECM/IR)
Battle Value: 41
Notes: +3 to-hit modifier to attackers if platoon doesn't move, +2 to-hit modifier to attackers if platoon expends 1 MP, +1 to-hit modifier to attackers if platoon expends 2 MP. Non-infantry units suffer +1/+1/+2 to-hit modifiers at short/medium/long ranges. Invisible to Standard/Light Active Probes. Demolition equipment.

Platoon Type (Specialty): Jump
    (Combat Engineers: Demolition)
    Ground MP: 1
    Jump MP: 3
Platoon Size (Squad/Platoon): 14 (7/2)
Armor Divisor: 1
To-Hit Modifier (Range in Hexes):
    0 (0 Hexes)
Maximum Weapon Damage (# of Troopers):
    3 (14-12), 2 (11-8), 1 (7-3), 0 (2-1)

LIAO

HOUSE LIAO

Minelayer Infantry

Notable Unit: 117th Field Explosive, Dynasty Guards
Tech Base (Rating): Inner Sphere (D/X-D-D)
Transport Weight: 16 tons
Equipment:
    Primary Weapon: 14 Gyrojet Rifles
    Secondary Weapon: None
    Armor: Capellan Confederation Standard Infantry Kit
Battle Value: 36
Notes: Mine-laying equipment.

Platoon Type (Specialty): Mechanized/Tracked
    (Combat Engineers: Minelayer)
    Ground MP: 3
Platoon Size (Squad/Platoon): 14 (7/2)
Armor Divisor: 1
To-Hit Modifier (Range in Hexes):
    −2 (0 Hex), 0 (1 Hex), +2 (2 Hexes), +4 (3 hexes)
Maximum Weapon Damage (# of Troopers):
    5 (14-13), 4 (12-10), 3 (9-7), 2 (6-5), 1 (4-2), 0(1)

Sniper

Notable Unit: House Dai Da Chi Snipers
Tech Base (Rating): Inner Sphere (D/X-X-E)
Transport Weight: 1 ton
Equipment:
    Primary Weapon: Minolta 9000 Advanced
        Sniper System
    Secondary Weapon: None
    Armor: Sneak Suit (Camo)
Battle Value: 24
Notes: 7 troopers with Minolta 9000 Advanced Sniper Systems per squad; +3 modifier to attackers if squad doesn't move, +2 modifier to attackers if squad expends 1 MP
Platoon Type (Specialty): Foot
    Ground MP: 1
Platoon Size (Squad/Platoon): 7 (7/1)
Armor Divisor: 1
To-Hit Modifier (Range in Hexes):
    −2 (0 Hex), 0 (1-2 Hexes), +2 (3-4 Hexes),
    +4 (5-6 hexes)
Maximum Weapon Damage (# of Troopers):
    2 (7-6), 1 (5-2), 0 (1)

Missile Artillery Infantry

Notable Unit: Kommando Special Forces, Fifth MAC
Tech Base (Rating): Inner Sphere (E/E-F-E)
Transport Weight: 40 tons
Equipment:
    Primary Weapon: 16 Auto-Rifles
    Secondary Weapon: 8 Support Machine Guns
    Armor: Capellan Confederation Standard Infantry Kit
Battle Value: 210
Notes: 1 Arrow IV with 5 rounds of ammunition (requires 15 men to operate). Burst Damage.

Platoon Type (Specialty): Mechanized/Wheeled,
    Field Artillery (None)
    Ground MP: 1
Platoon Size (Squad/Platoon): 24 (6/4)
Armor Divisor: 1
To-Hit Modifier (Range in Hexes):
    −1 (0 Hex), 0 (1-2 Hexes), +2 (3-4 Hexes), +4 (5-6 hexes)
Maximum Weapon Damage (# of Troopers):
    16 (24), 15 (23-22), 14 (21), 13 (20-19), 12 (18), 11 (17-16),
    10 (15), 9 (14-13), 8 (12), 7 (11-10), 6 (9), 5 (8-7), 4 (6),
    3 (5-4), 2 (3), 1 (2-1)

HOUSE MARIK

Throughout The Republic, Devlin Stone is receiving laurels for creating a pro-infantry RAF that uses the common foot soldier to the utmost advantage. This decision alone has led many theorists to claim that he was raised in the Free Worlds League, where the common infantryman has been an integral part of the FWLM since the Andurien War.

New technology and creative thinking featured heavily in FWLM infantry deployment, with varied units and concepts the norm rather than the exception. Although the Free Worlds League has recently dissolved into several smaller states, the use of infantry remains largely unchanged. At nearly 1,800 strong, infantry regiments are significantly larger in the former FWL states than in other nations. By comparison, the same title is given to a group of 750 soldiers in House Kurita, and House Davion affixes the moniker to just over 1,000.

It is then no surprise that the former Leaguers prized conventional infantry and boasted several types of specialty infantry.

SPECIAL INFANTRY

The Royal Gurkha Battalion of the Fourth Regulan Hussars is arguably the most recognized infantry unit in the former FWL. Hailing from Muscida in the Principality of Regulus, and almost exclusively of Nepalese descent, this elite cadre has one of the best kits available in the Inner Sphere. A distinctive battle dress uniform features slide-in armor plating for maximum customization without sacrificing protection and a thirty-kilo jump pack adds tactical flexibility with a sixty-meter range. Each soldier carries a trustworthy Starfire ER laser rifle and the traditional *kukri*

knife. Squad support weapon specialists contribute the firepower of a King David Light Gauss Rifle. The combined package makes the Gurkhas a potent force on the battlefield, even without anti-'Mech training.

Once a unified presence, SAFE (the Marik intelligence agency) splintered into multiple competing factions with the dissolution of the Free Worlds League. Of the new states, the Marik-Stewart Commonwealth retained the most significant SAFE assets, including the organization's original Eyrie headquarters: a hidden bunker on Wendigo, Atreus's moon. This facility is home to the Eagle Corps, SAFE's special-forces branch. Safeguarding it is the responsibility of the Eyrie Defense Force—a group of highly-skilled, xenoplanetary-trained soldiers who spend most of their day ensconced in space suits. This foot-infantry unit operates in standard platoons of twenty-eight men armed with gyroslug rifles and ER support lasers. Their weapon mix gives each platoon a 360-meter range and enough firepower to make even the most brazen of 'Mech pilots cautious. This firepower comes at a price, as the EDF must devote significant effort to redeploying and are unable to engage on the move. Additionally, the weight of their armament prohibits anti-'Mech attacks.

Recently rediscovered technology allowed the return of a specialty infantry unit that had been disbanded since the early Succession Wars. The 292nd League Regulars are a conventional infantry unit attached to the Gryphons, a BattleMech regiment of the Silver Hawk Irregulars. The Gryphons have a lackluster history, but still managed to reap some fame by reintroducing anti-aircraft jump infantry after procuring a significant supply of man-portable anti-aircraft guns. Backed by auto-rifles, the 292nd's platoons have done well in their new role and inspired many copycat units.

From advanced technology to advanced inspiration, the Branth Irregulars are the sort of infantry usually encountered in the Periphery. This strange group of soldiers is attached to the Beta Regiment of the Fifth Legion. Equipped with high-power (but low-tech) elephant gun, they fly into battle on the agile branth. A large flying reptile reminiscent of the mythical Terran dragon, branths are capable of speeds nearing fifty-four kph. They pose little threat to hardened targets, but against conventional infantry, terror-instilling branth platoons are the equal or better of many traditional forces.

Heavy Jump Infantry

Notable Unit: Royal Gurkha Battalion
Tech Base (Rating): Inner Sphere (E/X-X-E)
Transport Weight: 4 tons
Equipment:
    Primary Weapon: 18 Starfire ER Laser Rifles
    Secondary Weapon: 3 King David Light Gauss Rifles
    Armor: Free Worlds League Standard Infantry Kit (3035 Issue)
Battle Value: 97
Notes: Cannot conduct Anti-'Mech or Swarming Attacks.

Platoon Type (Specialty): Jump (None)
    Ground MP: 1
    Jump MP: 2
Platoon Size (Squad/Platoon): 21 (7/3)
Armor Divisor: 2
To-Hit Modifier (Range in Hexes):
    –1 (0 Hexes), 0 (1-3 Hexes), +2 (4-6 Hexes), +4 (7-9 Hexes)
Maximum Weapon Damage (# of Troopers):
    7 (21-20), 6 (19-17), 5 (16-14), 4 (13-11), 3 (10-8), 2 (7-5), 1 (4-2), 0 (1)

MARIK

HOUSE MARIK

Xenoplanetary Infantry

Notable Unit: Eagle Corps Eyrie Defense Force
Tech Base (Rating): Inner Sphere (E/X-X-E)
Transport Weight: 3 tons
Equipment:
   Primary Weapon: 20 Gyroslug Rifles
   Secondary Weapon: 8 ER Support Lasers
   Armor: Spacesuit, Combat
Battle Value: 88
Notes: Encumbered; cannot move and shoot in the same turn. Cannot conduct Anti-'Mech or Swarming Attacks. Xenoplanetary (Vacuum) Condition-Trained.

Platoon Type (Specialty): Foot, XCT (Vacuum)
   Ground MP: 1
Platoon Size (Squad/Platoon): 28 (7/4)
Armor Divisor: 1
To-Hit Modifier (Range in Hexes):
   −1 (0 Hexes), 0 (1-4 Hexes), +1 (5-6 Hexes), +2 (7-8 Hexes), +3 (9-10 Hexes), +4 (11-12 Hexes)
Maximum Weapon Damage (# of Troopers):
   13 (28), 12 (27-25), 11 (24-23), 10 (22-21), 9 (20-19), 8 (18-17), 7 (16-15), 6 (14-12), 5 (11-10), 4 (9-8), 3 (7-6), 2 (5-4), 1 (3-2), 0 (1)

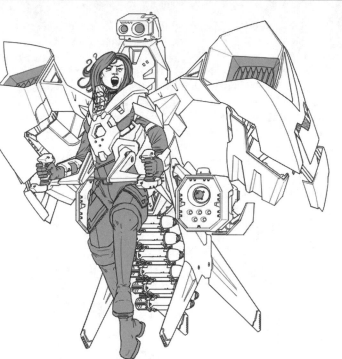

AA Jump Infantry

Notable Unit: 292nd League Regulars, Gryphons
Tech Base (Rating): Inner Sphere (D/E-F-D)
Transport Weight: 4 tons
Equipment:
   Primary Weapon: 15 Auto-Rifles
   Secondary Weapon: 6 Man-Portable AA Guns
   Armor: Flak Vest
Battle Value: 86
Notes: Anti-Aircraft equipment; may attack airborne targets that attack their hex.

Platoon Type (Specialty): Jump
   Ground MP: 1
   Jump MP: 2
Platoon Size (Squad/Platoon): 21 (7/3)
Armor Divisor: 1
To-Hit Modifier (Range in Hexes):
   −1 (0 Hexes), 0 (1-2 Hexes), +2 (3-4 Hexes), +4 (5-6 Hexes)
Maximum Weapon Damage (# of Troopers):
   13 (21), 12 (20-19), 11 (18-17), 10 (16), 9 (15-14), 8 (13), 7 (12-11), 6 (10-9), 5 (8), 4 (7-6), 3 (5), 2 (4-3), 1 (2-1)

Aerial Beast Infantry

Notable Unit: Branth Irregulars, Beta Regiment, Fifth Legion
Tech Base (Rating): Inner Sphere (C/X-E-C)
Transport Weight: 7 tons
Equipment:
   Primary Weapon: 7 Elephant Guns
   Secondary Weapon: None
   Armor: Free Worlds League Standard Infantry Kit (3035 Issue)
Battle Value: 41
Notes: Cannot conduct Anti-'Mech or Swarming Attacks. +2D6 damage vs Infantry. +1 damage vs Vehicles/'Mechs.

Platoon Type (Specialty): Beast-Mounted, Branth (None)
   Ground MP: 1
   VTOL MP: 5
Platoon Size (Squad/Platoon): 7 (7/1)
Armor Divisor: 2
To-Hit Modifier (Range in Hexes):
   −1 (0 Hexes), 0 (1 Hex), +2 (2 Hexes), +4 (3 Hexes)
Maximum Weapon Damage (# of Troopers):
   1 (7-5), 0 (4-1)

No doubt the Lyrans desire to get rid of infantry. Much like the long-gone Terran Hegemony, they place a higher value on human life than some other states. With their education and infrastructure, it is likely a more realistic statement than some would like to admit. However, while technological increases and better training can increase ability, it only goes so far. In the 31st Century, no nation, not even the Lyrans, can afford to be without a significant infantry force.

However, the Lyran budget goes a long way toward making their forces more flexible, able and valuable. This is even more apparent in their best and brightest. Any enemy expecting to find the Lyran forces from the history books will be sorely disappointed. The new tactics and strategies began under Alessandro Steiner and confirmed by the influence of the Federated Suns have integrated Lyran infantry with their other forces more than at any other time in their seven hundred years.

SPECIAL INFANTRY

Briefly overshadowed in the 3060s, Lyran infantry has had to adapt during the Civil War and Jihad. The best units, also typically the better equipped, were stripped to build up the Federated Commonwealth's (and Alliance's) battle armor units. However, after an ugly childhood, the LCAF has come to realize that despite battle armor being more effective per trooper than other infantry, battle armor is a specialized unit not suited for every battlefield role and not every infantry candidate is suited for battle armor operation. The LCAF has returned to more careful infantry

assignment and this has benefited their specialized infantry forces—to The Republic's detriment should it come in conflict with the Lyrans.

Combat engineers have a separate reporting structure from regular Lyran infantry, which makes them difficult to locate in the Lyran bureaucracy. However, the Royal Engineers will integrate with regular infantry or any other unit. Armed with submachine guns and organized in platoons of just two seven-mans squads, they are not a powerful fighting force. Ask a platoon if they are concerned about the Royal Engineers and most would scoff. But ask a general and they might even shiver at the thought of the Royal Engineers. Capable of engineering fieldwork as well as demolitions, they are a great force multiplier.

Most Lyran troops go through paratrooper training, but those actually deployed to the Lyran Paratrooper Corps are experienced and talented. With recoilless rifles backed up by Mauser and Gray rifles, the paratroopers attached to the Third Skye CMR are typical of the Corps. Arrayed similar to jump infantry in three-squad platoons, they are more a strategic unit than a tactical one, able to deploy quickly via the Commonwealth's large inventory of fixed-wing craft on a moment's notice.

The Second Lyran Armored Infantry, attached to the Thirty-second Lyran Guards, is an example of very specialized infantry. With eight Firedrake Support rifles supplemented by standard needlers, this unit can terrify opposing infantry. Of little use against hardened targets, they can cut through the infantry supporting them like a fiery spray of knives through butter. They can also turn the Firedrakes against the terrain, igniting buildings or plant life.

Opponents of the Third Lyran Guards should hope they are on the defensive and away from cover. Many a 'Mech lance has been sent to secure an important site and been sent running by "merely" a platoon of Heavy Urban Response infantry of the attached 608th Lyran MTR. Between their excellent skills, man-portable plasma rifles and a determined attitude, it might take a company to dislodge them from a heavy building. Even on the offensive, they can be potent, taking down a light 'Mech in one salvo.

Combat Engineer

Notable Unit: Royal Engineers, 1st Lyran Royal Guards RCT
Tech Base (Rating): Inner Sphere (C/X-E-C)
Transport Weight: 5 tons
Equipment:
    Primary Weapon: 14 Gunther MP-20 SMGs
    Secondary Weapon: None
    Armor: Lyran Alliance Standard Infantry Kit (3060 Issue)
Battle Value: 46
Notes: Trench/Fieldwork equipment.

Platoon Type (Specialty): Motorized
    (Combat Engineer: Trench/Fieldworks)
    Ground MP: 3
Platoon Size (Squad/Platoon): 14 (7/2)
Armor Divisor: 2
To-Hit Modifier (Range in Hexes):
    0 (0 Hexes)
Maximum Weapon Damage (# of Troopers):
    8 (14), 7 (13-12), 6 (11-10), 5 (9-8), 4 (7), 3 (6-5), 2 (4-3), 1 (2-1)

HOUSE STEINER

HALO Paratrooper

Notable Unit: Lyran Paratrooper Corps
Tech Base (Rating): Inner Sphere (C/X-X-C)
Transport Weight: 4 tons
Equipment:
  Primary Weapon: 18 Mauser & Gray G-150 Rifles
  Secondary Weapon: 3 Heavy Recoilless Rifles
  Armor: Lyran Alliance Standard Infantry Kit (3060 Issue)
Battle Value: 103
Notes: May use Atmospheric Drops rules.

Platoon Type (Specialty): Foot (Paratroopers)
  Ground MP: 1
Platoon Size (Squad/Platoon): 21 (7/3)
Armor Divisor: 2
To-Hit Modifier (Range in Hexes):
  −1 (0 Hex), 0 (1-2 Hexes), +2 (3-4 Hexes), +4 (5-6 hexes)
Maximum Weapon Damage (# of Troopers):
  7 (21-20), 6 (19-17), 5 (16-14), 4 (13-11), 3 (10-8),
  2 (7-5), 1 (4-2), 0 (1)

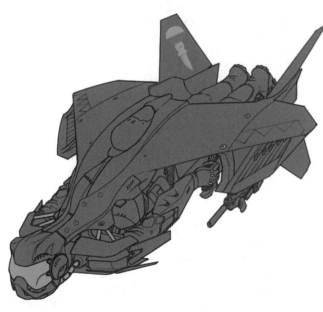

Anti-Infantry Unit

Notable Unit: Second Lyran Armored Infantry,
  Thirty-second Lyran Guards
Tech Base (Rating): Inner Sphere (D/X-X-C)
Transport Weight: 6 tons
Equipment:
  Primary Weapon: 20 Mauser & Gray Flechette
    Needler Rifles
  Secondary Weapon: 8 Firedrake Support Needler
  Armor: Lyran Alliance Standard Infantry Kit (3060 Issue)
Battle Value: 88
Notes: May set fire to target hex (5+ Success Number). Divide
Maximum Weapon Damage by 3 (round down) for attacks against
BattleMechs, ProtoMechs, Combat Vehicles, Support Vehicles with
a BAR of 10, battle armor and Hardened Buildings. Fire Damage.

Platoon Type (Specialty): Motorized (None)
  Ground MP: 2
Platoon Size (Squad/Platoon): 28 (7/4)
Armor Divisor: 2
To-Hit Modifier (Range in Hexes):
  +1 (0 Hex)
Maximum Weapon Damage (# of Troopers):
  9 (28-27), 8 (26-24), 7 (23-21), 6 (20-17), 5 (17-15),
  4 (14-11), 3 (10-8), 2 (7-5), 1 (4-2), 0 (1)

Heavy Infantry

Notable Unit: Heavy Urban Response Platoon,
  608th Lyran MTR, Third Lyran Guards
Tech Base (Rating): Inner Sphere (E/X-X-D)
Transport Weight: 6 tons
Equipment:
  Primary Weapon: 20 Auto-Rifles
  Secondary Weapon: 8 Man-Portable Plasma Rifles
  Armor: Lyran Alliance Standard Infantry Kit (3060 Issue)
Battle Value: 149
Notes: Flame-Based Weapon (may inflict damage and heat
to heat-tracking units).

Platoon Type (Specialty): Motorized (None)
  Ground MP: 2
Platoon Size (Squad/Platoon): 28 (7/4)
Armor Divisor: 2
To-Hit Modifier (Range in Hexes):
  −1 (0 Hex), 0 (1-2 Hexes), +2 (3-4 Hexes), +4 (5-6 hexes)
Maximum Weapon Damage (# of Troopers):
  23 (28), 22 (27), 21 (26-25), 20 (24), 19 (23), 18 (22),
  17 (21), 16 (20-19), 15 (18), 14 (17), 13 (16), 12 (15),
  11 (14-13), 10 (12), 9 (11), 8 (10), 7 (9-8), 6 (7), 5 (6),
  4 (5), 3 (4), 2 (3-2), 1 (1)

Like all militaries, the Com Guards used large numbers of unarmored infantrymen in a variety of roles. The Com Guards were always built as a combined arms force, and this cohesion was only enhanced when Precentor Martial Anastasius Focht assumed command. While many criticized the Com Guards for their lack of focus on BattleMech formations, the Battle of Tukayyid and the actions of the Com Guards throughout the Jihad quickly proved the validity of combined arms doctrine, and even The Republic Armed Forces are questioning the necessity of large BattleMech formations.

SPECIALIST INFANTRY

The sheer size of ComStar and its varied interests guarantee a large range of specialist infantry roles in the Com Guards, but none are more specialized than the hostile environment reconnaissance teams of the Explorer Corps. Highly regarded as the elite infantry of the Corps, the hostile recon infantryman is a well-trained soldier capable of operating in a combat role in almost any environment, including the vacuum of space. These platoons are routinely motorized, using whatever vehicle is most appropriate to the environment, from low-slung tracked crawlers on high-gravity worlds to near-flying skimmers in low-gravity, dense-atmosphere planets. Armed with advanced weaponry and supported by Hellbore assault lasers, the hostile environment infantry can face nearly any threat to an Explorer Corps survey team.

The business of ComStar has always been communication, whether transmitting, archiving or stealing it,

and the Com Guards were no different than any other branch of the Order. Warfare requires the most up-to-date information, and the gathering of battlefield intelligence was a prime concern for ComStar strategists. One class of infantry squad—the battlefield data miner—was especially useful in gathering up-to-the-second intelligence on the Com Guards' enemies. By using a system of remote sensors deployed from mechanized carriers, the data miners could capture all enemy transmissions and submit them for processing. Though they rarely managed to crack enemy encryption in real time, they successfully used simple signal measurements to identify enemy commanders for targeting by Com Guard battlefield units.

The revelation in the 3050s that ComStar retained a fleet of WarShips shook the Inner Sphere powers, despite many of them having purchased ComStar-built interplanetary drives for their own nascent WarShip fleets. These vessels remained active and crewed, if hidden, for many decades, and the fleet marine assets of the Com Guards are expert in dealing with shipboard security and combat. Several of the ship-to-ship battles in the Jihad degenerated to boarding actions, and the laser-armed marines served valiantly against the Word of Blake. The RAF's own few WarShip-based marine units have drawn significantly from Com Guard marine doctrine, which far outpaces that of other Inner Sphere navies.

The Forty-eighth Division fought ferociously in the Jihad and earned a reputation for fast, mobile warfare despite suffering horrendous losses. A large part of that reputation is built on the bridging units of Take the Time III-chi, who, by necessity, became experts at moving the Forty-eighth's heavy combat units across rivers, streams and chasms blocking their path. Often under fire, these heavy troops saved the day again and again by making it possible for Com Guard combat units to outflank or outdistance Word of Blake opposition. Though armed with laser rifles, the bridging units often used their engineering vehicles in combat, quickly digging fighting positions along the banks of their bridging encampments; several times the infantry and armored units waiting to move would only leave their fighting positions to cross the river and then cover the bridging unit as it crossed behind them.

Motorized XCT Infantry

Notable Unit: Explorer Corps Hostile Environment Recon Units
Tech Base (Rating): Inner Sphere (E/X-X-E)
Transport Weight: 8 tons (4 tons)
Equipment:
  Primary Weapon: 30 Mauser 960 Assault Systems
  Secondary Weapon: 6 Hellbore Assault Lasers
  Armor: Environment Suit, Hostile
Battle Value: 121
Notes: Cannot make Anti-'Mech or Swarm attacks. Xenoplanetary (All Environments) Condition-Trained. Breaks up into two 18-trooper platoons in play.

Platoon Type (Specialty): Motorized, XCT (None)
  Ground MP: 2
Platoon Size (Squad/Platoon): 36 (6/6)
Armor Divisor: 2
To-Hit Modifier (Range in Hexes):
  –1 (0 Hex), 0 (1-2 Hexes), +2 (3-4 Hexes), +4 (5-6 hexes)
Maximum Weapon Damage (# of Troopers):
  7 (18), 6 (17-15), 5 (14-12), 4 (11-10), 3 (9-7), 2 (6-4), 1 (3-2), 0 (1)

Surveillance Specialists

Notable Unit: Com Guards Battlefield Data Miners
Tech Base (Rating): Inner Sphere (F/X-X-D)
Transport Weight: 14 tons
Equipment:
    Primary Weapon: 12 Federated-Barrett M42B
        Assault Rifles
    Secondary Weapon: None
    Armor: ComStar Standard Infantry Kit
Battle Value: 68
Notes: Sensor equipment.

Platoon Type (Specialty): Mechanized/Hover
    (Combat Engineers: Sensor)
    Ground MP: 5
Platoon Size (Squad/Platoon): 12 (6/2)
Armor Divisor: 2
To-Hit Modifier (Range in Hexes):
    -2 (0 Hexes), 0 (1 Hex), +2 (2 Hexes), +4 (3 Hexes)
Maximum Weapon Damage (# of Troopers):
    13(12), 12(11), 11(10), 10(9), 9(8), 8(7), 7(6), 5(5), 4(4),
    3(3), 2(2), 1(1)

Space Marine

Notable Unit: Com Guards Warship Fleet Marine
Tech Base (Rating): Inner Sphere (D/X-F-D)
Transport Weight: 3 tons
Equipment:
    Primary Weapon: 24 Sunbeam Laser Pistols
    Secondary Weapon: 4 Blazer Rifles
    Armor: Environment Suit, Marine
Battle Value: 121
Notes: None.

Platoon Type (Specialty): Foot (Marine)
    Ground MP: 1
Platoon Size (Squad/Platoon): 24 (6/4)
Armor Divisor: 2
To-Hit Modifier (Range in Hexes):
    −2 (0 Hex), 0 (1 Hex), +2 (2 Hexes), +4 (3 hexes)
Maximum Weapon Damage (# of Troopers):
    7 (24-23), 6 (22-19), 5 (18-16), 4 (15-12), 3 (11-9),
    2 (8-6), 1 (5-2), 0 (1)

Bridge-builder Engineers

Notable Unit: Take the Time III-chi, Forty-eighth Division
Tech Base (Rating): Inner Sphere (F/X-F-D)
Transport Weight: 14 tons
Equipment:
    Primary Weapon: 12 Pulse Laser Rifles
    Secondary Weapon: None
    Armor: ComStar Standard Infantry Kit
Battle Value: 49
Notes: Bridge-building equipment.

Platoon Type (Specialty): Mechanized/Tracked
    (Combat Engineers: Bridge-Building)
    Ground MP: 3
Platoon Size (Squad/Platoon): 12 (6/2)
Armor Divisor: 2
To-Hit Modifier (Range in Hexes):
    −2 (0 Hex), 0 (1 Hex), +2 (2 Hexes), +4 (3 hexes)
Maximum Weapon Damage (# of Troopers):
    3 (12-10), 2 (9-6), 1 (5-2), 0 (1)

WORD OF BLAKE

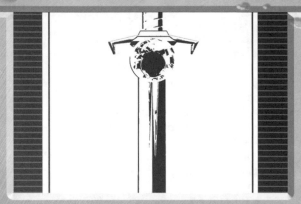

Descended from the same combined-arms philosophies that spawned the Com Guards, the Word of Blake Militia placed a solid emphasis on infantry assets as a key element in their order of battle. Sparing no expense, the Word's infantry forces were arguably among the best equipped of the Inner Sphere powers during the Jihad, even though the vast majority of these troops were employed as defensive troops and in urban pacification duties.

Although the elite Manei Domini grabbed headlines throughout the Jihad, most of the infantry the Word of Blake fielded beyond the confines of their Protectorate were those of the regular military, the Word of Blake Militia. By the time the various states of the Inner Sphere were on the offensive, however, most of the Blakist infantry had been folded into or backed up by the troops of the Blake Protectorate. Most of these troops were either veterans of the Com Guards' epic battle against the Clans on Tukayyid, recruits from the Free Worlds League and other pro-Blake states, or volunteers taken from the worlds of the Protectorate. While many were fanatical, fighting to the death as Coalition forces converged on Terra, many of these regular troops tended to surrender as their Protectorate crumbled and the Word's hierarchy collapsed.

Special Infantry

At all three levels of their organization—Protectorate Militia, Word of Blake Militia, and Manei Domini—the Word employed specialized troops tailored to select missions. These special missions tended to vary not merely by local conditions and needs, but also with the level of experience, fanaticism, and authority each tier operated with. For example, the elite

and deadly Domini rarely assigned its troops to police duties or post-battle mop up, often leaving that to the Protectorate Militia and the regular WoBM, respectively.

The Word of Blake NBC (Nuclear, Biological, Chemical) Special Weapons Teams, for instance, were the standard force for handling a combat zone after an initial nuclear or chemical strike occurred. Trained and equipped for operations in toxic environments, these mechanized troops often appeared during a standard Word of Blake raid, or immediately in its aftermath, scouring the field for survivors and taking prisoners as needed—or eliminating those enemies too foolish to realize that they were already dead.

Meanwhile, in the Blake Protectorate (where, contrary to the propaganda, not every government was a willing accomplice to the Word's agenda) the order of the day was often riot control. To minimize the visibility of collateral damage and avoid playing into the hands of their detractors, many of these Protectorate Militia "pacification units" carried an assortment of non-lethal weapons intended to subdue rather than kill. Their tendency to operate in eighteen-man "sub-platoons" also enabled them to flank difficult mobs so they could engage them more effectively, or sweep buildings and other structures for hidden insurgents.

At the opposite end of the scale, of course, were the Manei Domini's fearsome shock troops, the infamous "Tau Zombies" (although the use of the Tau designator is more an indication of rank that was not always the case with these squads). Rarely deployed in formations larger than the squad level, the "Zombies" featured the most effective collection of cybernetics available for infantry use: myomers augmenting strength and armor, prosthetics with built-in weapons, enhanced cybernetic sensors, and pain shunts to block out the worst injuries. These troops never surrendered and never fled, often butchering entire platoons or gutting enemy vehicles despite horrific injuries.

Equally effective in their own niche were the so-called "Tau Wraiths". The reconnaissance equivalent of Zombie shock troops, the Wraiths boasted superior stealth equipment and communications systems that allowed them to link into friendly C³ networks, achieving a tactical advantage few conventional forces could match. Though they could be deadly in combat, these troops often operated in the shadows, coordinating the fight and providing key telemetry for heavier support forces.

Mechanized Assault XCT

Notable Unit: Word of Blake Militia NBC Special Weapons Team
Tech Base (Rating): Inner Sphere (F/X-X-D)
Transport Weight: 24 tons
Equipment:
    Primary Weapon: 20 Mauser 1200 LSS
    Secondary Weapon: 4 Man-Portable Plasma Rifles
    Armor: Environment Suit, Marine
Battle Value: 134
Notes: Xenoplanetary (All Environments) Condition-Trained.

Platoon Type (Specialty): Mechanized/Wheeled, XCT (None)
    Ground MP: 4
Platoon Size (Squad/Platoon): 24 (6/4)
Armor Divisor: 2
To-Hit Modifier (Range in Hexes):
    –1 (0 Hex), 0 (1-2 Hexes), +2 (3-4 Hexes), +4 (5-6 hexes)
Maximum Weapon Damage (# of Troopers):
    19 (24), 18 (23), 17 (22-21), 16 (20), 15 (19), 14 (18), 13 (17-16), 12 (15), 11 (14), 10 (13), 9 (12-11), 8 (10), 7 (9), 6 (8-7), 5 (6), 4 (5), 3 (4), 2 (3-2), 1 (1)

WORD OF BLAKE

Riot Police

Notable Unit: Word of Blake Protectorate Militia Pacification Unit
Tech Base (Rating): Inner Sphere (F/X-F-D)
Transport Weight: 8 tons (4 tons)
Equipment:
Primary Weapon: 30 Tranq Guns
Secondary Weapon: 6 Stunsticks
Armor: Word of Blake Standard Infantry Kit
Battle Value: 99
Notes: Breaks up into two 18-trooper platoons in play. Can only damage conventional infantry units.

Platoon Type (Specialty): Motorized (None)
Ground MP: 3
Platoon Size (Squad/Platoon): 36 (6/6)
Armor Divisor: 2
To-Hit Modifier (Range in Hexes):
0 (0 Hexes)
Maximum Weapon Damage (# of Troopers):
2 (18-14), 1 (13-5), 0 (4-1)

Tau Zombie

Notable Unit: Manei Domini "Tau Zombie" Attack Squad
Tech Base (Rating): Inner Sphere (F/X-X-F)
Transport Weight: 1 ton
Equipment:
Primary Weapon: 2 Mauser 1200 LSS
Secondary Weapon: 4 Heavy Support Laser
Armor: Word of Blake Standard Infantry Kit
Battle Value: 93 + MD Modifier of 1.75
(multiply Skill modified BV by 1.75)
Notes: Cybernetically enhanced infantry: Features Pain Shunt (reduces damage from fire and fire-based attacks by half, round down), Improved Enhanced Prosthetic Arms with TK Enforcer and Magnet accessories (TK Enforcers add +0.20 damage per trooper at range 0; Magnets provide −2 TN modifier for Anti-'Mech Swarm and Leg Attacks), Multi-Modal Cybernetic Eyes (IR/Laser Targeting; IR provides Active Probe capabilities at 2-hex range; Laser provides −1 to-hit modifier), Full-Body Dermal Armor and Triple-Strength Myomer Implants (Combination provides +1 Damage Divisor; unit does not suffer double damage effects when attacked in open terrain; reduce all Burst-Fire damage sustained by 1D6—to a minimum of 1 point; +0.14 Damage per trooper vs other conventional infantry at Range 0; +2 Support Weapon maximum per Squad; −2 crew needs per Support Weapon, to minimum of 1; MP not reduced by support weapons, support weapons are not Encumbering). Also features Suicide Implants (delivers 0.4 damage to all hostile units in the same hex per trooper killed by combat damage).

Platoon Type (Specialty): Foot, Cybernetically Enhanced (None)
Ground MP: 1
Platoon Size (Squad/Platoon): 6 (6/1)
Armor Divisor: 3
To-Hit Modifier (Range in Hexes):
−2 (0 Hexes), −1 (1-5 Hexes), +0 (6-7 Hexes),
+1 (8-10 Hexes), +2 (11-12 Hexes), +3 (13-15 Hexes)
Maximum Weapon Damage (# of Troopers):
7 (6), 6 (5), 5 (4), 3 (3), 2 (2), 1 (1)
8 (6), 7 (5), 6 (4), 4 (3), 2 (2), 1 (1) at Range 0
9 (6), 8 (5), 6 (4), 5 (3), 2 (2), 1 (1) at Range 0 vs Conventional Infantry only

Tau Wraith

Notable Unit: Manei Domini "Tau Wraith" Recon Squad
Tech Base (Rating): Inner Sphere (F/X-X-F)
Transport Weight: 1 ton
Equipment:
Primary Weapon: 6 Mauser 1200 LSS
Secondary Weapon: None
Armor: Sneak Suit (Camo/ECM/IR)
Battle Value: 26 + MD Modifier of 1.75
(multiply Skill modified BV by 1.75) + C³i Modifier
Notes: Cybernetically enhanced infantry: Features Cosmetic Enhancements (No effect in combat), Pheromone Effuser (No effect in combat), Toxin Effuser (+0.27 damage per trooper vs other conventional infantry at Range 0, Negated by Enviro suits), Multi-Modal Cybernetic Eyes (IR/Laser Targeting; IR provides Active Probe capabilities at 2-hex range; Laser provides −1 to-hit modifier), Boosted Communicator Implants (Provides +1 non-cumulative Initiative modifier for friendly force; Allows unit to act as part of C³i network). Paratroop equipment allows unit to employ Atmospheric Drop rules. Sneak Suits apply Mimetic to-hit modifiers (applied to attacker based on number of hexes the unit moves: +3 to-hit when stationary; +2 to-hit when moved 1 hex; +1 to-hit when moved 2 hexes; +0 to-hit when moved 3+ hexes) and additional range modifiers to non-infantry attackers (+1 to-hit at short and medium range; +2 to-hit at long range). Unit cannot be spotted by Light and Standard Active Probes.

Platoon Type (Specialty): Foot, Cybernetically Enhanced (Paratrooper)
Ground MP: 1
Platoon Size (Squad/Platoon): 6 (6/1)
Armor Divisor: 1
To-Hit Modifier (Range in Hexes):
−3 (0 Hex), −1 (1-2 Hexes),
+1 (3-4 Hexes), +3 (5-6 hexes)
Maximum Weapon Damage (# of Troopers):
4 (6), 3 (5-4), 2 (3), 1 (2-1)
6 (6), 5 (5), 4 (4), 3 (3), 2 (2), 1 (1) at Range 0 vs Conventional Infantry only

GHOST BEAR (RASALHAGUE)

The Ghost Bear Dominion is not known for its infantry, at least the unarmored kind. The popular image is of the giant Elemental riding a 'Mech into battle. While this may be true for the fighting arms of the touman, internal security forces like the Watch frequently use unarmored troops to achieve their aims.

The KungsArmé made extensive use of infantry, from its partisan roots to its modern infantry regiments. Their absorption into the Dominion touman has not been easy, but they still exist, providing screening forces for the KungsArmé's conventional armor. At the same time, others have gone back to their roots, fighting to free their homelands from the Clan invaders and whoever supports them.

One only need watch the Chatterweb to see the result. Until recently, public bombings and firefights were a daily occurrence on Alshain and elsewhere throughout the Dominion. Only with the end of the Jihad and Mimir allying with the Watch has a measure of peace been achieved, but the hidden civil war still continues.

SPECIAL INFANTRY

While all Clans make use of their old warriors in *solahma* formations, few match the Dominion's Heavy Points. The Dominion's oversized battle armor force means that there is a continual supply of retired or failed Elementals. Unlike most *solahma* troopers, these Elementals combine a lifetime of infantry training with the physical bulk to handle the heaviest weapons and armor available. Usually equipped as jump infantry to make the most of their existing training, these warriors act as internal security across

the Dominion, where ongoing terrorist actions keep them sharper than one might expect.

Mimir had been coordinating organized resistance to invaders for centuries when the Clans arrived in 3049. After a number of early successes, Mimir settled down into an extended guerrilla war against the rapidly improving Clan Watch. A standard Mimir troop is fast and hard-hitting. Armed with readily available assault rifles and rocket launchers, they can easily overwhelm an isolated outpost before fading back into the hinterland. With Mimir merging into the Dominion Watch, the fate of the troops themselves has been mixed. Many aligned themselves with the Motstånd so that they can continue the fight. To confuse the issue further, rumors persist of Mimir-funded troops in the Clan Wolf and Hell's Horses' occupation zones, which the Dominion vehemently denies.

After Tukayyid, Clan Ghost Bear tried to handle Mimir uprisings with their existing *solahma* troops. While effective in a stand-up fight, the *solahma* proved too slow to keep up with the fast-moving Mimir troops. Years of fighting resulted in specialist Watch counter-insurgency Points to hunt down Mimir units. Mounted in fast, armored vehicles, the counter-insurgency Points use advanced weapons and armor to overwhelm any light forces they encounter. After merging with the Dominion, access to Mimir's intelligence networks and field operatives has only improved their performance, while recent strategic gaffes by the Motstånd and successful high-profile anti-terrorist operations have seen public support swing in favor of the Dominion troops.

Finally, the Third Ueda infantry regiment is a typical example of the KungsArmé's infantry forces. Veterans of the war against Clan Wolf, their numbers were culled in the Trials of Position to become part of the Rasalhague Dominion touman and then further reduced as their strongest were seconded into the Third Drakøn Cluster's battle armor Binaries. But some remain, providing support to the First Ueda Cavaliers. Low on the food chain, they have yet to gain access to Clan equipment, and retain much of their old equipment. This might appear to make the Third Ueda infantry less than capable on a modern battlefield, but appearances are deceptive. As jump troops with anti-'Mech training, they pose a threat to any force they can close with.

Clan Assault Infantry
Notable Unit: Ghost Bear Heavy *Solahma* Infantry
Tech Base (Rating): Clan (F/X-F-E)
Transport Weight: 4 tons
Equipment:
  Primary Weapon: 12 Mauser IICs
  Secondary Weapon: 8 Support Lasers (ER) Clan
  Armor: Clan Standard Infantry Kit
Battle Value: 186
Notes: None

Platoon Type (Specialty): Jump (None)
  Ground MP: 1
  Jump MP: 2
Platoon Size (Squad/Platoon): 20 (5/4)
Armor Divisor: 2
To-Hit Modifier (Range in Hexes):
  −1 (0 Hex), 0 (1-4 Hexes), +2 (5-8 Hexes), +4 (9-12 hexes)
Maximum Weapon Damage (# of Troopers):
  19 (20), 18 (19), 17 (18), 16 (17), 15 (16), 14 (15), 13 (14), 12 (13), 11 (12), 10 (11-10), 9 (9), 8 (8), 7 (7), 6 (6), 5 (5), 4 (4), 3 (3), 2 (2), 1 (1)

GHOST BEAR (RASALHAGUE)

Motorized Heavy Infantry
Notable Unit: Motstånd/Mimir Troop
Tech Base (Rating): Inner Sphere (C/X-X-B)
Transport Weight: 6 tons
Equipment:
Primary Weapon: 24 Auto Rifles
Secondary Weapon: 4 Rocket Launchers (LAW)
Armor: Free Rasalhague Republic Standard Infantry Kit
Battle Value: 80
Notes: None

Platoon Type (Specialty): Motorized (None)
Ground MP: 3
Platoon Size (Squad/Platoon): 28 (7/4)
Armor Divisor: 1
To-Hit Modifier (Range in Hexes):
−2 (0 Hex), 0 (1 Hex), +2 (2 Hexes), +4 (3 hexes)
Maximum Weapon Damage (# of Troopers):
13 (28), 12 (27-25), 11 (24-23), 10 (22-21), 9 (20-19), 8 (18-17), 7 (16-15), 6 (14-12), 5 (11-10), 4 (9-8), 3 (7-6), 2 (5-4), 1 (3-2), 0 (1)

Clan Mechanized Infantry
Notable Unit: Mimir/Watch Counter Insurgency Point
Tech Base (Rating): Clan (E/X-X-E)
Transport Weight: 20 tons
Equipment:
Primary Weapon: 12 Gauss Sub Machineguns
Secondary Weapon: 8 Clan Support Pulse Lasers
Armor: Clan Standard Infantry Kit
Battle Value: 106
Notes: +1D6 against infantry

Platoon Type (Specialty): Mechanized Tracked (None)
Ground MP: 3
Platoon Size (Squad/Platoon): 20 (5/4)
Armor Divisor: 2
To-Hit Modifier (Range in Hexes):
-1 (0 Hex), 0 (1-3 Hexes), +2 (4-6 Hexes), +4 (7-9 hexes)
Maximum Weapon Damage (# of Troopers):
12 (20), 11 (19-18), 10 (17-16), 9 (15), 8 (14-13), 7 (12-11), 6 (10), 5 (9-8), 4 (7-6), 3 (5), 2 (4-3), 1 (2-1)

Anti-'Mech Jump Infantry
Notable Unit: Third Ueda Infantry, Third Drakøns
Tech Base (Rating): Inner Sphere (D/X-X-D)
Transport Weight: 4 tons
Equipment:
Primary Weapon: 18 Blazer Rifles
Secondary Weapon: 3 Heavy Support Lasers
Armor: FRR Standard Infantry Kit
Battle Value: 158
Notes: None

Platoon Type (Specialty): Jump (None)
Ground MP: 1
Jump MP: 3
Platoon Size (Squad/Platoon): 21 (7/3)
Armor Divisor: 1
To-Hit Modifier (Range in Hexes):
−1 (0 Hexes), 0 (1-2 Hexes), +2 (3-4 Hexes), +4 (5-6 Hexes)
Maximum Weapon Damage (# of Troopers):
11 (21), 10 (20-19), 9 (18-17), 8 (16-15), 7 (14-13), 6 (12-11), 5 (10-9), 4 (8-7), 3 (6-5), 2 (4-3), 1 (2-1)

Clan Hell's Horses has always made heavy use of infantry forces. Marching alongside conventional armor, these forces are used to screen more valuable units. Officially Clan Hell's Horses' conventional infantry is made up of Elementals who failed their initial Trial of Position. However, many are *solahma* at the end of their career, especially in the less physically demanding mechanized Binaries.

As the Clan deploys its vehicles in a number of wide ranging roles, their infantry has to be equally varied. The high percentage of trained Elementals in the Hell's Horses touman means it is trivial to equip them as anti-'Mech-trained jump infantry. New weapons like the Bearhunter and Gauss SMG have caused a marked increase in the firepower of Clan Hell's Horses' infantry forces. Advanced armor utilizing Clan copper is universally employed, as are the hardest-hitting weapons the warriors can carry. Indeed, a lack of heavy weapons is often an indication of a lack of Elementals. Mechanized troops are used when extra speed or weapons capacity is needed, while ad hoc points manned by *solahma* warriors are deployed when heavy infantry is not available.

SPECIAL INFANTRY

The Sixty-seventh BattleMech Cluster maintains an unusually large number of infantry. Cavalry Points are designed to be able to keep up with scouting elements and scoot across the battlefield in small hovercraft. Naturally these vehicles are limited in what they can carry and these troops are accordingly lacking in firepower. In the enclosed environments the Sixty-seventh prefers, they proved to be quite capable scouts, but all too often it seems they are used as a distraction to allow damaged scout tanks to limp off the battlefield and are highly vulnerable in a stand up fight.

Another type of infantry serving in the Sixty-seventh BattleMech Cluster is Mechanized AA. Traveling in special light tanks fitted with lightweight antiaircraft weapons, these troops are expected to provide a screen for support units, supply dumps and artillery vehicles. They rarely see combat and there are serious questions about how battle worthy they are. It is unclear if they can even survive against a VTOL, let alone an aerospace fighter. Against Clan Ice Hellion, these troops took heavy losses from rapid strikes as they lacked the speed to respond, but they succeeded in their mission and the tanks they protected were left untouched.

Elementals who lose their armor face a more honorable future in infantry forces because of their existing training. Armed with the heaviest weapons available the heavy infantry of the Ninety-first Mechanized Assault represents some of the most dangerous infantry on the battlefield. Already skilled in infantry combat, fitted with jump packs and body armor, a squad of this heavy infantry is able to operate alongside Elementals and BattleMechs. Their secret is the use of the Bearhunter autocannon, which boosts the Point's firepower without restricting its mobility compared to other heavy infantry. This style of heavy infantry is very popular in Clan Hell's Horses and only limited by the number of warriors available.

Most Clusters like the Forty-second BattleMech Cluster deploy a number of ad hoc Points which lack the specialization of those already listed. These troops are armed with modern weapons, are quite capable and are motivated by the high chance of seeing combat. Made up of tested-down warriors from all branches, these *solahma* troops aren't expected to live long; they are just happy to be given one last chance for honor. Combat reports from the Occupation Zone suggest Clan Wolf preferred to use Elementals on headhunting missions against the conventional support units the Forty-second's infantry routinely protects. One can only imagine what Elementals would do to these lightly protected infantry.

Fast Recon
Notable Unit: Cavalry Point,
    Sixty-seventh BattleMech Cluster, Iota Galaxy
Tech Base (Rating): Clan (F/X-F-D)
Transport Weight: 20 tons
Equipment:
    Primary Weapon: 20 Mauser IICs
    Secondary Weapon: None
    Armor: Clan Standard Infantry Kit
Battle Value: 114
Notes: None.

Platoon Type (Specialty): Mechanized/Hover (None)
    Ground MP: 5
Platoon Size (Squad/Platoon): 20 (5/4)
Armor Divisor: 2
To-Hit Modifier (Range in Hexes):
    -2 (0 Hexes), 0 (1-3 Hexes), +2 (4-6 Hexes), +4 (7-9 Hexes)
Maximum Weapon Damage (# of Troopers):
    18 (20), 17 (19), 16 (18), 15 (17), 14 (16-15), 13 (14),
    12 (13), 11 (12), 10 (11), 9 (10), 8 (9), 7 (8), 6 (7), 5 (6-5),
    4 (4), 3 (3), 2 (2), 1 (1)

HELL'S HORSES

AA Mechanized Infantry
Notable Unit: Mechanized AA Infantry Point,
 Sixty-seventh BattleMech Cluster, Iota Galaxy
Tech Base (Rating): Clan (E/X-F-E)
Transport Weight: 20 tons
Equipment:
 Primary Weapon: 12 Auto-Rifles
 Secondary Weapon: 8 Mk. 2 Man-Portable AA
 Armor: Clan Standard Infantry Kit
Battle Value: 99
Notes: Anti-Aircraft equipment; may attack airborne targets that attack their hex.

Platoon Type (Specialty): Mechanized Wheeled (AAA)
 Ground MP: 3
Platoon Size (Squad/Platoon): 20 (5/4)
Armor Divisor: 2
To-Hit Modifier (Range in Hexes):
 −1 (0 Hex), 0 (1-2 Hexes), +2 (3-4 Hexes), +4 (5-6 hexes)
Maximum Weapon Damage (# of Troopers):
 13 (20), 12 (19-18), 11 (17), 10 (16-15), 9 (14), 8 (13-12), 7 (11-10), 6 (9), 5 (8-7), 4 (6), 3 (5-4), 2 (3), 1 (2-1)

Clan Heavy Jump Infantry
Notable Unit: Heavy Infantry Point,
 Ninety-first Mechanized Assault, Epsilon Galaxy
Tech Base (Rating): Clan (F/X-X-E)
Transport Weight: 4 tons
Equipment:
 Primary Weapon: 16 Mauser IICs
 Secondary Weapon: 4 Bearhunter Autocannons
 Armor: Clan Standard Infantry Kit
Battle Value: 136
Notes: None.

Platoon Type (Specialty): Jump
 Ground MP: 1
 Jump MP: 3
Platoon Size (Squad/Platoon): 20 (5/4)
Armor Divisor: 2
To-Hit Modifier (Range in Hexes):
 −1 (0 Hex), 0 (1-3 Hexes), +2 (4-6 Hexes), +4 (7-9 hexes)
Maximum Weapon Damage (# of Troopers):
 24 (20), 23 (19), 22 (18), 20 (17), 19 (16), 18 (15), 17 (14), 16 (13), 14 (12), 13 (11), 12 (10), 11 (9), 10 (8), 8(7), 7 (6), 6 (5), 5 (4), 4 (3), 2 (2), 1 (1)

Clan Foot Infantry
Notable Unit: Ad Hoc Point, Forty-second
 BattleMech Cluster, Theta Galaxy
Tech Base (Rating): Clan (E/X-X-E)
Transport Weight: 3 tons
Equipment:
 Primary Weapon: 20 Gauss SMGs
 Secondary Weapon: 5 Automatic Grenade Launchers
 Armor: Clan Standard Infantry Kit
Battle Value: 108
Notes: None.

Platoon Type (Specialty): Foot (None)
 Ground MP: 1
Platoon Size (Squad/Platoon): 25 (5/5)
Armor Divisor: 2
To-Hit Modifier (Range in Hexes):
 −2 (0 Hexes), 0 (1 Hex), +2 (2 Hexes), +4 (3 Hexes)
Maximum Weapon Damage (# of Troopers):
 12 (25-24), 11 (23-22), 10 (21-20), 9 (19-18), 8 (17-16), 7 (15-14), 6 (13-12), 5 (11-10), 4 (9-8), 3 (7-6), 2 (5-4), 1 (3-2), 0 (1)

It is a common misconception that unarmored infantry has no role within the Clans, but the simple truth is that battle armor is expensive and not suited to all roles. For most tasks away from the battlefield a simple foot soldier is adequate. Though Elementals are preferred, most Clan infantry are *solahma* warriors at the end of their careers or who have failed their Trials. While many seek an honorable death, their typical employment makes it unlikely.

While some Clans see infantry as useful, most Clans see infantry as a necessary evil populated with failures. Despite those attitudes, Clan infantry is almost always better equipped than Inner Sphere infantry, with advanced armor, weapons and supporting equipment. Though this is an incidental result of advanced Clan technology rather than any conscious intention, it means even a disaffected Clan unit can be a match for its Inner Sphere equivalent if used carefully.

SPECIAL INFANTRY

The Ebon Keshik is a group of elite, black-clad Elementals that guard the most revered sites on Strana Mechty. As battle armor is too bulky for these human-scale facilities and operating basically in a civilian environment, there is little need for the protection and firepower of a battle armor suit. Instead these warriors are most commonly equipped as foot infantry in specially sculpted black body armor. Unlikely to see combat, a warrior in the Ebon Keshik has little to look forward to beyond a Trial of Position from a younger warrior and the inevitable relegation to a *solahma* unit. Patrolling the corridors of power on

Strana Mechty is the ultimate achievement in the career of an Elemental, yet it is a tainted honor.

Throughout history navies have sought soldiers of their own, marines whom they can tailor to suit the navy's needs and requirements. This tradition continues to modern navies like that of Clan Snow Raven. Typically made up of warriors of all phenotypes, these troops guard Clan Snow Raven's fleet from internal threats. Unlike battle armor, these troops have limited mobility and are best suited to defense. They can be found on spacecraft ranging from battleships to observation space stations, providing security and defense against boarding. With the introduction of the Aerie (P)AL it has been suggested that the unarmored marine's days are numbered in Clan Snow Raven. However, the Aerie's cost means that it will never be deployed in the numbers regular marines are.

Poor Lyran national spirit is often blamed for the lack of civilian disturbances in the Clan Jade Falcon Occupation Zone. Many would begrudgingly admit that the Jade Falcons might be good at controlling civilian dissent. Dating back to the Culling, Clan Jade Falcon has employed specialist Watch units to control its civilian population. As the front line of Clan Jade Falcon repression, the police show little interest in restraint or building good will. Armed with a mixture of lethal and non-lethal weapons, they swoop in using fast vehicles to put down any riots or disturbances as soon as they occur. More ominously, the police have been involved in countless nighttime arrests of Lyran nationalists over the last twenty years. Inner Sphere pundits like to compare these to Capellan "disappearances" but the police rarely make any attempt at secrecy and the prisoners are usually publicly punished and executed.

The Dark Caste is a mystery to nearly everybody, including the Clans. Yet from time to time the Clans encounter a large Dark Caste group and a firefight occurs. The harsh conditions the Dark Caste lives under limits their weaponry to what they can build on their own or steal from the Clans. Protection is little better than safety equipment for their ramshackle light vehicles. Outmatched by all but the weakest of Clan forces they still act as bogeymen to the Clans. Perhaps the fear is not what they can do but what they represent, because for the regimented Clans the freedom of the Dark Caste must be truly terrifying.

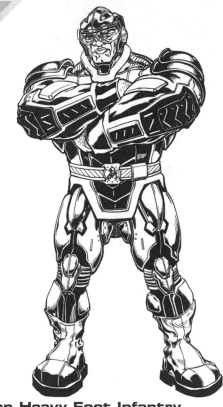

Clan Heavy Foot Infantry
Notable Unit: Ebon Keshik Point
Tech Base (Rating): Clan (E-X-F-E)
Transport Weight: 1 ton
Equipment:
    Primary Weapon: 5 Mauser IICs
    Secondary Weapon: None
    Armor: Clan Standard Infantry Kit
Battle Value: 26
Notes: None.

Platoon Type (Specialty): Foot (None)
    Ground MP: 1
Platoon Size (Squad/Platoon): 5 (5/1)
Armor Divisor: 2
To-Hit Modifier (Range in Hexes):
    –2 (0 Hexes), 0 (1-3 Hexes), +2 (4-6 Hexes), +4 (7-9 Hexes)
Maximum Weapon Damage (# of Troopers):
    5 (5), 4 (4), 3 (3), 2 (2), 1 (1)

Clan Space Marine

Notable Unit: Clan Snow Raven Space Marines
Tech Base (Rating): Clan (E/X-F-E)
Transport Weight: 2 tons
Equipment:
  Primary Weapon: 20 Mauser IICs
  Secondary Weapon: None
  Armor: Environment Suit, Marine
Battle Value: 138
Notes: None.

Platoon Type (Specialty): Foot (Marine)
  Ground MP: 1
Platoon Size (Squad/Platoon): 20 (5/4)
Armor Divisor: 2
To-Hit Modifier (Range in Hexes):
  −2 (0 Hexes), 0 (1-3 Hexes), +2 (4-6 Hexes), +4 (7-9 Hexes)
Maximum Weapon Damage (# of Troopers):
  18 (20), 17 (19), 16 (18), 15 (17), 14 (16-15), 13 (14),
  12 (13), 11 (12), 10 (11), 9 (10), 8 (9), 7 (8), 6 (7), 5 (6-5),
  4 (4), 3 (3), 2 (2), 1 (1)

Clan Anti-Infantry

Notable Unit: Clan Jade Falcon Police
Tech Base (Rating): Clan (E/X-X-E)
Transport Weight: 20 tons
Equipment:
  Primary Weapon: 12 Avenger CCW Shotguns
  Secondary Weapon: 8 Tranq Guns
  Armor: Clan Standard Infantry Kit
Battle Value: 65
Notes: Can only damage conventional infantry units.

Platoon Type (Specialty): Mechanized/Wheeled (None)
  Ground MP: 4
Platoon Size (Squad/Platoon): 20 (5/4)
Armor Divisor: 2
To-Hit Modifier (Range in Hexes):
  0 (0 Hexes)
Maximum Weapon Damage (# of Troopers):
  5 (20-18), 4 (17-14), 3 (13-10), 2 (9-6), 1 (5-2), 0 (1)

Motorized Infantry

Notable Unit: Dark Caste Bandits
Tech Base (Rating): Clan (C/X-C-D)
Transport Weight: 6 tons
Equipment:
  Primary Weapon: 20 Bolt-Action Rifles
  Secondary Weapon: 5 Standard SRM Launchers
  Armor: Clothing, Leather/Synthetic Hide
Battle Value: 72
Notes: None.

Platoon Type (Specialty): Motorized (None)
  Ground MP: 3
Platoon Size (Squad/Platoon): 25 (5/5)
Armor Divisor: 1
To-Hit Modifier (Range in Hexes):
  −1 (0 Hexes), 0 (1 Hex), +2 (2 Hexes), +4 (3 Hexes)
Maximum Weapon Damage (# of Troopers):
  6 (25-23), 5 (22-19), 4 (18-15), 3 (14-11), 2 (10-7),
  1 (6-3), 0 (2-1)

TAURIAN CONCORDAT

The Taurian Concordat is one of the more militaristic Periphery realms, and the Taurian Defense Force has always been a respected, if sometimes underwhelming, military. The role of infantry cannot be understated in Taurian defensive plans. Even during the Reunification War, with the entire might of the Star League Defense Force arrayed against them, Taurian citizens fought *en masse* against the invaders, sometimes with nothing more than farm implements. Such a tradition does not easily vanish, and the staggering losses sustained by the Concordat before and during the Jihad have led to a surge of specialist infantry teams.

While battle armor has been spreading in the Concordat proper and the breakaway Calderon Protectorate, the unarmored infantryman remains a staple of Taurian doctrine. The Concordat Constabulary, the paramilitary force directly responsible for reinforcing Concordat defenses, has refused to adapt many squads and platoons to specialist roles, but the noble family regiments and planetary militias have taken every scrap of technology the TDF offers them and used them to augment their defenses. The famous Taurian paranoia was reawakened with the attack on Taurus during the Jihad, and no one in the Concordat nowadays bats an eye at more defense spending.

SPECIAL INFANTRY

The core of Taurian defensive strategy is the Citizens' Militia, units of reserve formations on every world. The most basic of defenses, these battalions are normally armed with little more than personal rifles and throwaway missile launchers, but given national service requirements, many a Taurian adult is a qualified rifleman. Though last in line for use, behind the front-line TDF, the noble family regiments and the Concordat Constabulary, the militia units' customary Zeus heavy rifles are no less deadly to the Concordat's enemies.

Though they constitute the worst-kept secret in the Concordat, the Special Asteroid Support Force has some of the most highly trained, though not combat experienced, troopers in the TDF. Extensively trained in low-G and vacuum operations, they man the many weapons emplacements seeded in the asteroid fields that ring Taurus. At the core of these defenses are missile and laser emplacements, a poor man's space defense system, but each SAF trooper is a trained infantryman as well. Armed with laser weaponry, they are perfectly able to defend the asteroid emplacements from ground attack—a likely tactic of any invader, given how deeply some installations are dug into the asteroids.

The Trinity Alliance with the Magistracy of Canopus and the Capellan Confederation in the 3060s led to many innovations in the TDF prior to the Concordat's withdrawal from that alliance. One of those bonuses was gaining experience with the Confederation's expert mine-handlers. The infantry auxiliaries of the Red Chasseurs put this knowledge to good use, training several companies of mine-sweeping troops that have become adept at locating and defusing minefields in the path of the Chasseurs' advance. In a recent action on the FedSuns border, the Support Force located a minefield before a company of tanks blundered into it—which resulted in commendations for the minesweepers.

The defection of the Calderon Protectorate, the annihilation of Samantha near the end of the Jihad, and the losses sustained in Capellan space have all made every Taurian strategist more tight-fisted with the Concordat's scant military resources. To that end, units of the First Taurian Lancers have been seen training with field gun batteries along with all their motorized companies, usually light autocannon batteries. With specialized ammunition copied from the Federated Suns, these units can be deadly when striking from ambush.

SRM Foot Infantry
Notable Unit: Taurian Citizens' Militia
Tech Base (Rating): Inner Sphere (C/C-C-D)
Transport Weight: 3 tons
Equipment:
Primary Weapon: 27 Zeus Heavy Rifles
Secondary Weapon: 3 Light SRM Launchers
Armor: Clothing, Fatigues/Civilian/Non-Armored
Battle Value: 68
Notes: None.

Platoon Type (Specialty): Foot (None)
Ground MP: 1
Platoon Size (Squad/Platoon): 30 (10/3)
Armor Divisor: 1
To-Hit Modifier (Range in Hexes):
−2 (0 Hexes), 0 (1 Hex), +2 (2 Hexes), +4 (3 Hexes)
Maximum Weapon Damage (# of Troopers):
8 (30-28), 7 (27-25), 6 (24-21), 5 (20-17), 4 (16-13), 3 (12-10), 2 (9-6), 1 (5-2), 0 (1)

XCT Marine

Notable Unit: Special Asteroid Support Forces
Tech Base (Rating): Inner Sphere (D/D-E-D)
Transport Weight: 3 tons
Equipment:
    Primary Weapon: 27 Marx XX Laser Rifles
    Secondary Weapon: 3 Vibro-Blades
Armor: Environment Suit, Marine
Battle Value: 150
Notes: Xenoplanetary (Vacuum) Condition-Trained.

Platoon Type (Specialty): Foot (XCT: Vacuum)
    Ground MP: 1
Platoon Size (Squad/Platoon): 30 (10/3)
Armor Divisor: 2
To-Hit Modifier (Range in Hexes):
    −2 (0 Hexes), 0 (1-3 Hexes), +2 (4-6 Hexes), +4 (7-9 Hexes)
Maximum Weapon Damage (# of Troopers):
    8 (30-28), 7 (27-25), 6 (24-21), 5 (20-17), 4 (16-13),
    3 (12-10), 2 (9-6), 1 (5-2), 0 (1)

Minesweeper Infantry

Notable Unit: Minesweepers, Thirty-fifth Cluster
    Support Force, Red Chasseurs
Tech Base (Rating): Inner Sphere (E/X-X-F)
Transport Weight: 6.5 tons
Equipment:
    Primary Weapon: 20 Auto-Rifles
    Secondary Weapon: None
    Armor: Taurian Concordat/Calderon Standard
    Infantry Kit
Battle Value: 72
Notes: Minesweeper equipment.

Platoon Type (Specialty): Motorized (Combat Engineers:
    Minesweeping)
    Ground MP: 3
Platoon Size (Squad/Platoon): 20 (10/2)
Armor Divisor: 1
To-Hit Modifier (Range in Hexes):
    −2 (0 Hexes), 0 (1 Hex), +2 (2 Hexes), +4 (3 Hexes)
Maximum Weapon Damage (# of Troopers):
    10 (20-19), 9 (18-17), 8 (16-15), 7 (14-13), 6 (12-11),
    5 (10-9), 4 (8-7), 3 (6-5), 2 (4-3), 1 (2-1)

Field Gun Infantry

Notable Unit: Motorized Batteries, Seventy-fifth
    Light Guard, First Taurian Lancers
Tech Base (Rating): Inner Sphere (C/B-B-B)
Transport Weight: 42.5 tons
Equipment:
    Primary Weapon: 24 Auto-Rifles
    Secondary Weapon: 6 Support Particle
    Projection Cannons
    Armor: Taurian Concordat/Calderon Standard
    Infantry Kit
Battle Value: 300
Notes: 6 Light Autocannon-5 pieces with 20 rounds of ammunition each. Each LAC/5 requires 5 men to operate.
Cannot make Anti-'Mech or Swarm Attacks.

Platoon Type (Specialty): Motorized, Field Artillery (None)
    Ground MP: 2
Platoon Size (Squad/Platoon): 30 (10/3)
Armor Divisor: 1
To-Hit Modifier (Range in Hexes):
    −1 (0 Hexes), 0 (1-3 Hexes), +2 (4-6 Hexes), +4 (7-9 Hexes)
Maximum Weapon Damage (# of Troopers):
    22 (30), 21 (29), 20 (28-27), 19 (26), 18 (25-24), 17 (23),
    16 (22), 15 (21-20), 14 (19), 13 (18), 12 (17-16), 11 (15),
    10 (14), 9 (13-12), 8 (11), 7 (10-9), 6 (8), 5 (7), 4 (6-5),
    3 (4), 2 (3), 1 (2-1)

MAGISTRACY OF CANOPUS

In the Periphery, resources and equipment are hard to come by. Any area where this wasn't true wouldn't remain out of the grasp of someone more powerful for long, so infantry is disproportionally more important in the Magistracy of Canopus than in the Inner Sphere.

With a greater number of people going into infantry service there is more manpower for specialization, an opportunity the Magistracy has not passed up. Tapping into what resources they have—in geography, manufacturing, people and training—they have units that can take on the best of the best. Of course, they also have desperate people doing anything they can to fight off predatory pirates and powerful invaders. But perhaps even more so than their Capellan allies, the groups that are willing to break any rule and push themselves to the limit are the ones that The Republic should be most wary of.

SPECIAL INFANTRY

Specialized infantry forces are nothing new for the Magistracy. Unable to mass produce battle armor at the rate of Inner Sphere nations, there has been no great embracing of battle armor units. Few platoons are relying on any great new technical breakthroughs. Rather, most infantry platoons remain a resource that the MAF has a long history of carefully nurturing.

With the Manei Domini out of the picture, the Ebon Magistrate's Shock Troops are perhaps the deadliest soldiers being fielded today. Deployed in seven-man squads, these men and women can take on whole platoons. Three man-portable plasma guns backed by Ebony rifles provide a potent offense while dermal armor protects them. Mixing fanatical devotion with upgraded eye implants gives them an edge that few can match. Most troopers won't run into them on the standard battlefield, as they are usually only deployed on covert missions.

On the battlefield, the RAF has often registered a unit of infantry as destroyed without killing all the members. Many are wounded and unable to be combat effective, while some are too busy with the wounded or dead to be able to fight. With a history of great medical training behind them, the MAF can dispatch the Magistracy Medical Corps to help the injured. While not a direct threat, a mere squad can treat injured soldiers and get them back into a fight sooner than transporting them back to a field hospital. They can change the flow of a battle if properly utilized.

While modern militaries can dispatch BattleMechs to almost any location, infantry is often more restricted by terrain. Engaging the Magistracy Cavaliers high in the mountains would be a case in point. Conventional infantry would be nearly useless due to the altitude, snow, and rough terrain, but the Cavalier "Mountain Men" Infantry Guard is not so hindered. Even with just two-squad platoons they can not only press the fight where they aren't expected, but they can demoralize as soldiers feel let down by their own infantry. Their use of mortars is doubly dangerous when one realizes their familiarity with avalanches and rock slides. Drawn mostly from citizens of the rough world of Thraxa, they often initiate new members by having them survive on Thraxa's rough northern continent with just a knife, snowsuit and boots.

Finally, when it comes to pure firepower, the elite foot soldiers attached to Raventhir's Iron Hand aren't fancy, just ready to unleash a wall of lead. The only specialist infantry listed here that deploys in full platoons, they use simple autorifles and portable machine guns to great effect. Consisting of the best troops from all of the MAF, this group has protected each Magestrix. Even the Word of Blake could not fully break this unit, getting the Magestrix to agree to surrender before the Infantry Guard stepped down.

Assault Commando
Notable Unit: Ebon Magistrate Shock Troops
Tech Base (Rating): Inner Sphere (F/X-X-F)
Transport Weight: 1 ton
Equipment:
    Primary Weapon: 4 Ebony Assault Lasers
    Secondary Weapon: 3 Man-Portable Plasma Guns
    Armor: Magistracy of Canopus Standard Infantry Kit
Battle Value: 46 + Modifier of 1.75
    (multiply Skill modified BV by 1.75)
Notes: Cybernetically enhanced infantry: Features Multi-Modal Cybernetic Eyes (IR/Laser Targeting; IR provides Active Probe capabilities at 2-hex range; Laser provides –1 to-hit modifier), Full-Body Dermal Armor (+1 Damage Divisor; reduce all Burst-Fire damage sustained by 1D6 – to minimum of 1 point; +1 Support Weapon maximum per Squad; –1 crew needs per Support Weapon, to minimum of 1). Flame-Based Weapon (may inflict damage and heat to heat-tracking units).

Platoon Type (Specialty): Foot (None)
    Ground MP: 1
Platoon Size (Squad/Platoon): 7 (7/1)
Armor Divisor: 2
To-Hit Modifier (Range in Hexes):
    –3 (0 Hexes),–1 (1-2 Hexes), +1 (3-4 Hexes), +3 (5-6 Hexes)
Maximum Weapon Damage (# of Troopers):
    6 (7), 5 (6), 4 (5), 3 (4-3), 2 (2), 1 (1)

MAGISTRACY

Field Medic

Notable Unit: Magistracy Medical Corps
Tech Base (Rating): Inner Sphere (C/X-C-B)
Transport Weight: 1 ton
Equipment:
    Primary Weapon: 5 Federated Long Rifles
    Secondary Weapon: None
    Armor: Magistracy of Canopus Standard Infantry Kit
Battle Value: 15
Notes: 2 Paramedics per squad. Paramedic equipment.

Platoon Type (Specialty): Foot (Paramedics)
    Ground MP: 1
Platoon Size (Squad/Platoon): 7 (7/1)
Armor Divisor: 1
To-Hit Modifier (Range in Hexes):
    −2 (0 Hexes), 0 (1 Hex), +2 (2 Hexes), +4 (3 Hexes)
Maximum Weapon Damage (# of Troopers):
    2 (7-6), 1 (5-4), 0 (3-1)

Heavy Mountain Infantry

Notable Unit: Cavalier "Mountain Men" Infantry Guard,
    Magistracy Cavaliers
Tech Base (Rating): Inner Sphere (C/X-X-B)
Transport Weight: 1.5 tons
Equipment:
    Primary Weapon: 12 Imperator AX-22 Assault Rifles
    Secondary Weapon: 2 Heavy Mortars
    Armor: Snowsuit
Battle Value: 36
Notes: Mountain climbing equipment. Unit can traverse
3 levels per hex. Unit is immune to the effects of Thin
Atmosphere. Cannot make Anti-'Mech or Swarm Attacks.

Platoon Type (Specialty): Foot (Mountain Troops)
    Ground MP: 1
Platoon Size (Squad/Platoon): 14 (7/2)
Armor Divisor: 1
To-Hit Modifier (Range in Hexes):
    −1 (0 Hexes), 0 (1 Hex), +2 (2 Hexes), +4 (3 Hexes)
Maximum Weapon Damage (# of Troopers):
    7 (14-13), 6 (12-11), 5 (10-9), 4 (8-7), 3 (6-5), 2 (4-3),
    1 (2-1)

Foot Infantry

Notable Unit: Raventhir's Infantry Guard, Raventhir's Iron Hand
Tech Base (Rating): Inner Sphere (C/B-B-B)
Transport Weight: 3 tons
Equipment:
    Primary Weapon: 24 Auto-Rifles
    Secondary Weapon: 4 Portable Machine Guns
    Armor: Magistracy of Canopus Standard Infantry Kit
Battle Value: 82
Notes: None.

Platoon Type (Specialty): Foot
    Ground MP: 1
Platoon Size (Squad/Platoon): 28 (7/4)
Armor Divisor: 1
To-Hit Modifier (Range in Hexes):
    −1 (0 Hexes), 0 (1 Hex), +2 (2 Hexes), +4 (3 Hexes)
Maximum Weapon Damage (# of Troopers):
    15 (28), 14 (27-26), 13 (25-24), 12 (23-22), 11 (21-20),
    10 (19-18), 9 (17), 8 (16-15), 7 (14-13), 6 (12-11),
    5 (10-9), 4 (8-7), 3 (6-5), 2 (4-3), 1 (2-1)

Given that the Periphery spawned the death of the old Star League, the RAF maintains an awareness of military and political developments as closely there as it does in the Successor States, despite the unlikelihood of RAF troops encountering these forces in combat.

Necessity is the mother of invention, and nowhere is the necessity greater than on the fringe of civilization. While these innovations may not be as grand in scale as those in the Inner Sphere, RAF troops can learn much from the tactics and equipment used by the conventional forces in the Periphery. Infantry in the Periphery has always formed a larger percentage of military might than in the Successor States. Thus, infantry will certainly be the largest complement an aggressor will face in these nations.

SPECIAL INFANTRY

Like the political tides that see new nations arise and fall in the Periphery, so too do new infantry types and tactics ebb and flow. Battle armored infantry has assumed a significant role in the various Inner Sphere militaries, but such technology is still rare in the Periphery. Conventional infantry forces, however, are continuously evolving.

While some might suspect the death of their Caesar would drive them to despair, the Caesar's Royal Guard only increased their brutality and ruthlessness. The notion of any unit being the "best of the best" is generally only so much hyperbole, but in the Marian Hegemony it is fact. Royal Guards are selected only after punishing trials to prove the physical quality of the candidates and their loyalty to the Caesar. Their fanaticism is unmatched among Periphery troops. Appearing archaic by design, their armor is still able to turn aside fire from modern weapons. Their constant training ensures the delivery of withering fire from support machine guns and auto-rifles. It will be through no fault of theirs that any Caesar dies.

Among the more despicable infantry in the Periphery are the so-called Pacification Squads of the Death's Consorts. Clad in whatever armor each trooper can scrounge, these mismatched troopers make up for in destruction what they lack in appearance. Formed under Lady Death, it was not until Gary Tiqualme took control that these troopers showed their true nature. Focused around heavy flamers, these platoons rain fire upon any who speak out against their masters. Great swaths of urban territory were turned to ash on Malagrotta thanks to these criminals.

The Outworlds Alliance fields troopers relying upon beasts for transport. The tariq-mounted infantry of Brasha's Qum'ran Guard hearken back to the days of horse-mounted cavalrymen with the reptilian tariqim replacing horses. Arranged similarly to an Inner Sphere jump infantry platoon, the twenty-one troopers maintain constant contact with their tariqim. These mounted troopers demonstrate uncanny battlefield acumen for such ill-provisioned troops. They care for their tariqim as they would a family member, mourning the loss of a mount as they do a fellow trooper. While their firepower suffers from inadequate supplies, they are capable of disrupting rear areas and performing exceptional recon.

Among the less-verifiable of Periphery troops are the Skåret assassins of the JàrnFòlk. Not much is known about the secretive JàrnFòlk and that comes from ComStar Explorer Corps reports. Given the wide-ranging rumors of these assassin teams, the inability to locate or observe them speaks either to their acumen or their non-existence. Based largely on conjecture and crime scene evidence in the Hanseatic League, it is believed that the Skåret assassins operate in three-man—or more—teams. While they are able to kill from a distance with rifles, they are also blamed for many deaths via blade, pistol and poison. Their ability to evade detection leads many to believe they possess sneak suits that rival those of DEST operatives.

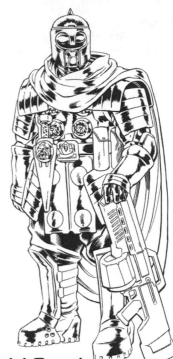

Ceremonial Guard

Notable Unit: Caesar's Royal Guard, Marian Hegemony
Tech Base (Rating): Inner Sphere (C/C-C-C)
Transport Weight: 12 tons (4 groups of 3 tons)
Equipment:
　　Primary Weapon: 90 Auto-Rifles
　　Secondary Weapon: 10 Support Machine Guns
　　Armor: Marian Hegemony Standard Infantry Kit
Battle Value: 467
Notes: Breaks up into four 25-trooper platoons in play. Cannot make Anti-'Mech or Swarm Attacks.

Platoon Type (Specialty): Foot (None)
　　Ground MP: 1
Platoon Size (Squad/Platoon): 100 (10/10)
Armor Divisor: 2
To-Hit Modifier (Range in Hexes):
　　–1 (0 Hexes), 0 (1 Hex), +2 (2 Hexes), +4 (3 Hexes)
Maximum Weapon Damage (# of Troopers):
　　14 (25), 13 (24-23), 12 (22-21), 11 (20-19), 10 (18-17), 9 (16), 8 (15-14), 7 (13-12), 6 (11-10), 5 (9), 4 (8-7), 3 (6-5), 2 (4-3), 1 (2-1)

Pirate

Notable Unit: Lady Death's "Pacification" Squads, Pirate
Tech Base (Rating): Inner Sphere (D/C-B-B)
Transport Weight: 6 tons
Equipment:
    Primary Weapon: 20 Laser Rifles
    Secondary Weapon: 8 Heavy Flamers
    Armor: Other Periphery/Generic Kit
Battle Value: 56
Notes: Flame-Based Weapon (may inflict damage and heat to heat-tracking units).

Platoon Type (Specialty): Motorized (None)
    Ground MP: 2
Platoon Size (Squad/Platoon): 28 (7/4)
Armor Divisor: 1
To-Hit Modifier (Range in Hexes):
    +1 (0 Hexes)
Maximum Weapon Damage (# of Troopers):
    11 (28-27), 10 (26-25), 9 (24-22), 8 (21-20), 7 (19-17),
    6 (16-15), 5 (14-12), 4 (11-9), 3 (8-7), 2 (6-4),
    1 (3-2), 0 (1)

Beast Mounted Infantry

Notable Unit: Tariq-mounted Infantry, Outworlds Alliance
Tech Base (Rating): Inner Sphere (C/B-B-B)
Transport Weight: 15 tons
Equipment:
    Primary Weapon: 21 Makeshift Rifles
    Secondary Weapon: None
    Armor: Other Periphery/Generic Kit
Battle Value: 79
Notes: None.

Platoon Type (Specialty): Beast-Mounted, Tariq (None)
    Ground MP: 5
Platoon Size (Squad/Platoon): 21 (7/3)
Armor Divisor: 2
To-Hit Modifier (Range in Hexes):
    −2 (0 Hexes), 0 (1 Hex), +2 (2 Hexes), +4 (3 Hexes)
Maximum Weapon Damage (# of Troopers):
    1 (21-10), 0 (9-1)

Assassin

Notable Unit: Skåret Assassins, JàrnFòlk
Tech Base (Rating): Inner Sphere (D/X-E-E)
Transport Weight: 1.5 tons
Equipment:
    Primary Weapon: 6 Sniper Rifles
    Secondary Weapon: 1 Sternsnacht Heavy Pistol
    Armor: Sneak Suit (Camo/ECM/IR)
Battle Value: 21
Notes: +3 to-hit modifier to attackers if platoon doesn't move, +2 modifier to attackers if platoon expends 1 MP. Non-infantry units suffer +1/+1/+2 penalty to hit at short/medium/long ranges. Invisible to Active Probes. May use Atmospheric Drops rules.

Platoon Type (Specialty): Foot (Paratroops)
    Ground MP: 1
Platoon Size (Squad/Platoon): 7 (7/1)
Armor Divisor: 1
To-Hit Modifier (Range in Hexes):
    −2 (0 Hexes), 0 (1-2 Hexes), +2 (3-4 Hexes), +4 (5-6 Hexes)
Maximum Weapon Damage (# of Troopers):
    1 (7-4), 0 (3-1)

Corporate security in the thirty-first century can rival the skill and equipment of the most elite Inner Sphere army and the size of a small Periphery nation's armed forces. But for all the flashy high-end firepower seen from the likes of Irian BattleMechs Unlimited, Defiance Industries or StarCorps, in the end corporations rely on the common trooper more than any nation. With factory complexes that can span dozens of kilometers, only manpower is economical enough to cover that territory. New Avalon's Achernar BattleMechs, for example, maintains a battalion of mostly *Valkyrie* and *Legionnaire* BattleMechs, backed up by two mixed battle armor battalions. However, these forces rarely deploy for passive defense; instead, they wait until called upon by the frontline corporate foot soldiers.

Given their reliance on "boots on the ground," it is not surprising that corporations have gotten the most out of the PBI (Poor Bloody Infantry).

SPECIAL INFANTRY

Preferring to reserve their armor and BattleMech security forces for so-called real problems, Johnston Industries relies on Rapid Response Forces as their first line of reinforcements for security. Riding on small, heavily armored hover bikes, Johnston's RRF troopers wear light protection to allow greater dismounted mobility. The hover bikes combine speed and the ability to carry heavy support weapons, like infantry LRM launchers.

Under the stewardship of Chandrasekhar Kurita, Hachiman Taro Enterprises experienced explosive growth. With such growth comes the inevitable long list of enemies, corporate or otherwise. Uncle Chandy's death at

the hands of the Word of Blake is a prime example of the level of conflict in which HTE can find itself. Given this reality, and the extensive technical expertise on which it can call, Hachiman has become adept at extracting itself from problems. The HTE Extraction Force takes it a step further, specializing in getting assets out of troubled territory. Using one-man VTOL systems allows incredible freedom of mobility and response. These teams can insert, rescue the kidnapped CFO and be airborne again before any alarm is raised.

"There is no problem a greater application of ballistic lead can't solve." Attributed to mercenary-turned-Solaris jock Kip Caselton, this saying best describes Irian BattleMechs Unlimited's approach to threat response. Deploying from full-sized APCs, Irian SWAT teams wear the heaviest unpowered armor in existence and take the application of throwing lead to the extreme. Imperator assault rifles backed up by no less than eight David light Gauss rifles ensure that Irian can bring major firepower to bear on any threat.

StarCorps prefers a middle ground between the nimble Johnston RRFs and the lumbering Irian SWAT teams. Equipped with reinforced jump packs to carry a maximum equipment load, StarCorps jump assault infantry is deadly in any urban or industrialized battlefield. Troops armed with auto-rifles are backed up by heavy grenade launchers mounted to their jump packs. Various grenades round out the devastating ensemble. As the Jihad grew in intensity and StarCorps saw its own facilities hit numerous times, they began to deploy their jump infantry with inferno grenade rounds. Able to threaten even BattleMechs in combat, StarCorps continues to show its wariness of any government authority.

Hover Assault Infantry
Notable Unit: Johnston Industries Rapid Response Force
Tech Base (Rating): Inner Sphere (D/X-X-D)
Transport Weight: 20 tons
Equipment:
  Primary Weapon: 12 Auto-Rifles
  Secondary Weapon: 8 LRM Launchers
  Armor: Other Periphery/Generic Kit
Battle Value: 55
Notes: None.

Platoon Type (Specialty): Mechanized/Hover (None)
  Ground MP: 4
Platoon Size (Squad/Platoon): 20 (5/4)
Armor Divisor: 1
To-Hit Modifier (Range in Hexes):
  –1 (0 Hexes), 0 (1-3 Hexes), +2 (4-6 Hexes), +4 (7-9 Hexes)
Maximum Weapon Damage (# of Troopers):
  8 (20-19), 7 (18-17), 6 (16-14), 5 (13-12), 4 (11-9), 3 (8-7), 2 (6-4), 1 (3-2), 0 (1)

VTOL Infantry

Notable Unit: Hachiman Taro Enterprise Extraction Force
Tech Base (Rating): Inner Sphere (E/X-X-E)
Transport Weight: 32 tons
Equipment:
    Primary Weapon: 16 Auto-Rifles
    Secondary Weapon: None
    Armor: Myomer, Vest
Battle Value: 81
Notes: None.

Platoon Type (Specialty): Mechanized VTOL,
    Micro-Copter (None)
    VTOL MP: 5
Platoon Size (Squad/Platoon): 16 (4/4)
Armor Divisor: 2
To-Hit Modifier (Range in Hexes):
    −2 (0 Hexes), 0 (1 Hex), +2 (2 Hexes), +4 (3 Hexes)
Maximum Weapon Damage (# of Troopers):
    8 (16-15), 7 (14-13), 6 (12-11), 5 (10-9), 4 (8-7), 3 (6-5),
    2 (4-3), 1 (2-1)

Heavy Support Infantry

Notable Unit: Irian Technologies SWAT Team
Tech Base (Rating): Inner Sphere (E/X-X-E)
Transport Weight: 6 tons
Equipment:
    Primary Weapon: 20 Imperator AX-22 Assault Rifles
    Secondary Weapon: 8 David Light Gauss Rifles
    Armor: Ballistic Plate
Battle Value: 88
Notes: Cannot conduct Anti-'Mech or Swarm Attacks.

Platoon Type (Specialty): Motorized (None)
    Ground MP: 1
Platoon Size (Squad/Platoon): 28 (7/4)
Armor Divisor: 2
To-Hit Modifier (Range in Hexes):
    −1 (0 Hexes), 0 (1-3 Hexes), +2 (4-6 Hexes), +4 (7-9 Hexes)
Maximum Weapon Damage (# of Troopers):
    15 (28-27), 14 (26-25), 13 (24), 12 (23-22), 11 (21-20),
    10 (19-18), 9 (17-16), 8 (15-14), 7 (13), 6 (12-11),
    5 (10-9), 4 (8-7), 3 (6-5), 2 (4-3), 1 (2-1)

Jump Support Infantry

Notable Unit: StarCorps Jump Assault Infantry
Tech Base (Rating): Inner Sphere (D/X-X-D)
Transport Weight: 4 tons
Equipment:
    Primary Weapon: 15 Auto-Rifles
    Secondary Weapon: 6 Heavy Grenade Launcher
      w/Infernos
    Armor: Other Periphery/Generic Kit
Battle Value: 78
Notes: Flame-based weapons (may inflict damage and heat to heat-tracking units).

Platoon Type (Specialty): Jump (None)
    Jump MP: 2
Platoon Size (Squad/Platoon): 21 (7/3)
Armor Divisor: 1
To-Hit Modifier (Range in Hexes):
    −1 (0 Hexes), 0 (1 Hex), +2 (2 Hexes), +4 (3 Hexes)
Maximum Weapon Damage (# of Troopers):
    11 (21), 10 (20-19), 9 (18-17), 8 (16-15), 7 (14-13),
    6 (12-11), 5 (10-9), 4 (8-7), 3 (6-5), 2 (4-3), 1 (2-1)

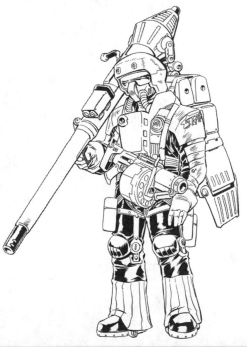

PROJECT PHOENIX

What Giovanni Estrella de la Sangre began in the 3060s as an effort to increase his planet's revenues has taken on a life far beyond those first steps. The concept of "Phoenixizations" has grown well beyond those initial twenty-two Inner Sphere designs. The new *Spider* and *Wolfhound* are examples of the growing trend toward updating older designs that began with the original Phoenix Project.

The initial Phoenix designs have played a significant role in the fighting of the past twenty years, joined by a growing procession of higher-tech machines. Leveraging the latest technological innovations to come out of the Jihad, these new Phoenix upgrades made their mark in the final battle to liberate Terra, as well as in the continuing struggles that have plagued the new peace of The Republic.

—General Albrecht Hoft
RAF Department of Military Intelligence
1 December, 3085

PROJECT PHOENIX: THE INNER SPHERE

Morgan Kell's *Archer*, Hanse Davion's *BattleMaster*, Natasha Kerensky's *Warhammer*, the Bounty Hunter's *Marauder*. Each of these famous 'Mechs is an image burned into our collective minds. And with the recent declassification of the infamous Silver Eagle incident, we were awed by the ROM footage of Daniel Allard slamming his *Valkyrie* into Yorinaga Kurita's *Warhammer*. While only the oldest veterans can recall such events firsthand, the images are so much the stuff of history that they have become legend. A massed battalion of *Stingers*, the hulking mass of a *Crusader* in an urban jungle, a lance of *Rifleman*s standing their ground before onrushing aerospace fighters. Whether through sheer numbers or their iconic participation in pivotal events, a handful of designs have remained part of the battlefield even as new ones have risen to prominence and fallen to obscurity. Three things one can count on: death, taxes and the fact that the *Archer* will forever be the gold-medal standard against which all fire-support units are measured.

When I first wrote of these emerging Project Phoenix designs, I quoted the ancient adage, "The more things change, the more they stay the same." In 3067, it came as a surprise that some of the greatest advancements in battlefield technology were built on the chassis of re-imagined icons like the *Wolverine*, *Phoenix Hawk* and *Locust*. Nearly twenty years later, little has changed. An army of new weapon designs has marched forth from the factories of the Inner Sphere, yet the most tried and true platforms continue not only to exist, but to dominate. The latest wave of Project Phoenix designs fits the weapons of the Jihad and engineers' drawing boards to our most familiar war machines. With updated exteriors and the newest weapons and equipment, these icons of war will continue to be part of the modern battlefield. Even as broad demilitarization rolls across the Inner Sphere, we can expect these designs to remain among the units that continue to see action.

—Colonel Martin Overstreet
Director of Technology
Department of Military Intelligence

LCT-5W2 LOCUST

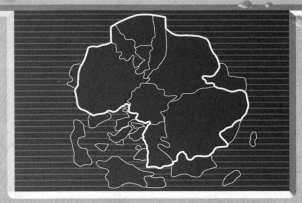

Mass: 20 tons
Chassis: Corean-IIa Delux Endo Steel
Power Plant: GM 180 XL
Cruising Speed: 97 kph
Maximum Speed: 151 kph, 194 kph with MASC
Jump Jets: None
Jump Capacity: None
Armor: Kallon Special Lite Ferro-Fibrous
Armament:
2 Diverse Optics Extended Range Medium Lasers
Manufacturer: Corean Enterprises MacAdams-Suharno
Primary Factory: Stewart (Corean)
Communications System: Garret T10 B with Guardian ECM and C^3
Targeting and Tracking System: Corean CalcMaster with TAG

Overview

Despite its ancient design, the *Locust* remains a modern and potent BattleMech on every battlefield where 'Mechs dare to tread. The Word of Blake used several upgraded models, both their own production and those bought (or stolen) from their so-called allies. One such variant was the 5W model built on Achernar, as well as several Marik and Periphery-born variants. With Achernar IndustrialMechs still rebuilding, The Republic has provided the plans for the 5W to Corean Enterprises to put an accessible *Locust* back into production.

Capabilities

Designated the 5W2, the RAF's newest *Locust* is very similar to the earlier Word of Blake model. It shares the same speed—a standard top speed of over 150 kilometers per hour, with sprints of almost 200 kph thanks to its myomer accelerator signal circuitry. Powered by a GM 180 extralight engine and protected by advanced light ferro-fibrous armor, this *Locust* is a maneuverable platform.

Dual extended-range medium lasers provide the 5W2 with medium-range offensive firepower, but the *Locust*'s real threat is its advanced electronics. Most opponents are used to seeing advanced scout 'Mechs like the *Raven* or the *Hitman* stalking them with heavier guns in support, but the *Locust* has long been a simple recon and strike BattleMech. By fitting the Corean-produced models with advanced C^3 computers and a target acquisition gear bundle, The Republic Armed Forces have gained a nimble and unexpected spotter. To help keep the lightly armored *Locust* alive, a Guardian ECM suite is embedded with the communications system.

Detractors among the RAF procurement offices have criticized the *Locust* for mounting expensive double heat sinks when its speed and weaponry clearly only call for single-strength models. Achernar's technicians, however, counter that without engine damage, their *Locust* is nearly impossible to overheat—removing another worry from the MechWarrior who is undoubtedly scrambling to stay alive on a battlefield filled with plasma rifles and Infernos and still TAG his target.

Deployment

Though Corean is still finishing the first full production run for the RAF, early shipments were made to both the Lament and the Liberators. The next machines to reach their assigned post will stand with the Hastati, but recent talks between the RAF and Corean hinge on the company's ability to sell 'Mechs outside The Republic. With the Reclamation Riots still fresh in the public's mind, it seems unlikely that The Republic will approve.

Variants

Many examples of the Blakist-standard LCT-5W still serve The Republic, with their original C^3i computers still intact, but the scarcity of C^3i systems makes them the odd man out of their lances. Rumors are circulating that the RAF will quietly refit them all to the 5W2 standard for conformity's sake.

RAF units near the Capellan border report continuing clashes with the Periphery-born LCT-5T in the hands of onetime Taurian allies, the Capellan Confederation. With a single ER medium laser and six light machine guns tied into two arrays, the 5T fills the *Locust*'s traditional role very well.

House Marik's LCT-6M still appears in several Republic lances as well, legacies of the inclusion of former Free Worlds soldiers into the RAF as well as salvage and outright purchase. Still claiming to be the fastest BattleMech ever made, the 6M is minimally armed with a pair of lasers but can outpace even the Federated Suns' *Fireball*.

Notable MechWarriors

Sergeant Wilkie Baskerville: Sergeant Baskerville fought on Terra with Stone's Lament from the cockpit of a captured LCT-5W and was responsible for three BattleMech kills in one day during a particularly nasty battle in Australia. His final kill—a Blakist *Red Shift*—crippled his 'Mech and broke Baskerville's leg in three places, but his extended convalescence allowed him time to write several white papers on the strengths and weaknesses of the LCT-5W. Corean engineers have repeatedly cited his paper for several modifications made to the 5W2, and there is a quiet movement afoot in his prefecture to have him ennobled.

Type: **Locust**
Technology Base: Inner Sphere
Tonnage: 20
Battle Value: 787

Equipment			Mass
Internal Structure:	Endo Steel		1
Engine:	180 XL		3.5
Walking MP:	9		
Running MP:	14 (18)		
Jumping MP:	0		
Heat Sinks:	10 [20]		0
Gyro:			2
Cockpit:			3
Armor Factor (Light Ferro):	67		4

	Internal Structure	Armor Value
Head	3	9
Center Torso	6	10
Center Torso (rear)		2
R/L Torso	5	8
R/L Torso (rear)		2
R/L Arm	3	5
R/L Leg	4	8

Weapons and Ammo	Location	Critical	Tonnage
ER Medium Laser	RA	1	1
Guardian ECM Suite	RT	2	1.5
C³ Slave	RT	1	1
MASC	CT	1	1
TAG	CT	1	1
ER Medium Laser	LA	1	1

STG-3P STINGER

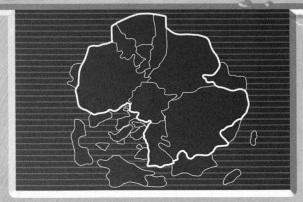

Mass: 20 tons
Chassis: Earthwerks STG-II Endo Steel
Power Plant: VOX 120
Cruising Speed: 65 kph
Maximum Speed: 97 kph
Jump Jets: Rawlings 52
　　Jump Capacity: 180 meters
Armor: Durallex Standard
Armament:
　　1 Lord's Light 3 Light Particle Beam Weapon
Manufacturer: Refit
　　Primary Factory: None
Communications System: Garret T10 B
Targeting and Tracking System: O/P 911 Targeting System

Overview

The Jihad put much military equipment into the hands of those who wouldn't ordinarily have access to it. Boys and girls were thrust rifles and bows and told to defend their homes while down-on-their-luck mercenaries and psychopathic killers got their hands on advanced military hardware, even BattleMechs. The plentiful *Stinger*-class 'Mech was passed around very often, often rebuilt with whatever tools were at hand, and many were customized in the refit yards that sprang up all around the Inner Sphere. One such model was the STG-3P.

Capabilities

The STG-3P used both endo steel internal structure to save enough mass to increase the 'Mech's overall protection

by almost a quarter. Maintaining the same speed and maneuverability profiles as classic *Stingers*, the 3P replaced the original machine guns and medium laser with a longer-ranged light particle projection cannon. With a similar damage profile to the medium laser, veteran *Stinger* pilots quickly adapted, although they were forced to keep a closer eye on their heat buildup than previously.

Deployment

The 3P flowed out of refit yards in the Lyran Commonwealth (or, as it was known then, Lyran Alliance) and the Draconis Combine, and many fought on both sides of the Jihad. The Stinger was a popular 'Mech in the Blakist Protectorate Militia, as well as a popular "incentive" to the many disreputable mercenary bands the Word attracted in their last spasm of defense. Their defeat led to a great proliferation across many factions thanks to salvage and captured equipment. In the RAF the highest concentration is found in the Liberators.

Variants

The Periphery-produced STG-5T, found in Magistracy units along The Republic's powder keg border with the Capellan Confederation, is a missile-support version that is often paired with the Capellan-influenced *Wasp*. Instead of any direct-fire weapons it carries a pair of three-tube multi-missile launchers, making it an adequate support machine at any range. The Taurians also field this design, using it effectively as a sniper against the Federated Suns.

House Steiner's STG-6S is a factory product, using a higher-rated light fusion engine to push the *Stinger* into speeds usually seen only in *Jenners*—and that impressive speed is further enhanced with MASC. The weapons configuration is largely unchanged—a pair of machine guns supported by an extended-range medium laser, but the real strength is the *Stinger*'s thick heavy ferro-fibrous armor.

The 7S *Stinger* is an attempt to create a more dangerous anti-'Mech and battlesuit vehicle. Although retaining the original *Stinger*'s speed, the 7S carries an ER medium laser and uses improved jump jets to reach a 240-meter jump range.

Notable MechWarriors

Sergeant Theresa Davenport: Sergeant Davenport fought with the Ruchbah resistance throughout the Blakist occupation of that world. Although she only gained a BattleMech during the last year of the resistance, her 3P model soon became a familiar sight at Protectorate Militia garrisons. She was known for her taunts, using her light PPC to fire at the fortifications that might shelter a Level II in order to draw out any mobile defenders. The first three times she succeeded in drawing out heavy forces into an ambush, but the fourth time the Protectorate Militia troopers refused to rise to her bait, and her *Stinger* was crippled when a field gun ripped its right leg off. Sergeant Davenport refused to give up and managed to destroy the field gun before escaping from the 'Mech's cockpit ahead of her would-be captors.

Ensign Alexander Rice: Ensign Rice was part of the Magistracy contingent of a Capellan raiding force on New Hessen in 3084 and was instrumental in turning a Republic relief column before it could lift the Capellan siege of Denton. Using his 5T-model *Stinger*, Rice combined Thunder long-range missile ammunition with smoke SRMs to make his lone 'Mech seem like an entire Capellan lance. The Republic force—which lacked BattleMechs—kept lumbering out of the smoke and into minefields. The Republic relief commander was sacked after the Capellans withdrew, but impartial reviews of the ROMs of his force concluded that he acted accordingly. Ensign Rice, we believe, was promoted.

INNER SPHERE

Type: **Stinger**
Technology Base: Inner Sphere
Tonnage: 20
Battle Value: 489

Equipment		Mass
Internal Structure:	Endo Steel	1
Engine:	120	4
Walking MP:	6	
Running MP:	9	
Jumping MP:	6	
Heat Sinks:	10	0
Gyro:		2
Cockpit:		3
Armor Factor:	64	4

	Internal Structure	Armor Value
Head	3	6
Center Torso	6	8
Center Torso (rear)		4
R/L Torso	5	7
R/L Torso (rear)		3
R/L Arm	3	6
R/L Leg	4	7

Weapons and Ammo	Location	Critical	Tonnage
Light PPC	RT	2	3
Jump Jets	RT	3	1.5
Jump Jets	LT	3	1.5

WSP-8T WASP

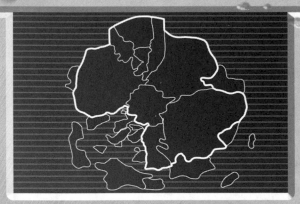

Mass: 20 tons
Chassis: Hellespont Type W Endo Steel
Power Plant: Hermes 120 XL
Cruising Speed: 64 kph
Maximum Speed: 97 kph
Jump Jets: Hellespont Leapers
  Jump Capacity: 180 meters
Armor: Durallex Light
Armament:
  1 CeresArms Striker Light PPC
  1 Doombud MML 3
Manufacturer: Hellespont BattleMech Works,
  Detroit Consolidated MechWorks
  Primary Factory: Sian, Detroit
Communications System: Hellespont Tight Beam
Targeting and Tracking System: Radcom TXXI

Overview

Like the *Stinger* and the *Locust,* the *Wasp* has long been a staple of light lances across the Inner Sphere and Periphery. The Jihad was just as transfiguring for this staple 'Mech as for any other. The Phoenix programs of the 3060s did much to return the *Wasp* to prominence, and the war against the Blakists brought this easily produced and culturally familiar chassis back into the limelight.

The WSP-8T *Wasp* is produced in the Confederation and the Magistracy of Canopus, and serves in both militaries while enjoying vigorous sales to other nations. The Word of Blake especially became adept at capturing supply convoys from Detroit on their way to the Inner Sphere and fielded many *Wasps* against their enemies. The Republic captured a great many from the Blakists, as did the Federated Suns and the Taurian Concordat.

Capabilities

The most prominent feature of the WSP-8T is its small cockpit, a design consideration that reflected the subordination of everything, even pilot comfort, to the need to get combat-viable equipment into the field against the Word of Blake during the Jihad—though many scout 'Mech pilots complain that neither Detroit nor Sian appears to have experimented with a full-scale cockpit version since the 'Mech's inception in 3075.

A light PPC replaces the customary medium laser, and the two-rack short-range missile launcher has been replaced by a three-tube multi-missile launcher. The ammunition magazines and the MML 3's larger mass necessitated the use of an extralight engine, though designers neglected to increase the *Wasp*'s armor protection at the same time.

Deployment

After ten years of prodigious production, the WSP-8T appears in nearly every Inner Sphere realm, including the Republic of the Sphere. Though our RAF purchases only a few WSP-8Ts, a small number have been kept active for training purposes since the Confederation and its allies use this 'Mech or ones like it so prolifically.

A number of *Wasp*-8Ts have been offered for sale on Galatea recently for cut-rate prices. RAF analysts have not been able to determine the source of these 'Mechs, but the mercenaries on Galatea are snapping them up as soon as they can be delivered. We suspect that a treasure-seeker has located a lost Blakist cache, but our agents lost the trail of the money from all buyers to date. The culprit seems quite adept at financial legerdemain.

Variants

The WSP-7MAF, manufactured inside the Magistracy's traditional borders, is faster and can jump farther than any other *Wasp*. The light PPC of the 8T is replaced by a more traditional extended-range medium laser, but the three-tube MML is upgraded to a five-tube model. It too uses the small cockpit, but pilot complaints are less common than might be supposed because strike 'Mechs do not normally keep the field as long as traditional recon models, and so the 7MAF MechWarriors can tolerate their cramped confines a little more easily.

A new model appeared in 3082 in the Outworlds Alliance, using a smaller engine and carrying a medium pulse laser for armament. Most telling about this new design, however, is the use of improved jump jets to offer the Outworlds *Wasp* a 240-meter jump range. RAF analysts have been unable to ascertain whether it was Taurian advisors who provided the specifications or the Outworlds Alliance's new Snow Raven allies.

Notable MechWarriors

MechWarrior Gerald: A MechWarrior of Clan Snow Raven, MechWarrior Gerald has been seen often on Alpheratz at the controls of a WSP-3A. His Trial of Grievance against Star Commander Reginald was the first reported combat use of the Outworlds-designed *Wasp*, and RAF analysts were keen to get the ROMs from a trader coming along the Suns-Combine border.

Facing a *Baboon*, Gerald used his *Wasp*'s mobility (and its jump jets) to close with the support 'Mech while using terrain to evade Reginald's missile fire. His pulse laser's accuracy was barely inhibited by the jumping 'Mech's instability, and he quickly bored through the *Baboon*'s thin rear armor. Reginald was injured ejecting, but Gerald won much acclaim using a "Spheroid" BattleMech to defeat his superior.

Type: **Wasp**
Technology Base: Inner Sphere
Tonnage: 20
Battle Value: 476

Equipment			Mass
Internal Structure:	Endo Steel		1
Engine:	120 XL		2
Walking MP:	6		
Running MP:	9		
Jumping MP:	6		
Heat Sinks:	10 [20]		0
Gyro:			2
Cockpit (Small):			2
Armor Factor:	56		3.5

	Internal Structure	Armor Value
Head	3	9
Center Torso	6	9
Center Torso (rear)		2
R/L Torso	5	7
R/L Torso (rear)		1
R/L Arm	3	5
R/L Leg	4	5

Weapons and Ammo	Location	Critical	Tonnage
Light PPC	RA	2	3
MML 3	RT	2	1.5
Ammo (MML) 80/66	RT	2	2
Jump Jets	RT	3	1.5
Jump Jets	LT	3	1.5

VLK-QT2 VALKYRIE

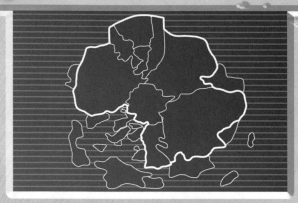

Mass: 30 tons
Chassis: Corean Model 101AA Endo Steel
Power Plant: Hermes 210 XL
Cruising Speed: 75 kph
Maximum Speed: 118 kph
Jump Jets: Rawlings 54
   Jump Capacity: 210 meters
Armor: Durallex Ferro-Fibrous with CASE
Armament:
   1 Guided Technologies Second Generation Streak SRM 6
   1 Blankenburg Light PPC
Manufacturer: Vandenberg Mechanized Industries (Refit)
   Primary Refit Location: New Vandenberg
Communications System: Lynx-Shur
Targeting and Tracking System: Sync-Tracker (39-42071)

Overview

With a lot of *Valkyrie* frames littering the Taurian battlefields, the Concordat decided to standardize their rebuilds of the many *Valkyrie*s they salvaged. These newly upgraded machines have since returned to the battlefield to fight pirates, rebels or the very Davion forces from which they were taken.

Capabilities

The *Valkyrie* plant on New Avalon has been spitting out 'Mechs for centuries. Though its function was once thought beyond understanding, the NAIS figured out enough to upgrade the design and keep the factory going. This automated plant barely survived the Blakist occupation. The Word of Blake used it throughout that time, but it was bombed as they retreated, and Corean has only recently brought the plant back online. Despite being out of commission for more than a decade, there are enough *Valkyrie*s in existence for the Taurians to have acquired plenty in battlefield salvage.

Five and a half tons of armor offer good but not great protection. A more useful feature is the new extralight fusion engine, which propels Taurian refits at a top speed more than thirty kilometers per hour faster than the original. That increased speed, combined with another sixty meters of jump capacity, allows the QT2 *Valkyrie* to avoid being hit.

For long-range fire, the Concordat is apparently using light particle cannons left over from their dealings with the Blakists. Supporting that is a Streak missile rack that provides short-range punch with economy and accuracy. With CASE to protect the ammunition, the frame and pilot can survive an ammunition explosion, often well enough to be refitted again.

The QT2 version plays a different role than most *Valkyrie*s. Rather than fire support, the Taurians use theirs primarily for reconnaissance and counter-recon. It is especially useful against pirates, who often operate antiquated light 'Mechs that are slower and less powerful than this *Valkyrie*.

Deployment

Once the darling of the Federated Suns, the *Valkyrie* remains theirs in pride, but in reality it has migrated well beyond their borders. Battle losses have spread the design to neighboring realms, while the FedCom alliance allowed it to cross to Lyran space in large numbers. Now Corean is selling *Valkyrie*s to the Republic of the Sphere, while the Taurians have sent their refits to their best units, especially those featured in the media. The Lyrans use their design sparingly, primarily as quick fire support, while most other realms use their few *Valkyrie*s to fill holes in their rosters. The newest Davion version has just started coming off the rebuilt lines in 3085, destined for internal use and sale to The Republic.

Variants

In addition to the many pre-Clan versions of the *Valkyrie*, three recent versions have graced the battlefields. The first received a lukewarm reception from pilots, but still managed to find a useful niche in the Suns and here in The Republic. Lacking the speed of the Taurian refit, the QD2 carries two light class-2 autocannons and a medium laser. A targeting computer ties all the weapons together.

The Lyrans have their own version, the QS5. Mounting a nine-tube multi-missile launcher, it can provide fire support and then move in to brawl. It also mounts ferro-fibrous armor for increased protection, though pilots aren't happy about the lack of double heat sinks. A common remark is that the Lyrans bought the design from a discount Luthien Armor Works sale. During the occupation, the Blakists put out their own version, similar to the Lyran design. Theirs uses a smaller launcher with enhanced guidance, while a light engine and small cockpit save weight to add an improved C^3 system. The armor is replaced with standard plate to allow the use of double heat sinks.

Finally, the Federated Suns followed the Commonwealth's lead after repairing the Blakists' damage to the factory and have built their own version of the QS5, listed as the QD4. It too mounts a multi-missile launcher and a medium laser, though this version has seven tubes. It trades down to light ferro-fibrous armor and upgrades the heat sinks to freezers. The most significant change is replacement of the jump jets with seven improved versions.

Notable MechWarriors

Captain Randy Vicenta: Captain Vicenta is one of the Filvelt Coalition's most senior MechWarriors. Piloting Mag, his QD2-model *Valkyrie*, he has taken down dozens of pirates using his excellent shooting with the targeting computer in his 'Mech. His comrades in arms refer to him as "The Closer," for his ability to take out enemies damaged by other members of his unit. While they may get annoyed at times that Randy steals their kills, there is no shortage of targets for the overworked Filtvelt forces.

Type: **Valkyrie**
Technology Base: Inner Sphere
Tonnage: 30
Battle Value: 863

Equipment			Mass
Internal Structure:	Endo Steel		1.5
Engine:	210 XL		4.5
Walking MP:	7		
Running MP:	11		
Jumping MP:	7		
Heat Sinks:	10 [20]		0
Gyro:			3
Cockpit:			3
Armor Factor:	88		5.5

	Internal Structure	Armor Value
Head	3	9
Center Torso	10	13
Center Torso (rear)		4
R/L Torso	7	10
R/L Torso (rear)		2
R/L Arm	5	8
R/L Leg	7	11

Weapons and Ammo	Location	Critical	Tonnage
Light PPC	RA	1	3
Streak SRM 6	RT	2	4.5
Ammo (Streak) 15	RT	1	1
CASE	RT	1	.5
Jump Jets	RL	2	1
Jump Jet	RT	1	.5
Jump Jet	CT	1	.5
Jump Jet	LT	1	.5
Jump Jets	LL	2	1

PLG 2010

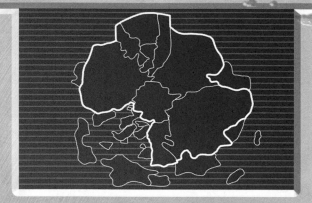

Mass: 35 tons
Chassis: Krupp 255 Endo Steel
Power Plant: GM 315 XL
Cruising Speed: 97 kph
Maximum Speed: 151 kph
Jump Jets: Rawlings 45
   Jump Capacity: 240 meters
Armor: Krupp 156 Ferro-Fibrous
Armament:
   2 Moscovia Light Particle Projector Cannons
Manufacturer: Krupp Armament Works
   Primary Factory: Terra
Communications System: Exeter Longscan 300
Targeting and Tracking System: TRSS Eagle Eye with TAG

Overview

The *Ostscout* has a long and well-deserved reputation as a scout 'Mech from the Succession Wars, and the recovery of Star League technologies in the 3040s and 3050s gave the *Ostscout* even more of an edge. It wasn't until after the Jihad's eruption, when Word of Blake and ComStar-sponsored Free Rasalhague Republic factories began to manufacture the OTT-10CS model, that the MechWarriors of the Inner Sphere actually came to respect the *Ostscout* as a 'Mech that could harm them directly as well as indirectly. That experiment must have been deemed a success, as the OTT-11J now produced by The Republic from old Word of Blake factories is a more powerful example.

Capabilities

The Succession Wars-era *Ostscout* was more or less unarmed, fitted with sensor equipment and light armor and a defensive laser armament that never really frightened anyone. The 'Mech's sensors were so well-designed and hardy, though, that battlefield commanders quickly learned to protect them from combat, leading *Ostscout* MechWarriors to become truly expert BattleMech pilots but terrible BattleMech gunners.

The 11J reverses that trend. Though the 'Mech still carries the artillery-designation target acquisition gear that allows it to fulfill its historical spotter role, each of the formerly spindly arms now ends in a fully-articulated hand, while each torso houses a light PPC. The 11J came as an unwelcome surprise to the recon lances of Stone's Lament and Stone's Liberators during the final assault on Terra, when they fired at ranges not even expected by the most jaded of *Ostscout* opponents.

Deployment

The bulk of the OTT-11Js produced before the fall of Terra were used in the final ring of so-called Maginot worlds around Terra during the Coalition's push against the Blakists. Though they were overlooked at the time, Republic historians have identified PPC-armed *Ostscout*s on Phecda and Thorin, and we know many worked with TerraSec formations in Europe and Asia. The Manei Domini of the Fifty-first Shadow shunned the design, however, so none served with Azrael's Terran Guard.

Though the RAF has little need for so specialized a 'Mech, the *Ostscout* remains in limited production on Terra. The Republic has been selling the *Ostscout* to our neighbors for much-needed hard currency, and both the Federated Suns and the Lyran Commonwealth have purchased nearly a dozen of the slender BattleMech.

Variants

The OTT-10CS, upon which the 11J was based, was still being produced in the Rasalhague Republic at the time of that nation's absorption by Clan Ghost Bear. RAF analysts have been unable to get solid numbers out of the Ghost Bears, but reliable rumors from the Bears' Delta Galaxy suggest that the 'Mech is still being produced for the KungsArmé.

The 10CS is similar to the 11J, though incrementally slower; it carries ER medium lasers in place of the light PPCs and a C³i computer in place of the TAG. When designing it, ComStar engineers had intended this *Ostscout* as a spotter for a Level II rather than an artillery battery, and the *Ostscout* performed that role middling well for the Com Guards.

Notable MechWarriors

Adept Akio Fuchita: Fuchita served with the Com Guards' First Army during the last years of the Jihad and his 10CS *Ostscout* was adorned with nearly a dozen kill markers from Blakist 'Mechs. Though he was detached for duty on Phecda, his *Ostscout* still wore its First Army markings when it fought an 11J *Ostscout* in the ruins of the Atlantic Coast. Despite the Blakist 'Mech's superior range, Fuchita used his *Ostscout*'s jump jets to keep his enemy off balance long enough for the rest of his Level II to arrive. Once the rest of the Level II was involved in keeping the *Ostscout*'s mates away, Fuchita closed with and defeated the 11J's pilot in single combat. After that, Fuchita would claim six more kills, including a *Buccaneer*, before being slain in the assault on Terra.

Type: **Ostscout**
Technology Base: Inner Sphere
Tonnage: 35
Battle Value: 908

Equipment			Mass
Internal Structure:	Endo Steel		2
Engine:	315 XL		11
Walking MP:	9		
Running MP:	14		
Jumping MP:	8		
Heat Sinks:	10 [20]		0
Gyro:			4
Cockpit:			3
Armor Factor (Ferro):	71		4

	Internal Structure	Armor Value
Head	3	9
Center Torso	11	10
Center Torso (rear)		4
R/L Torso	8	8
R/L Torso (rear)		2
R/L Arm	6	7
R/L Leg	8	7

Weapons and Ammo	Location	Critical	Tonnage
Light PPC	RT	2	3
TAG	CT	1	1
Light PPC	LT	2	3
Jump Jets	RT	4	2
Jump Jets	LT	4	2

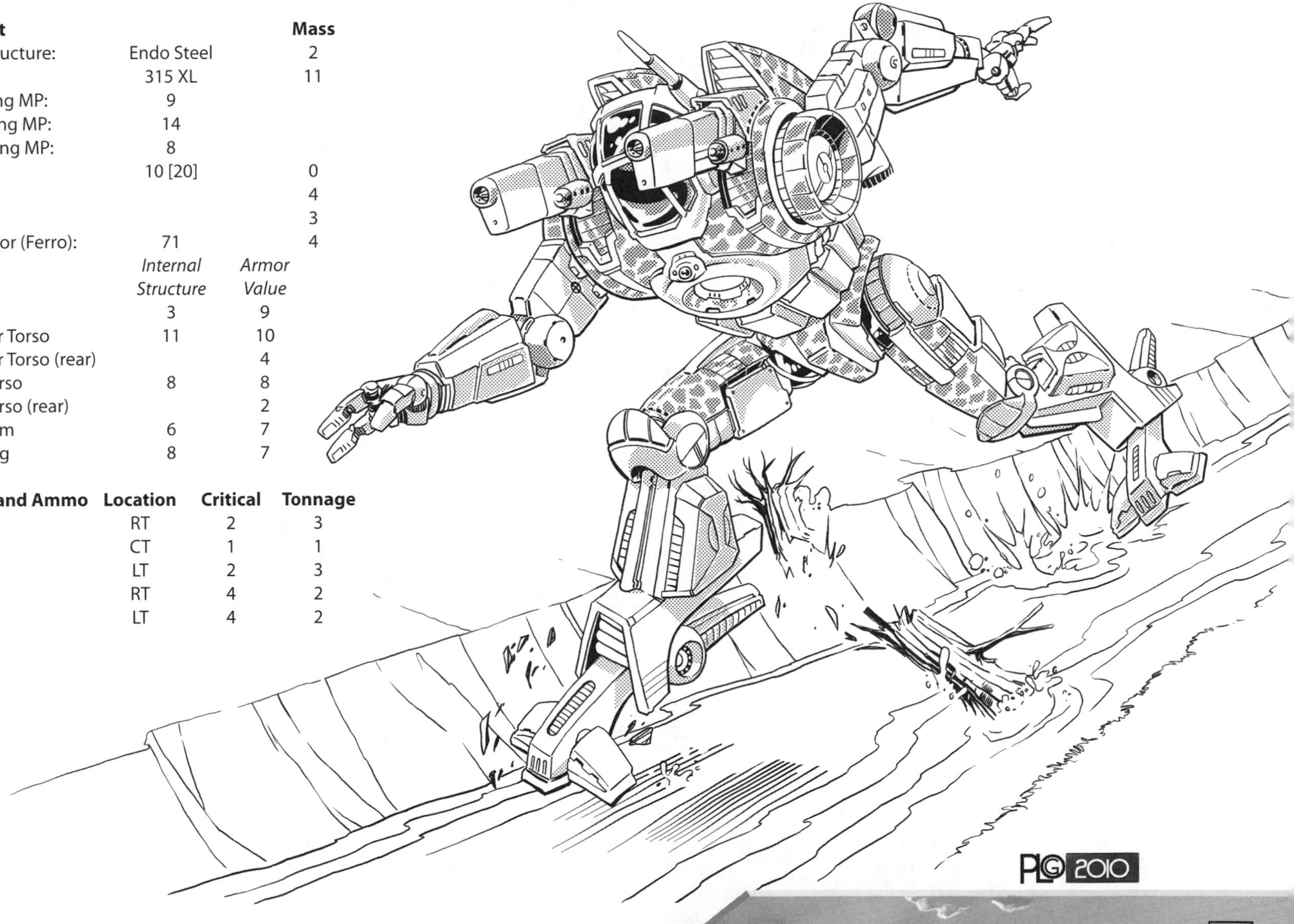

PLG 2010

Mass: 45 tons
Chassis: Ceresplex IV Endo Steel
Power Plant: Plasmastar 270
Cruising Speed: 64 kph
Maximum Speed: 97 kph
Jump Jets: Anderson Propulsion 30
Jump Capacity: 150 meters
Armor: Ceres Metals Stealth Armor
Armament:
    1 Ceres Arms Crusher Plasma Rifle
    2 Ceres Arms Extended Range Medium Lasers
Manufacturer: Ceres Metals Industries
    Primary Factory: St. Ives
Communications System: Ceres Metals Model 686
    with Guardian ECM
Targeting and Tracking System: Apple Churchill 2000

Overview

Intrigued by the potential of the new plasma rifle, Ceres Metals Industries began experimenting with the idea of mounting the weapon on their production model *Phoenix Hawk*. Development was slowed by the disruption to interstellar commerce that accompanied the Word of Blake's crusade against humanity, but the new PXH-5L *Phoenix Hawk* was deployed just in time to participate in the counterattacks that halted the fanatics' depredations.

Capabilities

The PXH-5L retains most of the performance of the earlier PXH-4L. Worsening relations with the Taurian Concordat forced Ceres to source an alternative to the Warner 270M power plant. Luckily, Ceres Metals found that the *Phoenix Hawk* could accept the Plasmastar 270 engine constructed by StarCorps for their EMP-7L *Emperor*. Ground speed was unaffected by the engine swap but the removal of a jump jet reduced the maximum jumping distance by thirty meters.

The power plant change opened the door for other changes as well. One heat sink and the auxiliary anti-personnel weapons were stripped out. The loss of the machine guns is less of a problem than it would appear—the Ceres Arms Crusher Plasma Rifle which replaced the extended-range large laser is a fearsome anti-personnel system in its own right.

Deployment

The Capellan Confederation has chosen to group the new PXH-5L with other stealth-equipped units. Traditionally this has proven to be a winning combination, but fundamental flaws in the tactics used by these units were demonstrated most painfully in the fighting with Republic of the Sphere forces on Tikonov. Republican troops dubbed standard Capellan tactics of engaging their stealth systems and heading for cover as "camping." Although effective if the enemy obliges with a head-on attack, Paladin David McKinnon completely negated their advantage by using artillery-delivered smoke screens to rob the Capellans of free shots on his troops as they closed. On other occasions RAF troops just bypassed enemy positions or encircled them and called in artillery or aerospace strikes. Ultimately Chancellor Sun-Tzu Liao was forced to accept humiliation by signing the Treaty of Tikonov and formally recognizing the Republic of the Sphere and its territorial claims.

The Duchy of Oriente has started to field the new PXH-7K, originally developed for the DCMS, in limited numbers. In spite of their best efforts several have fallen in battle and been captured by other members of the fragmented Free Worlds League.

Intended for service with the Com Guards, the 8CS was designed and built in the Combine but the conflict with the Word of Blake ended before it entered service in quantity and the advanced design was adopted by the DCMS. A number were captured by the Ghost Bears during clashes along the Clan frontier, and these have been pressed into service by the Dominion's Rasalhague troops. Most of the Com Guard units were absorbed by the Republic of the Sphere.

The Word of Blake created the PXH-4W for their own use, but the Periphery-based manufacturing plants were seized by the Taurian Concordat and Magistracy of Canopus. The Republic of the Sphere is also fielding a handful of former Blakist units.

Variants

The PXH-7K swaps the plasma rifle for a snub-nose PPC and removes the right arm medium laser for a C3 slave unit. Improved jump jets allow it to clear 270 meters in a single bound. The endo steel internal structure has been retained, but the stealth armor has been replaced with light ferro-fibrous armor. A light fusion power plant replaces the standard-model engine.

The PXH-8CS is a smorgasbord of advanced experimental technology. It swaps all weapons for a pair of arm-mounted snub-nose PPCs. The 'Mech carries standard jump jets, but a 315 XXL engine allows it to hit 118 kph. An XL gyro and C³ slave round out the design. Endo steel internal structure is still used, but an additional four heat sinks are installed.

The PXH-4W also uses endo steel and Guardian ECM suite. A smaller 225 light fusion engine reduces ground speed, but eight improved jump jets give this variant an extended jump envelope of 240 meters. Each arm mounts an extended-range medium laser and a light PPC.

Notable MechWarriors

Sao-wei **Eustace Haversack:** A lance commander in McCarron's Armored Cavalry, Haversack was enraged by the humiliation heaped upon the Confederation by the Treaty of Tikonov. He is constantly agitating for action against the Republic of the Sphere and his superiors have chosen to overlook his politically inconvenient attitude. We suspect this is due to his highly successful participation in several "false flag" raids believed to have been conducted by the Confederation against The Republic.

PXH-5L PHOENIX HAWK

Type: **Phoenix Hawk**
Technology Base: Inner Sphere
Tonnage: 45
Battle Value: 1,589

Equipment			Mass
Internal Structure:	Endo Steel		2.5
Engine:	270		14.5
Walking MP:	6		
Running MP:	9		
Jumping MP:	5		
Heat Sinks:	10 [20]		0
Gyro:			3
Cockpit:			3
Armor Factor (Stealth):	128		8

	Internal Structure	Armor Value
Head	3	6
Center Torso	14	23
Center Torso (rear)		5
R/L Torso	11	18
R/L Torso (rear)		4
R/L Arm	7	10
R/L Leg	11	15

Weapons and Ammo	Location	Critical	Tonnage
Plasma Rifle	RA	2	6
ER Medium Laser	RA	1	1
Ammo (Plasma) 20	RT	2	2
Guardian ECM Suite	LT	2	1.5
ER Medium Laser	LA	1	1
Jump Jets	RT	2	1
Jump Jet	CT	1	.5
Jump Jets	LT	2	1

Note: If playing under Advanced Rules, treat head as having a Full-Head Ejection System.

PLG 2010

GRF-4R GRIFFIN

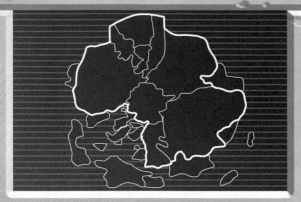

Mass: 55 tons
Chassis: Earthwerks GRF Endo Steel
Power Plant: Edasich 330 XL
Cruising Speed: 64 kph
Maximum Speed: 97 kph
Jump Jets: Rawlings 65+
    Jump Capacity: 270 meters
Armor: Starshield A
Armament:
    1 Fusigon Smarttooth Snub-Nose PPC
    1 Martell ER Medium Laser
    1 Holly MML 5
Manufacturer: Refit
    Primary Factory: Terra
Communications System: Neil 6000
Targeting and Tracking System: RCA Instatrac Mark XI

Overview

The classic *Griffin* is one of the most ancient designs still found on the modern battlefield. Its first incarnation debuted in 2492 and has been in near-continuous production for almost 600 years. Even today, manufacturers in the Periphery produce a limited number of the original GRF-1N model.

However, technology moves on, and the *Griffin* has been upgraded numerous times over the centuries. One of the most deadly new variants appeared in the Word of Blake's hands during the last years of the Jihad. The GRF-4R improves on the original design in nearly every way, with few of the trade-offs seen in similar updated BattleMechs.

Capabilities

When upgrading their *Griffin*s, the Word of Blake started with a larger engine and a full battery of improved jump jets, giving this heavy-end medium 'Mech the mobility of a machine half its mass. They swapped out the PPC for a snub-nose model and the LRM rack for a mid-sized multi-missile launcher, reducing the 'Mech's long-range bite for more substantial and accurate medium and close-range attacks. A single ER medium laser fills out the machine's payload, giving the GRF-4R a strong backup weapon.

Some compromises did have to be made. This variant of the *Griffin* is less well protected than most other contemporary models, though it is still better armored than the original series. Its extralight engine can also be a liability, especially as it lacks CASE for its missile magazines.

Deployment

The GRF-4R first appeared in the Word of Blake Militia's Protectorate forces, where it was very popular for its speed, maneuverability and firepower. That it lacked the C³i so common among other high-end Blakist 'Mechs was seen as an advantage on increasingly ECM-heavy battlefields, and contributed to its continued popularity.

Today the GRF-4R can be found throughout the Inner Sphere. Its tactical flexibility means that many nations are keeping these impressive machines active even as they decommission its lesser brethren. In the post-Jihad age, having a single machine that can fill so many battlefield roles makes the latest *Griffin* a valuable and treasured 'Mech. Indeed, the only major state that lacks the GRF-4R is the Lyran Commonwealth; they prefer their own home-built variants, such as the earlier 6S.

Variants

In the early days of the Jihad, the Draconis Combine and Capellan Confederation each debuted new versions of the *Griffin* based on the FedCom Civil War-period Vicore plans. The Kurita model, the 5K, made extensive use of advanced materials in its construction, featuring a light fusion engine and a heavy-duty gyro. Its armament was a slight upgrade from the original *Griffin*, centered around a light PPC and an LRM 10, with a single ER medium laser as backup. The Capellan version, as with many of its contemporaries in the Confederation, was protected by stealth armor. It mounted a plasma rifle and a five-tube multi-missile launcher supported by a cluster of medium lasers. These GRF-5L variants were shared with the Magistracy of Canopus, but not with the Taurian Concordat.

Toward the end of the Jihad, the Concordat introduced its own plasma rifle-equipped *Griffin*. Unable to acquire stocks of stealth armor from their former Trinity allies, the GRF-4N instead mounted a trio of ER medium lasers in place of the usual missile launcher. These models were also faster and could jump further than the GRF-5L.

Notable Pilots

Adept Joseph McMannus: Adept McMannus was a devout believer in the Word of Blake, and records recovered after the Jihad indicated that the Manei Domini had begun to express an interest in the young pilot. Had the Protectorate lasted longer, there is little doubt he would have advanced quickly through the ranks. Unfortunately for him, Devlin Stone's Coalition forces assaulted Terra before he could make his rise. McMannus didn't attempt to meet Stone's forces in direct combat, instead choosing to hide his *Griffin* in an industrial park outside London. He made the mistake of trusting that the students and faculty at the University of Southampton were as dedicated to the Blakist regime as he was. Not long afterward, he was turned in and arrested. To this day, Republic security forces continue to hunt for other potential fifth columnists left behind by the Word.

238

INNER SPHERE

Type: **Griffin**
Technology Base: Inner Sphere
Tonnage: 55
Battle Value: 1,412

Equipment		Mass
Internal Structure:	Endo Steel	3
Engine:	330 XL	12.5
Walking MP:	6	
Running MP:	9	
Jumping MP:	9	
Heat Sinks:	11 [22]	1
Gyro:		4
Cockpit:		3
Armor Factor:	168	10.5

	Internal Structure	Armor Value
Head	3	9
Center Torso	18	25
Center Torso (rear)		8
R/L Torso	13	19
R/L Torso (rear)		5
R/L Arm	9	16
R/L Leg	13	23

Weapons and Ammo	Location	Critical	Tonnage
Snub-Nose PPC	RA	2	6
ER Medium Laser	RA	1	1
MML 5	LT	3	3
Ammo (MML) 48/40	LT	2	2
Improved Jump Jet	RL	2	1
Improved Jump Jets	RT	8	4
Improved Jump Jet	CT	2	1
Improved Jump Jets	LT	4	2
Improved Jump Jet	LL	2	1

SCP-10M SCORPION

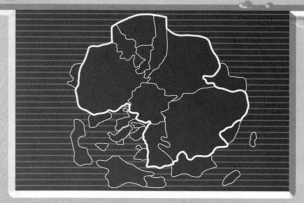

Mass: 55 tons
Chassis: Brigadier 800F Endo Steel
Power Plant: Vox 385 XL
Cruising Speed: 76 kph
Maximum Speed: 119 kph
Jump Jets: None
    Jump Capacity: None
Armor: StarSlab/4
Armament:
    1 Fusigon Strongtooth Heavy PPC
    1 Doombud LRM 10
Manufacturer: Brigadier Corporation
    Primary Factory: Oliver
Communications System: Garrett 500A
Targeting and Tracking System: Garret GRNDTRK9

Overview

Long a 'Mech of last resort, the last stop before piloting a Quasit, Dispossession or an early retirement, the *Scorpion* has rehabilitated its image in the past few decades. Upgrades to the gyroscope and actuator software have made the ride smoother, but the weapons and ability to use them have mattered far more. The first attempts to upgrade the *Scorpion* were minor, replacing the particle cannon with an extended-range version. But the heat generated actually hurt the machine, slowing it down every time the main gun was fired. As engineers have learned from their mistakes with the *Scorpion*, the refits have gotten better. The most recent one was first developed in the crumbling Free Worlds League and dubbed the SCP-10M. With its success, almost every nation has duplicated the 10M.

Capabilities

The 10M is a pricey upgrade that most feel is worth it. Made possible thanks to the Blakists' reconstruction of Brigadier Corporation's factories on Oliver, where they built new *Scorpion*s to their 12C refit and provided a stream of chasses for other variants, like the 10M. The expensive 330 engine, a huge chunk of the SCP-12C's mass, is removed. In its place is an even more expensive 385 extralight engine. The chassis is also a new, weight-saving endo steel. The particle cannon is upgraded to a heavy version and the short-range missile launcher replaced with a ten-tube long-range version, which was moved to the other side of the 'Mech in an effort to improve balance. Finally, the heat sinks are upgraded, allowing the 'Mech to finally be as close to worry-free of its weapons as it ever has.

The 10M is best used as a cavalry 'Mech and mid-range striker. With the reach of both its weapons, as well as their minimum range, the *Scorpion* has no business closing within 200 meters of its targets. The limited arc of fire would further limit this quad at close ranges. It is not the most heavily armored 'Mech for its size, so it should use speed to provide extra defense. Of course the *Scorpion*, like any 'Mech, works best in conjunction with a larger force, such as a lance or company. The combination of speed and firepower becomes even more useful at the company level, where it can cover a large range, perhaps even supporting different elements.

Deployment

The greatest concentrations of the *Scorpion* can be found in the Lyran Commonwealth and Draconis Combine. With The Republic's demilitarization reforms, the Oliver *Scorpion* lines were some of the first to be closed down, limiting the numbers found in the RAF. However, *Scorpion*s can be found in almost any large army, having some resiliency by being stuck on the fringe of forces. The Periphery also has its fair share of *Scorpion*s, though many of these are the original 1N version, banished to the edges of humanity where any 'Mech had value. The 10M can be found in fire support lances, quick strike units as well as recon forces of the fractured Free Worlds and RAF. It might be something of overkill on a recon lance, but an enemy *Raven* would have a bad day if it ran into a recon lance with a *Scorpion*.

Variants

While the Lyrans were the first to experiment with an endo steel chassis, the Combine chose to replicate the use of an extralight engine. They have made their *Scorpion* into more of a cavalry 'Mech, with a snub-nosed PPC and nine-tube MML launcher. Ferro-fibrous armor increased protection while a C[3] master allows it to coordinate a lance of linked 'Mechs. Finally, an additional laser was added to take advantage of the double heat sink capacity.

Notable MechWarriors

MechWarrior Chuck Russell: A young noble, Russell was unexpectedly given his 12S *Scorpion* when a relative was killed. He has since proven to be very adept at piloting his 'Mech for the Fifteenth Arcturan Guard. He seems to prefer the speed of the *Scorpion* and is the point man for his lance. His favored tactic is to circle around the enemy, not letting them in too close where the *Scorpion*'s inability to pivot and fire would put him at a disadvantage. During the fighting on Terra, a Blakist *Initiate* hit him from behind, destroying both his autocannon and missile launcher in a single shot. After hiding behind a mesa and dumping his ammo, he proceeded to destroy three more opponents by high speed ramming before the battle was finished. Now part of the RAF, he is currently awaiting the 10M upgrade to his 'Mech.

SCP-10M SCORPION

Type: **Scorpion**
Technology Base: Inner Sphere
Tonnage: 55
Battle Value: 1,458

Equipment		Mass
Internal Structure:	Endo Steel	3
Engine:	385 XL	22
Walking MP:	7	
Running MP:	11	
Jumping MP:	0	
Heat Sinks:	10 [20]	0
Gyro (XL):		2
Cockpit:		3
Armor Factor:	144	9

	Internal Structure	Armor Value
Head	3	9
Center Torso	18	21
Center Torso (rear)		6
R/L Torso	13	14
R/L Torso (rear)		4
FR/L Leg	13	18
RR/L Leg	13	18

Weapons and Ammo	Location	Critical	Tonnage
Heavy PPC	RT	4	10
LRM 10	LT	2	5
Ammo (LRM) 12	LT	1	1

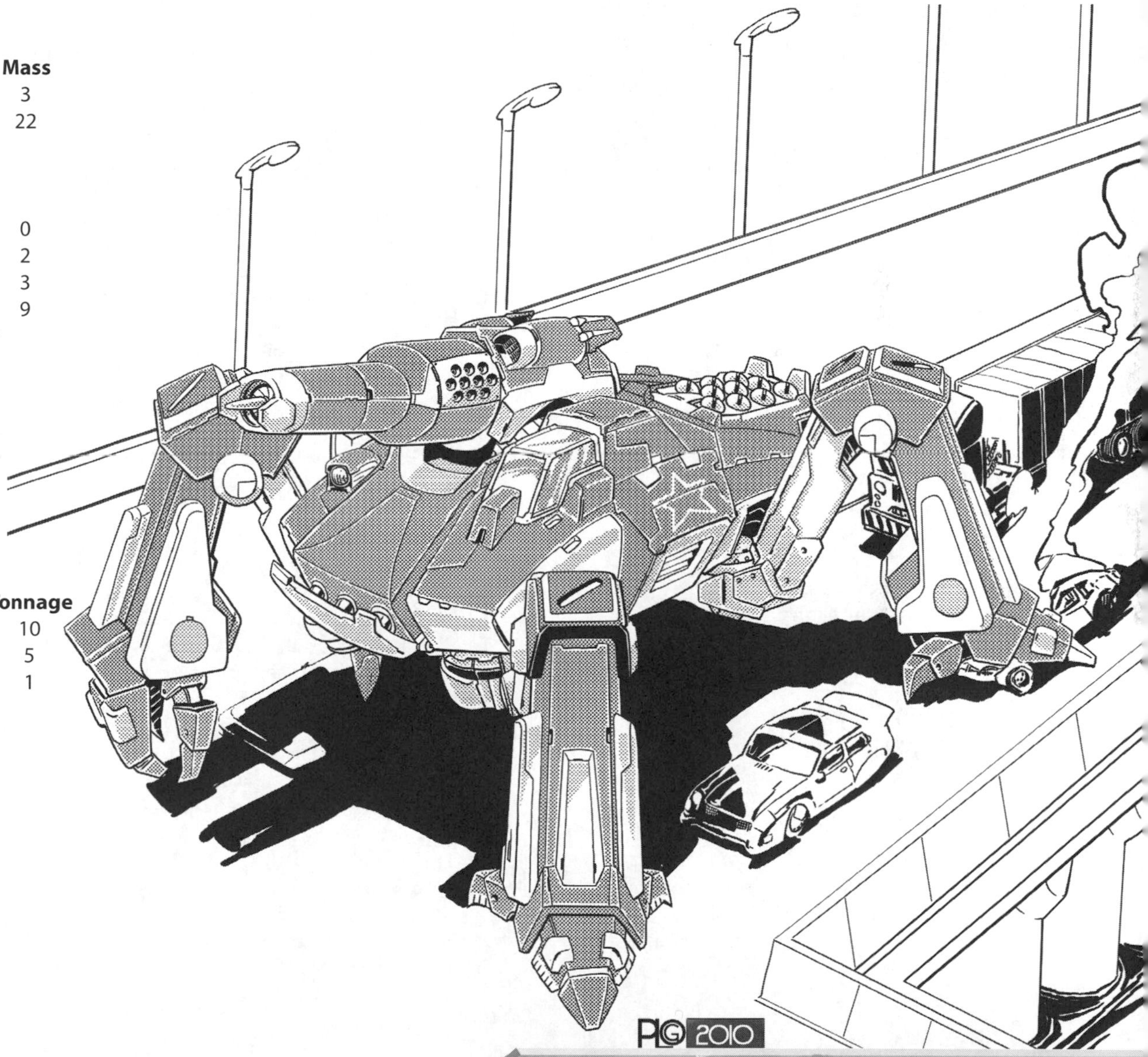

PLG 2010

SHD-12C SHADOW HAWK

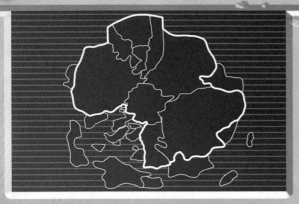

Mass: 55 tons
Chassis: Kallon Type VII Endo Steel
Power Plant: GM 330 XL
Cruising Speed: 64 kph
Maximum Speed: 97 kph
Jump Jets: Rawlings 55
    Jump Capacity: 120 meters
Armor: Wall Type 8 Light Ferro-Fibrous with CASE
Armament:
    1 Diverse Optics Extended Range Medium Laser
    1 Lord's Light 3 Heavy PPC
    1 Helga Series 7-Tube Multi-Missile Launcher
Manufacturer: Odin Manufacturing
    Primary Factory: Orestes
Communications System: Dash 2 Standard
Targeting and Tracking System: Blade 12

Overview

Faced with the task of merging the Free Rasalhague Republic with the Ghost Bear Dominion, the Ghost Bears sought to defuse tensions with their new Inner Sphere citizens by publicly embracing the KungsArmé. To that end they have striven to treat their new Galaxies not as a dumping ground for old and worn-out equipment like *solahma* troops, but as equal partners. New equipment has been secured, and while it's not always of Clan manufacture it is the best that can be produced locally or imported. One such example is a new variant of the *Shadow Hawk* that Odin Manufacturing has put into production.

Capabilities

Boasting improved performance over the standard *Shadow Hawk*, Odin's SHD-12C mounts a more powerful GM 330 XL power plant. This unit has proven slightly problematical, often running hotter than its official specifications and requiring higher levels of maintenance. The performance achieved more than justifies these issues.

The BattleMech retains the classic weapons layout: right-arm mounted medium laser, torso missile launcher and over-the-shoulder weapon mount on the left torso. In this case the laser is the popular extended-range medium laser marketed by Diverse Optics. The missile system is a flexible Helga-series launcher, a design taken as spoils of war from the Word of Blake. In place of the traditional autocannon for the over the shoulder weapon is a powerful Lord's Light Heavy PPC.

The heavy PPC combined with the multi-missile firing long-range missiles gives the 12C a powerful long-range damage profile. Opponents trying to close under the PPC's minimum range are forced to contend with the SRM load of the MML. This gives the 12C a well-rounded attack profile reminiscent of the original SHD-2H.

Deployment

First call on Odin's production has gone to the most seriously depleted KungsArmé Clusters, such as the Third Hussars, Second Freeman, and First Kavalleri. Other Clusters will have to wait until 3086 to receive their allocations. A small number have also found their way into Ghost Bear second-line Clusters. The PPC technology used by Odin was acquired from the Draconis Combine. In exchange, Odin is supplying ten percent of its output to the DCMS. The Republic of the Sphere has acquired a handful of this BattleMech design from Ghost Bear warriors who have chosen to follow Devlin Stone.

Variants

The SHD-11CS is powered by a 275-rated light fusion plant. This variant carries a second laser on the left arm. Instead of the MML launcher, it mounts an LRM 15 system paired with Artemis IV fire control. A snub-nose PPC replaces the heavy version and improved C³ enables it to operate as part of a network.

The SHD-9D swaps the PPC for a Light AC/5. Two MML 5 launchers replace the seven-tube model and the BattleMech carries sophisticated electronics in the form of a targeting computer and a C³ slave.

The SHD-8L mounts a 275-rated XL fusion power plant. Improved jump jets propel the 'Mech up to 210 meters. A variable-speed pulse laser replaces the extended-range model, and the MML launcher is reduced to five tubes. The PPC has been swapped out for a plasma rifle and a Beagle Active Probe and ECM suite have been installed.

The success of the heavy PPC has lead the Combine to update their venerable SHD-2K. The 3K uses a double heat sink equipped engine, freeing tonnage to replace the 2K's armament with a heavy PPC and MML 5 launcher. Upgrading to heavy ferro-fibrous armor opened up enough free tonnage to include an extended-range medium laser, a C³ slave and CASE protection.

Notable MechWarriors

Warrior Carl Jarlhelm: A fanatical citizen of Rasalhague, Carl was lucky to survive the purges of the 1st Kavalleri in 3076. During a 3079 Clan Wolf raid on Satalice, Jarlhelm defeated a *Shadow Hawk IIC* and seriously damaged a *Clint IIC* at the cost of his ancient SHD-2K. Having proved his skill, Jarlhelm was one of the first warriors to receive a SHD-12C and was reassigned to the elite First Freemen. While clearly respected as a warrior, Jarlhelm's *Shadow Hawk* stands out in the medium cluster as a new 'Mech that is not Clantech, suggesting that he is not yet fully trusted.

SHD-12C SHADOW HAWK

Type: **Shadow Hawk**
Technology Base: Inner Sphere
Tonnage: 55
Battle Value: 1,574

Equipment		Mass
Internal Structure:	Endo Steel	3
Engine:	330 XL	12.5
Walking MP:	6	
Running MP:	9	
Jumping MP:	4	
Heat Sinks:	12 [24]	2
Gyro:		4
Cockpit:		3
Armor Factor (Light Ferro):	178	10.5

	Internal Structure	Armor Value
Head	3	9
Center Torso	18	25
Center Torso (rear)		10
R/L Torso	13	20
R/L Torso (rear)		6
R/L Arm	9	18
R/L Leg	13	23

Weapons and Ammo	Location	Critical	Tonnage
ER Medium Laser	RA	1	1
MML 7	RT	4	4.5
Ammo (MML) 34/28	RT	2	2
CASE	RT	1	.5
Heavy PPC	LT	4	10
Jump Jet	RL	1	.5
Jump Jets	CT	2	1
Jump Jet	LL	1	.5

Note: If playing under Advanced Rules, treat head as having a Full-Head Ejection System.

WVR-9W2 WOLVERINE

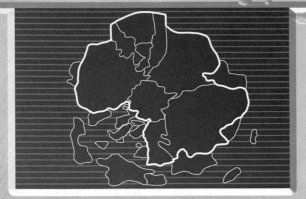

Mass: 55 tons
Chassis: Crucis-A
Power Plant: Nissan 275 XL
Cruising Speed: 54 kph
Maximum Speed: 86 kph
Jump Jets: Northrup StarLifter M41s
   Jump Capacity: 210 meters
Armor: Starshield A with CASE
Armament:
   2 Lord's Light 4 Light PPCs
   1 Shigunga Multiple-Missile Launch Series-5
   1 Diverse Optics ER Small Laser
   1 Diverse Optics ER Medium Laser
Manufacturer: Luthien Armor Works
   Primary Factory: Dieron (destroyed 3077),
      New Samarkand
Communications System: Garret T11-b
   with Guardian ECM and C³ Slave
Targeting and Tracking System: Cat's Eyes 5
   with Artemis IV Module

Overview

A capable medium-weight BattleMech, the *Wolverine* chassis has found long life among military units in the Inner Sphere and beyond. Forever seeing upgrades, field refits, and customization, the *Wolverine* continues to fill production queues across the corporate spectrum. Even designs developed and used by the Word of Blake have continued to find use, just under new ownership.

Capabilities

The latest *Wolverine* comes from the Combine's Luthien Armor Works, thanks to a licensing grab by the corporation toward the end of the Jihad. With LAW still reeling financially, the sudden flood of design concepts and licensing agreements from the brute dismantling of Vicore Industries afforded the vulnerable corporation a lifeline. Utilizing specifications captured on Dieron, LAW rammed through a field upgrade version of the 9W at nearly all of its operating medium BattleMech lines. The bulk of the refits went immediately to DCMS regiments operating in Devlin Stone's Operation SCOUR and then to other heavily damaged Kuritan regiments. The refit was well-received by DCMS MechWarriors, who saw the addition of the upgraded design as the perfect complement to incoming *Panthers*, *Chargers*, and *Dragons*. They were instrumental in *Kanrei* Minamoto's sustained siege of Cairo, where the newly replenished First Sword of Light utilized them to great effect among the shattered ruins of the city.

Buoyed by its success during the waning years of the war, LAW used that refit as the basis for its 9W2, built with Kuritan parts and labor. This "new" design walked off the assembly line last year to great acclaim. Improved jump jet technology gives the 9W2 a large mobility profile, especially useful in C³ networks. With two long-range compact PPCs, the *Wolverine* can snipe at range indefinitely, using its lasers and missile launcher to finish off damaged targets as distances close. The use of the versatile Shigunga MML plays to the pilot's preferences; most Kuritan MechWarriors opt to go with short-ranged missile loads, in order to provide a solid punch with its lasers.

The true gem of the design is the incorporation of a C³ slave module and Guardian ECM package. With its increased mobility, the *Wolverine* can move in and out of range to targets with ease, providing important target telemetry to its lancemates while disrupting enemy communications and targeting packages.

Deployment

Currently, the WVR-9W2 is the backbone medium BattleMech of most DCMS line regiments. LAW's exclusive contract with the DCMS keeps nearly eighty-five percent of them within the Kuritan realm, though the Coordinator has granted permission for a small quota to be sold on the secondary market through a cooperative arrangement with StarCorps and on a limited scale at LAW-Dieron for The Republic Armed Forces.

Variants

Two other new variants of the *Wolverine* made appearances during the Jihad. The WVR-9M isn't produced by a particular corporation—it isn't listed on any corporate rolls—but was a field upgrade born from Duchess Alys Rousset-Marik's freedom fighters. Built in mobile refit installations housed in specially-modified DropShips, the 9M totes a heavy PPC, an extended-range medium laser, and an ammunition-conserving Streak SRM 6. Kallon Industries has recently begun producing the 9M field refit at their repaired factory on Thermopolis.

The WVR-9K wades into close-quarter combat with a mix of light machine guns, B-pods, an SRM 4 pack, and a snub-nose PPC. Sapphire Metals first tested this TSM-augmented version with a stylized *wakizashi* on the mercenary market. After its initial success, Sapphire then licensed the design to Victory Industries, which has used its more efficient manufacturing lines on Marduk to supply 9Ks to garrison commands in the RAF and samurai MechWarriors in the DCMS.

Notable MechWarriors

Chu-sa **Eliza Mallawaratchi:** One of the few escapees from Fortress Dieron in 3070, *Chu-sa* Mallawaratchi is most remembered for her wild flight through the rocky canyons and dense forests of Dieron. Riding with her in the stolen *Wolverine's* cockpit was none other than Hohiro Kurita, the soon-to-be Coordinator of the Draconis Combine. As her fleeing escorts fell one by one to the pursing Blakists, the *chu-sa* managed to get Hohiro to the designated coordinates just ahead of recapture and then turned to defend his escape with her life. When the Coordinator returned to Dieron in 3081, he dedicated the place of her sacrifice as a monument to the Dragon's bushido warriors who perished on Dieron and planted a rare Yoshino cherry tree where her *Wolverine* fell.

Type: **Wolverine**
Technology Base: Inner Sphere
Tonnage: 55
Battle Value: 1,480

Equipment		Mass
Internal Structure:		5.5
Engine:	275 XL	8
Walking MP:	5	
Running MP:	8	
Jumping MP:	7	
Heat Sinks:	12 [24]	2
Gyro:		3
Cockpit:		3
Armor Factor (Light Ferro):	169	10

	Internal Structure	Armor Value
Head	3	9
Center Torso	18	25
Center Torso (rear)		7
R/L Torso	13	20
R/L Torso (rear)		5
R/L Arm	9	17
R/L Leg	13	22

Weapons and Ammo	Location	Critical	Tonnage
2 Light PPCs	RA	4	6
C³ Slave	RT	1	1
Guardian ECM Suite	RT	2	1.5
ER Medium Laser	H	1	1
CASE	LT	1	.5
ER Small Laser	LA	1	.5
MML 5	LA	3	3
Artemis IV FCS	LA	1	1
Ammo (MML) 48/40	LA	2	2
Improved Jump Jet	RL	2	1
Improved Jump Jets	RT	4	2
Improved Jump Jet	CT	2	1
Improved Jump Jets	LT	4	2
Improved Jump Jet	LL	2	1

PLG 2010

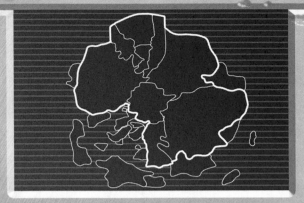

Mass: 60 tons
Chassis: Ost-III Ostroc Endo Steel
Power Plant: Defiance 300 Light Fusion
Cruising Speed: 54 kph
Maximum Speed: 86 kph
Jump Jets: HildCo Model 13
   Jump Capacity: 150 meters
Armor: Kallon Unity Weave Ferro-Fibrous
Armament:
   2 Ceres Arms Thrasher Snub-Nose PPCs
   2 Diverse Optics Extended Range Medium Lasers
Manufacturer: Kressly WarWorks
   Primary Factory: Epsilon Eridani
Communications System: Ceres Metals Model 667 with C³i
Targeting and Tracking System: Ceres Bullseye

Overview

The Word of Blake managed to extract the design work of Ceres Metals' OSR-4L not too long after it received approval from the Capellan Strategios for production on Capella, Detroit and Warlock. This data provided the Word with numerous insights and engineering solutions that simplified the process of fielding the OSR-4C among the Circinus Confederation's armed forces. While outwardly similar, the differences between the 4C and 4L models are substantial.

Logistical planners noticed that the reinvigoration of Terra's military industry recreated a number of supply chains that were used by several of Terra's arms manufacturers during its heyday. The Word tapped into this capability by effectively reverse-engineering Terra's logistical footprint, allowing them to drastically increase 'Mech production on Terra and nearby Protectorate worlds. By 3071, the Word had begun production of their OSR-5W model at Kressly WarWorks on Epsilon Eridani.

Capabilities

The OSR-4L's operational profile rewards its MechWarrior when he strikes at his quarry from range. The 5W is more at home in urban combat. Its snub-nosed PPCs' optimum range band ensures excellent accuracy at most typical urban combat ranges, and also improves the *Ostroc*'s damage potential. The 'Mech has been armored to the maximum capacity of its endo steel frame, providing better durability for close-range combat where the 4L's stealth armor offers little advantage. Initially, the designers had intended to swap out the ECM suite for a Beagle active probe, but the utilization of small cockpits similar to those of the Celestial designs allowed the Blakists to upgrade the 5W's electronics to include a C³i suite. Another component from the Celestial supply line is the OSR's compact gyroscope, a device it shares with the C-ANG-O *Archangel*. The mass of the armor, gyroscope and PPCs demanded weight savings that were realized by installing a light fusion engine produced on Hesperus II.

Deployment

Kressly WarWorks' industrial capabilities are modest, and the Word fielded their new *Ostroc* in equally humble numbers. This restricted supply seems to have promoted a specialist deployment among Blakist military units, with the OSR-5W deployed almost exclusively among Level IIs specializing in urban combat.

A few notable exceptions have occurred. An OSR-5W appeared among the Asta Planetary Militia on Dieron, where it did not perform well without the benefit of C³i-equipped allies. A more objective analysis of the material provided by the Ghost Bears suggests that the MechWarrior's inferior skill may have contributed to that machine's swift demise. Another encounter occurred during the liberation of Bryant, where an OSR-5W rushed Allied lines over relatively open terrain. Its excellent armor protection allowed it to act long enough as a C³i spotter to help its Level III seriously damage an assault company.

Variants

The Taurian Concordat has continued its re-armament efforts, most recently producing an updated version of the OSR-4C built on New Vandenburg since 3067. First deployed in 3082, the 5C features an extralight engine and two PPCs, one heavy and one light, for its primary armament, providing a substantial departure from the 4C's weapon loadout. Combined with the presence of five jump jets and an endo steel internal frame, we have come to believe that the Concordat took the Capellan espionage accusations of 3067 to heart and implemented them retroactively, pulling significant design information from the Detroit plant.

The Draconis Combine introduced a field refit in late 3077. The OSR-4K was so well received that it has since become a production variant. Using a Pitban 240 engine slowed the 4K down, but allowed room for a battery of improved jump jets that gave it a jump range of 180 meters. Twin snub-nosed PPCs and paired extended-range medium lasers are light firepower for a heavy 'Mech, but its heavy-duty gyro allows it to take far more punishment while dishing out that damage.

Notable MechWarriors

Adept-II Lucas Moens: The typical 5W pilot engages in bully-style combat while in an urban environment. Highly mobile and well-armored, they often swiftly close range with poorly supported enemies, unloading with fist and weapon until the foe is vanquished or help arrives. Adept Moens, by contrast, became notorious for his seeming lack of spine. He attacked units that were properly supported, and often found himself outmatched in a fight. After sustaining significant damage, he would attempt to disengage, frequently dragging hostiles behind him that sought to finish him off. Only later did his pursuers become aware of the rest of Moens' Level II, largely equipped with LRMs.

Type: **Ostroc**
Technology Base: Inner Sphere
Tonnage: 60
Battle Value: 1,665

Equipment		Mass
Internal Structure:	Endo Steel	3
Engine:	300 Light	14.5
Walking MP:	5	
Running MP:	8	
Jumping MP:	5	
Heat Sinks:	13 [26]	3
Gyro (Compact):		4.5
Cockpit (Small):		2
Armor Factor (Ferro):	201	11.5

	Internal Structure	Armor Value
Head	3	9
Center Torso	20	30
Center Torso (rear)		10
R/L Torso	14	21
R/L Torso (rear)		7
R/L Arm	10	20
R/L Leg	14	28

Weapons and Ammo	Location	Critical	Tonnage
Snub-Nose PPC	RT	2	6
ER Medium Laser	RT	1	1
Improved C³ Computer	H	2	2.5
Snub-Nose PPC	LT	2	6
ER Medium Laser	LT	1	1
Jump Jets	RT	2	2
Jump Jet	CT	1	1
Jump Jets	LT	2	2

OTL-9R OSTSOL

Mass: 60 tons
Chassis: Kell/K
Power Plant: GM 180 Fusion
Cruising Speed: 32 kph
Maximum Speed: 54 kph
Jump Jets: None
    Jump Capacity: None
Armor: Valiant Lamellor
Armament:
    1 Magna Supernova Heavy PPC
    1 Fusigon Smarttooth Snub Nose PPC
    1 Diverse Optics Sunbeam Large Laser
    1 Magna Mk VI ER Medium Laser
    1 Diverse Optics ER Small Laser
    1 Tronel I Small Laser
Manufacturer: Kong Interstellar
    Primary Factory: Connaught
Communications System: Barrett 509p with C³
Targeting and Tracking System: TRSS.2L3

Overview

Liberating Connaught provided the Coalition with direct access to Kong Interstellar. The transition did not go without incident, and among the material casualties were Kong's OTL-7M and 8M lines. While the damage largely resulted in temporary delays, Kong's orbital endo steel facility was a more permanent loss. Its source of 360 XL-rated engines was likewise unavailable. With the aid of RAF fusion specialist Rebecca "Mini" O'Donaghue, Kong redesigned the 8M to use a standard engine and several new PPCs sourced from the Combine. They also heavily redesigned their ancient Kell/H chassis so that it could incorporate the new weaponry and triple-strength myomer.

Capabilities

The new *Ostsol* was much slower than its 8M counterpart, which prompted Kong to implement some unusual design choices at the behest of Mrs. O'Donaghue. Experience had proved that capturing Blakist-held territories frequently demanded close-quarters combat and required units to breach dense fortifications. Such tasks were frequently relegated to assault units, which resulted in significant damage and casualties. A powerful and durable unit that was relatively easy to repair would greatly alleviate the taxed supply lines of Stone's Coalition.

Kong therefore decided to reduce the speed of the *Ostsol* even further, allowing it to wield a heavy-duty gyroscope for added combat endurance and a heat sink system that easily managed the load created by its weapon systems. Kong completed the first production run of the OTL-9R as early as 3077, in time for the 'Mech's participation in most of the Coalition's crucial battles.

It is rare for an OTL-9R to hit the field without its triple-strength myomer at optimum operating temperature. Its heavy PPC is an effective weapon at range, but is almost exclusively used while the *Ostsol* closes with its intended target, or when engaging faster enemies. It comes into its own up close, where it can provide a sustained barrage with its lasers and snub-nose PPC. When enhanced by triple-strength myomer, OTL-9Rs can make short work of most fortifications, easily suffering the harrowing moments until a wall is breached for the line 'Mechs and vehicles of the unit to exploit. As it does not rely on speed once it reaches its objective, the triple-strength myomer's deteriorating efficiency from overheating has minimal impact. While the 9R's limited speed also limits its battlefield application, few can deny that it excels in its niche.

Deployment

Initial deployment of the OTL-9R occurred in lance-sized disbursements to units tasked to engage Blakist fortifications. This caused them to initially be widespread among the Inner Sphere nations allied with Stone, though many 9Rs have joined The Republic military since its formation. Kong continues to produce it for mercenary use, as it remains attractive through its combination of high-tech weaponry and low cost.

Variants

Soon after re-acquiring a source for 360 XL engines, Kong began production of an updated version of the OTL-8M. No longer equipped with triple-strength myomer, the 9M is geared more toward a sustained long-range engagement than its predecessor, relying on extended-range large and medium lasers for the bulk of its firepower. Up close it adds the same snub-nose PPC used on the 9R, along with a medium pulse laser. Utilizing MASC for its speed boost, and assisted by an ECM suite, the 9M can dictate range with its opponents.

An updated version of the OTL-6D debuted several years ago, largely in response to the difficulties involved in procuring parts for the 6D. Equipped with a pair of light AC/5s, two ER medium lasers and a light PPC all linked to a targeting computer, the 8D is built for sustained mid-range engagements. Ample ammunition supplies for its autocannons allow it to deploy a variety of ammunition types.

Notable MechWarriors

Captain Ilona Humphreys: A distant relative of Andurien nobility, Captain Humphreys has distinguished herself in her 9M *Ostsol* on numerous occasions. Using her *Ostsol's* outstanding mobility to outflank opponents, she has managed to swiftly cripple or disable hostile assets by lining up shots on their rear armor moments after they engage the other members of her company.

Type: Ostsol
Technology Base: Inner Sphere
Tonnage: 60
Battle Value: 1,654

Equipment		Mass
Internal Structure:		6
Engine:	180	7
Walking MP:	3 (4)	
Running MP:	5 (6)	
Jumping MP:	0	
Heat Sinks:	14 [28]	4
Gyro (Heavy-Duty):		4
Cockpit:		3
Armor Factor:	192	12

	Internal Structure	Armor Value
Head	3	9
Center Torso	20	32
Center Torso (rear)		7
R/L Torso	14	24
R/L Torso (rear)		4
R/L Arm	10	16
R/L Leg	14	28

Weapons and Ammo	Location	Critical	Tonnage
Snub-Nose PPC	RT	2	6
ER Medium Laser	RT	1	1
ER Small Laser	RT	1	.5
C³ Slave	H	1	1
Large Laser	CT	2	5
Heavy PPC	LT	4	10
Small Laser	LT	1	.5
Triple-Strength Myomer	RL/LL/RT/LT	2/2/1/1	0

Mass: 60 tons
Chassis: Kallon Type XV Endo Steel
Power Plant: Hermes 360 XL
Cruising Speed: 64 kph
Maximum Speed: 97 kph
Jump Jets: McCloud Specials (Reinforced)
   Jump Capacity: 180 meters
Armor: Durallex Light Ferro-Fibrous
Armament:
   2 Magna Bolt Light PPCs
   2 Magna Flarestar Snub-Nose PPCs
Manufacturer: Field Refit
   Primary Factory: None
Communications System: Garret T-11A
Targeting and Tracking System: Garret D2j

Overview

Our young Republic of the Sphere faced the daunting challenge of equipping the forces Devlin Stone knew we would need to defend our new nation. A vital source of equipment was the salvage from a hundred battlefields where Coalition troops had faced the Word of Blake. The venerable *Rifleman* was a common design for which The Republic developed a standardized refit package. Much as the Draconis Combine created its upgraded *Wolverine* by refitting Succession War-era machines, The Republic's refit program resulted in a BattleMech with a markedly different appearance from the original.

Capabilities

Using many components from modern *Rifleman* variants grafted onto older examples of the design, the RFL-7X upgrade process is an involved affair. The fact that many recipients of the refit had suffered heavy damage was actually an advantage, as replacement of the internal structure would have required significant disassembly. The installation of the powerful Hermes 360 XL engine gives this variant a boost in ground speed by fifty percent. Mobility has been further enhanced by the addition of McCloud Special jump jets. Re-armoring with the latest light ferro-fibrous material, combined with the other major structural upgrades, transforms the BattleMech's silhouette.

The accuracy of the Garret D2j targeting system is legendary, prompting The Republic technicians to retain it. By contrast, the weapons array received a complete overhaul. Gone is the classic twinned autocannon and laser arrangement, replaced by pairs of light and snub-nosed PPCs.

In its new configuration, the mission of the RFL-7X has changed almost as radically as its appearance. Previously an anti-aircraft platform pressed into service as a main-line BattleMech, The Republic intended its refit to serve as a fast fire-support unit.

Deployment

Comprising a mishmash of equipment, the RAF still has not approached a standard deployment plan. The RFL-7X is used to plug the holes where medium and heavy BattleMechs are required. The Republic has also made the refit kit available to mercenary commands that aided Devlin Stone's Coalition against the Word of Blake.

Variants

Clan Jade Falcon produces a variant at Red Devil Industries on Pandora. The RFL-C 2 mounts a 360 XXL engine and improved jump jets, allowing it to clear 270 meters in a single leap. Arm-mounted improved heavy medium lasers are paired with extended-range large lasers. Endo steel structure and ferro-fibrous armor complete the variant.

The Federated Suns produces the RFL-6D. Equipped with a 300 XL engine, it carries only ten heat sinks. Each arm mounts a pair of Type 5 light autocannons, and extended-range medium lasers are carried in the torsos. A sophisticated C^3 slave is included and the six tons of ammunition in the side torsos are protected by CASE.

The RFL-9T refit was developed by the Taurian Concordat. Retaining the original standard 240 power plant, it carries light AC/5s in place of the snub-nose PPCs. A pair of extended-range medium lasers rounds out the weapons, all of which are tied into an advanced targeting computer. A Guardian ECM suite combines with stealth armor to make the RFL-9T an elusive target.

A secondary RAF design is the RFL-8X. Inspired by a mercenary battlefield refit, the 8X uses a more durable light fusion engine to achieve speeds up to 86 kph. While it only carries two ER PPCs and a brace of extended-range medium lasers, these are all backed a targeting computer that allows deadly accuracy at any range.

Notable MechWarriors

Colonel Joey Nichole: Only 26 when she formed the Battle Corps, Colonel Nichole has a reputation for selfless dedication to the protection of civilian populations; the ability to hold together the disparate people of the Battle Corps and forge them into a fighting force that proved itself time and again during Operation SCOUR; and lastly, an almost uncanny skill with energy weapons. Piloting *the* original RFL-8X, on more than one occasion she took down targets outside the standard effective range of her PPCs. Her *Rifleman*—nicknamed the Pink Lady—was rebuilt several times, Nichole steadfastly refusing to move to a "proper" command 'Mech. Only after the battle for New Home, when the Pink Lady was annihilated by artillery, did she finally gave in. The battle for Terra saw Nichole piloting a modified pink *Warlord*.

Type: **Rifleman**
Technology Base: Inner Sphere
Tonnage: 60
Battle Value: 1,645

Equipment		Mass
Internal Structure:	Endo Steel	3
Engine:	360 XL	16.5
Walking MP:	6	
Running MP:	9	
Jumping MP:	6	
Heat Sinks:	12 [24]	2
Gyro (XL):		2
Cockpit:		3
Armor Factor (Light Ferro):	161	9.5

	Internal Structure	Armor Value
Head	3	9
Center Torso	20	22
Center Torso (rear)		6
R/L Torso	14	20
R/L Torso (rear)		4
R/L Arm	10	18
R/L Leg	14	20

Weapons and Ammo	Location	Critical	Tonnage
Light PPC	RA	2	3
Snub-Nose PPC	RA	2	6
Light PPC	LA	2	3
Snub-Nose PPC	LA	2	6
Jump Jet	RL	1	1
Jump Jets	RT	2	2
Jump Jets	LT	2	2
Jump Jet	LL	1	1

CRD-8L CRUSADER

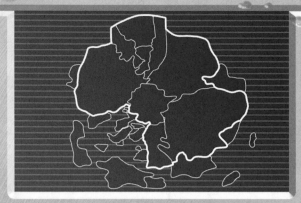

Mass: 65 tons
Chassis: Foundation CMRFa6
Power Plant: VOX 325 XL
Cruising Speed: 54 kph
Maximum Speed: 86 kph
Jump Jets: None
   Jump Capacity: None
Armor: Riese 500 with CASE
Armament:
   2 CeresArms Crusher Plasma Rifles
   2 Doombud MML 7s
   2 Diverse Optics Extended-Range Medium Lasers
Manufacturer: Tao 'MechWorks
   Primary Factory: Sarmaxa
Communications System: Garret T11-A
Targeting and Tracking System: Garret D5j

Overview

As The Republic Armed Forces attempted to contain Capellan adventurism, RAF units spotted a new configuration of the *Crusader* heavy BattleMech. After two years of diligent effort, Republic agents have finally succeeded in capturing the specifications. The CRD-8L, as it's been dubbed, is a surprising departure from recent Capellan BattleMech architecture and came as a nasty surprise to the elements of Stone's Lament who first faced it.

Capabilities

Two chief departures mark this *Crusader* as different from other recent Capellan 'Mech designs. First, it does not use the near-ubiquitous stealth armor the Capellans

seem to find necessary for their 'Mechs, perhaps because the Capellans have enough heavy, stealthy 'Mechs for their *Ying Qiang* lances.

The second change is in the weaponry. Though a pair of seven-tube multi-missile launchers allows the 8L to keep to the *Crusader*'s traditional support role, two arm-mounted plasma rifles provide this Capellan *Crusader* with devastating direct-fire anti-'Mech weaponry. The Lament MechWarrior who first encountered the *Crusader*-8L only expected short-range missiles and medium lasers when his *Maelstrom* was blasted with plasma. Enough missile storage is allocated in the *Crusader* 8L's CASE-protected torso magazines to keep its opponents on their toes at any range.

Finally, the Capellans have used an advanced engine to increase the *Crusader*'s speed to a level more common with medium 'Mechs, which makes the 8L a very mobile platform. McCarron's Armored Cavalry has put this feature to excellent use.

Deployment

The bulk of the 8L *Crusader*s observed so far have been with McCarron's Armored Cavalry, though RAF analysts suspect they have identified at least one with House Dai Da Chi and two others in the hands of allied Magistracy units. What is most surprising is the quantity. The sole known Capellan manufacturer of *Crusader*s was Tao 'Mechworks on Styk. With Styk joining The Republic despite the sentiments of the separatists still staging the occasional uprising and demonstration—and it seems like that many of these have infiltrated Tao 'Mechworks' production facility—it was believed the Confederation had lost the ability to produce new *Crusader*s. Intelligence found the source of these new units when they uncovered a Capellan-controlled Tao 'Mechworks facility on Sarmaxa. Backed by Sian, this Tao 'Mechworks factory employs many key staffers thought lost to the fall of the Protectorate. Analysts now believe that the damage to Tao 'Mechworks' Styk factory was not the result of Blakist sabotage, but instead reflects actions taken by the Confederation prior to handing the world over to The Republic, allowing the Capellans to hide their theft of much of the company's vital technology and personnel to rebuild Tao on Sarmaxa.

Variants

The Word of Blake fielded the CRD-7W against the Coalition before the Word's demise, and many of these 'Mechs survive in mercenary service. More traditional in design, the 7W carries four separate Artemis IV-equipped multi-missile launchers—two nine-tube and two five-tube—along with supporting lasers. This combination of missile launchers means that the 7W can overwhelm a target at either range or split its fire between long- and short-range and still be effective.

The CRD-6M is still produced in small quantities in the former Free Worlds League. It carries dual MML 7 launchers in the arms along with light PPCs, and the leg-mounted SRMs have been replaced with four-tube Streak launchers. To make the changes, the Leaguers had to slow the 'Mech down, which severely limits its mobility, though they attempted to compensate by adding improved jump jets.

Notable MechWarriors

Sao-wei Bennett Laramie: *Sao-wei* Laramie was the warrior who faced the Lament *Maelstrom* in 3083. By firing only his MMLs, he lured the Lament 'Mechjock into close range and then unleashed his plasma rifles, which drove the *Maelstrom* back with heavy damage before it succumbed to heat overload. This break in the Lament's lines allowed Laramie and his lance to break through and wreak considerable havoc before being brought down by a former Clansman in a *Thor*. Laramie was captured and eventually ransomed back to the Confederation, as part of a quiet peace agreement that included The Republic gaining access to the 8L's technical specifications.

CRD-8L CRUSADER

Type: **Crusader**
Technology Base: Inner Sphere
Tonnage: 65
Battle Value: 1,701

Equipment			Mass
Internal Structure:	Endo Steel		3.5
Engine:	325 XL		12
Walking MP:	5		
Running MP:	8		
Jumping MP:	0		
Heat Sinks:	10 [20]		0
Gyro:			4
Cockpit:			3
Armor Factor:	184		11.5

	Internal Structure	Armor Value
Head	3	9
Center Torso	21	28
Center Torso (rear)		7
R/L Torso	15	23
R/L Torso (rear)		6
R/L Arm	10	20
R/L Leg	15	21

Weapons and Ammo	Location	Critical	Tonnage
Plasma Rifle	RA	2	6
ER Medium Laser	RA	1	1
MML 7	RA	4	4.5
Ammo (MML) 34/28	RT	2	2
Ammo (Plasma) 20	RT	2	2
CASE	RT	1	.5
Ammo (MML) 34/28	LT	2	2
Ammo (Plasma) 10	LT	1	1
CASE	LT	1	.5
Plasma Rifle	LA	2	6
ER Medium Laser	LA	1	1
MML 7	LA	4	4.5

TDR-10M THUNDERBOLT

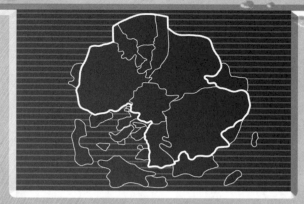

Mass: 65 tons
Chassis: Earthwerks TDR II Endo Steel
Power Plant: 260 Magna Lite Light Fusion
Cruising Speed: 43 kph
Maximum Speed: 64 kph
Jump Jets: Chilton 466
Jump Capacity: 120 meters
Armor: Starshield A
Armament:
   1 Ceres Arms Thrasher Snub Nose PPC
   1 Fusigon Strongtooth Heavy PPC
   1 Fusigon Shorttooth Light PPC
   1 Doombud Multi-Missile Launcher 5
   1 Diverse Optics ER Medium Laser
Manufacturer: Earthwerks Incorporated
   Primary Factory: Keystone
Communications System: Neil 8000
Targeting and Tracking System: RCA Instatrac Mark X

Overview

The *Thunderbolt* design goes back to the Age of War, and is often affectionately referred to simply as the T-Bolt. Known for durability despite an extensive amount of ammunition, the design can be found in all major armies and many smaller ones. Its durability and easily modified frame have made it a popular 'Mech for field modifications, which vary with the tendencies of the army fielding it. With the Inner Sphere rebuilding, Earthwerks decided to modify their Keystone-manufactured *Thunderbolt*. The new design has received praise, but the 'Mech needs to see combat before a true verdict can be rendered.

Capabilities

The weaponry was totally revised on the new *Thunderbolt*. A smorgasbord of particle cannons, light and snub-nosed versions, sits in the left torso. On the right arm is a powerful heavy PPC, capable of punching holes through smaller 'Mechs. An extended-range medium laser supports the PPCs in the torso, reminiscent of the original model's trio of lasers. Rounding out the firepower is a versatile multi-missile launcher. The PPCs, coupled with the LRMs from multiple missile launchers, give the 'Mech a strong long-range punch. When combat moves to close quarters, the snub-nose PPC and laser can sustain fire while the missile launcher can switch to SRMs to exploit any holes the PPCs opened up.

The endo steel frame mounts as much armor as it is capable of holding. This protects the vulnerable light engine, made even more fragile by the lack of protection over the two tons of ammunition for the five-tube launcher. MechWarriors assigned this new model often complain about that, noting that a great reputation isn't enough to protect them from a chain-reaction detonation.

Deployment

The 10M has been sold on the general market, currently to former Free Worlds states, the nearby Republic and various mercenary units. Keystone does not expect to compete in other states with other versions of the *Thunderbolt*. They have been trying to market the 10M in the Capellan Confederation and the Draconis Combine, with mixed results. The Combine has shown little interest, preferring older *Thunderbolt* chassis as experimental test-beds, but the Confederation appears receptive, not yet having replenished their gradually shrinking fleet of *Thunderbolt*s.

Variants

With so many nations making the *Thunderbolt*, many different designs continue to evolve. Perhaps the most unexpected, the Taurian variant seems to have less firepower than the original, with only a ten-tube LRM rack, dual light PPCs and a trio of ER medium lasers. However, with a top speed of over 90 kph, it won't be mistaken for any of its predecessors. Prior to the Jihad, the Free Worlds League had a similar design to the 10M that was sold to most nations. Rather than the heavy and light PPCs, this variant has greater jump capacity, extra lasers and a larger missile rack. In addition, a slew of electronics makes this *Thunderbolt* more effective on the battlefield.

The Draconis Combine variant breaks their norms, often being mistaken for a Federated Suns design. Originally a test bed for the *No-Dachi*, it was updated and became a common refit during the Jihad. Built around triple strength myomer, a full array of energy weapons and jump jets go with an upgraded engine. Both arms are weaponless, reducing the arc of fire but also freeing them to pummel enemies. The Lyrans have a similar version, with the triple strength myomer and energy layout, but an ER PPC gives it more range while a compact engine and heavy-duty gyro make it almost impossible to destroy.

During their occupation of New Avalon the Word of Blake took the TDR-NAIS chassis and modified it to their purposes. The RAC and targeting computer were removed for a large VSP and a light PPC. A full suite of electronics and B-Pods were added to improve its urban fighting ability.

Notable MechWarriors

Captain Eddie Edelmira: A company commander with the Andurien Rangers, Edelmira has been with them since their inception. During a Capellan incursion in 3083, he frustrated the Liao forces with his use of infernos and constant movement throughout the battlefield. He collected three kills while his company took down a total of fifteen enemy 'Mechs and vehicles before the invaders retreated.

TDR-10M THUNDERBOLT

Type: **Thunderbolt**
Technology Base: Inner Sphere
Tonnage: 65
Battle Value: 1,727

Equipment			Mass
Internal Structure:	Endo Steel		3.5
Engine:	260 Light		10.5
Walking MP:	4		
Running MP:	6		
Jumping MP:	4		
Heat Sinks:	13 [26]		3
Gyro:			3
Cockpit:			3
Armor Factor:	208		13

	Internal Structure	Armor Value
Head	3	9
Center Torso	21	31
Center Torso (rear)		10
R/L Torso	15	22
R/L Torso (rear)		8
R/L Arm	10	20
R/L Leg	15	29

Weapons and Ammo	Location	Critical	Tonnage
Heavy PPC	RA	4	10
MML 5	RT	3	3
Ammo (MML) 48/40	LT	2	2
Snub-Nose PPC	LT	2	6
Light PPC	LT	1	3
ER Medium Laser	LT	1	1
Jump Jets	RL	2	2
Jump Jets	LL	2	2

ARC-9M ARCHER

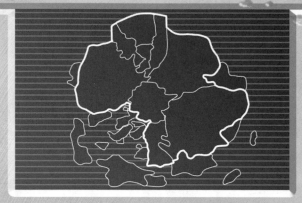

Mass: 70 tons
Chassis: Earthwerks Archer
Power Plant: Defiance 210 Light
Cruising Speed: 32 kph
Maximum Speed: 54 kph
Jump Jets: Chilton Model 21 Improved Jump Jets
    Jump Capacity: 150 meters
Armor: Durallex Guardian II Light Ferro-Fibrous with CASE
Armament:
    2 Defiance 250 Light Particle Projection Cannons
    2 Delta Dart LRM 15 Racks
    2 Diverse Optics Extended Range Medium Lasers
Manufacturer: Bowie Industries, Earthwerks,
    Incorporated, Lexatech Industries
    Primary Factory: Carlisle (Bowie),
        Calloway VI (Earthwerks), Hun Ho (Lexatech)
Communications System: Neil 9000
Targeting and Tracking System: RCA Instatrac Mark XII
    with Artemis IV

Overview

The *Archer* has a long and distinguished history. Originally conceived as an assault 'Mech in the late 25th century, the *Archer* has gone through many variants and modifications over the years. Developed by Bowie Industries during the Jihad, the ARC-9M takes advantage of new particle cannon technology to augment its direct-fire capabilities and uses CASE to improve battlefield survival.

Capabilities

Bowie reduced the 9M's top speed to 54 kph. Chilton improved jump jets effectively balance this speed reduction by providing increased mobility. Two arm-mounted Defiance light PPCs give the 9M reasonable direct-fire weaponry. A brace of reliable Diverse Optics lasers further augments its offensive punch. The main offensive punch of the 9M, however, comes from a pair of Delta Dart long-range missile racks. The missile launchers are durable, accurate and easy to maintain. Eleven tons of Durallex light ferro-fibrous armor give the 9M average protection for its weight, and the addition of CASE ensures the 9M can withdraw from battle under its own power if an ammo bin is breached.

Deployment

The ARC-9M is found in the militaries of the Lyran Commonwealth, Draconis Combine and Republic of the Sphere. Additionally, many mercenary commands feature this 'Mech in its traditional fire-support role, and until the end of the Jihad, Blakist forces included the 9M in many units. The fragmented Free Worlds League states all include this 'Mech to some capacity. Of all the militaries fielding this *Archer*, it is most prevalent in Lyran units, particularly along the Clan border where its long-range support capabilities pit it against comparable Clan designs.

Variants

Multiple new variants followed the 9M's 3076 introduction. The 9W first appeared in the Blake Militia in 3078. Sporting a pair of ER large lasers and LRM 15s with Artemis IV FCS, the 9W tops out at a respectable 86 kph. An Angel ECM and void signature system made the 9W a powerful asset for the Blakist forces. A handful of 9Ws survived the Jihad, but the Coalition assault on the Blake Protectorate destroyed the known factory, and all extant designs were successfully acquired or destroyed by Stone loyalists.

The Lyran-produced 7S model returns to a more traditional armament and speed for the *Archer*. Two LRM 20s with Artemis, two Streak SRM 2s, an ER medium laser, and a head-mounted, rear-facing small pulse laser mated with a 64 kph maximum speed make the 7S reminiscent of the 2R.

Upgrading the 2K model, the 9K features a trio of light PPCs, and four MML 5s with a head-mounted C^3 slave computer.

Notable MechWarriors

Hauptmann Kevin Roof: During the Jihad, Hauptmann Roof participated in many classified actions against the Blakists. While many of his engagements remain shrouded in mystery, Roof's actions on Mizar have been declassified and made available to the Lyran public. Piloting a prototype 9M, Roof participated in the liberation of Mizar in early 3077. During the battle for NouveauParis, the capital of Mizar, Roof's company engaged three Blakist Level IIs based on the Krupp Docks where a Kaleen Bay-class blue-water tanker was moored. Leading his company in a frontal assault against the Blakists, Roof launched an "alpha strike" against the Blakist commander. The Blakist dropped behind a warehouse and most of Roof's volley struck the tanker. A fluke shot pierced the tanker's forward liquid bay, and nearly 6,300 tons of petrochemicals exploded. The resulting fireball annihilated the Blakist forces along with the tanker's berth and a considerable portion of the Krupp Docks. When intelligence revealed the Blakists were preparing to detonate a Santa Ana nuclear warhead, Roof was awarded the Alliance Medal of Honor with silver bar.

Type: **Archer**
Technology Base: Inner Sphere
Tonnage: 70
Battle Value: 1,811

Equipment			Mass
Internal Structure:			7
Engine:	210 Light		7
Walking MP:	3		
Running MP:	5		
Jumping MP:	5		
Heat Sinks:	10 [20]		0
Gyro:			3
Cockpit:			3
Armor Factor (Light Ferro):	186		11

	Internal Structure	Armor Value
Head	3	9
Center Torso	22	28
Center Torso (rear)		9
R/L Torso	15	22
R/L Torso (rear)		6
R/L Arm	11	21
R/L Leg	15	21

Weapons and Ammo	Location	Critical	Tonnage
Light PPC	RA	2	3
Light PPC	LA	2	3
LRM 15	RT	3	7
Artemis IV FCS	RT	1	1
Ammo (LRM) 16	RT	2	2
ER Medium Laser	RT	1	1
CASE	RT	1	.5
ER Medium Laser	LT	1	1
LRM 15	LT	3	7
Artemis IV FCS	LT	1	1
Ammo (LRM) 16	LT	2	2
CASE	LT	1	.5
Improved Jump Jet	RL	2	2
Improved Jump Jet	RT	2	2
Improved Jump Jet	CT	2	2
Improved Jump Jet	LT	2	2
Improved Jump Jet	LL	2	2

WHM-11T WARHAMMER

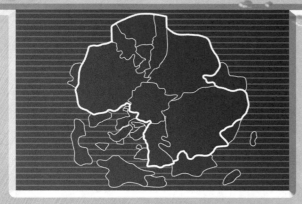

Mass: 70 tons
Chassis: StarFrame Standard
Power Plant: Vox 280 Extralight Fusion
Cruising Speed: 43 kph
Maximum Speed: 64 kph
Jump Jets: Waterly Heavy Lifters Improved Jump Jets
   Jump Capacity: 150 meters
Armor: Valiant Ringmail Light Ferro-Fibrous w/CASE
Armament:
   2 Parti-Kill Snub Nose PPCs
   2 Moscovia Light PPCs
   1 Doombud MML 5
   2 Diverse Optics ER Medium Lasers
Manufacturer: Taurus Territorial Industries
   Primary Factory: Taurus
Communications System: Garret T5C
Targeting and Tracking System: Garret JQ31

Overview

After the asteroid attack on Taurus, TTI CEO Matthias Commager won several reconstruction bids, not only funding the refurbishing of his facilities but also constructing them in a way that would draw attention to TTI. With a new plant successfully under way, the only thing missing was a new flagship product. After a brief discussion with TTI's board of directors, the *Warhammer* was chosen and the public relations campaign began.

Capabilities

The *Warhammer* is a popular design with more than ten frequently produced variants. At a glance, the Taurian-built variant is a doppelganger for the StarCorps WHM-8D model. It keeps the same 64 kph maximum speed, but a closer inspection reveals significant differences. With five Waterly improved jump jets, the 11T can vault 150 meters. The 11T's arms each mount a snub nose PPC and light PPC in an over-under configuration. This combination of PPCs gives the 11T its best offensive punch at a distance of 180 meters. Unfortunately, it doesn't have enough heat sinks to take advantage of its weapons load; a volley from all four PPCs exceeds the 11T's heat dispersal ability. When its two ER medium lasers and a versatile MML 5 are added to the mix, the heat output is more than enough to initiate an automatic shutdown of the Vox engine and could potentially detonate the MML ammo.

Deployment

The Taurian *Warhammer* just entered production last year and has yet to see significant deployment beyond the TDF. The Canopians have indicated they plan to acquire some 11Ts when available. The Capellans seem content to focus on their own *Warhammer* variants, not that analysts expect the Concordat to sell to the Confederation.

Even with most nations looking at major disarmament or at least limiting new production, the *Warhammer* is expected to remain a common sight on any battlefield. When the Federated Suns and Lyran Commonwealth tapped their mothballed equipment, to restore their depleted forces, *Warhammer*s were some of the first units to be pulled out and upgraded with new technology. In the RAF, *Warhammer*s are a favored direct-fire support BattleMech.

Variants

The *Warhammer* has a long history of variants in almost every nation, as well as some corporations and mercenary units, all customizing it in some fashion to better suit their needs. A joint venture between the Magistracy and the Capellan Confederation, the WHM-5L trades in its PPCs for plasma rifles. A trio of ER medium lasers and a Streak SRM 4 are its secondary weapons. As with the 11T, jumping range is 150 meters. Stealth armor is notably absent in this newer Capellan design.

A field refit variant of the 9D has been sighted in growing numbers along the Taurian/Davion border. Designated the 10T, it removes the bulky targeting computer and standard jump jets. In their place, seven improved jump jets give the 'Mech a jumping range of 210 meters.

Across the Inner Sphere, the Draconis Combine has been hard at work developing the *Warhammer* 8K. Building on the foundation of the 6K, Combine developers upgraded the standard PPCs to heavy PPCs. The bulkier cannons necessitated the use of endo steel internal structure and double heat sinks. The 'Mech's SRM 6 has been replaced with a Streak SRM 4, and a C^3 slave computer was installed. With nearly thirteen tons of light ferro-fibrous armor, the 8K is a much-needed upgrade from the 6K. The RAF is currently in negotiations with the Combine to obtain the 8K.

Regulus' poor relations with other former League member-states have hindered sales of Ronin Inc's WHM-8M *Warhammer*, but many commands have begun producing it as a refit. The 8M *Warhammer* has proved popular enough to drive a separate upgrade series that strips the AMS, SRM 6 and machine gun from the 7M. Its medium lasers are upgraded to ER models, and with the use of endo steel, enough space is created to house a light Gauss rifle in the right torso in place of the SRM 6.

Notable MechWarriors

Subaltern Bill Hawkins: Hawkins made a name for himself during the Pleiades Campaign. When the TDF first started engaging Davion targets on the border, Lance Sergeant Hawkins was a fresh graduate of the École Militaire on his first combat mission with the Pleiades Lancers. As the TDF made substantial gains early in the campaign, Hawkins reaped the benefits of his tactical knowledge, earning a quick promotion to cornet. When fighting on Lindsay got ugly, Hawkins was in the middle of it. Though wounded in battle, he led a successful rally against the Davion mercenaries and was promoted to subaltern for his skill and bravery.

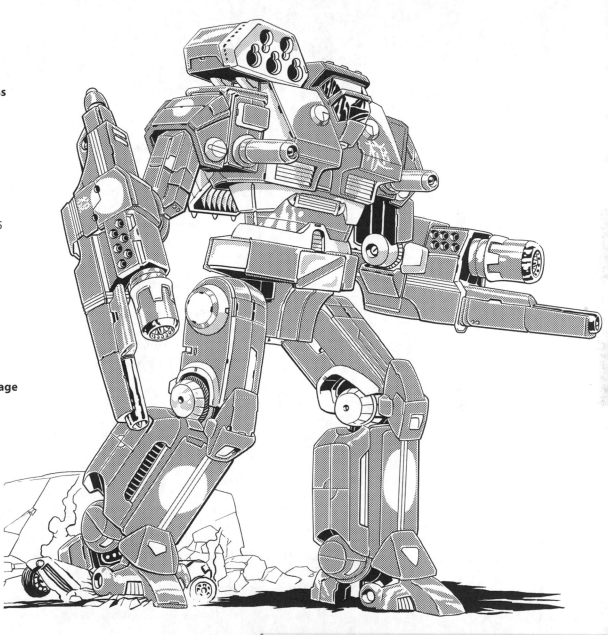

Type: **Warhammer**
Technology Base: Inner Sphere
Tonnage: 70
Battle Value: 1,698

Equipment		Mass
Internal Structure:		7
Engine:	280 XL	8
Walking MP:	4	
Running MP:	6	
Jumping MP:	5	
Heat Sinks:	13 [26]	3
Gyro:		3
Cockpit:		3
Armor Factor (Light Ferro):	178	10.5

	Internal Structure	Armor Value
Head	3	9
Center Torso	22	28
Center Torso (rear)		9
R/L Torso	15	22
R/L Torso (rear)		6
R/L Arm	11	20
R/L Leg	15	18

Weapons and Ammo	Location	Critical	Tonnage
Snub-Nose PPC	RA	2	6
Light PPC	RA	2	3
Snub-Nose PPC	LA	2	6
Light PPC	LA	2	3
ER Medium Laser	RT	1	1
ER Medium Laser	LT	1	1
MML 5	RT	3	3
Ammo (MML) 48/40	RT	2	2
CASE	RT	1	.5
Improved Jump Jet	CT	2	2
Improved Jump Jet	RT	2	2
Improved Jump Jet	LT	2	2
Improved Jump Jet	RL	2	2
Improved Jump Jet	LL	2	2

MAD-9W2 MARAUDER

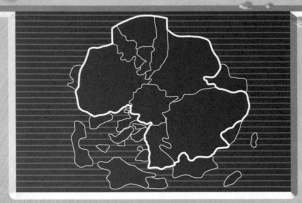

Mass: 75 tons
Chassis: GM Marauder-X
Power Plant: Vlar 225 LFE
Cruising Speed: 32 kph
Maximum Speed: 54 kph
Jump Jets: Phoenix Tail Improved Jumpers
  Jump Capacity: 150 meters
Armor: Ibuki Dragonweave
Armament:
  2 Victory Nickel Alloy ER Large Lasers
  2 Victory Heartbeat Medium Pulse Lasers
  1 Fusigon Smarttooth Snub Nose PPC
Manufacturer: Ibuki Robotics & Manufacturing,
  Bowie Industries
  Primary Factory: Togura (Ibuki), Carlisle (Bowie)
Communications System: Mendham DB with Guardian ECM
  and C³ slave
Targeting and Tracking System: Dalban HiRez

Overview

When Vicore Industries collapsed from Republic pressures, many of its tightly held licenses were released onto the corporate bidding market. Taking a gigantic risk, relative manufacturing newcomer Ibuki leveraged most of its assets to gain the highly contested *Marauder* license. Within a year, Ibuki unveiled a new energy version of the venerable *Marauder* design, using the latest in new technologies based on captured Word of Blake concepts. The MAD-9W2 was well received by many critics, and Ibuki formed several manufacturing partnerships

that have resulted in the 9W2 appearing in many current House militaries.

Capabilities

Utilizing a newly designed heavy-duty gyro at its core, the *Marauder* is an exceptionally stable firing platform with improved mobility. Its integrated C³ slave and ECM electronics allow it to serve in sniping or command roles. With the versatile snub-nosed PPC and paired extended-range lasers, the 9W2 provides excellent firepower over longer distances, but without sacrificing close-quarters combat punch.

Deployment

Ibuki determined up front to offer the design to any interested manufacturers, along with a complicated web of agreements. The legal red tape kept all but the most interested corporations from acquiring the design's license; those that entered into the tangle of interstellar agreements have found the decision extremely beneficial to both parties, as the MAD-9W2's popularity among military experts has kept the lines producing their maximum quotas. The *Marauder* has become a staple in the RAF, DCMS, AFFS and LCAF militaries, especially among units that incorporate C³ technology.

The 9W2 has also proven popular on the mercenary market, though the recent scandal may hurt future sales. Mercenary supply officers are encouraged to double-check newly purchased 9W and 9W2 parts, as it appears that Ibuki was actually selling production line defectives to secondary and tertiary markets.

Variants

The 9W2 owes its success to the proven design concept of its progenitor, the 9W. A Word of Blake design built on several captured Combine worlds, the 9W used a sophisticated C³i system, which was replaced with the more reliable (and standard) C³ module and ECM suite. The weapon loadout is the same, though Ibuki found that many companies refused to sell a known Blakist variant due to the stigma of any association with the terrorist organization.

The Capellan Confederation developed the stealth TSM variant now deployed with CCAF and MAF forces early in the Jihad. This version mounts dual plasma rifles in the standard "armpod" look and uses an off-center PPC for long-range support. The design has found no favor outside the Confederation and the Magistracy of Canopus.

Irian BattleMechs Corporation recently restarted its MAD-9M2 production lines after repairing extensive damage to its Irian facility. Ronin Inc. of Wallis has been producing the 9M2 ever since reverse-engineering it during the Jihad. The 9M2 is a weaker competitor to Ibuki's offering, as it mounts dual heavy PPCs and a conservative Streak SRM 6 system. Ammunition dependence and high heat output tend to make it a less desired option, but rumor has it that Irian will offer a lower price point to interested parties.

Notable MechWarriors

Adept Titus Earlacher: One of a number of Blakists slated for The Republic's war crimes trials, Adept Earlacher was known as the "Butcher of Singapore" during Stone's reclamation of Terra. Venturing out in his *Marauder* during the firestorm that engulfed the city after the Castle Brian self-destructed, he targeted emergency support teams and vehicles, adding to the horrific carnage. Refusing all calls to surrender, he evaded Coalition forces for more than three days, destroying key support centers, refugee shelters and other civilian services. It is believed his actions brought down the Jalan Sultan Ibrahim Causeway, killing more than 1,500 civilians as they attempted to flee the burning city. His motivations for these acts are unclear, as they did nothing to slow the Coalition advance. Then again, many of the Word of Blake's final defensive acts, like the use of nuclear weapons on Terra, were of scant military value.

MAD-9W2 MARAUDER

Type: **Marauder**
Technology Base: Inner Sphere
Tonnage: 75
Battle Value: 1,868

Equipment		Mass
Internal Structure:		7.5
Engine:	225 Light	7.5
Walking MP:	3	
Running MP:	5	
Jumping MP:	5	
Heat Sinks:	16 [32]	6
Gyro (Heavy-Duty):		6
Cockpit:		3
Armor Factor:	200	12.5

	Internal Structure	Armor Value
Head	3	9
Center Torso	23	30
Center Torso (rear)		11
R/L Torso	16	24
R/L Torso (rear)		6
R/L Arm	12	21
R/L Leg	16	24

Weapons and Ammo	Location	Critical	Tonnage
ER Large Laser	RA	2	5
Medium Pulse Laser	RA	1	2
Snub-Nose PPC	RT	2	6
C³ Slave	RT	1	1
Guardian ECM Suite	RT	2	1.5
ER Large Laser	LA	2	5
Medium Pulse Laser	LA	1	2
Improved Jump Jet	RL	2	2
Improved Jump Jet	RT	2	2
Improved Jump Jet	CT	2	2
Improved Jump Jet	LT	2	2
Improved Jump Jet	LL	2	2

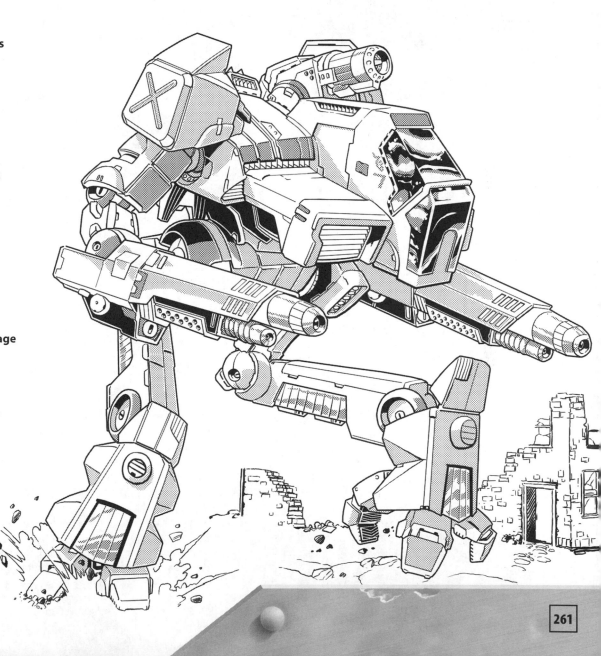

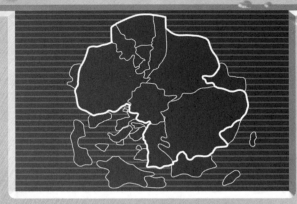

Mass: 80 tons
Chassis: Earthwerks GOL Quad-A
Power Plant: Pitban 320 Light Fusion
Cruising Speed: 43 kph
Maximum Speed: 65 kph
Jump Jets: None
    Jump Capacity: None
Armor: Durallex Heavy with CASE
Armament:
    1 Fusigon Strongtooth Heavy PPC
    2 Delta Dart LRM 10s
    6 SperryBrowning Light Machine Guns
    2 Hellespont Array Assemblies
    4 Defiance Razorback Anti-Battle Armor Pods
Manufacturer: Refit
    Primary Factory: None
Communications System: Angst Clear Channel 3G
Targeting and Tracking System: Angst Clear View Multitask

Overview

Long trying to escape the bad press garnered by the *Scorpion* and *Xanthos*, and perhaps the damning accounts of the defeat of Cochraine's *Goliath*s at the hands of a force of Davion light 'Mechs, more than fifty years ago, the *Goliath* has quietly emerged as a quality fire-support platform. Many of the initial sales went to the Periphery after Inner Sphere armies refused to buy them, and there many have remained. This offered an excellent opportunity for field refits. Begun at the onset of the Jihad, the 6H has shown itself more than capable in its role.

Capabilities

The *Goliath* 6H is in many ways the most similar to the original. Both mount a particle cannon with dual missile launchers and secondary weapons. The 6H uses a heavy PPC to cut large holes in the opposition. Supplementing that weapon is a pair of LRM 10s. With Periphery nations lacking adequate access to Artemis-enhanced munitions, these launchers are no more sophisticated than those that came off the assembly line over three centuries ago. The original *Goliath* mounted Holly racks, not Delta Dart. Instead of dual machine guns as point defense, however, six light machine guns give the 6H greater range and punch. A trio of each linked through an array gives the impression of a heavy machine gun with greater range.

The 'Mech is not without its defenses, either. A passive B-pod is mounted on each leg, waiting for battle armor to attempt to assail it. Fifteen tons of thick plates give the 'Mech plenty of protection, while the quad design makes it much more stable. Finally, though it uses a light fusion engine to save mass for the upgrades, it can still survive an ammunition explosion with CASE in the left torso.

Deployment

Ever since the destruction of Cochraine's *Goliath*s, *Goliath*s rarely appear en masse. However, they are still relatively common in the Periphery, Capellan Confederation, Commonwealth and former League states. The new 6H is found most frequently in Hegemony forces, but any large military in the Periphery is likely to have some.

Variants

So far, three new variants have been reported. The first is a massive undertaking by the Capellan Confederation. Their new 3L is 25 percent faster than the 6H and mounts stealth armor. An extended-range PPC and dual MML 7s provide most of the firepower, but it lacks the capacity to use all those weapons without building up a large amount of heat. Engaging the stealth armor makes the situation worse, especially with one ton of ammo right under the reactor, outside the CASE in the side torso.

In the RAF, some former Com Guard pilots are using a Word of Blake design that makes better use of stealth armor. It can sustain fire from dual plasma cannons while the armor is engaged. Dropping the stealth to move in close allows three medium lasers to be added and the C³i to come on line, which helps networked allies hit the 5W's foes.

Perhaps the most interesting variant is a refit from the former Free Worlds League. Much like the Capellan variant, it has dual MML 7s with some lasers on the legs. The Gauss rifle is nice, but the most impressive feature is the placement of one of the launchers and the Gauss rifle in an experimental turret system. Anyone marking the 6M as easy to flank is in for a surprise.

[Editor's Note: The unit pictured here is the GOL-6M variant. - AH]

Notable MechWarriors

MechWarrior Joni Franchesca: A MechWarrior in the III Legio, Franchesca showcased the 6H against Word of Blake's allies in the Circinus Federation. During the Battle of Zorn's Keep, she alternated PPC and LRM fire at enemy fire support units from behind a small hill. While this sporadic fire was less than efficient, it did force them to move and decreased the pressure on her brothers-in-arms. Infantry forces were sent in to dislodge her, but her machine guns carved into them while three B-pods devastated the small battle-armor contingent. Her commander credited her and the new *Goliath* with the victory, though the battle for the planet was lost.

GOL-6H GOLIATH

Type: Goliath
Technology Base: Inner Sphere
Tonnage: 80
Battle Value: 1,681

Equipment		Mass
Internal Structure:		8
Engine:	320 Light	17
Walking MP:	4	
Running MP:	6	
Jumping MP:	0	
Heat Sinks:	12 [24]	2
Gyro:		4
Cockpit:		3
Armor Factor:	240	15

	Internal Structure	Armor Value
Head	3	9
Center Torso	25	30
Center Torso (rear)		19
R/L Torso	17	20
R/L Torso (rear)		13
FR/L Leg	17	29
RR/L Leg	17	29

Weapons and Ammo	Location	Critical	Tonnage
Heavy PPC	RT	4	10
LRM 10	RT	2	5
3 Light Machine Guns	RT	3	1.5
Light Machine Gun Array	RT	1	.5
B-Pod	RFL	1	1
B-Pod	RRL	1	1
LRM 10	LT	2	5
3 Light Machine Guns	LT	3	1.5
Light Machine Gun Array	LT	1	.5
Ammo (LRM) 24	LT	2	2
Ammo (Light MG) 100	LT	1	.5
CASE	LT	1	.5
B-Pod	LFL	1	1
B-Pod	LRL	1	1

BLR-10S BATTLEMASTER

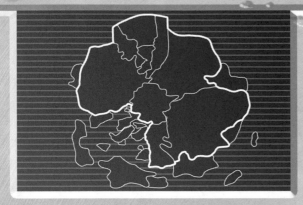

Mass: 85 tons
Chassis: StarFrame Heavy
Power Plant: Edasich Compact 255
Cruising Speed: 32 kph
Maximum Speed: 54 kph
Jump Jets: None
    Jump Capacity: None
Armor: ArcShield Maxi
Armament:
    1 Defiance 1001 ER PPC
    1 Coventry TH4b Streak SRM 4
    6 Diverse Optics ER Medium Lasers
    1 Diverse Optics ER Small Laser
    2 Defiance Razorback ABA Pods
Manufacturer: J.B. BattleMechs
    Primary Factory: Storfors
Communications System: O/P 3000 COMSET
    with Guardian ECM
Targeting and Tracking System: Cyclops Multi-Tasker 10

Overview

The *BattleMaster* has transformed not only the face of command units, but also the fortunes of Hollis Inc. Turning a company that suffered from the poor investment of developing the first quad 'Mech into a success, the *BattleMaster* 10S is now helping J. B. BattleMechs improve their prospects. Likewise, the machine that once defined the term "command 'Mech" is on the way back, as the 10S version heavily redefines the *BattleMaster*. This redefinition returns to the basics of the formidable original design, using modern technology to do so.

Capabilities

The 10S is an upgrade over the 1 and the 3 series in terms of firepower. An ER PPC gives it plenty of range without ammunition limits. Once battle is engaged, six ER medium lasers increase firepower by 300 percent. Up close, a four-tube Streak launcher ensures that every missile hits. Even more impressive, it has the heat sinks to use most of its firepower continuously. The standard anti-personnel weaponry has been replaced with two anti-battle armor pods.

While all that firepower is useful in a command 'Mech, the most important part is keeping the commander in play. The new *BattleMaster* excels at this. Thick armor protects critical systems, but once that is penetrated, the 10S can still tolerate enormous abuse. Heat sinks protect more sensitive equipment. The engine is compact and hard to hit, while the heavy-duty gyro can withstand more damage than a typical version and keep functioning. The small ammo bin is protected by a CASE; a rear-firing small laser and ECM equipment provide the finishing touches.

Deployment

The *BattleMaster* can be found almost anywhere, even in the Periphery. It is frequently piloted by a commander of some sort, but sometimes its pilot is just a MechWarrior using the powerful machine as a simple assault 'Mech.

Variants

Such a popular 'Mech has seen its share of upgrades and modifications. The former Free Worlds League built one to coordinate a C[3] unit, giving it a light Gauss rifle and dual light PPCs to keep it away from most of the infighting. An MML and dual pulse lasers provide some short-range capability, while heavy ferro-fibrous armor protects the M3 version. The Falcons have used their Pandora facility to make a *BattleMaster* of their own, replacing the PPC with a mid-sized HAG and the SRM with an ATM that has the same number of tubes. In addition to a sextet of lasers, an advanced targeting computer ties all the direct-fire weapons together.

More recently, the Capellan Confederation decided that their *BattleMasters* needed stealth armor. The Capellan variant's firepower is similar to the M3, but the armor is reduced, especially on the legs where jump jets give it additional mobility. The Combine took the jump jets to another extreme, slowing down their new version and using improved versions to reach 150 meters of jump capacity. With a snub-nosed PPC, large pulse laser and Gauss rifle, this variant is something of a skirmisher, with a pair of lasers to round out the firepower.

The most compelling new modification is a Defiance Industries design in which the Lyrans apparently have some interest. For a reasonable price, Defiance will refit *BattleMasters* at their Kwangjong-ni facility. The new specifications include an advanced engine allowing it to reach speeds of more than 80 kph. Two different PPCs give it reach and punch. A Streak SRM 6 is also included, but on the right torso, giving this variant an odd profile.

[Editor's Note: The unit pictured here is the BLR-10S2 sub-variant. - AH]

Notable MechWarriors

Doctor Roger Fleming: A retired major, Roger Fleming got his doctorate in war science and taught at the Nagelring. After the Blakist invasion of Tharkad, he returned to the cockpit with the resistance, where his 10S proved its toughness and firepower. He racked up seven kills during the occupation, and the technicians who worked on his machine claim that almost any other 'Mech would have been destroyed at least three times. He stayed on active duty until the conclusion of the Jihad and has since returned to teaching, helping to fill out the skeleton staff at the Nagelring.

BLR-10S BATTLEMASTER

Type: **BattleMaster**
Technology Base: Inner Sphere
Tonnage: 85
Battle Value: 1,930

Equipment		Mass
Internal Structure:		8.5
Engine:	255 Compact	19.5
Walking MP:	3	
Running MP:	5	
Jumping MP:	0	
Heat Sinks:	20 [40]	10
Gyro (Heavy-Duty):		6
Cockpit:		3
Armor Factor:	263	16.5

	Internal Structure	Armor Value
Head	3	9
Center Torso	27	39
Center Torso (rear)		15
R/L Torso	18	26
R/L Torso (rear)		10
R/L Arm	14	28
R/L Leg	18	36

Weapons and Ammo	Location	Critical	Tonnage
ER PPC	RA	3	7
3 ER Medium Lasers	RT	3	3
B-Pod	RL	1	1
3 ER Medium Lasers	LT	3	3
Streak SRM 4	LT	1	3
Ammo (SRM) 25	LT	1	1
CASE	LT	1	.5
B-Pod	LL	1	1
ER Small Laser	H(R)	1	.5
Guardian ECM Suite	CT	2	1.5

LGB-12R LONGBOW

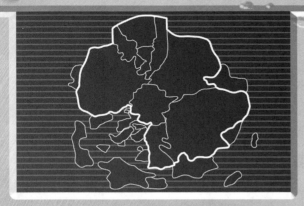

Mass: 85 tons
Chassis: StarCorp 100
Power Plant: Strand 255 Class B Light Fusion
Cruising Speed: 32 kph
Maximum Speed: 54 kph
Jump Jets: Audi-Fokker Mark IV
   Jump Capacity: 90 meters
Armor: StarSlab/12.5 with CASE
Armament:
   4 Holly "Ballista" LRM 15 Missile Rack
   1 Defiance Model 6 Extended Range Large Laser
   1 Defiance Model XII Extended Range Medium Laser
Manufacturer: StarCorps Industries
   Primary Factory: Crofton (FS), Loburg (LC), Terra (RoS)
Communications System: O/P 3950 COMSET M7
Targeting and Tracking System: Martin-Quarry
   Tarsys XLR 1.0

Overview

The new *Longbow* 12R has been in production for three years. A powerful fire-support 'Mech, the *Longbow* has often been criticized for its ammunition dependence and lack of maneuverability. While adequately armored, most *Longbow* variants mount minimal secondary weapons and require escorts when withdrawing from combat for resupply. StarCorps addressed these issues and designed the 12R to be its own escort.

Capabilities

Beginning with a ninety-meter jump capacity to address mobility issues, StarCorps then installed four Holly "Ballista" LRM racks to give the *Longbow* 12R its trademark offense. With a staggering eight tons of ammunition, the missile boat boasts sixteen volleys per rack for two and a half minutes of battlefield endurance at continual fire. The 12R lacks the Artemis IV system found on many other variants, but does include CASE in both torsos. Two Defiance-produced extended-range lasers, one large and one medium, round out the 12R's armament and create a heat curve that demands careful attention. With only eleven freezers, an "alpha strike" comes dangerously close to triggering the Strand 255 engine's failsafe system.

Deployment

The Triarii Protectors, Principes Guards and Hastati Sentinels jointly hold the first option to purchase *Longbow* 12R production runs from StarCorps' Republic factory—now back under StarCorps board leadership after the Liberation of Terra. Only the Hastati Sentinels have exercised their option, and two complete production runs went for sale on the open market. Nearly all of these were acquired by the DCMS. Republic intelligence believes they've been deployed along the Combine/Bear border, though several remain unaccounted for.

12Rs produced at the Federated Suns plant on Crofton are beginning to appear on border worlds in the Capellan and Periphery Marches. Clearly employing a different philosophy, the Lyrans have deployed small quantities of 12Rs throughout the Commonwealth, with preference shown to units with the most need (though some units still acquire upgrades through force of politics).

Variants

Three additional variants of the *Longbow* are currently in production. The LGB-14C is produced by the Capellans, Lyrans and Davions. Quite possibly the most sought-after *Longbow* ever developed, it is available across the Inner Sphere and Periphery, though without the right connections to speed procurement in the Suns or the Commonwealth, the waiting list exceeds two years. Capellan-produced 14Cs are dispersed per the Chancellor's wishes. Armed with six MML 9s, the 14C excels in both fire support and close support thanks to the MML's flexibility. Six tons of CASE-protected ammo fills the torsos. The 14C can fire volleys of up to fifty-four missiles; only the 12C exceeds this firepower. However, with only ten double heat sinks, the 14C has a challenging heat curve that must be closely monitored even without using its three extended-range medium lasers.

Built at the Crofton and Emris IV facilities, the LGB-13C increases maximum speed to 64 kph and mounts six MML 7 racks backed up by three extended-range small lasers. The flexible firing options of the MML make the 13C effective at ranged and close support. Second in popularity to the 14C, the 13C is selling well everywhere except the Lyran Commonwealth, where importing the 13C has been blocked to encourage purchase of the locally produced 12R and 14C.

Finally, built in limited numbers exclusively for the Federated Suns, the LGB-13NAIS model swaps LRMs for six light AC/5s, with three mounted in each arm. The ER large laser and jump jets are replaced with a C³ slave computer, Guardian ECM system, two ER medium lasers and an ER small laser.

Notable MechWarriors

Captains Aaron Williams and Alice Hughes: Williams and Hughes were both test pilots at the NAIS when the Blakists attacked. They deployed along with the Tenth Lyran Guard and NAIS Cadre to engage hostiles in Avalon City. As the encounter turned against the defenders, Williams and Hughes held off a Level II of Thirty-first Division 'Mechs and bought time for an orderly withdrawal of NAIS and Lyran Guard survivors. Reorganized into the First Davion Guards, Williams and Hughes saw action in most of the significant battles that took place during seven long years of occupation. The end of the Jihad finds both teaching urban combat to cadets at the half-rebuilt NAIS.

LGB-12R LONGBOW

Type: **Longbow**
Technology Base: Inner Sphere
Tonnage: 85
Battle Value: 1,979

Equipment		Mass
Internal Structure:		8.5
Engine:	255 Light	10
Walking MP:	3	
Running MP:	5	
Jumping MP:	3	
Heat Sinks:	11 [22]	1
Gyro:		3
Cockpit:		3
Armor Factor:	216	13.5

	Internal Structure	Armor Value
Head	3	9
Center Torso	27	35
Center Torso (rear)		10
R/L Torso	18	25
R/L Torso (rear)		8
R/L Arm	14	22
R/L Leg	18	26

Weapons and Ammo	Location	Critical	Tonnage
LRM 15	RA	3	7
LRM 15	RT	3	7
Ammo (LRM) 32	RT	4	4
CASE	RT	1	.5
ER Medium Laser	H	1	1
ER Large Laser	LT	2	5
LRM 15	LA	3	7
LRM 15	LT	3	7
Ammo (LRM) 32	LT	4	4
CASE	LT	1	.5
Jump Jet	CT	1	2
Jump Jet	RL	1	2
Jump Jet	LL	1	2

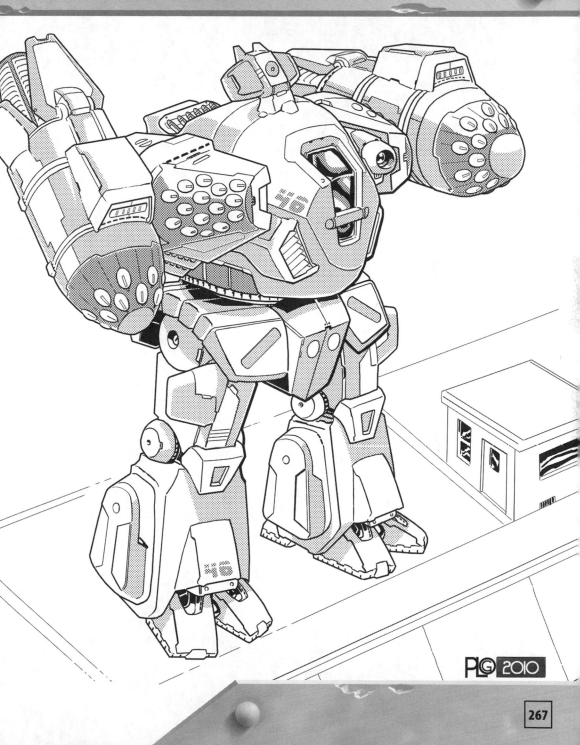

PLG 2010

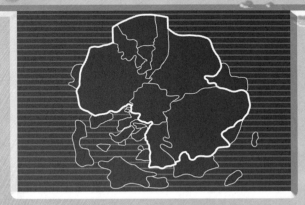

Mass: 100 tons
Chassis: GM Marauder
Power Plant: GM 300 Extralight Fusion
Cruising Speed: 32 kph
Maximum Speed: 54 kph
Jump Jets: Chilton 1350
  Jump Capacity: 150 meters
Armor: Valiant Lamellor
Armament:
  2 Johnston Wide-Beam Snub-Nosed PPCs
  2 Johnston Lite Light PPCs
  1 Mydron Tornado Rotary AC/5
Manufacturer: Refit
  Primary Factory: None
Communications System: Blackwell Multi-Linq 55
Targeting and Tracking System: Dragwell Hi-Rez IV

Overview

The *Marauder*, a fearsome BattleMech from the 2600s, could win some battles in the Third Succession War just by showing up. Then Wolf's Dragoons appeared and spawned the *Marauder II*, a monster out of MechWarrior nightmares. In the six decades since its first appearance, the *Marauder II* has backed up that reputation with powerful weapons and amazing endurance. In great demand even before the Jihad, the 'Mech became even more so when the Word of Blake destroyed the factories that manufactured it in an effort to annihilate anything associated with Wolf's Dragoons. With so many *Marauder II*s having survived and so many

new weapons available, most nations went through refit programs to increase the *Marauder II's* capabilities. The most recent of those is the Federated Suns, with the help of The Republic.

Capabilities

With the sturdy chassis and thick armor of the *Marauder II* 5A, Davion designers didn't want to "mess with a good thing." Instead, they reworked the weaponry. The extended-range particle cannons were swapped for snub-nosed versions, while the heavy autocannon was replaced with a rotary autocannon. Finally, the lasers were removed and light particle cannons added in their stead, replacing some of the range lost with the other weapon changes.

Those changes alone made an impressive 'Mech, but the design team didn't stop there. The almost archaic standard heat sinks were removed and replaced with more efficient freezers that allow the current design to dissipate more heat than its predecessor at a fraction of the weight. Leveraging that freed-up weight, the designers followed the lead of the Word of Blake and upgraded the *Marauder II's* jump capacity to 150 meters. If it weren't for the difficulty of aiming at the enemy, and perhaps keeping the pilot's brain from becoming covered in bruises, there would be little reason for this machine to ever be seen walking. Sadly, this ambitious array of firepower didn't allow the more vulnerable extralight engine to be altered, but the increase in offensive power can't help but add to the 'Mech's defenses.

Deployment

Still unable to manufacture their *Marauder II*s, the Davion design team has shared their version with The Republic, which will do the refit work on Tikonov. In exchange, The Republic will get compensation as well as the ability to use the same design to upgrade the *Marauder II*s in their arsenal. It is unknown if this will be a standard design, as the RAF has a number of different designs, including those used by private individuals who joined up and captured Blakist versions of varying sorts. Nearly all nations possess some *Marauder II*s, even the Lyrans, who have adopted the original 4S heavy Gauss rifle version as their own.

Variants

The former Free Worlds League states refitted many of their *Marauder II*s, though some of these have fallen into the hands of mercenaries or The Republic. The Free Worlds variant still mounts one dorsal particle cannon, while each arm mounts a heavy and a medium advanced pulse laser. The 'Mech also has a faster ground speed, but only mounts standard jump jets. An ECM system is included, though this refit was as massive an undertaking as the first *Marauder II*s because the chassis was replaced with an endo steel version.

The Combine's version resembles the Steiner *Marauder* with a Gauss rifle on the back. However, the energy weapons were changed to heavy PPCs and ER small lasers. Finally, the Blakists had an upgrade that ComStar used as well. Its jump capacity is similar to the 6D, as are the snub-nosed PPCs, but the autocannon is replaced by a heavy particle cannon. The lower arm weapons were removed to allow for a standard engine, but a reworked endo steel frame holds a deadlier weapon—an improved C^3 system.

Notable MechWarriors

Maggie Elmore: A solid but unremarkable member of Stone's Lament during the reclamation of Terra, Elmore has shown her talents in her new 6D, fighting Capellan forces. The Capellans thought they were safe with their stealth armor, but Maggie used the accuracy of her snub-nosed PPCs and the mobility of her jump jets to fell half a company of Capellan 'Mechs. Their formations disrupted, the frustrated Capellans had to retreat before Elmore's company.

Type: Marauder II
Technology Base: Inner Sphere
Tonnage: 100
Battle Value: 2,378

Equipment			Mass
Internal Structure:			10
Engine:	300 XL		9.5
Walking MP:	3		
Running MP:	5		
Jumping MP:	5		
Heat Sinks:	14 [28]		4
Gyro:			3
Cockpit:			3
Armor Factor:	304		19

	Internal Structure	Armor Value
Head	3	9
Center Torso	31	45
Center Torso (rear)		16
R/L Torso	21	31
R/L Torso (rear)		11
R/L Arm	17	34
R/L Leg	21	41

Weapons and Ammo	Location	Critical	Tonnage
Snub-Nose PPC	RA	2	6
Light PPC	RA	1	3
Rotary AC/5	RT	6	10
Snub-Nose PPC	LA	2	6
Light PPC	LA	1	3
Ammo (RAC) 60	LT	3	3
CASE	LT	1	.5
Improved Jump Jet	RT	2	4
Improved Jump Jet	RL	2	4
Improved Jump Jet	LT	2	4
Improved Jump Jet	CT	2	4
Improved Jump Jet	LL	2	4

PROJECT PHOENIX: THE CLANS

What began with Clan Diamond Shark has become a driving trend among all the surviving Inner Sphere Clans. With access to their homeworlds cut off, the Clans have been forced to rely on the tools available to them. Their second-line formations were often among the least damaged elements in their toumans, and the number of second-line Clan 'Mechs that survived the past fifteen years offered an attractive avenue for pursuing further technological upgrades. The first Clan Phoenix designs were an effort by the Diamond Sharks to resell outmoded technology, but they have since become a significant piece of the Inner Sphere Clans' efforts at defense and offense.

Some of the Clans use the new Phoenix machines to augment their tattered defenses, as with Clan Wolf's rebuilding of their second-line garrisons. Other Clans use these upgraded designs to fill new niches in their expanding toumans; the Snow Ravens' growing space 'Mech forces offer the most striking example. Even the Inner Sphere has begun to see the fruits of these newer designs, with the Diamond Sharks willing to sell them to nearly anyone with the necessary credits. The spread of these BattleMechs is a disturbing trend that works against The Republic's goal of reducing, if not rolling back, the rate of military expansion. The technological edge of these Clan designs makes them a growing threat.

Where once I would have given my right arm for a lance of *Warhammer IIC*s, now I fear how easy it is for anyone with the funds to obtain them. The threat to peace presented by the Diamond Sharks' "open markets" calls for careful consideration.

—Lt. Colonel Jake Crow
Assistant Director, Clan Affairs
Department of Military Intelligence

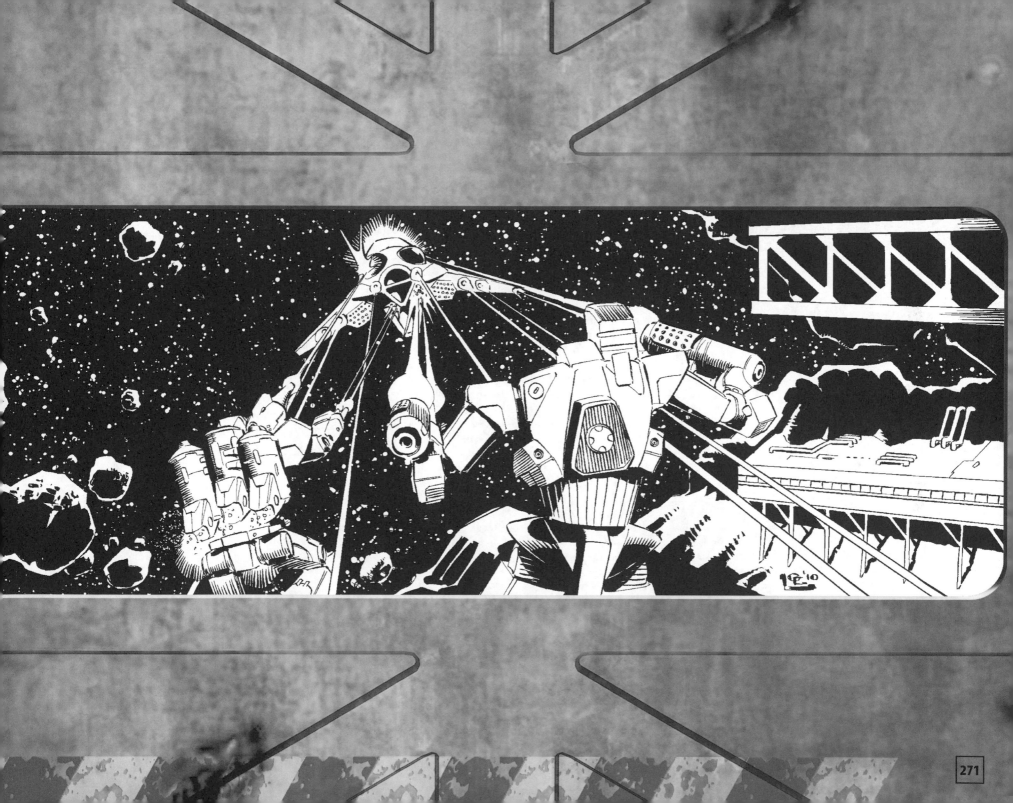

Mass: 25 tons
Chassis: Olivetti Stage 2
Power Plant: Fusion 200 Standard
Cruising Speed: 86 kph
Maximum Speed: 129 kph
Jump Jets: None
Jump Capacity: None
Armor: Compound Alpha Ferro-Fibrous with CASE
Armament:
  6 Tau-II Anti-Personnel Gauss Rifles
  1 Series 7Ja Extended Range Medium Laser
Manufacturer: Manufacturing Site #3
  Primary Factory: New Oslo
Communications System: Angst 2400
Targeting and Tracking System: Omicron XX

Overview

Still rebuilding from the losses incurred in carving out a permanent Inner Sphere enclave, the efforts of Clan Hell's Horses have been hampered by their limited military-industrial capacity. The production center on New Oslo, wrestled from the claws of the Wolf Clan, could produce only light and medium second-line designs. Efforts to upgrade Manufacturing Site #3 have started to bring production of heavier BattleMechs and OmniMechs online, but the bulk of the equipment produced to date has been lighter second-line 'Mechs. One such example is a variant of the *Locust IIC*, a BattleMech the Horses have manufactured since 3076.

Capabilities

Simple and robust, the *Locust IIC* is an ideal BattleMech for mass production with limited resources. Based on the *Locust IIC* 4, the Horses' *Locust IIC* 7 replaces the heavy lasers and two heat sinks with six anti-personnel Gauss weapons. While intended to deal with soft targets, the high-velocity Gauss weapons also possess the range and punch to deal with lightly armored targets. With the laser and Gauss weapons tied into an advanced targeting computer, this variant can pose a significant threat even to medium and heavy 'Mechs with the right MechWarrior at the controls.

Deployment

Combat losses against the Wolves and Ice Hellions forced Khan Cobb to reorganize the Horses' touman, with many a Trinary reduced to Binaries. As its Inner Sphere production centers are coming online, it has a chance to reverse this trend. Much of the new equipment is of second-line quality, like the *Locust IIC* 7, but ultimately the rate of recovery is dictated by the availability of warm bodies rather than hardware. Clan Hell's Horses employs their *Locust IIC* variant in a supporting role for armor and infantry.

While Devlin Stone convinced the Clans not to land on Terra, that did not extend to Mars, the Word of Blake's final bastion other than Terra. The Hells Horses' Eleventh Mechanized Cavalry took part in the brief campaign. Short on front-line hardware, the Eleventh had several *Locust IIC* 7s in their ranks. The targeting computer-backed AP Gauss rifles proved highly effective in the tunneled warrens of Kyoro Dome. They were the leveling factor against the highly experienced battle armor defenders, preventing the loss of many Coalition 'Mechs.

Variants

Both the Wolves and the Ghost Bears continue to manufacture the *Locust IIC* at other locations in the Inner Sphere. Their new *IIC* 6 mounts two triple heavy machine gun arrays in place of the Gauss weapons and targeting computer. Armor protection has been increased by half a ton.

The Ghost Bears have recently started to produce the *IIC* 8 variant. A 300 XL power plant boosts ground speed, and weapons range is enhanced by the installation of an extended-range large laser. All other weaponry and the targeting computer have been removed to accommodate this weapon.

The Jade Falcons have just rolled out their experimental *IIC* 9 variant. Powered by a monster 350 XXL engine, this BattleMech also uses an XL gyro and heavy ferro-fibrous armor. The extended-range medium laser has been replaced with a laser anti-missile system, and the Gauss weapons and targeting computer have been swapped out for two improved heavy lasers and an additional heat sink.

Notable MechWarriors

Star Commander Brin: From one of the last Hell's Horses' sibkos to graduate in the Homeworlds, Brin has found relocation to the Inner Sphere a slightly bewildering experience. With an uneasy peace settling across the Occupation Zone, there are few opportunities for glory for the warriors who have not traveled to aid Devlin Stone. Brin is agitating for the opportunity to launch Trials of Possession against the Falcons, Ghost Bears and Clan Wolf for some of the materials and equipment the Horses desperately need. That his Clan leaders are even listening to these requests indicates his potential *ristar* status.

Type: **Locust IIC**
Technology Base: Clan
Tonnage: 25
Battle Value: 980

Equipment			Mass
Internal Structure:	Endo Steel		1.5
Engine:	200		8.5
Walking MP:	8		
Running MP:	12		
Jumping MP:	0		
Heat Sinks:	10 [20]		0
Gyro:			2
Cockpit:			3
Armor Factor (Ferro):	76		4

	Internal Structure	Armor Value
Head	3	8
Center Torso	8	10
Center Torso (rear)		2
R/L Torso	6	8
R/L Torso (rear)		2
R/L Arm	4	8
R/L Leg	6	10

Weapons and Ammo	Location	Critical	Tonnage
3 AP Gauss Rifles	RA	3	1.5
Targeting Computer	H	1	1
ER Medium Laser	CT	1	1
Ammo (AP Gauss) 40	LT	1	1
3 AP Gauss Rifles	LA	3	1.5

Mass: 40 tons
Chassis: NCIS Endo Steel Type M
Power Plant: Firebox 200
Cruising Speed: 54 kph
Maximum Speed: 86 kph
Jump Jets: Northrup Starlifter M41
   Jump Capacity: 240 meters
Armor: Alpha Compound Ferro-Fibrous
Armament:
   2 Type 3 Series Advanced Tactical Missile System
   1 Model X Heavy Large Laser
Manufacturer: Irece Alpha, Barcella Alpha
   Primary Factory: Irece, Irece
Communications System: JNE Integrated
Targeting and Tracking System: Build 3 CAT TTS

Overview

In the early 3070s, Nova Cat scientists developed a new variant of the *Griffin IIC*. Production facility expansion had just begun when the Blakists (masquerading as DCMS) came to Irece. Their nuclear assault on civilians was meant to draw the Cats into a war with the Combine, but the Cats discovered the subterfuge. Abandoning their expansion project, they quickly retooled the *Griffin IIC* 4 line to produce the *IIC* 6 for use against the Word of Blake.

Capabilities

Compared to other variants, the *Griffin IIC* 6 suffers a 10 kph reduction in top speed and a twenty-one percent loss of armor protection, but a sixty-meter increase in jump capacity thanks to the installation of Starlifter improved jump jets. Based on the *IIC* 4, the *IIC* 6 keeps its ATM-3 launchers and ample ammunition bins, but replaces the *IIC* 4's ER large laser with a heavy large laser, trading range for stopping power. A targeting computer offsets the inherent inaccuracy of the heavy laser.

Deployment

The *Griffin IIC* has always been a prominent fixture in the Cats' PGCs, and the *IIC* 6 is no different. Initial production went live in early 3073 with 'Mechs deployed to a strike force sent after the Blakists' 42nd Shadow Division. Unfortunately, all were lost in combat. During the Jihad, many front-line Galaxies included the *IIC* 6 out of necessity, though most surviving units were redeployed to PGCs following cession of hostilities.

At the first Geneva conference in 3080, the Nova Cats gifted a Trinary of *IIC* 6s to The Republic for use in the still-forming RAF. These 'Mechs were primarily assigned to Stone's Lament. The *IIC* 6 has also found its way into DCMS units in the Benjamin and Pesht military districts.

With the total blackout of the Clan Homeworlds, Republic Intelligence cannot confirm if *Griffin IIC*s are still being produced there.

Variants

The *Griffin IIC* 5 (produced by both the Sharks and the Cats) keeps the ER large laser and ER small laser common to most of the *IIC* through *IIC* 4 variants. Built for handling soft targets, the *IIC* 5 mounts a pair of light machine gun arrays with three guns each. Starlifter improved jump jets give it a jump capacity of 210 meters. Rumors of the Cloud Cobras producing this variant cannot be confirmed.

In 3083, the Cats started refitting some older *IIC*s to test their newly acquired, experimental Streak LRMs. Dubbed the *IIC* 7, the new variant has a top speed of 118 kph. Right torso LRM 5s are replaced with a single Streak LRM 10 launcher, and a Streak SRM 6 replaces the LRM 5s in the left torso. Each is backed up by an ER medium pulse laser. The *IIC* 7 uses standard jump jets, but coaxes out 210 meters of jump capacity. The Cats have also made this version available to the RAF.

Strangely, the Falcons began producing the *Griffin IIC* 8 in 3078. An update of the *IIC* 3, it drops its heavy small laser and ER large laser in favor of improved jump jets with a range of 270 meters. Built in great numbers, it is found in modest quantities with Clan Wolf, Clan Wolf in Exile and the Lyran Commonwealth, primarily as a result of combat salvage. Taking advantage of current good relations with the Falcons, the RAF is seeking to acquire a few samples.

Notable MechWarriors

Star Commander Duck: The freeborn son of Snow Raven bondsman Charles and Nova Cat scientist Olsen, Duck lost his *Stormcrow* and most of his left leg when the Cats' Sigma Galaxy helped the Combine liberate Benjamin in late 3072. Duck was fitted with a prosthetic leg, assigned a *Griffin IIC* 6, and returned to the front lines. A year later, in the Tukayyid system, the Nova Cats issued a Trial of Refusal against Devlin Stone. Duck was one of the MechWarriors chosen to represent the Cats. Though the Cats lost and half their number had to return to Irece, Duck's performance earned him a place in Stone's coalition. Duck piloted his *IIC* 6 for the duration of the Jihad, and has become so fond of it that he refuses upgrades to an OmniMech.

GRIFFIN IIC 6

Type: **Griffin IIC**
Technology Base: Clan
Tonnage: 40
Battle Value: 1,468

Equipment		Mass
Internal Structure:	Endo Steel	2
Engine:	200	8.5
Walking MP:	5	
Running MP:	8	
Jumping MP:	8	
Heat Sinks:	10 [20]	0
Gyro:		2
Cockpit:		3
Armor Factor (Ferro):	105	5.5

	Internal Structure	Armor Value
Head	3	9
Center Torso	12	14
Center Torso (rear)		4
R/L Torso	10	13
R/L Torso (rear)		3
R/L Arm	6	9
R/L Leg	10	14

Weapons and Ammo	Location	Critical	Tonnage
ATM 3	RT	2	1.5
ATM 3	LT	2	1.5
Ammo (ATM) 60	RT	3	3
Heavy Large Laser	LT	3	4
Targeting Computer	LT	1	1
Improved Jump Jets	LT	6	3
Improved Jump Jets	RT	6	3
Improved Jump Jet	LL	2	1
Improved Jump Jet	RL	2	1

PLG 2010

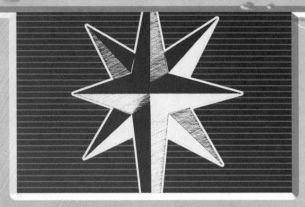

Mass: 45 tons
Chassis: NCIS Endo Steel Type M
Power Plant: Fusion 225 XL
Cruising Speed: 54 kph
Maximum Speed: 86 kph
Jump Jets: Northrup Starlifter M46
  Jump Capacity: 240 meters
Armor: Alpha Compound Ferro-Fibrous Armor
Armament:
  1 Series 6b Extended Range Large Laser
  1 Type 6 Series Advanced Tactical Missile System
  1 Series 2d Extended Range Medium
  1 Series 14a Medium Pulse Laser
Manufacturer: Snow Raven Industrial Complex Alpha
  Primary Factory: Dante
Communications System: JNE Integrated
Targeting and Tracking System: Build 3 CAT TTS

Overview

Traditionally, BattleMechs are considered the kings of ground warfare, with the black seas of space ruled by aerospace fighters. 'Mechs, despite their impressive flexibility when planetside, are simply outmatched in space. Fighters are faster and more maneuverable—huge assets in zero-G warfare—and boast far greater combat endurance outside the atmosphere. 'Mechs with jump jets can maneuver and fight to some degree in space, but they don't carry enough reaction mass for their thrusters to even begin to match fighters.

However, every now and then, a job comes up in zero-G that a fighter simply cannot handle, or where the greater durability of a 'Mech is an advantage. These kinds of missions—such as combat in asteroid mines or boarding actions against space stations—are usually handled by BattleMechs, but often pilots and machines are be lost through the basic unsuitability of 'Mechs for space combat. Land-Air 'Mechs were once considered the best machines for these tasks, but this year Clan Snow Raven has introduced a pair of second-line BattleMechs optimized for combat in space.

Capabilities

While it is obviously a development from the Nova Cats' *IIC* 4 model, the most notable features of the *Shadow Hawk IIC* 7 are its massive fuel tanks and banks of advanced thrusters. These allow Raven and Alliance pilots to fly these impressive machines in space. They're still not equal to even a slow aerospace fighter, but now MechWarriors have far more control over their 'Mechs when conducting zero-G operations. To allow for these improvements, the fusion engine was reduced in size, but even on the ground the *IIC* 7's jump jets allow for faster tactical movement.

To allow for the greatest possible efficiency in space combat, this 'Mech mounts an array of low-recoil weapons. Its primary armament is an ER large laser backed up with a six-tube advanced missile launcher. A full three tons of ATM ammunition gives the missile launcher impressive endurance and flexibility. The *Shadow Hawk IIC* 7 also mounts a pair of medium lasers—one extended-range, the second a pulse model—to add to its already substantial bite. These secondary weapons are mounted in one arm of the 'Mech, most likely to allow their use as close-range cutting tools to gain entry through locked hatches and bay doors.

Deployment

As might be expected, the majority of the new *Shadow Hawk IICs* are seeing deployment with Snow Raven R-Teams and as marine contingents on WarShips, often partnered with the similar *Warhammer IIC* 7. The Outworlds Alliance fields a sizeable number as security on space stations and in asteroid mining outposts. The firepower these units bring to the field is expected to be a substantial deterrent to the space-suited infantry that usually conducts zero-G raids. Indeed, it is enough to pose a threat even to landing craft and small DropShips.

At this time, no other state or Clan fields these unusual variants or their equivalents. Industry experts are watching the Outworlds Alliance closely to see if this development is worth pursuing or another technological dead end.

Variants

In the years since the Federated Commonwealth Civil War, a number of other variants of this chassis have appeared throughout the Clans. Two are being aggressively marketed across the Inner Sphere by Clan Diamond Shark. The first has paired plasma cannons and three AP Gauss rifles. Originally it was meant as an incendiary machine, but a leaked battleROM showed a Lyran *Berserker* C3, coated in flaming gel, cleaving a *Shadow Hawk IIC* 5 to pieces while the Clan 'Mech desperately plinked away with its nearly ineffectual small guns. After that incident, the Clan's merchants wisely re-designated it as an infantry and vehicle hunter, at which point it began to see moderate sales success.

The second Diamond Shark model is a blistering fast cavalry platform, covered in lasers and mounting a mid-sized LRM rack almost as an afterthought. It is also sold to anyone with the money and has proved quite popular with pilots who don't mind aggressively riding their machines' heat curves.

The final common variant is a Hell's Horses model, first seen during their return to the Inner Sphere. It mounts a large hyper-assault Gauss rifle and an array of pulse lasers. This variant has spread through the Clans over the years as an alternative to 'Mechs and vehicles mounting LB-20X cannons.

Notable Pilots

Star Captain Laura: Though she has yet to win a Bloodname, Laura is currently enjoying a certain amount of fame for her unique situation: she is an aerospace fighter phenotype piloting a 'Mech in a front-line ground unit. While some conservative elements view her as a divisive influence, her skill at the controls of a 'Mech and her genetic adaptations to space combat made her a natural test pilot for Clan Snow Raven's new *Shadow Hawk* model. She has excelled at all tests and simulations, making the Clan leadership hopeful that their space-combat BattleMech program will be a success.

Type: **Shadow Hawk IIC**
Technology Base: Clan
Tonnage: 45
Battle Value: 1,999

Equipment		Mass
Internal Structure:	Endo Steel	2.5
Engine:	225 XL	5
Walking MP:	5	
Running MP:	8	
Jumping MP:	8	
Heat Sinks:	10 [20]	0
Gyro:		3
Cockpit:		3
Armor Factor (Ferro):	153	8

	Internal Structure	Armor Value
Head	3	9
Center Torso	14	21
Center Torso (rear)		7
R/L Torso	11	17
R/L Torso (rear)		5
R/L Arm	7	14
R/L Leg	11	22

Weapons and Ammo	Location	Critical	Tonnage
ER Medium Laser	RA	1	1
Medium Pulse Laser	RA	1	2
ER Large Laser	RT	1	4
ATM 6	RT	3	3.5
Liquid Storage	RT	1	1
Ammo (ATM) 30	LT	3	3
Liquid Storage	LT	1	1
Improved Jump Jets	RT	4	2
Improved Jump Jets	LT	6	3
Improved Jump Jet	CT	2	1
Improved Jump Jet	RL	2	1
Improved Jump Jet	LL	2	1

Mass: 65 tons
Chassis: CCo-B Endo
Power Plant: Consolidated Fusion 325 XL
Cruising Speed: 54 kph
Maximum Speed: 86 kph
Jump Jets: Trellshire Long Lifters
  Jump Capacity: 150 meters
Armor: Trellshire Royalstar
Armament:
  2 Series 7K Extended Range Large Lasers
  4 Series-9 AP Gauss Rifle
  2 Type VI SRM 6 Streak Launchers
Manufacturer: Trellshire Heavy Industries
  Primary Factory: Twycross
Communications System: Hector CC-22E with ECM Suite
Targeting and Tracking System: Mk. CXC-4

Overview

[Editor's Note: Our forensic data scientists have been hard at work on the handful of Blakist memory cores that survived the Jihad. Recently decrypted information dating from early 3078 gives some insight into the Blakist mindset. –JC]

As all Blake's children receiving this briefing already know, the corrupt Clans have come to New Earth. First came the Wolves and Falcons, but now the homicidal Bears have joined them. No doubt they'll try to murder all of the faithful here as they've done on Luthien and Pesht, but let fear reside only in them. The Tenth and Twelfth Divisions are strong. We shall prevail. Let us greet the Clan threat with our wrath.

These data briefings shall aid us in throwing back these corruptions of Blake's Will. *[data corruption, information irretrievable].* Next we review a new *Rifleman IIC* variant that has been reported among their forces. It is provisionally designated IIC 8 *[data corruption, information irretrievable].*

Capabilities

Inner Sphere influences suggest the Diamond Sharks are behind this 'Mech variant, possibly collaborating with the Federated Suns. *[The Blakists were correct. –JC]* With a top speed of 86 kph and a 150-meter jumping range, this *Rifleman's* primary firepower comes from a pair of extended-range large lasers. BattleROMs salvaged from our initial engagements show anti-infantry weaponry, including a quartet of AP Gauss rifles and twin Streak SRM 6 racks. It also has an insidious ECM system capable of disrupting our C3i computers, a capability the abhorrent Clans have used to their advantage. Analysts suggest our MechWarriors must overcome roughly ten tons of ferro-fibrous armor to put down this menace.

Deployment

This variant appeared in forces from all three Clans who soiled New Earth with their presence. We suspect it has recently gone into production and expect to encounter it in any of Stone's so-called Coalition force. *[Though offered to all Inner Sphere factions, prior to 3080 the IIC 8 only appeared with the Sharks, Wolves, Falcons, Bears and AFFS. Since then, the DCMS and Duchy of Oriente have both acquired the design in small numbers. –JC]*

Variants

In a futile attempt to confuse us, the putrid Falcons deployed a second variant of the *Rifleman IIC*. Examining the smoking ruin of one yielded the following data. The weaponry consists of three ER large lasers (one each in the arms and one in the head). Two medium pulse lasers round out the armaments. The design was slow, with a maximum speed of 54 kph, but it had non-standard jump jets.

[The second variant identified by the Blakists is the IIC 5. In addition, Clan Nova Cat introduced the IIC 7 in 3078. As with the IIC 5, the IIC 7 maxes out at 54 kph and mounts improved jump jets with a 150-meter range. It features paired heavy large lasers and plasma cannons along with a targeting computer. Republic Intelligence also has some old data regarding a Star Adder IIC 6 model that began production before the blackout. Dropping the jump jets, it replaces the heavy lasers and plasma cannons with HAG-30s. Two anti-missile systems, an ER small laser and an active probe round out the configuration. The design hasn't appeared in the Inner Sphere, and we suspect it's apocryphal. –JC]

Notable MechWarriors

Star Captain David *[(Hill Bloodline) –JC]:* Divine Retribution XLII (a Level II from the 10th Division) was the first of Blake's chosen to smite the Ghost Bears on New Earth. Encountering a partial Star, they quickly purified two MechWarriors before a *Rifleman IIC 8* rocketed over a hill and engaged. Retribution's commander attempted to provide targeting information through her *Raijin's* C3i, but failed due to the *Rifleman's* ECM. Seconds later, Clan ER large lasers opened her 'Mech's ammo bin. The Bear warrior then savaged Retribution's Phalanx battle armor squads with salvo after salvo from AP Gauss rifles and Streak SRMs; none survived. Our forces staged a fighting withdrawal, losing a *Blue Flame* and, sadly, leaving the *Rifleman IIC 8* heavily damaged but functional. *[David is unusual for a Ghost Bear. Bred from a bloodline traditionally found in the Coyotes, he was a very young Wolf MechWarrior when taken as bondsman by the Bears some years ago. He subsequently regained his warrior status and had earned the rank of Star Captain prior to the Jihad. Despite his excellent service record, he has yet to earn his Bloodname. –JC]*

Type: Rifleman IIC
Technology Base: Clan
Tonnage: 65
Battle Value: 2,541

Equipment		Mass
Internal Structure:	Endo Steel	3.5
Engine:	325 XL	12
Walking MP:	5	
Running MP:	8	
Jumping MP:	5	
Heat Sinks:	16 [32]	6
Gyro:		4
Cockpit:		3
Armor Factor (Ferro):	201	10.5

	Internal Structure	Armor Value
Head	3	9
Center Torso	21	32
Center Torso (rear)		10
R/L Torso	15	22
R/L Torso (rear)		7
R/L Arm	10	20
R/L Leg	15	26

Weapons and Ammo	Location	Critical	Tonnage
ER Large Laser	RA	1	4
2 AP Gauss Rifles	RA	2	1
Ammo (AP Gauss) 40	RA	1	1
Streak SRM 6	RT	2	3
Ammo (Streak) 15	RT	1	1
ECM Suite	H	1	1
ER Large Laser	LA	1	4
2 AP Gauss Rifles	LA	2	1
Ammo (AP Gauss) 40	LA	1	1
Streak SRM 6	LT	2	3
Ammo (Streak) 15	LT	1	1
Jump Jet	CT	1	1
Jump Jets	RL	2	2
Jump Jets	LL	2	2

PLG 2010

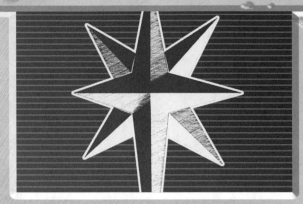

Mass: 80 tons
Chassis: DSAM 4
Power Plant: Type 81 320 XL Fusion
Cruising Speed: 43 kph
Maximum Speed: 64 kph
Jump Jets: Trellshire Long Lifters Improved Jump Jets
    Jump Capacity: 180 meters
Armor: AM15
Armament:
    2 Type KOV LB-10X Autocannons
    2 Mk 3 ER Medium Lasers
    2 Series-4 Streak SRM 4s
Manufacturer: Trellshire Heavy Industries
    Primary Factory: Twycross
Communications System: MegaBand System 21
Targeting and Tracking System: Dtrac Suite 4

Overview

The Diamond Sharks have managed to extract an excellent return on their acquisition of the ancient *Phoenix Hawk IIC* from the Steel Vipers, producing at least six different versions at their Trellshire plant. This truly is an amazing feat of manufacturing prowess, especially as the Sharks appear to be producing enough of all versions and several other 'Mechs to fill their needs and trade with other Clans and Inner Sphere customers. The extent to which the Clan has upgraded its Trellshire Heavy facilities has to be tremendous.

The latest of their *Phoenix Hawk*s still uses the spacious torso weapon bays to mount large autocannons, but the support weaponry is much more prominent: a pair of ER medium lasers and a pair of Streak SRM 4 packs. Mobility is enhanced with the same Improved jump jets found on the *IIC* 6. Here, even Clan engineering apparently reached its limits, as the heavy weapons load and the more than doubled weight of the improved jump jet system forced Shark engineers to reduce the jump range and engine rating.

Capabilities

Variant 7 is a competent mid-range fighter, but is particularly effective when engaging vehicles or exploiting armor breaches in other 'Mechs. The Sharks have deployed the *IIC* 7 defensively at a number of their holdings and interests, where it has proven adept at engaging airborne threats. It does not seem to compare favorably to its siblings, however. Even with the improved jump jets, it has marginally better jumping capability than the standard *Phoenix Hawk IIC*, and it is the only one in the series with a lower land speed. While the *IIC* 6's impressive jump capability may have come at a high price, the *IIC* 7's firepower isn't exemplary, and neither is its mobility. It appears to be a compromise design compared to other Diamond Shark versions such as the *IIC* 3 and -4, or even the original Ultra AC/10-equipped model.

Deployment

The majority of the *IIC* 7s were deployed with Diamond Shark garrison forces as early as 3078. While other Clans appear to have access to the design, they invariably deploy it in small numbers. It appears more frequently in the ranks of Inner Sphere mercenaries, and to some degree in regular line units, where the *IIC* 7's capabilities may be unremarkable by Clan standards, but are still outstanding by Inner Sphere standards. Its mediocre performance may reduce the degree of agitation from other Clans toward the Sharks' chosen clientele. The *IIC* 7 was one of several Diamond Shark products that Stone's Coalition could acquire at favorable pricing.

Variants

Another recent version of the *Phoenix Hawk IIC* is Variant 5, which brings two HAG 20s and a quartet of AP Gauss weapons to the field. The *IIC* 5 is becoming an increasingly common sight among the Diamond Sharks and other Clans, despite reportedly originating from the Star Adders. It has only begun appearing among Inner Sphere units in recent years.

Variant 6 is another intriguing diversion from the *Phoenix Hawk IIC*'s usual mold. Utilizing improved armor protection and a 240-meter jump capability, again courtesy of improved jump jets, the *IIC* 6 is one of the most mobile assault 'Mechs ever created. Its weapons capability is substantially less impressive as a consequence, fielding only a quartet of heavy medium lasers for offensive purposes. These are supported by arm-mounted plasma cannons, which have ample ammunition to degrade the *IIC* 6's target prior to closing in to medium laser range. A targeting computer ensures accurate firepower, but the 'Mech's heat system has a hard time dealing with a sustained barrage.

Notable MechWarriors

MechWarrior Steven Hauspie: Attached to Able Battery of Thor's Hammers, MechWarrior Hauspie has the distinction of having taken out the largest number of hostile aircraft of any soldier in the unit. He has earned most of his score since the Hammers acquired his *Phoenix Hawk IIC* 7 from an unnamed source. Hauspie tends to use his 'Mech's mobility to full effect, rapidly moving along multiple fronts around his charges in an attempt to interject himself between them and any possible attack. While most anti-air 'Mechs and vehicles engage aircraft while stationary, Hauspie distinguishes himself with his excellent mobility and high success rate.

Type: **Phoenix Hawk IIC**
Technology Base: Clan
Tonnage: 80
Battle Value: 2,219

Equipment		Mass
Internal Structure:	Endo Steel	4
Engine:	320 XL	11.5
Walking MP:	4	
Running MP:	6	
Jumping MP:	6	
Heat Sinks:	10 [20]	0
Gyro:		4
Cockpit:		3
Armor Factor:	232	14.5

	Internal Structure	Armor Value
Head	3	9
Center Torso	25	36
Center Torso (rear)		9
R/L Torso	17	26
R/L Torso (rear)		7
R/L Arm	13	25
R/L Leg	17	31

Weapons and Ammo	Location	Critical	Tonnage
ER Medium Laser	RA	1	1
LB 10-X AC	RT	5	10
Ammo (LB-X) 20	RA	2	2
2 Streak SRM 4	CT	2	4
Ammo (Streak) 25	H	1	1
LB 10-X AC	LT	5	10
Ammo (LB-X) 20	LA	2	2
ER Medium Laser	LA	1	1
Improved Jump Jet	RL	2	2
Improved Jump Jets	RT	4	4
Improved Jump Jets	LT	4	4
Improved Jump Jet	LL	2	2

PLG 2010

Mass: 80 tons
Chassis: SFX-80 Endo
Power Plant: Type 79 400 XL
Cruising Speed: 54 kph
Maximum Speed: 86 kph
Jump Jets: None
Jump Capacity: None
Armor: Forging ZM15 Ferro-Fibrous
Armament:
2 Zeta-series X Plasma Cannon
2 Series 4D-2 Heavy Large Lasers
2 Series 2b ER Medium Lasers
1 Type VI SRM 6 Streak
Manufacturer: Auxiliary Production Site #4,
Trellshire Heavy Industries
Primary Factory: DSS *Poseidon*, Trellshire
Communications System: TDWS-37 Mk 2.2
Targeting and Tracking System: "Hephaestus" CT-44

Overview

The Clan version of the classic *Warhammer* has never been subtle. Its hyper-advanced technology only accentuated and improved the BattleMech's role as a frontline brawler; increasing its mass by ten tons (with corresponding increases in armor protection) made it even more powerful.

So when Clan Diamond Shark began marketing their new model, bristling with terrifying firepower and faster than any previous incarnation, people across the Inner Sphere sat up and took notice.

Capabilities

The eighth model of the *Warhammer IIC* is an improved version of the Diamond Sharks' previous *IIC 3* variant. Like that model, its main armament is a pair of brutally effective—if inaccurate and hot-firing—heavy large lasers. However, it replaces the targeting computer and pulse laser array with a more balanced secondary load-out of plasma cannons, ER medium lasers and a Streak missile pack. This gives the new *Warhammer* a ferocious bite and a great deal of tactical flexibility in combat.

The literal heart of the *Warhammer IIC 8* is a massive Type 79 XL fusion plant, the same model used in the acclaimed *Phoenix Hawk IIC*. While the 'Mech still cannot jump, this huge power plant boosts its ground speed to cavalry levels, allowing it to exploit its firepower advantages. It lost a heat sink in the upgrade, but with a careful pilot at the controls it can easily maintain a punishing volume of fire.

The tradeoffs for these improvements are relatively minor. The 'Mech mounts slightly less armor than previous models, but has been carefully balanced so that the loss in practical protection is minimal. The *Warhammer IIC 8* also carries limited ammunition loads for its plasma and missile weapons (less than two minutes' worth of sustained fire each), but its impressive laser complement mitigates this to a considerable degree. Even when "ammo dry," this BattleMech is more than capable of savaging opponents in any weight class.

Deployment

The *Warhammer IIC 8* is now the most widely distributed Clan BattleMech in the Inner Sphere. Every major Inner Sphere power, Clan, and many major mercenary groups field these impressive machines. It is only rare in the Periphery, where its equally impressive price tag is simply too much for these nations to justify.

During the closing days of the Jihad, this model served with particular success as a Manei Domini hunter-killer, especially when paired with 'Mechs mounting ECM suites. (Clan Ghost Bear, for example, fielded *Warhammer IIC 8s* alongside their own *Marauder IIC 7s* in a 3-and-2 Star configuration.) The awesome hitting power of its heavy lasers easily matched the Vapula designs it was pitted against, and its plasma cannons could be used against hot-running 'Mechs and (otherwise difficult to kill) Domini infantry alike.

Variants

Clan Snow Raven introduced their own new model of the *Warhammer IIC* in 3079. Like the *Shadow Hawk IIC 7* (which was actually developed a year later), the *Warhammer IIC 7* is designed for combat in vacuum. Its load-out is similar to the original WHM-6R, with paired ER PPCs supported by a large number of assorted pulse and ER lasers and supplemented with a six-tube advanced tactical missile system. It also carries two fuel tanks for sustained space operations.

The Diamond Sharks and Snow Ravens fielded less well-received variants earlier in the Jihad, each built around large-bore hyper-assault Gauss rifles. Of these, the Sharks' 5 model has appeared across the Inner Sphere, though in lesser numbers than the *Warhammer IIC 8*, while the Ravens' 6 variant is found only in the Outworlds Alliance and Clan Ghost Bear.

Notable MechWarriors

MechWarrior Jason: A substandard pilot who barely passed his Trial of Position, Jason was turned over to the Diamond Shark Scientist Caste as an extreme-conditions test pilot. His usual job is to take a 'Mech—often with safety measures disabled—into a dangerous environment and try not to die. That he's been successful for so many years is a testament to either his strong survival instincts or quite a bit of good luck. His latest assignment was to test a production experiment of special ablative shielding used during the liberation of Devil's Rock. He brought the *Warhammer IIC 8* into an active lava flow to test the heat-protecting armor and see how long it could continuously fire its weapons before shutting down. As it turned out, the first salvo caused his SRM ammunition to explode, ending the test early and forcing him to return to the DropShip with roughly 3/5 of a BattleMech remaining, the nearly useless ablative armor streaming off in rivers of molten material.

Type: **Warhammer IIC**
Technology Base: Clan
Tonnage: 80
Battle Value: 2,380

Equipment		Mass
Internal Structure:	Endo Steel	4
Engine:	400 XL	26.5
Walking MP:	5	
Running MP:	8	
Jumping MP:	0	
Heat Sinks:	19 [38]	9
Gyro:		4
Cockpit:		3
Armor Factor (Ferro):	220	11.5

	Internal Structure	Armor Value
Head	3	9
Center Torso	25	34
Center Torso (rear)		11
R/L Torso	17	23
R/L Torso (rear)		7
R/L Arm	13	23
R/L Leg	17	30

Weapons and Ammo	Location	Critical	Tonnage
Heavy Large Laser	RA	3	4
Plasma Cannon	RA	1	3
Ammo (Plasma) 10	RA	1	1
Streak SRM 6	RT	2	3
Ammo (Streak) 15	RT	1	1
ER Medium Laser	RT	1	1
Heavy Large Laser	LA	3	4
Plasma Cannon	LA	1	3
Ammo (Plasma) 10	LA	1	1
ER Medium Laser	LT	1	1

MARAUDER IIC 7

Mass: 85 tons
Chassis: Type GB-850 Light
Power Plant: 255 XL Fusion Engine
Cruising Speed: 32 kph
Maximum Speed: 54 kph
Jump Jets: None
    Jump Capacity: None
Armor: Compound 12A1 Standard with CASE
Armament:
    1 Series 1g Extended Range Small Laser
    1 Type 0 HAG-30
    1 Omega 12-Coil Gauss Rifle
    1 Kolibri Delta Series Large Pulse Laser
    2 Smartshot Mk V Streak SRM 4
Manufacturer: Gorton, Kingsley & Thorpe Enterprises
    Primary Factory: Satalice
Communications System: Series D8 CC-25a with ECM
Targeting and Tracking System: "Hermes" CT-42 Mk II

Overview

Throughout the 3060s, the Ghost Bear Dominion imported a number of updated *Marauder IIC*s via Clan Diamond Shark, but when Clan Diamond Shark started a shadow trade war, the Dominion decided to cut out the middleman in favor of building *Marauder IIC*s on their own. The resulting *Marauder IIC* 4 was built around a pair of massive HAG 40s for a formidable first attempt, but a lack of ammunition meant it didn't have the staying power required. Going back to the drawing board, Gorton,

Kingsley & Thorpe looked to the *Viking* for inspiration and revamped the *Marauder IIC* as a powerful direct-fire support 'Mech.

Capabilities

Forgoing just about every common feature of past *Marauder IICs*, the *IIC* 7 drops ground speed in favor of weaponry. The influence of the VKG-2G can be seen in the combination of pulse laser, Gauss rifle and HAG. The Clan 'Mech even has an ECM suite, but that is where the similarities end. An XL engine frees up the mass for a targeting computer that guides these already accurate weapons. A pair of arm-mounted missile launchers and a small laser round out the weapon load.

Typically, a *Marauder IIC* 7 finds its way into a firing position where it uses its long-range weapons to dominate the field. Draconis Combine field reports recommend using artillery to shift a dug-in *IIC* 7, as the 'Mech has proven highly effective against aircraft trying to bomb it out. Fortunately, the *Marauder IIC* 7 is relatively light on ammo and runs into difficulties on extended operations. As we have yet to see the 'Mech deployed far from its supply depots, it seems the Dominion is well aware of this weakness.

Deployment

It is not clear how long this 'Mech has been deployed. The first combat reports come from raids by Draconis Combine forces last year, but other hints suggest a late 3070s introduction. The Combine troops were certainly impressed by the big 'Mech's ability to hold a defensive position. Considered too slow for front-line service, the *Marauder IIC* 7 has been deployed to garrison units across the Dominion, where it replaces aging *Supernova*s and Inner Sphere assault 'Mechs.

Variants

Two new *Marauder IIC* variants are being built at Olivetti Weaponry. The *Marauder IIC* 5 retains the original's arm-mounted ER PPCs and supports them with an array of Gauss weapons. Reminiscent of the Star League *Marauders*, a HAG sits in the dorsal assembly, while an anti-personnel Gauss rifle sits under each ER PPC. In production since 3077,

the *Marauder IIC* 6 is a far more mobile *Marauder IIC* than we have seen before. Improved jump jets allow it to soar 180 meters at a time. The eclectic weaponry combines lasers, a Gauss rifle and an LB 10-X autocannon. Heavy combat throughout the Jihad spread the *Marauder IIC* 5 across all combatants on the Lyran front, while the later *IIC* 6 has mainly seen service against Clan Wolf, whose military has salvaged a few of their own.

The *Marauder IIC* 4 still shows up, usually as a surprise in close terrain. That a few have spread to Clan Nova Cat is nothing short of amazing, given that this variant's firepower and mobility make it a deadly infighter and usually a primary target for destruction.

Notable MechWarriors

MechWarrior Shan: MechWarrior Shan is our primary source of information about the *Marauder IIC* 7. Along with the rest of his Binary, he found himself protecting a football stadium full of civilians when Sheliak was raided in 3084. Too slow to draw his enemies away from the stadium, he instead dug in and relied on accurate firepower to force the attackers to retreat. After dismounting from his 'Mech, Shan found himself assailed again, this time by a local holo-vid crew that had been covering the football match and had broadcast the entire battle. Warrior training counted for little in the face of the media, and the new hero was soon spilling all to a planet-wide audience, especially about his 'Mech. Shan has since been reassigned and new protocols applied to all media interactions with Dominion warriors.

CLAN

Type: **Marauder IIC**
Technology Base: Clan
Tonnage: 85
Battle Value: 2,843

Equipment			Mass
Internal Structure:	Endo Steel		4.5
Engine:	255 XL		6.5
Walking MP:	3		
Running MP:	5		
Jumping MP:	0		
Heat Sinks:	12 [24]		2
Gyro:			3
Cockpit:			3
Armor Factor:	263		16.5

	Internal Structure	Armor Value
Head	9	9
Center Torso	27	41
Center Torso (rear)		13
R/L Torso	18	27
R/L Torso (rear)		9
R/L Arm	14	28
R/L Leg	18	36

Weapons and Ammo	Location	Critical	Tonnage
HAG 30	RA	8	13
Ammo (HAG) 12	RT	3	3
Streak SRM 4	RA	1	2
Ammo (SRM) 25	RT	1	1
Large Pulse Laser	RT	2	6
Gauss Rifle	LA	6	12
Ammo (Gauss) 16	LT	2	2
Streak SRM 4	LA	1	2
ER Small Laser	HD	1	.5
ECM Suite	CT	1	1
Targeting Computer	LT	7	7

PLG 2010

LAMS

While this report is almost a decade old, it may still have some validity since we cannot account for all Word of Blake forces.

—Colonel Martin Overstreet
Director of Technology
Department of Military Intelligence

Land-Air BattleMechs (LAMs). Transforming 'Mech/aerospace hybrids. Jacks-of-all-trades. The elite recon units of the Star League Defense Force's Striker regiments. The embodiment of the technological might of the Terran Hegemony. The quintessential image of lostech during the depths of the Succession Wars.

Almost no battlefield unit beyond a standard BattleMech has been more romanticized and less understood. With rumors circulating from credible sources that the Word of Blake—even as our Coalition forces prepare to smash the final Blakist strongholds—may have developed the technology to build the first new LAMs in centuries, I've been tasked with creating an in-depth look at the history of this unique, equally beloved and maligned technology.

The Bimodal Land-Air BattleMech was the Terran Hegemony's first attempt at 'Mech-to-fighter conversion. In 2680, First Lord Michael Cameron went against conventional wisdom and appointed a naval officer, Admiral David Peterson, as commander of the SLDF. Peterson implemented sweeping changes and commissioned several manufacturers to create "a series of 'Mechs that could fly as well as function as light ground 'Mechs." Allied AeroSpace, Inc. won the bid. Their Shadow Hawk LAM was capable of conversion between 'Mech and aerospace fighter configurations. Only a handful of these bimodal LAMs were built before competitors perfected the standard LAM that survived into the Succession Wars.

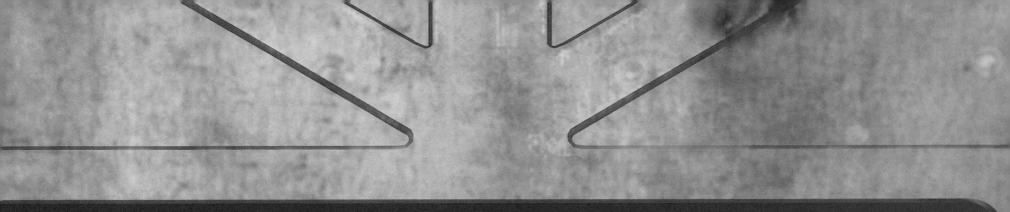

The standard Land-Air BattleMech design emerged less than a decade after the Terran Hegemony's project began. LexaTech Industries delivered the first fully-functional LAM based on the Stinger 'Mech, followed shortly by the Harvard Company, Inc who produced the Wasp LAM. Allied AeroSpace abandoned the Shadow Hawk chassis in favor of new development and introduced the Hegemony to the Phoenix Hawk LAM.

The LAMs rolling off the assembly lines in the late 27th Century marginally resembled their namesakes, but they were completely new designs with obvious differences. Dubbed the Mark I LAMs, they were produced for eight years. By that time, opposing forces were singling them out so Admiral Peterson sent the design teams back to the drawing board. All three LAM designs were painstakingly modified to more closely resemble the 'Mechs for which they were named. The cosmetic changes took almost five years to implement, and the new Mark II LAMs began production in 2701.

Although the LAM formed a prominent component of all SLDF divisions, few remained after the liberation of Terra. After the Successor States annihilated their navies in the First and Second Succession Wars, a growing emphasis on ground-based combat relegated the LAM to a battlefield curiosity that many commanders could neither effectively employ nor afford to risk. The difficulty of mastering both 'Mech and aerospace fighter, coupled with the complex AirMech mode, started the LAM's death spiral. By the Fourth Succession War the best academy for LAM pilots took three times as long as the worst MechWarrior academy to churn out qualified pilots. The depredations of the Succession Wars reduced LAM manufacturing to a bare trickle by the time of the Clan invasion, leaving fewer of these machines available to graduates each year. Pilots failing to earn LAM assignments found themselves mediocre MechWarriors or aerojocks and frequently died in combat without ever piloting a LAM in battle.

When Clan Nova Cat destroyed the last LAM parts factory on Irece it marked the end for the struggling LAM. Coupled with inordinate training and maintenance demands, the loss of parts production eliminated the LAM as a viable combat element in the Inner Sphere. A handful of non-airworthy LAMs remained in combat museums, tended by graying, retired pilots, when the Word of Blake Jihad began. Given their capricious use of WMDs, it is unlikely even those relics survived.

In the 3050s, the Jade Falcons briefly explored adding LAMs to their Touman. A variant of the Phoenix Hawk with a dual cockpit was developed. Controlled by an aerospace pilot and a MechWarrior, the project ultimately failed to fit the Clan's vision of warfare and was abandoned, as far as we know.

Beyond the cutting-edge technology required to build—much less repair—such units, it's of worth to note why LAMs were not prolific following the Star League. After all, a LAM can be both an aerospace fighter and a BattleMech. Why wouldn't they dominate the battlefield? The reality is that a LAM is a poor cousin to a 'Mech or aerospace fighter. While their conversion capabilities make them recon units without equal—the very reason companies were attached to every SLDF Striker regiment—they are weaker than standard units in a stand up fight. What's more, just because they have conversion technology does not make them exceptional in environments in which they're not designed to operate. For example, a LAM in BattleMech mode operating in space doesn't have some superior ability to do so…it's still just a BattleMech, out of its element. Not to mention that, due to LAM-conversion equipment, they cannot mount many of the sophisticated technologies that a pure BattleMech or aerospace fighter can mount, such as advanced armors, structural components and more; a loss in the tech race against such units even at the height of the Star League.

For LAMs to be fielded effectively by an empire requires four pillars: extensive cutting-edge technology, a culture that prizes said technology over more reliable technologies, massive military funding, and an ultra-large military force. All of these factors allow an empire the luxury of fielding such specialized units as LAMs. But this is a set of criteria that only the Terran Hegemony and the Star League Defense Force have met in the three centuries since Land-Air BattleMechs first appeared.

If the Blakists do manage to field such units, it's a testament to their technological savvy and their obsession with said technology. Despite their abundance of wealth, it's skewed due to their relatively small size. This, along with their limited military, leads me to believe that even if they could field such units, they would not be able to sustain them for long. Regardless, an understanding of LAM history and capabilities will provide our troops with the knowledge they need to defeat any unexpected surprises the Word of Blake might be holding in their last bag of tricks.

—Jas Hue
Aide-de-Camp to David Lear
27 October 3076

SHD-X2 SHADOW HAWK LAM

Mass: 55 tons
Chassis: Lang T1 Modified Bi-Modal LAM
Power Plant: DAV 220
Cruising Speed: 43 kph
Maximum Speed: 64 kph
Jump Jets: Allied Lifter B-Series
   Jump Capacity: 120 meters
Armor: StarSlab/2
Armament:
   1 Newhart Extended Range Large Laser
   1 Holly Long Range Missile Pack
   1 Martel Model 5 Medium Laser
   4 Internal Bomb Racks
Manufacturer: Allied Aerospace
   Primary Factory: Pollux (discontinued 2684, factory destroyed 2799)
Communications System: O/P 500 Comtalk II
Targeting and Tracking System: O/P 2000C-5

Overview

The *Shadow Hawk* LAM created the opportunity for one of the Star League's most astounding achievements in much the same way the *Mackie* paved the way for today's 'Mech. Though the prototype was completed in 2680, it was two years before it participated in the SLDF trials.

The first test run of the *Shadow Hawk* LAM ended when the prototype failed to lift off from Allied's runway. The local holo-news had an aviation history professor present who dubbed it the Spruce Hawk after an obscure pre-spaceflight Terran aircraft that nearly failed to fly. The Spruce Hawk was lampooned in the media, often appearing in sketch comedy of the time. In the ensuing years, continual false starts turned public opinion against the LAM far in advance of its evaluation by the SLDF.

Half a year later, the LAM's maiden flight lasted all of ten minutes and ended with significant damage to Chassis 001 when the main

landing gear failed to deploy and the test pilot had to perform a belly landing. The following month, the first airborne conversion attempt resulted in the destruction of Chassis 003 and the death of its pilot.

Allied continually modified the remaining two chassis until the LAM was ready for SLDF review in 2682. They performed adequately in the 'Mech trials, but received poor marks for armor protection and firepower. The LAM was subsequently dropped from consideration when it failed to generate the required three Gs of thrust in the aerospace trials.

Allied went back to work, and by 2684 the X2 was ready for evaluation. The dismal perception of the X1 left the evaluators looking for any reason to reject the X2. Though it passed the aerospace test, rapid fuel consumption was cited to eliminate it from consideration. Plans for an X3 never saw fruition.

Capabilities

The SHD-X2 is modeled after the 2H and features many of the same capabilities. The trademark "stow-and-go" Armstrong autocannon was replaced with a Newhart laser because of conversion complications. A familiar Holly LRM rack and Martel laser complete the offensive arsenal, and a DAV 220 engine gives the X2 a top ground speed of 64 kph. The reduction in speed is offset by a thirty-meter increase in jump range to 120 meters and ten double strength heat sinks.

As an aerospace fighter, the X2 sports nine and a half tons of StarSlab/2 armor and produces three Gs of thrust as its maximum output. Tactical maneuvering, battlefield endurance and combat range are all significantly limited by the X2's minimal fuel capacity. Four internal bomb bays provide multi-role ordnance capabilities.

Deployment

The *Shadow Hawk* LAM never saw active service with any Inner Sphere military. Allied produced twenty of the X2. Most were loaned to prospective customers for evaluation, but after failing to find buyers, Allied scrapped the project in 2688 to focus on the *Phoenix Hawk* LAM.

Variants

The original prototype—the SHD-X1—retained the 2H's ground speed but suffered from reductions in armor protection and weaponry. Three tons of armor were sacrificed, and the Mydron Model C was downgraded to a Model D autocannon.

Only three X1s were produced. Two (chassis 001 and 003) were destroyed in trials. Chassis 002 sat on display at Allied Aerospace's plant on Pollux, but was replaced by *Phoenix Hawk* LAM chassis 001 after the SLDF signed the contract for that design. The fate of SHD-X1 Chassis 002 remains a mystery.

Notable MechWarriors

Commander Nathan Bosworth (Ret.): A former commander in the Stewart Dragoons, Bosworth started his career as a MechWarrior but took up flying while young and ultimately transferred to the Free Worlds League navy to pursue his interest in aerospace fighters. After retiring

from active service, he was recruited by Allied as an aerospace test pilot and became their chief test pilot during the *Shadow Hawk* program. He is the only test pilot to have successfully completed the dangerous fighter-to-'Mech atmospheric conversion. Bosworth's performance during the SLDF's aerospace trial of the X2 LAM set records that stood through the end of the Star League.

Type: Shadow Hawk LAM
Technology Base: Inner Sphere (Experimental)
Tonnage: 55
Battle Value: 933

Equipment			Mass
Internal Structure:			5.5
LAM Conversion Equipment			9
Engine:	220		10
Walking MP:	4		
Running MP:	6		
Jumping MP:	4		
AirMech Cruising MP:	N/A		
AirMech Flanking MP:	N/A		
Safe Thrust:	4		
Max Thrust:	6		
Heat Sinks:	10 [20]		0
Gyro:			3
Cockpit:			3
Fuel:	80		0
Structural Integrity:	18		
Armor Factor:	152		9.5
		Internal Structure	Armor Value
Head		3	9
Center Torso		18	23
Center Torso (rear)			8
R/L Torso		13	18
R/L Torso (rear)			6
R/L Arm		9	16
R/L Leg		13	16

Weapons and Ammo	Location	Critical	Tonnage
Medium Laser	RA	1	1
LRM 5	RT	1	2
Ammo (LRM) 24	RT	1	1
ER Large Laser	LT	2	5
Bomb Bay	LT	4	4
Jump Jets	RT	2	1
Jump Jets	LT	2	1

SHD-X2 SHADOW HAWK LAM

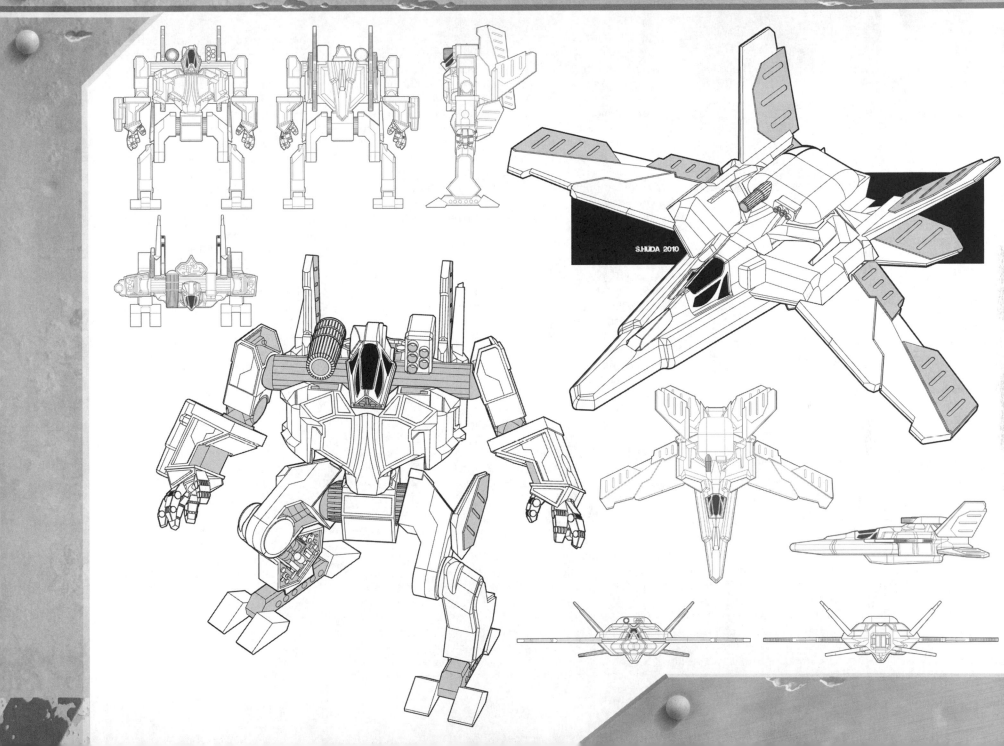

S.HUDA 2010

STG-A1 STINGER LAM MK I

Mass: 30 tons
Chassis: LexaTech 300
Power Plant: GM 180
Cruising Speed: 64 kph
Maximum Speed: 97 kph
Jump Jets: GM ATO 100
    Jump Capacity: 180 meters
Armor: Riese-100
Armament:
    1 Raker-IV Medium Pulse Laser
    2 Raker-II Small Pulse Lasers
Manufacturer: LexaTech Industries
    Primary Factory: Irece
Communications System: O/P 900
Targeting and Tracking System: O/P LAMTRACK 45

Overview

After the boondoggle of the *Shadow Hawk* LAM, SLDF procurement officers were understandably reticent about new Land-Air BattleMechs. It was clear that bimodal designs were too limited for anything but the most specialized combat roles, the exact opposite of the LAM concept. All that changed when LexaTech Industries perfected tri-modal (what became known as "standard") Land-Air BattleMech conversion equipment in 2688 with their hyper-advanced *Stinger* LAM. This sleek, powerful design—which managed to improve on nearly every aspect of its parent BattleMech while maintaining the same ground movement profile—took the military world by storm. It was almost as if the *Mackie* had been immediately followed by the *Pillager*, so great was the technological leap.

Capabilities

The *Stinger* LAM, like its later contemporaries, gained ten tons over the original chassis, but put this extra space and mass to excellent use. This new LAM lost no ground speed or jump range over the basic *Stinger*, and gained extra armor protection. The weapons payload was heavily upgraded as well, with pulse lasers replacing the standard laser and machine guns. Ten double-strength heat sinks provided more than enough cooling for this array.

The end result was an extremely flexible and well-rounded light BattleMech, with the added advantage of being a capable light aerospace fighter as well. The amazingly maneuverable AirMech mode was just icing on the cake.

Deployment

The Star League Defense Force was thrilled with the *Stinger* LAM and ordered thousands of the design, though LexaTech could only deliver about two hundred before the Mark II STG-A5 replaced the STG-A1. While the A1 remained the provenance of the Terran Hegemony's Royal Divisions, the A5 spread to all corners of the Inner Sphere and Periphery.

The *Stinger* LAM received its baptism of fire early in 2690, when rumors reached the Hegemony command of a nuclear weapons plant in Terra's own Oort cloud. Fearing that Periphery secessionists were planning a terrorist strike, the SLDF scrambled a hasty attack force of *Stinger* LAMs and a quartet of the brand-new *Wasp* LAMs. With the *Stinger*s providing aerospace superiority, the *Wasp*s crippled the factory with their Arrow IV ATGMs. The assault went better than anyone could have imagined, with every LAM returning unscathed.

Variants

Interestingly, the most common variant of the *Stinger* LAM—the STG-A5—was actually being designed before the SLDF put out the call for the Mark II models. While the A1 was a fine machine, it was also expensive, and LexaTech wanted to sell more copies of the 'Mech than just what the SLDF Royal Divisions would buy. The STG-A5 replaced all the pulse lasers with a larger array of standard medium lasers and downgraded its heat sinks to single capacity. The SLDF wasn't thrilled with the downgraded version, but the A5 was still a capable fast scout, and limited exposure of advanced weapons technology to the rest of the Inner Sphere. It saw one further variant, the STG-A10, which replaced the A5's arm-mounted medium lasers with two pairs of small lasers; this version was found mostly in the Draconis Combine.

LexaTech also drew up plans for an even more advanced *Stinger* LAM, built with a larger XL engine, ferro-fibrous armor, endo steel structure, and extra weapons and armor, but proved unable to reconcile the limitations of the Land-Air BattleMech chassis with the bulky new, lightweight equipment. In recent years, some have suggested using a composite structure along with improved jump jets. However, since no militaries or manufacturers are seriously interested in reviving LAMs, such ideas remain theoretical.

Notable MechWarriors

Hauptmann Simon Rastler II: Once a member of the Skye Rangers, Simon Rastler was promoted to company command following his heroic actions against House Kurita in the Fourth Succession War and the War of 3039, where his superiors' fears that he was a lucky rather than skilled pilot proved unfounded. Unfortunately, Hauptmann Rastler was sent to the border of the nascent Free Rasalhague Republic, where he met his end at the guns of a Clan Wolf aerospace fighter in 3051.

MechWarrior Kurt Brunner: Born into Clan Goliath Scorpion in an undistinguished branch of the Shaffer bloodline, MechWarrior Kurt dreamed of returning to the Inner Sphere. When the Dragoons Compromise was announced, Kurt leaped at the opportunity and underwent Trials to be part of Jaime and Joshua Wolf's force. Upon arriving in the Federated Suns, Kurt (who had taken the surname of Brunner) found himself disillusioned by how far the Successor States had fallen. He was killed in action on Misery, a bitter shadow of his enthusiastic younger self.

Type: Stinger LAM MK I
Technology Base: Inner Sphere (Advanced)
Tonnage: 30
Battle Value: 788

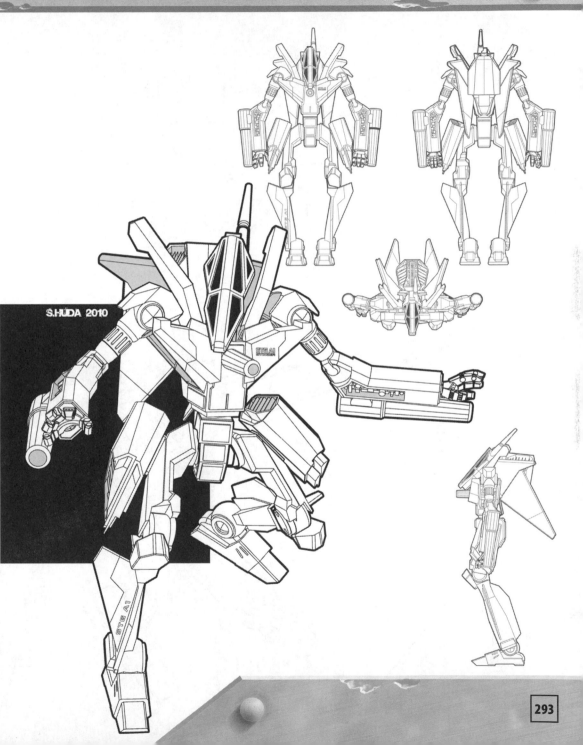

S.HUDA 2010

Equipment		Mass
Internal Structure:		3
LAM Conversion Equipment:		3
Engine:	180	7
Walking MP:	6	
Running MP:	9	
Jumping MP:	6	
AirMech Cruising MP:	18	
AirMech Flanking MP:	27	
Safe Thrust:	6	
Max Thrust:	9	
Heat Sinks:	10 [20]	0
Gyro:		2
Cockpit:		3
Fuel:	80	0
Structural Integrity:	10	
Armor Factor:	80	5

	Internal Structure	Armor Value
Head	3	9
Center Torso	10	12
Center Torso (rear)		3
R/L Torso	7	9
R/L Torso (rear)		3
R/L Arm	5	6
R/L Leg	7	10

Weapons and Ammo	Location	Critical	Tonnage
Medium Pulse Laser	RT	1	2
Small Pulse Laser	RA	1	1
Small Pulse Laser	LA	1	1
Jump Jets	RT	3	1.5
Jump Jets	LT	3	1.5

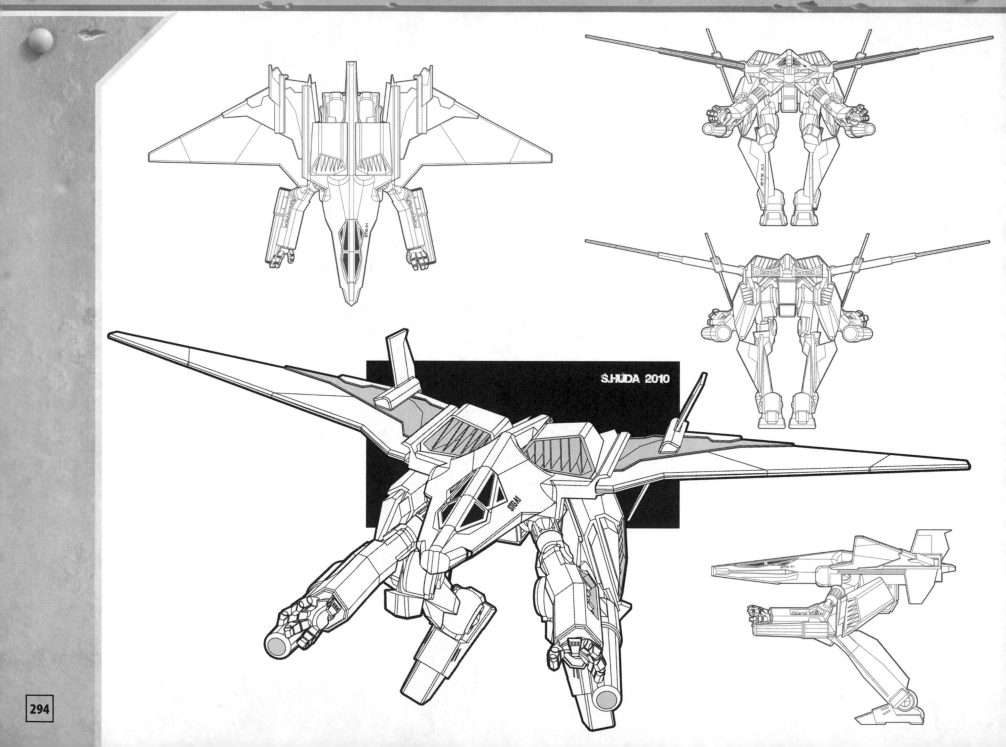

S.HUDA 2010

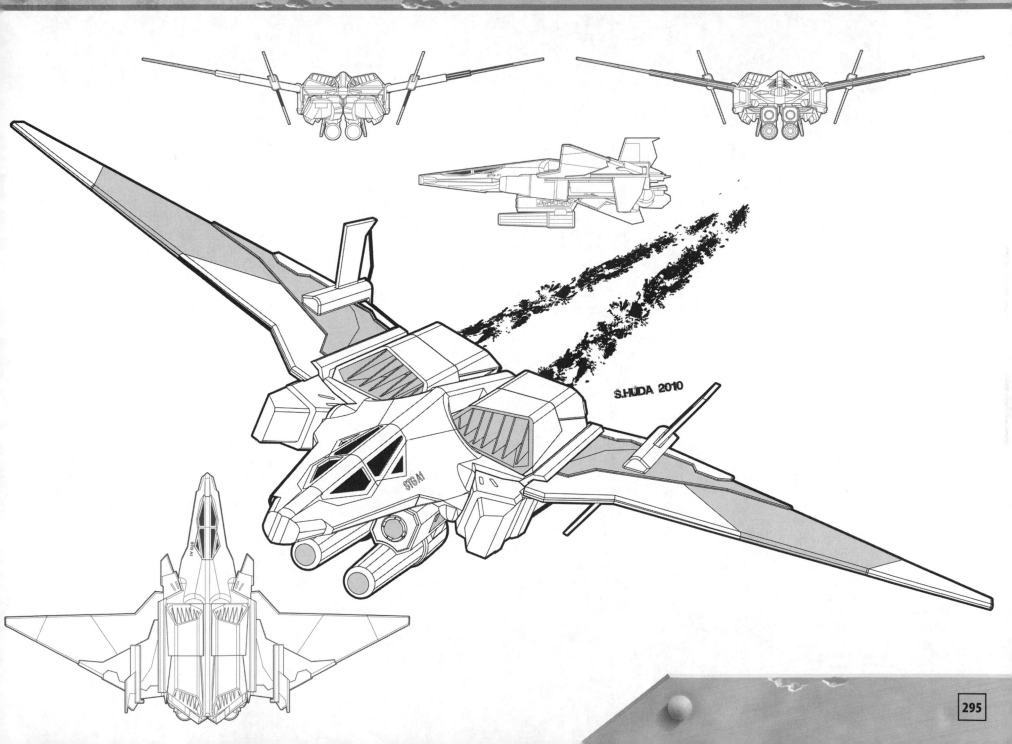

S.HUDA 2010

STG A1

WSP-100 WASP LAM MK I

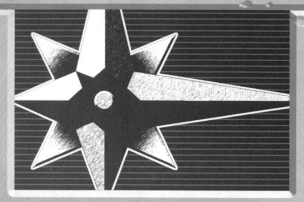

Mass: 30 tons
Chassis: Harvard 12H
Power Plant: LTV 150
Cruising Speed: 54 kph
Maximum Speed: 86 kph
Jump Jets: Rawlings 46 FX
    Jump Capacity: 120 meters
Armor: Durallex Light
Armament:
    1 Martell Medium Laser
    1 Holly Short Range Missile Pack (One-Shot)
Manufacturer: Harvard Company, Inc.
    Primary Factory: Epsilon Eridani (Destroyed)
Communications System: Rand 1200
Targeting and Tracking System: Rand LAMTar 100

Overview

After LexaTech won the contract for their LAM version of the *Stinger*, Harvard Co. secured the rights to the *Wasp* BattleMech and began their own project, though with very different ideas. While Allied and LexaTech had concentrated on fairly standard 'Mech/aerospace fighter hybrids, Harvard—and their brilliant lead engineer, Dr. Katherine Piscalla—were interested in exploring the fighter-bomber role. Most aerospace fighters are not built with that mission in mind, as they are all capable of carrying external stores as needed. However, LAMs could not mount effective hard points. By reducing the size of the *Wasp*'s engine and stripping ammunition and thrusters, Harvard was able to fit a bomb bay in the expanded and better-armored frame.

Capabilities

While slower than its parent design and unable to jump as far in BattleMech mode, the increased maneuverability and flexibility offered by its AirMech and fighter forms were considered a fair trade-off. Similarly, Harvard Co. had been forced to reduce its short-range missile launcher to a one-shot model mounted to the rear, but the *Wasp* LAM more than made up for this firepower reduction with its bomb bay. No other light fighter could carry such a load, up to and including massive Arrow IV ATGMs, without serious speed restrictions, if they even had the hard-point capacity.

Every aspect of the design was carefully considered and planned. Though it mounted fewer jump jets than the standard *Wasp*, those it did include were concentrated in the legs, giving it unparalleled maneuverability in all three modes, as the existing leg joints could be used to shift the angle of thrust. Its huge bomb bay featured a rotating revolver-like mechanism, minimizing its external footprint.

Despite the era in which it was designed, the *Wasp* LAM mounted no technologies that would later become lostech. This made it rugged and easy to maintain. It was also the easiest of the LAMs to pilot, making it popular among soldiers despite its shortcomings.

Deployment

Along with the *Stinger* and later *Phoenix Hawk* LAMs, the *Wasp* LAM was distributed in large numbers throughout the Star League Defense Force. As might be expected, the greatest concentration appeared in the Terran Hegemony's Royal Divisions. The SLDF typically deployed *Wasp* LAMs in homogenous companies, often using a pair of *Leopard* DropShips to insert these units into combat zones. Star League troops loved them, granting *Wasp* LAM units the highest honor groundpounders can bestow upon fliers: the nickname of "angels on our shoulders."

When forced into combat on the ground, the *Wasp* LAM often found itself out-gunned and out-maneuvered, but they still made unparalleled fast scouts and raiders. Had the reign of the Star League lasted longer, there is little doubt that the *Wasp* and its contemporaries would have been the catalyst for even more LAM designs.

Variants

The WSP-100 saw one minor variant that was produced in limited numbers. This model, the WSP-100A, replaced the bomb bay and SRM 2 with an LRM 10 and an additional jump jet. While it never saw widespread deployment, its performance in ground combat impressed the SLDF brass. They commissioned a new BattleMech that copied it nearly wholesale. When Harvard Co. saw the first prototypes, they were incensed and sued to prevent its production. It took the fall of the Star League and the occupation of Corean's facilities for the VLK-QA *Valkyrie* to enter service.

Sadly, the very qualities that made the *Wasp* LAM such a success also made it a prime target in combat, and after a mere seven years it underwent a substantial redesign. The resulting Mark II model, designated the WSP-105, eliminated the original's bomb bay in favor of a larger engine and more thrusters, SRM ammunition and armor. The Mark II *Wasp* LAM survived through the Succession Wars, with the last few combat-worthy examples destroyed during the aftermath of the Clan Invasion.

[Editor's note: Image pictured here is that of a rare WSP-100b model, custom-modified for the SLDF's "Blackhearts" teams. - MO]

Notable MechWarriors

Tai-i **Mandrake Matherson:** Commander of the Twelfth Dieron Regulars' Special Air Lance, a four-LAM force, *Tai-i* Matherson accrued a good deal of press across the Inner Sphere when he discovered a cache of SLDF-grade armor in an abandoned bunker on Galtor. While reports of his subsequent retrofitting of his WSP-105's armor tended toward sensationalism, the truth was that he merely managed to restore his 'Mech's appearance to that of a 100-series *Wasp* LAM, along with some minor weapon modifications. He concealed this fact for more than a decade, until he was killed in combat during the War of 3039.

Type: **Wasp LAM MK I**
Technology Base: Inner Sphere (Advanced)
Tonnage: 30
Battle Value: 489

Equipment		Mass
Internal Structure:		3
LAM Conversion Equipment:		3
Engine:	150	5.5
Walking MP:	5	
Running MP:	8	
Jumping MP:	4	
AirMech Cruising MP:	12	
AirMech Flanking MP:	18	
Safe Thrust:	4	
Max Thrust:	6	
Heat Sinks:	10	0
Gyro:		2
Cockpit:		3
Fuel:	80	0
Structural Integrity:	10	
Armor Factor:	64	4

	Internal Structure	Armor Value
Head	3	8
Center Torso	10	9
Center Torso (rear)		3
R/L Torso	7	8
R/L Torso (rear)		2
R/L Arm	5	5
R/L Leg	7	7

Weapons and Ammo	Location	Critical	Tonnage
Medium Laser	RA	1	1
Bomb Bay	RT	5	5
SRM 2 (OS)	CT (R)	1	1.5
Jump Jets	RL	2	1
Jump Jets	LL	2	1

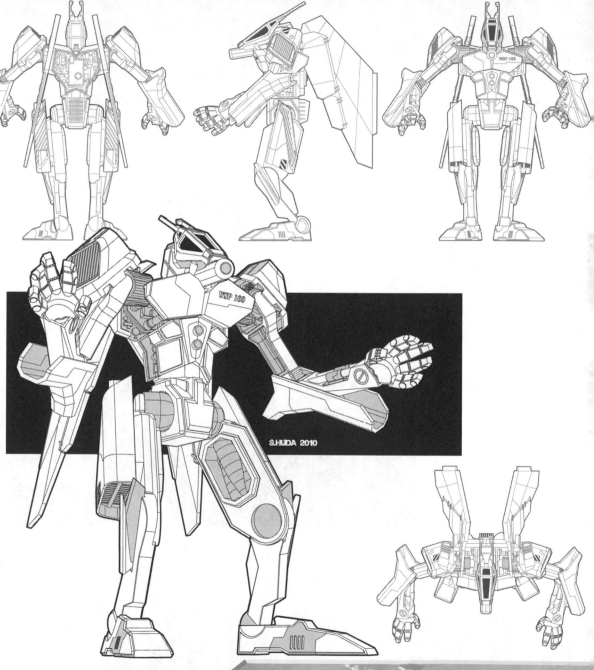

S.HUDA 2010

WSP-100 WASP LAM MK I

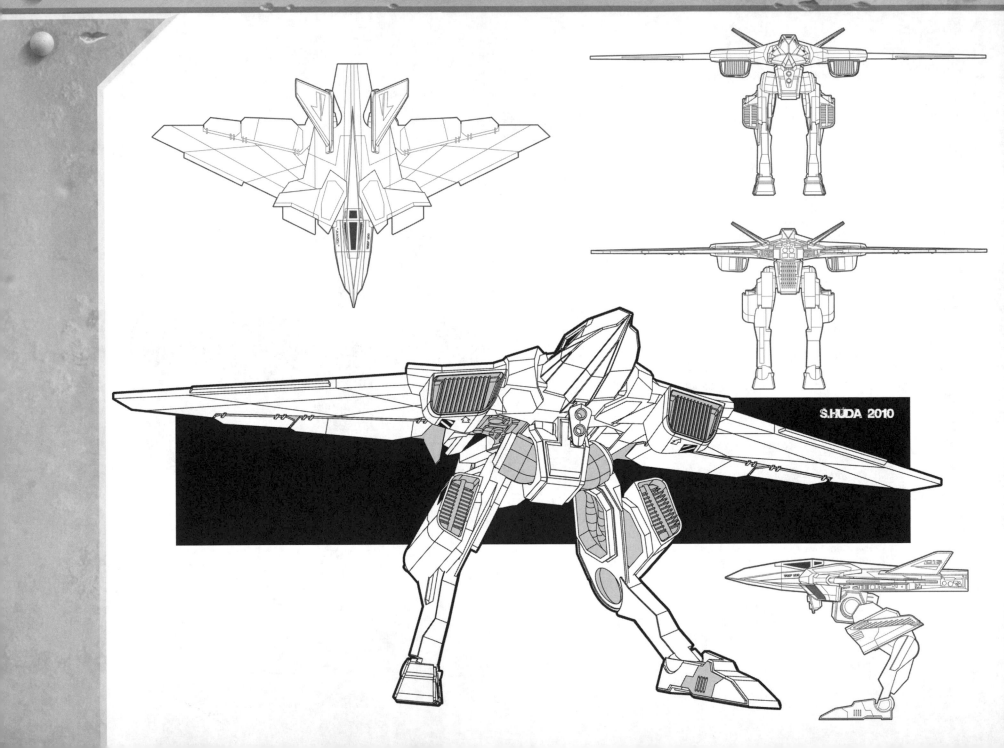

S.HUDA 2010

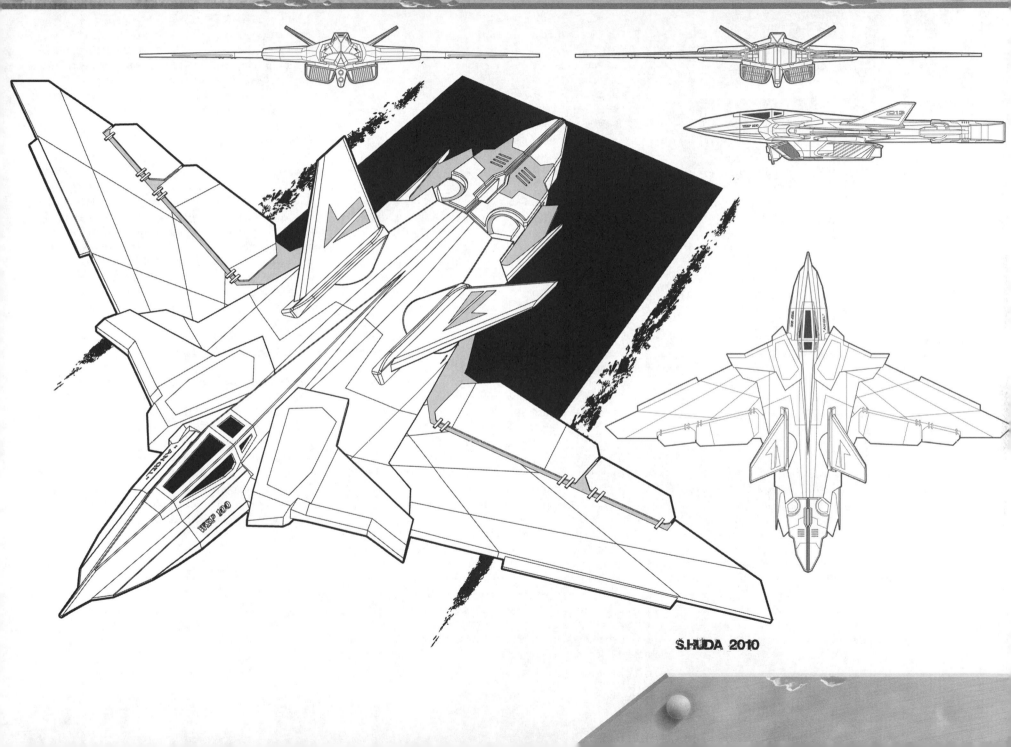

S.HUDA 2010

Mass: 50 tons
Chassis: Dort 85 LAM Prototype
Power Plant: Allied 250
Cruising Speed: 54 kph
Maximum Speed: 86 kph
Jump Jets: Allied AVRTech Model A
    Jump Capacity: 150 meters
Armor: Maximillian 100
Armament:
    1 Blankenburg 30 Extended Range Large Laser
    4 Maxim Medium Lasers
Manufacturer: Allied Aerospace
    Primary Factory: Pollux (destroyed 2799)
Communications System: Hartford Baseband 3
Targeting and Tracking System: Hartford-Allied Trakit 8 V

Overview

Allied Aerospace began work on the *Phoenix Hawk* LAM the same year that LexaTech's tri-mode *Stinger* LAM wowed SLDF evaluators. Needing to match LexaTech's innovation, Allied spent six years in development, the first two of which were devoted to advanced computer modeling.

When the prototype HK1 was finally realized, it featured multiple improvements over the failed *Shadow Hawk*. Foremost was its AirMech mode. A relaxed static stability design made it slightly unstable in aerospace and AirMech modes, but the trade-off provided increased atmospheric dogfighting performance. However, limited fuel capacity discouraged pilots from taking advantage of this.

The HK1 was delivered on time to SLDF evaluators and passed all functional specifications tests, earning high marks for firepower and heat management. It officially entered service in 2701, nineteen years after the initial evaluation of the *Shadow Hawk* LAM.

Allied sold the HK1 and its successor, the HK2, to the SLDF throughout the Amaris Crisis, and offered the design to all Successor States following the Exodus. The destruction of their factory during the First Succession War ended production, but the PHX LAMs would continue in service for more than two hundred years, though with downgraded equipment. Chassis 013 currently sits in the Historic Innovations hangar at the Wings over Donegal museum.

Capabilities

In 'Mech mode, the HK1's Allied 250 fusion engine propelled it at speeds up to 86 kph, which was equivalent to most medium 'Mechs of the era. The Blankenburg extended-range large laser gave the LAM striking power at more than half a kilometer. A quartet of Magna medium lasers augmented this with considerable short-range firepower, and twelve double heat sinks gave the pilot a comfortable heat curve, even with a jumping "alpha strike."

Converting to AirMech mode took less than ten seconds, and a competent pilot could maneuver and fire during the conversion process. After conversion, directional exhaust venting gave the LAM maneuverability similar to modern WiGE vehicles, though with many advantages such as the ability to hover. The *Phoenix Hawk* HK1 could max out at just under 250 kph in this mode. When grounded, the AirMech was slow, with a top speed of 32 kph. This mode was most often used when terrain prohibited landing in fighter mode.

As an aerospace fighter, the HK1 had an asymmetrical disposition of weapons, with the Blankenburg and one Magna firing from its right wing, and the other three Magnas firing from its left wing. Many opponents took advantage of this disparity in atmospheric combat and engaged from its port side. At 2.5 Gs of standard thrust and a maximum thrust of 4 Gs, the *Phoenix Hawk* was poorly matched in dogfights with equal-weight fighters, but had acceptable maneuverability for evading heavier craft.

Deployment

The *Phoenix Hawk* LAM HK1 saw considerable distribution throughout the SLDF. Striker Regiments always featured at least one recon company of LAMs, and in approximately half the regiments, the recon company was comprised entirely of HK1s.

Variants

Prior to the creation of the HK2 series—which modified the *Phoenix Hawk* to more closely resemble its namesake—a single variant of the HK1 was created. The PHX-HK1R removed one left-torso medium laser and exchanged the Blankenburg for an experimental snub-nose PPC. This configuration significantly reduced the HK1R's engagement range, but the unique focusing aperture of the snub-nose PPC more than made up for the difference. Two heat sinks were dropped to make room for a Beagle active probe and an additional half-ton of armor. A deadly and accurate scout, the HK1R was frequently the target of headhunter units.

Notable MechWarriors

Captain Blaise Stewart: LAM recon company commander of the 201st Striker Regiment and Order of the Sword recipient, Stewart led her company of *Phoenix Hawk* LAM HK1s in the first trial of the Terran SDS system. Stewart's team evaded the drone fighters launched by Caspar Drone 73 and successfully breached its landing bay. Wargame operators credited her company with the functional kill of Drone 73; the SDS development team spent two years reprogramming the Caspar system to account for LAMs and prevent subsequent use of Stewart's tactics.

Type: **Phoenix Hawk LAM MK I**
Technology Base: Inner Sphere (Advanced)
Tonnage: 50
Battle Value: 1,942

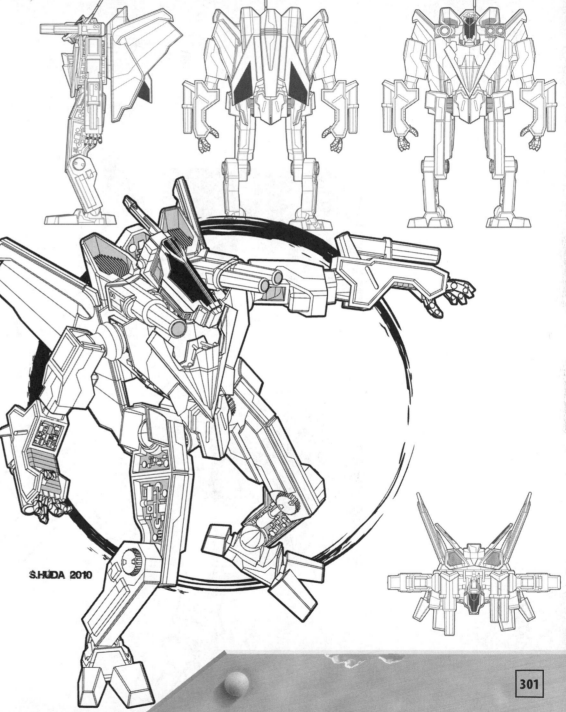

Equipment		Mass
Internal Structure:		5
LAM Conversion Equipment		5
Engine:	250	12.5
Walking MP:	5	
Running MP:	8	
Jumping MP:	5	
AirMech Cruising MP:	15	
AirMech Flanking MP:	23	
Safe Thrust:	5	
Maximum Thrust:	8	
Heat Sinks:	12 [24]	2
Gyro:		3
Cockpit:		3
Fuel:	80	0
Structural Integrity:	16	
Armor Factor:	128	8

	Internal Structure	Armor Value
Head	3	6
Center Torso	16	23
Center Torso (rear)		5
R/L Torso	12	18
R/L Torso (rear)		4
R/L Arm	8	10
R/L Leg	12	15

Weapons and Ammo	Location	Critical	Tonnage
ER Large Laser	RT	2	5
Medium Laser	RA	1	1
Medium Laser	LA	1	1
Medium Laser	LT	1	1
Medium Laser	LT	1	1
Jump Jet	CT	1	.5
Jump Jet	RT	1	.5
Jump Jet	RT	1	.5
Jump Jet	LT	1	.5
Jump Jet	LT	1	.5

S.HUDA 2010

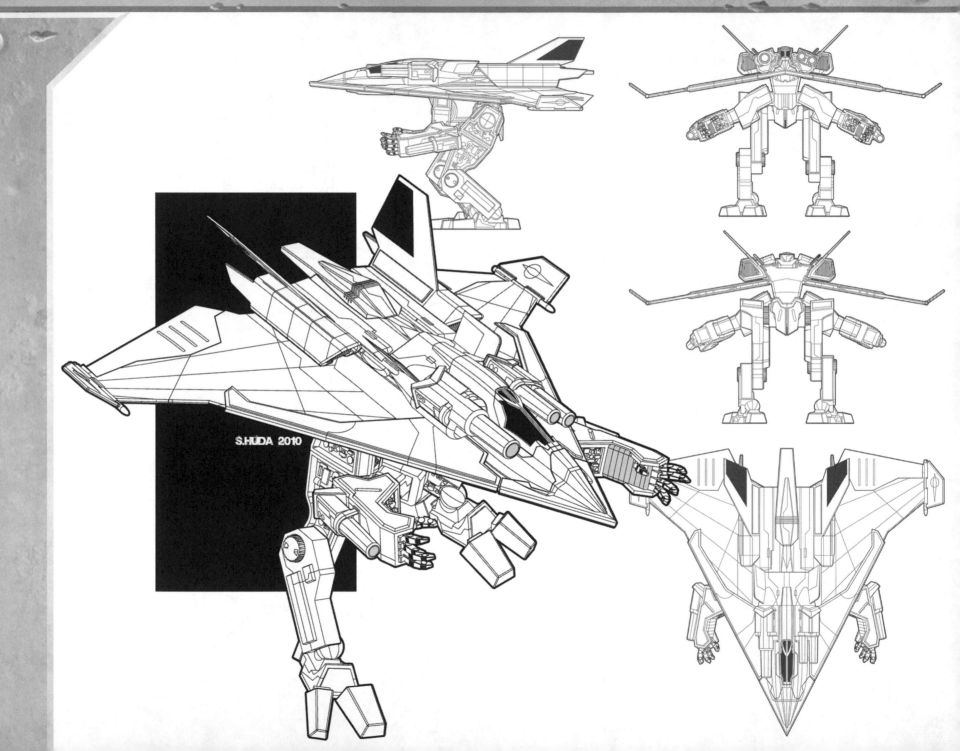

S.HUDA 2010

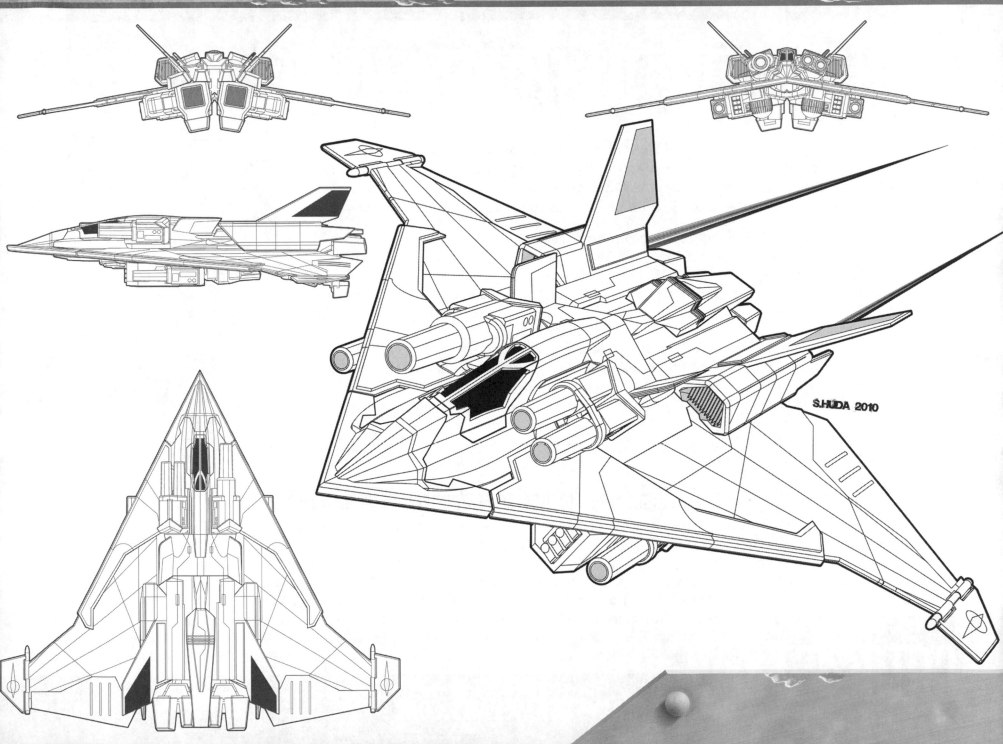

S.HUDA 2010

JIHAD: THE END COMES

In November 3067 the Word of Blake unleashed the Jihad: a war unlike any seen in centuries. In the furious campaign of terror and deception, billions have died, mighty armies have fallen and ancient empires have shattered.

Yet heroes have arisen, the tide has fully turned…and the end comes.

Jihad Hot Spots: Terra is more than just the next installment in the Jihad plot sourcebook series. 3078 is the pivotal year of the entire Jihad conflict. The massed allied armies of the Inner Sphere, having cracked the Blakist Hegemony, assault Terra on a scale not seen since Aleksandr Kerensky freed humanity's birthworld from Amaris the Usurper at the fall of the first Star League three centuries ago.

In addition to the "Jihad Hot Spot"-style sourcebook coverage for the years 3077-3078, a mini Terra System sourcebook will cover this most important of all star systems in a level of detail never before provided to *BattleTech* players. The book includes a rules section covering the complete system defenses of humanity's cradle, such as the Castle Brian complexes, Caspar II drones, SDS surface-to-orbit capital weapons, Meggido satellites and more

Jihad: Final Reckoning – *Coming In The Near Future!*

Jihad: Final Reckoning brings to a close the current massive story arc begun in 2005 with the publication of the *Dawn of the Jihad* sourcebook. Covering the years 3079 to 3081, this sourcebook not only wraps up the final battles that occur after the titanic events of the Terran System invasion, but includes troop movement and conflict information across the fourteen-year conflict.

The book also sets the stage for the various factions coming out of the Jihad, as well as covering new factions that have arisen, such as the Republic of the Sphere, with rules for their use.

Finally, The Legacy of the Word and Rules sections cover the Hidden Five Worlds, as well as revealing a host of previously hidden technologies in development but never fielded before the war ended. These include Caspar III SAS drones, Machina Domini, super-heavy BattleMechs, Celestial LAMs and more.

CATALYST game labs™

WWW.CATALYSTGAMELABS.COM